Encyclopedia
of
Elba

Paris. Typ. H. Plon.

Napoléon confie à sa mère son projet de quitter l'île d'Elbe. (P. 346.)

Encyclopedia
of
Elba

Justin Corfield

GENTEXT PUBLICATIONS
2016

Gentext Publications
An imprint of Corfield and Company

This edition first published in Australia, 2016
by Gentext Publications
59 Smeaton Close, Lara, Victoria, 3212, Australia

ISBN: 978-1-876586-32-4 (hardback)

CONTENTS

INTRODUCTION

On 4 May 1814, Napoleon Bonaparte, having abdicated as Emperor of the French, arrived on the island of Elba, off the coast of Tuscany. Although Napoleon was only on the island for 296 days, Elba became famous as a result although most tourists who now flock to the island each summer come for the weather and the beautiful beaches rather than the remarkable history of the Mediterranean island.

Elba is only some 28 kilometres long, and 19 kilometres across at its widest, and is the largest in the Tuscan Archipelago which includes six other islands. It has had an interesting history being inhabited by the Etruscans who were keen on exploiting the Elba's iron mines, and then it was occupied by the Romans, after which it was fought over by many rival powers since medieval times. It was occupied by the Republic of Pisa, and then Florence, with Cosimo

de Medici overseeing the rebuilding of the main town, Portoferraio. The island later became a possession of the Appiani family from Piombino, and then was divided with part controlled by Appiani, and the other part controlled from Porto Longone (now Porto Azzurro) by Spain.

The French Revolutionary and Napoleonic Wars resulted in a transformation of Elba. The British Royal Navy landed French Royalists there on 1 January 1794, establishing a British garrison on the island two years later. This was then withdrawn and in 1799 when the French invaded Tuscany, they took Elba but French Royalists took it back from them soon afterwards. In 1801–02 the French attacked again, laying siege to Portoferraio for 13 months. The siege ended not when Portoferraio fell but when news arrived that Portoferraio had been ceded to France as part of the Treaty of Amiens. For a short period Elba was a part of France, and was represented in the French legislature. The locals rose up against the French in 1814 and were on the point of driving the French from the island when news arrived that Napoleon had been given the island as part of the Treaty of Fontainebleau with the ex-emperor arriving soon afterwards.

Elba remains famous for being the residence of the ex-emperor Napoleon Bonaparte after his abdication on 11 April 1814. The European powers who had defeated Napoleon were keen on getting him away from mainland France. Tsar Alexander I of Russia had promised that if Napoleon abdicated and co-

operated with the victors, he would be treated generously. Corsica was an obvious choice for his exile but that was Napoleon's birthplace, and also more importantly a part of France – so ceding it might weaken the incoming French Bourbon government. Both the British and Russians were arguing over Corfu, so there was some discussion of the Canaries, or the Azores – owned respectively by Spain and Portugal. In the Caribbean, Trinidad was raised as a possibility, with even suggestions of Botany Bay, Australia; with the French diplomat Talleyrand favouring St. Helena in the South Atlantic. It was Tsar Alexander I who decided on Elba and refused to allow consideration of any other island. Elba was also close to one of Austria's main centres of influence in Italy so it might weaken Austria in the long term. Then it was all agreed, The terms of the abdication were, indeed, generous with Napoleon granted sovereignty over Elba, but there were no clauses about him intriguing, and indeed nothing in the Treaty of Fontainebleau which prevented him from leaving the island.

The ex-emperor arrived on the island on 4 May 1814, and remained there for 296 days until his departure 26 February 1815. Initially when he came to Elba, although it was so much smaller than the massive empire he had controlled, he seems to have planned to spend many years there. However with Bonapartist agents urging him to return to France, and the new French government refusing to make the annual payments that they had promised, Napoleon left Elba secretly in the evening of 26 February 1815, returned to France, and then gambled everything on the battle of Waterloo. His defeat there saw him exiled to St Helena.

During the 296 days that Napoleon spent on Elba, a significant number of British visitors travelled to the island to talk to the ex-emperor, with many writing accounts of their time there. And over the next two centuries, those interested in the story of Napoleon Bonaparte are still drawn to the island and the sites on it which are connected with the story of Napoleon.

In 1815 Elba was ruled by the Austrian Grand Duchy of Tuscany, and then in 1860 became part of the kingdom of Italy. The island was in the news again in 1899 when there was consternation over the treatment on the island of Giovanni Passannante who had been involved in a failed assassination attempt on King Umberto I. Paul Gruyer in 1906 wrote of the Elbans:

In their houses with low-ceilinged rooms, the whole family slept in one bed -- sometimes seven at a time, without distinction of sex and completely naked. The ordinary people had no kitchen utensils but earthenware pots, and no nourishment except dried vegetables brought from the mainland, cheese made of sheeps' milk, very rough and unhealthy bread,

THE ISLAND OF ELBA

ENTE NAZIONALE INDUSTRIE TURISTICHE
FERROVIE DELLO STATO

and salted meat. They added ginger to their wine, which made their regime still more heating to the blood. They made a soup or polenta with their chestnuts, or a sort of cake which kept from year to year. By a strange contrast, this people so primitive and whose fate was so uncertain, liked on Sundays to declaim the verses of Ariosto or Tasso in the public squares, and much enjoyed competitions of impromptu poetry.

In World War I, Austro-Hungarian officers were held as prisoners of war on the island with a lone Austrian submarine surfacing in Portoferraio harbour and firing on the town hoping to provide a distraction for the prisoners to escape. As Vernon Bartlett noted:

Even in 1920, an Italian writer, Vico Mantegazza [in Isola d' Elba], drew a depressing picture of a visit to Elba. There was no wharf at Piombino, and one had to bounce up and

The Ironworks.

down in a rowing boat until the boatman had collected ten passengers who, on arrival alongside their ship, had to climb up her side as best they could since there was no gangway. 'On arrival at Portoferraio, of twenty visitors who had come there for a holiday seven were reduced to thinking themselves very lucky that the ship's captain allowed them to spend the night on board, since they could find no accommodation ashore, the one hotel, the Ape Elbana, being overcrowded with officials from the iron mines.'

The events of World War II impinged much more on Elba in the last years of the war. After Italy had joined the war on the German side in 1940, men from Elba served in the Italian army in many theatres of war. However when the Fascist Grand Council arrested Mussolini on 25 July 1943 and declared for the Allies, the Germans, recognising the importance of Elba, sought the island's surrender. When this did not happen immediately, they launched a bombing raid and took the island, garrisoning it with some crack troops. On 17 June 1944, the British launched an attack on the island and ran into much stiffer resistance than they had expected. However with reinforcements from the French colonial forces – mainly from Morocco and Senegal – the island was captured and the French colonial troops went on a rampage for two days until their commanders reined them in.

The iron mines which had been the centre of much of the Elban economy for centuries were closed down in 1945 and the island had to come up with a strategy to prevent its economy collapsing. Romans had vacationed on the island in classical times, and with a good climate, and plenty of beaches, it quickly developed into a tourist resort. Initially it attracted many British tourists but soon it became a very popular place for Germans and other people from elsewhere in Europe. Although the climate and the beaches are the main attractions, its history – especially the connections with Cosimo de 'Medici and most of all Napoleon Bonaparte remain crucial to the continuing interest in the island.

On 4 May 2014, large numbers of history enthusiasts came to Elba to see Roberto Colla, a 59-year old doctor, dressed as the ex-emperor, arrive by barge at Portoferraio and start a period of re-enactments in Elba showing the contribution of Napoleon to the island's history.

Although Elba features in every book on Napoleon, there have been few books published in English about the island. Averil Mackenzie-Grieve's *Aspects of Elba and the other islands of the Tuscan Archipelago* (1964) captures the essence of Elba before tourism really changed the island. Vernon Bartlett's *A Book about Elba* (1965) also provides a good account of the island. The most detailed remains Christopher and Jean Serpell's *The Travellers' Guide to Elba and the Tuscan Archipelago* (1977). Although increasingly dated, it does provide much information on the island not easily accessible elsewhere. For Napoleon's time on Elba, Robert Christophe provided a good overall account in *Napoleon on Elba* (1964) and followed by Norman MacKenzie's *The Escape from Elba: The Fall & Flight of Napoleon 1814–1815* (1982).

CHRONOLOGY

48,000 BC   Evidence of the first wave of Mousterian culture on Elba.

38,000 BC   The second wave of Mousterian culture on Elba.

18,000 BC   The arrival on Elba of Homo sapiens. Elba at this stage was still connected to the mainland.

5,000   The existence of a Neolithic culture on Elba.

3,000–2,000 A Rinaldonian culture on Elba.

2,000–700   A sub-apennine culture on Elba, probably the Ilvates mentioned by the Roman writer Livy.

c1200   According to legend, fighters from Elba helped to defend Troy in the Trojan War.

c900   Jason and the Argonauts are credited with visiting Elba.

700–300   Greek traders in the Western Mediterranean start exploiting the copper and then iron resources on Elba.

540–535   The Battle of Alialia (also called the Battle of the Sardinian Sea) resulted in the Etruscans defeating the Greeks.

300   Rome takes the island of Elba previously controlled by the Etruscans. Roman tombs on Elba date from this period.

29   Octavian rules as the Emperor Augustus (until AD 14). He stops mining on Italian soil and this results in the closing down of the iron industry in Elba. Several large Roman villas at La Grotte and Cavo on Elba date from this period.

AD 400s	Rutilius Namazianus mentions monks and other religious fugitives coming to Elba.
c450	Mamilian (later St Mamilian), bishop of Palermo, flees the Vandals and settles on Elba and then moves to the island of Montecristo.
c550	Cerbone (later St Cerbone), bishop of Populonia, fleeing the Lombards, seeks refuge on Elba.
750s	The Arabs having conquered North Africa and Spain, then taking Sardinia and Corsica, start attacking Elba.
849	Another Arab attack on Elba.
850	The Pisans develop an interest in the iron mines on Elba.
874	The Saracens attack Elba.
1004	Pisa fights the Saracens.
1016	Elba sacked by the Arabs led by al-Mujahid'Āmirī.
1055	North African corsairs capture the island of Capraia.
1138	The Republic of Pisa in control of the whole of Elba.
1146	The Pisans fight the Corsairs off Capraia.
1293	Genoa challenges the Republic of Pisa for control of the iron mines in Elba.
1376	Pope Gregory XI while travelling from Avignon to Rome takes refuge on Elba during a storm, and prays at the church at Capoliveri.
1398	Gherado d'Appiano sells Pisa to Milan but remains Lord of Piombino, Elba, Pianosa and Montecristo.
1402	The Appiano family give the iron mines on Elba to Genoa.
1442	Corsairs from Tunisia attack Elba.
1501–03	Cesare Borgia, the duke of Valentino, and illegitimate son of

Pope Alexander VI takes Piombino and Elba in order to control central Italy.

1503   The death of Pope Alexander VI ends the control by Cesare Borgia.

1504   Aroodje Barbarossa and his Tunisian fleet capture Papal galleys off the coast of Elba.

1541   The Genoses build the Torre del Porto on Capraia.

1543   Khair-ed-Din Barbarossa, the senior admiral in the Turkish forces attacks Rio on Elba.

1544   Khair-ed-Din Barbarossa launches a second attack on Elba after Jacobo d'Appiano refuses to release a hostage.

1548   Cosimo de 'Medici establishes his base at Portoferraio with a fortified harbour to protect it from attack by the Turks.

1553   Dragut, the Turkish corsair, launches his first attack on Elba.

Map from 1595.

1555	Dragut attacks Elba for a second time.
1560	Jacobo d'Appiano (VI) moved to Elba after being forced to leave Piombino by the Spanish garrison.
1603	A Spanish viceroy of Naples orders the construction of walls to protect Porto Longone. Jacobo VIII, the last direct male heir of the Appiano family dies.
1632	Portoferraio Cathedral is enlarged.
1646	The French capture Porto Longone and refortify it.
1650	The Spanish with some help from the Tuscans, recapture Porto Longone.
1652	The outbreak of the Anglo-Dutch War leads to the battle of Elba (28 August).
1677	The Church of (The Reverenda) Misericordia is built in Portoferraio.
1678	The Spanish strengthen their defences on Porto Longone fearing an attack by the corsairs.
1708	The Austrians invade Elba but the Spanish governor Pinel manages to hold them off.
1713	An injured whale is seen in the bay of Portoferraio and is then chased to the Italian coast and killed between Piombino and Populonia.
1724	The windmills are converted into the Villa dei Mulini.
1738	The death of the last of the de 'Medici family sees the Grand Duchy of Tuscany pass to Austria and the Lorraine family take over control over their half of Elba with Austrian governors at Portoferraio and Spanish governors appointed by the Bourbons of Naples at Porto Longone.
1771	Captain Giovanelli writes *Breve Relazione dell'Isola dell'Elba*.
1782	In an unnaturally cold spell on Elba, a large number of olive trees

were destroyed (14–17 February).

1786   The British offer to purchase Portoferraio for use as a naval base.

1794   A British fleet land thousands of French royalists evacuated from Toulon at Portoferraio (1 January).

1796   The British place a garrison on Elba but withdraw it after nine months.

1799   The French, after having invaded Tuscany, land on Elba but after four months are driven back by Elbans supported by pro-Bourbon French.

1801–02   The French again attack Elba and lay siege to Portoferraio for 13 months (from 5 May 1801).

1802   Although the Elbans have held out, with the Treaty of Amiens, Elba becomes a part of France (26 August).

1803   Joseph Hugo moved to Elba with his family including the infant Victor Hugo.

1808   Arsène Thiébaut de Berneaud writes *Voyage à l'île d'Elbe*.

1809   Giuseppe Arrighi de Casanova, a cousin of Napoleon Bonaparte becomes the vicar general of Elba following the death of his brother Anton Arrighi de Casanova (28 December).

1814   Napoleon Bonaparte is offered complete sovereignty of the principality of Elba under the terms of the Treaty of Fontainebleau (6 April). Napoleon embarks on the *Undaunted* at Fréjus (29 April), arriving at Portoferraio (3 May). Napoleon lands at Portoferraio and attends a reception at the Town Hall (4 May), and moves to the Casa dei Mulini (21 May). Six hundred soldiers from the Imperial Guard arrive (26 May). Pauline Bonaparte arrives (2 June), leaving on the next day, with Napoleon spending the month of June travelling around Elba and annexing the island of Pianosa. Mme Bertrand arrives on the island bringing news to Napoleon Bonaparte of the death of Josephine (16 July). Napoleon's mother arrives at Elba (2 August). Napoleon moves to Marciana to await the arrival of Countess Marie Walewska

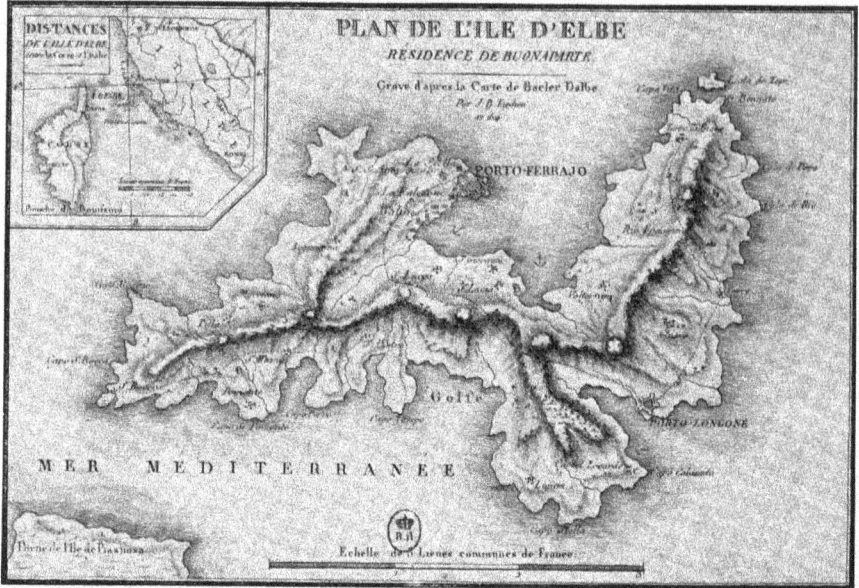

(21 August). Napoleon is joined at Marciana by his mother (25 August). Marie Walewska arrives on Elba from Naples (1 September), and leaves from Porto Longone (Porto Azzurro) (4 September). Napoleon Bonaparte visits Pianosa (12–17 September). John Barber Scott and other British visitors meet Napoleon Bonaparte (19 September). Pauline Bonaparte moves into the Villa dei Mulini (1 November).

1815   The Teatro dei Vigilanti opens (January). Pierre Fleury de Chaboulon arrives on Elba with information from Bonapartists in France (13 February). Napoleon Bonaparte decides to move to France when this is possible (14 February). Sir Neil Campbell leaves Elba for Livorno (16 February). Napoleon Bonaparte imposes an embargo on any ship leaving Elba (23 February). Pauline Bonaparte gives a ball at the Teatro dei Vigilanti in honour of Napoleon Bonaparte (25 February). Napoleon Bonaparte farewells his supporters at Elba and leaves in the evening (26 February). Napoleon, after evading the British, lands at the Antibes (1 March). Napoleon becomes emperor again (20 March). The battle of Waterloo (18 June). Napoleon seeks asylum on the HMS *Bellerophon* (15 July), and is later taken to St. Helena. Under agreement at the Congress of Vienna, Elba is handed over to the Austrian grand dukes of Tuscany.

1844 The first publication of Alexandre Dumas's *Le Comte de Monte-Cristo*.

1848 Many people in Portoferraio demonstrate in favour of the Italian patriot Giuseppe Garibaldi.

1849 Garibaldi comes to Cavo on his way from the Italian mainland to Caprera.

1852 George Watson-Taylor proclaims himself the Count of Monte Cristo. Prince Anatole Demidoff leaves money at the Church of (The Reverenda) Misericordia in Portoferraio for an annual memorial mass on 5 May for Napoleon Bonaparte.

1855 The Saint-Louis blast furnaces are built at Marseille to handle iron ore from Elba, and also from Algeria and Spain.

1860 Elba becomes a part of the new Kingdom of Italy.

1879 The Italian anarchist Giovanni Passannante is sentenced to death (29 March) and then had his sentence commuted to life imprisonment and is jailed at Portoferraio.

1889 The British engineer Daniel Adamson visits Elba and writes a report on the iron mines on the island.

1900 Newer blast-furnaces are built at Portoferraio.

1911 The Italian anarchist poet Pietri Gori dies at Portoferraio (8 January).

1915 Italy declares war on the Austro-Hungarian Empire (23 May).

1916 An Austrian submarine bombards Portoferraio (23 May).

1920 Mario Foresi gives a large collection of books to the library in Portoferraio which is later named the Biblioteca Comunale Foresiana.

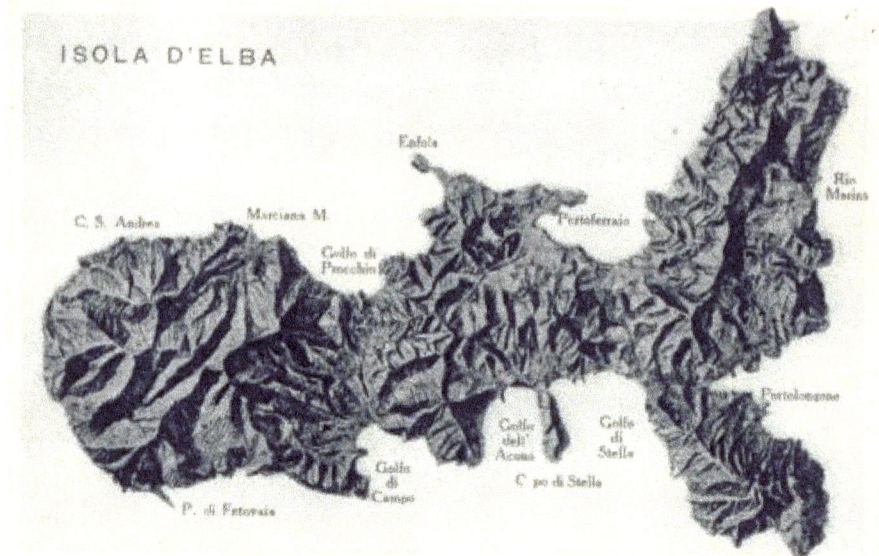

Map from 1925.

1920–21	Strikes and industrial problems at the steel works at Portoferraio.
1921	Renovation work starts on the Villa dei Mulini at Portoferraio.
1943	Following the collapse of the Mussolini government in Italy, the Germans bomb Portoferraio (15 September) and then occupy the island (16 September). *Sgarallino*, a passenger steamer is torpedoed off the coast of Elba with 200 drowned.
1944	Allied planes bomb Elba (19 March). A US air force plane crashes on Elba (4 April). In Operation Brassard, the Allied forces land in southern Elba and the Free French take control of the island (17 June). The German commander General Franz Gall has permission to evacuate the remaining German soldiers (19 June) and does so (20 June).
1945	The steelworks is closed down owing to economic problems.
1947	The Allied War Cemetery at Marina di Campo is closed and the bodies of Allied servicemen buried there are moved to the Bolsena War Cemetery on the Italian mainland. Dylan Thomas and his wife Caitlin visit Elba, staying at Rio Marina with their

family.

1950   The decision is made to develop the tourist industry on Elba.

1954   A BOAC Comet 1 on flight 781 crashes into the sea off the coast of Elba killing all on board including the war correspondent Chester Wilmot (10 January). Caitlin Thomas, widow of Dylan Thomas, returns to Elba.

1960   A Misrair Vickers Viscount crashes north of Elba with all 21 on board killed (29 September). An Itavia De Havilland DH114 crashes at Monte Capanne (14 October).

1962   The Isola d'Elba Prize is inaugurated.

1964   Averil Mackenzie-Grieve writes *Aspects of Elba and the other islands of the Tuscan Archipelago*. The Villa dei Mulini is turned into a museum and opened to the public.

1965   Vernon Bartlett writes *A Book about Elba*.

1968   The Museo Civico Archeologico opens at Marciana.

1977   Christopher and Jean Serpell's *The Travellers' Guide to Elba and the Tuscan Archipelago* is published.

1982   Norman MacKenzie writes *The Escape from Elba: the fall & flight of Napoleon 1814–1815*.

1986   The penal colony on Cerboli is closed down.

1989   A lighthouse is built on the island of Palmaiola.

2001   Free diver Jacques Mayol commits suicide on Elba (23 December).

2005   Philippe Toussaint's novel *Fuir* is published.

2012   The *Costa Concordia* runs aground off the island of Giglio (13 January).

2014   On the 70th anniversary of the crash of the US Bell P–39 Airacobra 42–8971, a memorial is unveiled at the site of the crash (1 April). Roberto Colla, dressed as Napoleon, restages the ex-emperor's arrival at Portoferraio (4 May).

2015 The government of the United Arab Emirates signs an agreement to renovate the library of the Napoleon Museum on Elba (August).

ENCYCLOPEDIA
OF
ELBA

- A -

ABREU, JOSÉ ANTONIO (1939–   ). A Venezuelan economist and orchestra conductor, he was born on 7 May 1939 at Valera, Venezuela, the son of José Antonio Abreu, an Italian migrant from **Marciana**, Elba. Abreu completed an economics degree from the Universidad Católica Andres Bello, and then a doctorate in petroleum economics from the same university in 1961. Completing some graduate work at the University of Michigan, United States, he was elected to the Venezuelan chamber of deputies and then was a professor of economics and law at Universidad Simón Bolívar and then the Universidad Católica Andres Bello. The minister of culture briefly in 1983, he then gave up economics and politics for music which had been his passion since his childhood. He became a conductor for a number of orchestras and was the founder of El Sistema which has seen the teaching of music to poor children in Venezuela.

References: Michel Ficher, *Latin American Classical Composers: a biographical dictionary*, Lanham, Maryland: Scarecrow Press, 2002; *Who's Who in Entertainment*, second edition, 1992–93; Tricia Tunstall, *Changing Lives: Gustavo Dudamel, El Sistema, and the transformative power of music*, New York: Norton, 2012,

ACQUAVIVA, GIOVANNI (1900–1971). An Italian futurist, he was born on 30 October 1900 at **Marciana Marina**, and started illustrating books from the age of 18. His work was much acclaimed and he took part in a large number of festivals including the Venice Biennale. He also worked as a magistrate and died on 21 August 1971 in Milan.

References: Claudia Salaris, *Il futurismo e la pubblicità: dalla pubblicità dell'arte, all'arte della pubblicità*, Milan: Lupetti, 1986; Mario Verdone, *Giovanni Acquaviva*, Comune di Savona: Assessorato alla Cultura, 1987.

ADAMSON, DANIEL (1820–1890). A British engineer who investigated whether it was possible to work the iron mines in Elba, he was born on 30 April 1820 at Shildon, county Durham, the thirteenth or the fifteen children of Daniel Adamson, the landlord of the Grey Horse Inn at Shildon, and his wife Ann (née Eggleston). With the inn close to the site of the Shildon locomotive works, Daniel Adamson snr operated a horse-drawn passenger coach service, with Daniel jnr going to the Edward Walton Quaker School and then apprenticed to Timothy Hackworth, an engineer on the Stockton and Darlington Railway. By 1850 he was the manager of the Stockton engine works and built his own ironworks at Newton Moore, Dukinfield, near Manchester. He made extensive use of the Bessemer system of mass-producing steel, and in 1889 the Italian government invited Adamson to go to Elba to draw up a report on whether the iron mines there could be made more profitable. Daniel Adamson contracted an infection whilst in Italy, and returned to England, and died on 13 January 1890, at his home, The Towers, Didsbury, Manchester. He was survived by his wife Mary (née Pickard), and their two daughters Alice and Lavinia. Some of Daniel Adamson's notes on the iron mines at Elba are held at the Greater Manchester County Record Office.

References: J. G. Read, 'Adamson, Daniel', in D. J. Jeremy (ed), *Dictionary of business biography*, vol. 1; J. Gordon Read, 'Adamson, Daniel (1820–1890)', *Oxford Dictionary of National Biography*, Oxford University Press, 2004.

ADYE, JOHN MILLER. A British naval officer, he commanded the British sloop *Partridge* at the time of **Napoleon**'s daring escape from Elba in 1815. He had been concerned that Napoleon might escape from early 1815 and landed at **Portoferraio** about once a week to check that the ex-emperor was still there. He turned down an invitation to the gala opening of the new **Teatro dei Vigilanti** in Elba on 22 January 1815 telling his wife, 'I will explain that I am indisposed. In fact I have no desire to go and be insulted by some French officer, as is their habit.' In January 1815 bad weather prevented such regular visits and when he called into Portoferraio on the morning of 24 February 1815, along with a dozen British tourists he had brought to the island, he caused some concern for Napoleon who was preparing for his departure. However Adye left at around 2 pm that same day not noticing anything odd except for the *Inconstant* returning to the port along with the *Étoile* and the *Caroline*. The spy who used the codename **'Oil Merchant'** who would usually have made contact with the *Partridge*, was by this time convinced that the British were colluding with Napoleon. Adye sailed back to Livorno.

References: Pierre Branda, L'île d'Elbe et le retour de Napoléon: 1814–1815, Saint-Cloud: Soteca, 2014; Sir Neil Campbell, *Napoleon on Elba: diary of an eyewitness to exile*, Welwyn Garden City: Ravenhall Books, 2004; Norman MacKenzie, *The Escape from Elba: The Fall & Flight of Napoleon 1814–1815*, Oxford: Oxford University Press, 1982; Norwood Young and Alexander Meyrick Broadley, *Napoleon in exile: Elba – from the entry of the allies into Paris on the 31st March 1814 to the return of Napoleon from Elba and his landing at Golfe Jouan on the 1st March 1815*, London: S. Paul & Co, 1914.

AERELBA. This is a small local airline, Company Aerelba S.p.A., with light aircraft and operated from the **airport** on Elba, Aeroporto di Marina di Campo, running flights between Pisa and Elba three days a week.

AFRICAN COMMUNITY. The Corsairs from North Africa long posed a threat to the island of Elba, and indeed sacked it in 1016, attacking again in 1442, captured papal galleys off the coast of Elba in 1504, and ships from North Africa supported the Ottomans who attacked Elba in 1543 and again in the following year, then in 1553–55, and during a brief revival of their strength in the 1670s. Even as late as 1814 there was still fear in Elba that they might attack again with **Napoleon** voicing some concern about it.

AGENZIA PER IL TURISMO DELL'ARCHIPELAGO TOSCANO. The official tourist organisation on Elba, it took over from the **Ente Valorizzazione Elba** (ECE), and remains located on the second floor of the Grattacielo, opposite the ferry pier at **Portoferraio**. It is open from Monday to Saturday, 8 am to 8 pm, and on Sundays from 8 am to 2 pm, from Easter until October, and for the rest of the year is open from 8 am until 6 pm on Mondays to Saturday.

References: www.aptelba.it.

AIRPORT. There is a small airport on the island of Elba known as Aeroporto di Marina di Campo [Marina di Campo Airport] or Aeroporto Teseo Tesei [Teseo Tesei Airport] named after the **World War II** hero **Teso Tesei**. It started life as a small airstrip and is in the central part of the island, north of **Marina di Campo**, and south of Procchio. In 1977 it was still a grass airstrip used for light aircraft with **Aerelba** operating flights on Mondays, Wednesdays and Fridays with the flight to Pisa taking around 30 minutes. The airport is operated by the Italian government. It has been enlarged and is still used for charter flights for tourists and had flights by Elbafly from Milan and Pisa from mid-June until mid-September. It now handles seasonal flights by InterSky from Altenrhein, Munich, and Zurich, with flights from Bern starting in May

2014. Sky Works Airlines also fly to Elba from Bern in the summer.

References: Elba Airport, www.elba-airport.it; Elbafly, www.elbafly.it; Christopher and Jean Serpell, *The Travellers' Guide to Elba and the Tuscan Archipelago*, London: Jonathan Cape, 1977, p. 14; Marco Finelli, 'Elba – Gateway to the Tuscan Islands', *Airports of the World* no 51 (January/February 2014).

An artist's impression of the battle of Alalia.

ALALIA, BATTLE OF. Also known as the Battle of the Sardinian Sea, it was fought between 540 BC and 535 BC between a Greek fleet and one of the **Etruscans** reinforced by the Carthaginians. Its name comes from the fact that many of the Greeks came from their colony of Alalia (now Aléria), off the east coast of Corsica. The Phoenicians and the Etruscans had been rivals and allies over several centuries, but were facing competition from the emerging strength of Phocaean Greek colonies at Massalia (Marseille) and Alalia. The battle is described by the writer Herodotus and began with the Greeks driving off the Etruscan-Carthaginian fleet with the loss of around 40 of their approximately 60 ships. They quickly realised that they were still vastly outnumbered by the Etruscans and Carthaginians who had twice as many ships at the start of the battle. The Greeks then retreated and evacuated Corsica, with the Etruscans killing their Greek prisoners and the Carthaginians selling their prisoners into slavery. The battle saw Etruscan rule over the island of Elba confirmed with the Etruscans also taking over Corsica, and the Carthaginians holding Sardinia.

References: Herodotus, *The Histories*, Harmondsworth, Middx: Penguin Books, 1979, p. 108; Lionel Casson, *The Ancient Mariners*, Princeton: Princeton University Press, 1991.

ALBERGO L'APE ELBANA [Hotel of the Bee of Elba]. This hotel is located in the old part of **Portoferraio** and is located in the Piazza della Republica. It is painted light yellow and is the oldest surviving hotel on Elba. According to tradition some of the foreigners who came to Elba to see Napoleon Bonaparte in 1814–15 stayed in this hotel – at that time it was known as the Auberge Bonroux. **Paul Gruyer**, the author of *Napoleon, King of Elba* (1906) stayed there. He wrote:

I asked for the Albergo de l'Ape Elbana (Hotel of the Bee of Elba), in memory of the Napoleonic bee. Here I found good service, food, and lodging. The only remarkable dish at dinner was one of raw peas served in their pods, and French beans, also uncooked, elegantly arranged on a vine leaf. The other guests seemed to enjoy this form of dessert.

At the end of his second day in Elba, he noted:

That evening I sat at the door of the Ape Elbana, enjoying the delicious evening breeze, while the townspeople walked and talked, guitars and accordions made music, and children shouted; suddenly the church bells began to toll, and from the farther end of the town came lamentable cries, growing gradually nearer, while the shop people closed their shutters and the music stopped. A strange procession next appeared on the public square. A coffin was carried by four strong men; on each side of it walked a crowd of people of all sizes down to small children, all wearing black cloaks and each carrying large candles, chanting psalms as they went. Those who headed the procession waved lanterns mounted on long sticks, or carried crosses or banners. This was the funeral. When I remarked on the lateness of the hour, the hotel porter told me that this was the fashion for any important person; 'it was much the best style.'

The hotel has also appeared in one novel by the Belgian writer, Jean-Philippe Toussaint's *Fuir* (2005), published in English as *Running Away* (2009). This won the Prix Médicis in 2005. The hotel has mixed reviews on the internet, with the obvious attractions of the hotel being its history, location and price.

References: l'Hotel, http://www.ape-elbana.it/ingl'hotel.htm; Paul Gruyer, *Napoleon, King of Elba*, Philadelphia: J. B. Lippincott Company, 1906, p. 3f; Miles Roddis & Alex Leviton, *Tuscany & Umbria*, Footscray: Lonely Planet, 2006, p. 188; Jean-Philippe Toussaint, *Running Away*, Champaign: Dalkey Archive Press, 2009, pp. 137–44.

ANCIENT ELBA. The expansion of the Greeks into the western Mediterranean from 700 BC, at the end of the Bronze Age and the start of the Iron Age, led to major changes for Elba. The island features in the story of Jason and the **Argonauts**, and later Elbans were supposed to have fought to defend Troy against the Greeks. Odysseus ventured into the Tyrrhenian Sea, crossing from Corsica to his meeting with Circe on the mainland, well south of Elba. Later it was claimed that Aeneas had raised levies on the island to help in the defence of Troy, and the **Etruscans** had certainly settled on the island to mine minerals. From 540–535 BC, in the battle of the Sardinian Sea, the Etruscans defeated the Greeks. Aristotle also mentions the island under Etruscan rule.

Phoenicians – in search or iron – had traded with the island for many centuries. Initially they were in search of copper which was important for the Bronze Age. Deposits of copper, however, ran out by the sixth century BC but iron was found at the start of the Iron Age. The Romans probably took Elba – called Fabricia – from the Etruscans in about 300 BC. They were particularly keen on supplies of iron, and also granite from the quarries. The iron was used by the Roman armies and the poet Virgil makes mention of Elba's mines of steel, noting 'Ilva, the island rich in unexhausted mines of steel'. The granite was used for construction in many places and was even used in the construction of the Parthenon in Athens. Romans came to live on the island as the remains of villas and other Roman buildings clearly attest.

During his reign, the Emperor Augustus (29 BC – AD 14) ordered a halt to mining from Italian soil, and this stopped the iron industry on Elba. By this time it had already become popular as a place of retirement for wealthy Romans, or for exile for courtiers banished from the capital. Late Roman villas had been found during excavations at Le Grotte and **Cavo** in the island of Elba, and remains have also been found on the islands of **Giglio** and Giannutri. It is also claimed that St. Paul may have preached on the island.

The poet Ovid visited Elba to stay with the son of the famous general Marcus Valerius Messalla Corvinus who fought under Octavian (later the Emperor Augustus) at the battle of Actium in 31 BC. Ovid (43 BC – AD 17/18) was subsequently went into exile at Tomis, in the Black Sea. The general is best-known as the basis for the fictional character Messalla in the book and film *Ben-Hur*.

There has been speculation that Villa Le Grotte, on Elba overlooking the Gulf of Portoferraio was owned by the Messalla family of Rome, and there is the possibility that it could have been the one where Ovid stayed. The villa dates from 1st century BC, and had been destroyed in a fire. It was excavated by a team of archaeologists during the 1960s, and again in 2015 by another team led by Franco Cambi, professor of methodology of archaeological research at the University of Siena.

References: 'Ancient villa ruins found to be the estate of chariot-racer and Ben-Hur rival', http://www.ancient-origins.net/news-history-archaeology/ancient-villa-ruins-found-be-estate-chariot-racer-and-ben-hur-rival-002694 (accessed 15 September 2015); Guido Giubella, *Elba: A Garden in the Blu*, Milan: Co. Graf Editrice, 1988, p. 11; Rossella Lorenzi, 'Villa owned by Ben0Hur's rival identified', http://news.discovery.com/history/archaeology/villa-owned-by-ben-hurs-rival-identified-150216.htm (accessed 15 September 2015) Averil Mackenzie-Grieve, *Aspects of Elba and the other islands of the Tuscan Archipelago*, London: Jonathan Cape, 1964, Chapter 4; Norman MacKenzie, *The Escape from Elba: The Fall & Flight of Napoleon 1814–1815*, Oxford: Oxford University Press, 1982, pp. 66–67; Christopher and Jean Serpell, *The Travellers' Guide to Elba and the Tuscan Archipelago*, London: Jonathan Cape, 1977, pp. 97–100.

ANTWIS, MOSTYN (1916–1944). A British chief motor mechanic 4th class in the Royal Navy, he was born in 1916 in Runcorn, Cheshire, the son of Peter Antwis (1876–1949) and Mary 'Polly' (née Lightfoot). He married Hilda Hatton in 1941 in Prescot, Lancashire, and they lived at Montpelier, Gloucestershire. Mostyn Antwis was posted as missing presumed killed on a landing craft in the Allied attack on Elba on 17 June 1944 and is commemorated on the Portsmouth Naval Memorial (panel 86, column 2).

ARCHIVES. The Italian national archival system has four tiers. The major national documents are held in Rome. However prior to the reunification of Italy, there were many independent states, and the capitals of these states maintained their own large archives. As a result many documents relating to Elba are held in the Italian State Archives in Florence, the former capital of the Grand Duchy of Tuscany. Then there are 102 regional archives with the relevant one for Elba being the Archivio di Stato di Livorno (State Archive of Livorno, Via Fiume 40, Livorno) which was created in 1941, and also has its own library, the Biblioteca dell'Archivio di Stato, Livorno. However some of the important records have not survived, with the archives of the Livorno Customs House being destroyed in 1877. Each commune has its own archives, and those of Elba are held in **Porto Azzurro**.

References: Averil Mackenzie-Grieve, *Aspects of Elba and the other islands of the Tuscan Archipelago*, London: Jonathan Cape, 1964, pp. 219–20; Francesca Trivellato, *The Familiarity of Strangers: The Sephardic Diaspora, Livorno, and Cross-Cultural Trade in the Early Modern Period*, New Haven: Yale University Press, 2009, p. 109.

ARGONAUTS. According to Apollonius of Rhodes (fl. 3rd century BC) in his epic poem Argonautica, the legendary Greek mariner Jason and the Argonauts travelled to Elba after Jason had captured the Golden Fleece. Indeed Apollonius notes that some skin coloured pebbles there were the same ones on which the Argonauts dried their hands, and there were also large stones which they used in discus competitions. Strabo, however, disagrees with this interpretation and argues 'because the scrapings, which the Argonauts formed when they used their strigils, became congealed, the pebbles on the shore remain variegated still to this day.'

References: Apollonius of Rhodes, *The voyage of Argo*, Harmondsworth, Middx: Penguin Books, 1971; J. R. Bacon, *The Voyage of the Argonauts*, London: Methuen, 1925; Vernon Bartlett, *A Book about Elba*, London: Chatto & Windus, 1965, pp. 49–50; R. J. Clare, *The Path of the Argo: Language, Imagery and Narrative in the Argonautica of Apollonius Rhodius*, Cambridge: Cambridge University Press, 2002.

ARRIGHI de CASANOVA, GIUSEPPE FILIPPO (1758–1836). He was a Corsican, the youngest of the four sons of Gio Tomasa Arrighi de Casanova (and his wife Mari'Anna (née Biadelli). His oldest brother Giacinto Arrighi de Casanova, took the French name Hyacinthe Arrighi de Casanova and represented Corsica in the French Corps Législatif from 1800 to 1814, and was the préfet of Corsica from 11 June 1811 to 1814. His second brother, Anton Luigi Arrighi de Casanova (Antoine-Louis Arrighi de Casanova, 1755–1809) was the bishop of Acqui and the vicar general of Elba until his death on 28 December 1809 whereupon his younger brother Giuseppe, who had also been ordained a priest, and was an honorary canon at the Cathedral of Pisa was appointed to that position. The brothers were also first cousins by marriage to **Napoleon Bonaparte**'s mother, **Letizia Bonaparte**.

Giuseppe Arrighi de Casanova was the vicar general on Elba when he heard that Napoleon Bonaparte was about to arrive at **Portoferraio** on 3 May 1814. Because of his connection to the Bonaparte family, Arrighi had the task of formally welcoming the ex-emperor to Elba in a flowery address which made mention of the 'changing politics of Europe' and that this was Divine Providence giving Elba a chance for 'glory and prosperity'. He added that 'wealth will pour into the land', a sentiment which was certainly accurate as it caused many travellers to visit Elba ever since. Arrighi first met Napoleon on board the *Undaunted*, hoping undoubtedly to make something of his Corsican background. He then was present when the ex-emperor landed, and on 6 May during a service of thanksgiving, noted:

To my well-beloved in the Lord, my brethren of the clergy, and all the faithful of the island, health and benediction. Divine Providence, which in its benevolence irresistibly disposes all things, and assigns their destinies to nations, has willed that in the midst of the political changes of Europe, we should become for the future the subjects of Napoleon the Great. The Island of Elba, already celebrated for its natural productions, will hereafter become illustrious in the history of nations by the homage it renders to its new Prince, whose glory is immortal. The Island of Elba, in fact, takes rank among nations, and its narrow territory is ennobled by the name of its sovereign. Raised to so sublime an honor, it receives in its bosom the Anointed of the Lord, and the other distinguished personages who accompany him... What wealth is about to inundate our country! What multitudes will hasten from all parts to gaze upon the hero! The first day that he set foot upon this shore he proclaimed our destiny and our happiness. 'I will be a good father', said he, 'be my beloved children.' Dear Catholics, what words of tenderness! What expressions of good-will! What a pledge of your future felicity! May these words charm your thoughts delightfully and be strongly imprinted in your souls; they will prove an inexhaustible source of consolation!

Napoleon appointed Arrighi to the Council of State of Elba, and it seems he remained on the island when Napoleon left in February 1815. Arrighi died in 1836.

References: Imbert de Saint-Amand, *Marie Louise, the island of Elba and the Hundred Days*, New York, C. Scribner's Sons, 1891, pp. 15–16; Norman MacKenzie, *The Escape from Elba: The Fall & Flight of Napoleon 1814–1815*, Oxford: Oxford University Press, 1982, pp. 71–73; Norwood Young and Alexander Meyrick Broadley, *Napoleon in exile: Elba – from the entry of the allies into Paris on the 31st March 1814 to the return of Napoleon from Elba and his landing at Golfe Jouan on the 1st March 1815*, London: S. Paul & Co, 1914.

- B -

BADILEY, RICHARD (c.1616–1657). A British naval officer, he fought the Dutch off Elba in 1652. Nothing for certain is known about the origins of Richard Badiley until he was recorded as the master's mate of the *Increase* at Cadiz in 1636, when aged 20. He served in actions against the Turks in 1637, and again in 1640 and 1644. Also involved in trade with North America, he soon began to be an important captain in the navy being established by Cromwell's government. He sailed under Robert Blake to Lisbon where they hoped to attack the ships of Prince Rupert. He then served under Blake in the taking of Jersey, before becoming involved in guarding convoys of merchant ships in the Mediterranean.

In 1652, the Anglo-Dutch War broke out and Badiley remained in the Mediterranean to protect British merchantmen. On 27 August of that year Badiley was in charge of only four ships when they came across a large Dutch force under the command of **Johan van Galen** near the island of Montecristo, near Elba. On the following day, 28 August, in the Battle of Elba, Badiley's own vessel, the Paragon, was badly damaged with a third of his crew being casualties. He fled for the safety of Porto Longone (**Porto Azzurro**), Elba, then under Spanish control. The Spanish government refused to let the Dutch attack and this allowed Badiley to repair his ships. Blake was defeated at the battle of Dungeness on 30 November (9 December, n.s.) by the Dutch, and Badiley was given command of the English fleet in the area allowing him to go to Leghorn where there were a number of English merchantmen, and also, more importantly, the *Phoenix*, an English warship which had been captured by the Dutch in the engagement on 28 August. In a night-raid, the English retook the *Phoenix* but incurred the wrath of the Grand Duke of Tuscany who ordered Badiley to leave in February 1653. Badiley returned to London and his daughter, Elizabeth, was born in Wapping, and baptised on 31 January 1654 at Bull Lane Independent Church, Stepney. Richard Badiley died on 7 or 11 August 1657 at Wapping, being buried on 14 August at St. John-at-Wapping.

References: B. Capp, *Cromwell's navy: the fleet and the English revolution, 1648–1660*, Oxford: Clarendon Press, 1989; Bernard Capp, 'Badiley, Richard (c.1616–1657)', *Oxford Dictionary of National Biography*, Oxford University Press, 2004; T. A. Spalding, *A life of Richard Badiley*, Westminster, A Constable and Co., 1899.

BALBIANI, GIUSEPPE. He was the sub-prefect of Elba from 1811, a Tuscan lawyer with a large family, he held the position when Napoleon arrived there in May 1814, and was one of the local dignitaries who gathered when the *Undaunted* arrived at Portoferraio on 3 May. He boarded the *Undaunted* that night and helped advise the ex-emperor on the new **flag** for Elba.

References: Norman MacKenzie, *The Escape from Elba: The Fall & Flight of Napoleon 1814–1815*, Oxford: Oxford University Press, 1982; Sir Henry Drummond Wolff, *The island empire, or the scenes of the first exile of the Emperor Napoleon I*, London: T. Bosworth, 1855.

BANTI, MIRELLA (1964–   ). An Italian actress, she was born on 16 December 1964 at **Marciana Marina** and has starred in many films including: *Si ringrazia la regione Puglia per averci fornito i milanesi* (1982); *Tenebre* (1982); *Al bar dello sport* (1983); *Acapulco, prima spiaggia... a sinistra* (1983); *Vivre pour survivre* (1984); *Due assi per un turbo* (1984); *Nucleo zero* (1984); *State buoni se potete* (1984); *La più bella del reame* (1989); *Appuntamento in nero* (1990); *Mezzaestate* (1991); *Favola crudele* (1991); *Nostalgia di un piccolo grande amore* (1991); *Addio e ritorno* (1995); *La signora della città* (1996); and *Angelo nero* (1998).

BARBER, STEPHEN (1922–1980). A long-time Washington correspondent for the British newspapers *The Daily Telegraph* and *The Sunday Telegraph*, he had been born in Egypt where his father worked in the colonial service. Educated on the Isle of Wight, he became a copy writer for an advertising company and then in 1942 was appointed the naval correspondent for Associated Press, and spent some time on assignments with **Vernon Bartlett**. Covering the Allied landing on Elba in June 1944, he was injured by shrapnel. He was later the first correspondent to report on the death of Benito Mussolini. He then reported from behind partisan lines during the Greek Civil War in 1947, and then during the Korean War. He then spent 17 years reporting from Washington DC writing *America in Retreat* about the plight of the United States during the Vietnam War. He died on 30 March 1980 in the US capital.

References: 'Mr Stephen Barber – Notable Correspondent', *The Times* (2 April 1980), p. 18; Oliver Woods and James D. Bishop, *The Story of The Times*, London: Michael Joseph, 1983, p. 318.

BARBIELLINI AMIDEI, GASPARE (1934–2007). An Italian writer and journalist, he was born on 26 November 1934, the son of Bernardo Barbiellini

Amidi (1896–1940), and Anna Maria (d. 1998; nee Pullè). He was born on the Italian liner *Conte Rosso* in the Indian Ocean, his parents were from **Marciana Marina** which is often listed as his place of birth. After completing his university education, he moved to Rome and became a journalist for *Il Tempo*.

Barbiellini wrote many books: *Il Minusvalore* (1971); *Il re è un feticcio, with Bachisio Bandinu* (1976); *I Labirinti della sociologia, with Ulderico Bernardi* (1977); *Carovana di carta* (1978); *I nostri ragazzi* (1982); *I nostri ragazzi crescono* (1983); *La riscoperta di Dio* (1984); *Storia di lei* (1986); *I nuovi ragazzi* (1987); *Il potere* (1988); *Gli uomini di carta* (1990); *Ragazzo, dove vai?* (1990); *Perché credere* (1991); *Noi ragazzi, noi genitori* (1992); *Come insegnare l'educazione ai vostri figli* (1994); *La grammatica della vita* (1994); *Quel profondo desiderio di Dio* (1996); *L'amore è salvo* (1996); *New Age next age: Facile dea* (1998); *Le domande di tutti* (2002); *Picasso, Guernica* (2006) and *Quella bottega di via Montenapoleone* (2007). He combined his writing and journalism with social work and promoting charities. A commentator on Italian society, he was seen as a voice of Catholic liberalism. He died on 12 July 2007 in Rome.

References: Rudolf Arnheim, *To the Rescue of Art: Twenty-six essays*, Berkeley: University of California Press, 1992, p. 11.

BARKER, HENRY ASTON (1774–1856). A panorama painter and proprietor who visited Elba where he met **Napoleon**, he was born in Glasgow, the younger son of Robert Barker (1739–1806), a Scottish panorama painter, and his wife, Catherine, (née Aston, 1744–1842). He was baptised on 23 March 1774 in Glasgow. When he was twelve he accompanied his father to Edinburgh where Robert Barker was working on a 360 degree panorama of Edinburgh. He later worked on one of London. Henry also made his way to the British capital and studied at the Royal Academy and then established his panorama building in Leicester Square on 25 May 1793. This was a system in which a painting was completed covering the city and people would pay to look at it – Henry Barker's rooms were called 'The Panorama'. In 1799 Henry Barker went to Constantinople to make two panoramas of the capital of the Ottoman Empire. By this time he had made his name from making scenes of major battles of the **Napoleonic**

Wars, and on his return from Constantinople, Barker stopped at Palermo and there met **Horatio Nelson** who, according to Barker, 'took me by the hand and said he was indebted to me for keeping up the fame of victory in the Battle of the Nile for a year longer than it would have lasted in the public estimation'.

On 3 January 1802 Henry Barker married Harriet Maria Bligh (1782–1856), daughter of Captain (later Rear-Admiral) William Bligh, the survivor of the Mutiny on the H.M.S. *Bounty*. Henry and Harriet Barker lived next door to his father in London, and took over the family business in 1806. With the defeat of **Napoleon** in 1814, Barker went to Elba to meet the former Emperor whom he had met in 1802 when, briefly, Britain and France were at peace, and Barker had been putting together a panorama of Paris. At Elba Barker made some drawings of the island, and wrote a brief account of his time there in which he was granted access to the ex-emperor by Antoine Drouot. However soon afterwards, with the '100 Days and the Waterloo', Barker made a massive panorama of that battle which made him some £10,000. His last panorama was The Coronation Procession of George IV. He retired and lived at Cheam, Surrey, and then moved to Bristol, and for the last 30 years of his life, lived at Bitton, near Bristol where he died on 19 July 1856, and was buried in the churchyard of St Mary's Church, Bitton.

References: Henry Aston Barker, *A short description of the island of Elba, and town of Porto-Ferrajo; illustrative of the view now exhibiting in Henry Aston Barker's Panorama*, Leicester Square, London: J. Adlard, 1815; G. R. Corner, *The panorama, with memoirs of its inventor, Robert Barker, and his son, the late Henry Aston Barker*, London: Printed by J.& W. Robins, 1857; Ralph Hyde, 'Barker, Henry Aston (1774–1856)', *Oxford Dictionary of National Biography*, Oxford University Press, 2004; S. B. Wilcox, *The panorama and related exhibitions in London*, MLitt Thesis, University of Edinburgh, 1976.

BARTLETT, (CHARLES) VERNON (OLDFIELD) (1894–1983). An English journalist and writer who was also a member of parliament from 1938 to 1950, he wrote a book on Elba in 1965 at a time when tourists from Britain were starting to visit the island in large numbers. Born on 30 April 1894 at Westbury, Wiltshire, he was the son of Thomas Oldfield Bartlett and Mary Beatrice (née Jecks). Educated at Blundell's School, he worked as an English teacher in Berlin, and then served in **World War I** but was invalided out of the army in 1915 and became a journalist for the *Daily Mail*, and then foreign correspondent for *The Times*. Appointed the director of the London office of the League of Nations, he then became the diplomatic correspondent for the *News Chronicle* for 20 years, reporting from Spain during the Spanish Civil War.

He was elected to the House of Commons as a Popular Front candidate in a by-election in November 1938 – he stood on a platform against appeasement – and was re-elected in the next elections in 1945 as an independent, joining the Labour Party in 1950. He worked for *The Straits Times* in Singapore from 1954 to 1961, and on his retirement enjoyed travelling in Europe, buying a farm in Lucca. From there he visited Elba and in his book on the island, noted that few people knew much more about Elba than that **Napoleon** had spent less than a year there in 1814–15. He wrote:

I knew that Elba looked beautiful from the air, but what island does not look beautiful from the poky little window of an aeroplane? The local tourist office supplied me with an attractively illustrated folder, but I knew how effectively the camera can lie. The tourist office also gave me the name of an hotel, and the assurance that I should have no difficulty in getting a room since the season was nearly over. To be on the safe side, I wrote two weeks in advance to book accommodation. Filled with optimism, we set out one stormy September morning along that damned Via Aurelia.

Most of us have been fascinated by islands, ever since the first time we stood on one built of sand and defied the rising tide, with no more success than that of King Canute; or discovered islands in the patches of damp on some wall or ceiling; or drew maps, with furry caterpillars to denote the mountain ranges and with X marking the spot where the pirates had buried the treasure; or tried to decide what discs we would take with us if we were wrecked on a desert island with a gramophone which, by some miracle, had escaped damage when the ship went down.

Millionaires and travel agents are scouring the islands of the Caribbean and the Mediterranean. Hotels with swimming pools and dance floors are replacing the penal institutions for which so many islands were used by our ancestors. The Lipari Islands, where Mussolini liked to exile his political opponents, may soon become as popular as Majorca, and jazz music has replaced the songs of 'burning Sappho' on the Isles of Greece. Writing in 1837, A. C. Pasquin, in his Voyages en Corse etc., remarked that, 'of all the islands which stud the Tyrrhenian Sea, so celebrated in the history of the first nations of Italy, there is not one more interesting and less known than the Isle of Elba'. This remark still applies today, although the number of cars brought over to the island- most of them with German number-plates, for the Germans have replaced the British as discoverers of out of the way places- doubled in the four years from 1958 to 1962.

On that first day, I was not in the least astonished to find Elba so unspoilt and so little known. The sea was so rough that I wondered why we ourselves were such fools as to visit it. The rain had driven all the other unhappy passengers into the saloon, where there was a depressing lack of privacy for those who wanted, or rather were doomed, to be ill. The only consolation was the extraordinary perceptiveness of the barman. Almost before a passenger was aware of that ominous queasiness, he was; five minutes before it was needed, he had surreptitiously placed a bowl where it was not offensively conspicuous, and yet would be within easy reach at the critical moment. The principal ship that carries passengers and their cars to the island is a converted landing craft, and when she is in dock, with her bow raised like an immense upper jaw, she makes one think of Jonah's whale. A whale waiting for her cargo of mechanized Jonahs. But in this case it is not the whale that suffers from sickness.

All bad things come to an end. Recuperating, we drove across the island, and down the worst road I have ever known, to our hotel. The manager blandly explained that no room was vacant, but that he had forgotten to write to tell us so. On our way up the hill again, I tried to avoid an oncoming car, and my side wheels skidded on the loose surface into a ditch. It was dark when we got our suitcases into a small room in another hotel that was expensive, pretentious, horribly noisy, and 'modern' in the beastliest sense of the word. I hated Elba, and thought with longing of my little farm and of its lovely view of the Tuscan hills. But things looked different after a night's sleep. Within twenty-four hours, in a small hotel bungalow a mere thirty yards from the sea, I was reproaching myself for my faint-heartedness. Within forty-eight hours I knew that Elba was as satisfying in its beauty as any place I have ever known.

Nothing can now check the flood of visitors to this incredible island. But the duration of that satisfying beauty will depend upon the kind of visitors welcome, and the kind of encouragement to these visitors given by the authorities. Between 1957 and 1962, the number of Italian tourists visiting Capri – that is to say, of tourists, many of whom were going there only for one day-increased from 68,ooo to 93,000, but the number of foreign visitors-that is to say, of visitors many of whom went there for some weeks or more decreased from 221,000 to 199,000. Elba, it is true, is much farther away than Capri from a large city, but its authorities would nevertheless be wise to listen to the mayor of Capri, who recently complained that the invasion by day tourists during the short summer season was g:ravely damaging the island's long-term residential attractions. .One may still hope that the visitors to Elba will come because they appreciate its natural beauties, and not because they expect every little village to contain what the Italians call a 'night', where they can dance, drink, dine and enjoy a floor show until the early hours of the morning. For such holiday-makers – and good luck to them – the coast of the mainland, from Forte de' Marmi and Viareggio to Follonica, provides its miles of wide beach with enough sun umbrellas to reach, if placed end to end from the Simplon to Rome; one ventures to hope they will long allow those of us who prefer quieter and less sophisticated holidays to do so on Elba.

Our second visit was in May, well before the beginning of the season, and I had not therefore taken the precaution of reserving car accommodation on the steamer (and every wise visitor will write to the Societa di Navigazione Toscana at Piombino to do so). We arrived at Piombino dock more than an hour before sailing time, but there were no car berths left, and it was no comfort to be told that those who want to spend a holiday on the island in July or August have to book at least three weeks in advance. I was, however, luckier than some others who had to pass the night on the mainland; there would still be room, they told me, on a smaller and slower boat to Porto Azzurro, which was nearly as far from my destination as it could be on so small an island. We spent several hot and boring hours waiting at Piombino, and then fumed and fretted while a crane hoisted our car on board. But, in the event, I found that I had no great reason to complain, for the voyage to Porto Azzurro, instead of to Portoferraio, helped to underline a feeling which is never quite absent when I am on Elba – the feeling that one is immensely remote from the continent of Europe.

Off the mining town of Rio our engines stopped while a mixed cargo which included several pieces of furniture was dumped over the side into a large rowing boat. I had so often watched this sort of thing happening from the deck of a cargo boat in some small African or Asian port. And when our ship manoeuvred alongside the quay at Porto Azzurro, what seemed to be the entire population of that charming little town came along to welcome her. Our reception reminded me of the welcome given to the 'Rajah Brooke' on her weekly visit to Kuching, the capital of Sarawak. The Elbans are as pleased as anybody else to be Italians, but, time after time, one hears Elbans talking not of the mainland, but of the 'continente'. Cavo, the nearest little town to the mainland (but not the one where normally one lands; most boats go on to Portoferraio or Porto Azzurro) is only some six miles from Piombino, but somehow Elba has very definitely retained an individuality of its own.

In the next berth to us at Porto Azzurro was a schooner, painted green, yellow and red. Her cargo consisted of bricks. And every time I visit either of the ports I find men unloading building materials for more houses and more hotels. No introduction to the Elba of today could be more typical than the overcrowded ferry boat and the schooner's cargo.

Vernon Bartlett wrote of Vico Mantegazza's account of Elba in *Isola d'Elba* (1920):

His description of Portoferraio at the beginning of the nineteen twenties confirms my impression on my arrival at Porto Azzurro – this island, so close to the mainland of Europe, still has, or had until very recently, features which one usually associates with remote colonial territories. Everyone who claimed to be anybody met at lunch time in the restaurant of the Hotel Ape Elbana (still existing in quiet dignity at one corner of the Piazza della Repubblica, the Piazza d'Armi in Napoleon's day), as they used to gather in the club at Dar-es-Salaam, or Kuala Lumpur or Saigon or Dakar in colonial days. There would be the sub-prefect, the officers of the garrison, the leading business men, the senior officials of the Societa degli Alti Forni which mined and exported the ore. Later in the day the meeting place would be the Alti Forni's sports club, with its tennis courts, its swimming pool and its reading room. Although Elba is so close to the continent, there was then no telegraphed news service and in bad weather, when the steamer could not make the crossing, it was completely cut off from the rest of the world. Inevitably, the rest of Italy was considered part of a remote continent.

The most surprising comments on Elba and its people were made by Pons de d'Herault himself surprising, because he knew and loved the island so much better than all the other writers. In a short book which was published apart from his Souvenirs d'Elbe, he wrote that 'the people of Portoferraio, amongst whom the Tuscan government formerly dumped its important exiles, have studied the manners of these exiles, and have acquired a shadow of what are called the usages of good society. But imitation is not always resemblance. It is gauche when it is timid and ridiculous when it is exaggerated ... The Elbans themselves complain that the people of Portoferraio travel around the island allowing people whom they scarcely know to entertain them and avoiding the repayment of the politeness they have received.... Some of them affect a superiority which offends the inhabitants of the other towns.... Despite these nuances,' he adds, making amends as an afterthought, 'the people of Portoferrioa are a good people, and I know none better in Tuscany.'

Of his own home on Elba, Rio, he wrote that the two Rios, Alta and Marina, 'have never agreed and they never will'. The people of Marciana Alta, which was the centre of government in the time of the Appiani, 'consider themselves at least as equals of the Portoferrese.' 'When Portoferraio says white, Marciana says black, even when black is against its interests.' Marciana looks towards Piombino as Portoferraio looks towards Florence. Its inhabitants have little to do with the rest of the island. 'I lived for several years in Rio, and never saw anyone there who came from Marciana; I am sure that during that period nobody from Rio ever went to Marciana.'

Of all the Elbans, those of Campo have the fewest relations with the continent. They have no trade, for one cannot apply that word to their small sales of wine .... Civilization has not yet reached their region.' He wrote of Porto Azzurro (then Porto Langone) as though it were inhabited only by detainees in the fortress. 'They inspire one with the repulsion one feels towards even the best behaved prisoners.' And poor Capoliveri was, as always, the scapegoat. In his view- but most certainly not in mine- 'the population of Capoliveri is the scum of the population of Elba. Idle, egoistic, untruthful, they have all the degrading vices.'

To end this chapter of unkindly comment, I revert to the crusty and bad-tempered Thiebaut. In Capoliveri he 'never saw but one pretty woman, and she was a foreigner'. On the other hand, his compatriot, Paul Gruyer (writing, it is true, ninety-eight years later) expressed the opinion that 'the Elban women are handsome, with regular features, milk-white skin, and masses of fine, black, wavy hair'. Pons de l'Herault wrote that they have 'the most beautiful hair in the world'. And perhaps it is not only in men's opinions of women that objectivity is a very rare quality indeed.

Vernon Bartlett wrote the last volume in his autobiography, *I Know What I Liked*, and died on 18 January 1983.

References: Vernon Bartlett, *A Book about Elba*, London: Chatto & Windus, 1965, pp. 12–17, 37–39; reviewed by M. J. Clegg, *The Geographical Journal* vol. 131, no 3 (September 1965), pp. 390–91; Vernon Bartlett, *I Know What I Liked*, London: Chatto & Windus, 1974; Leonard Miall, 'Bartlett, (Charles) Vernon Oldfeld (1894–1983)', revised by *Oxford Dictionary of National Biography*, Oxford University Press, 2004; *The Times* (20 January 1983), p. 12.

BEAUME, JOSEPH (1796–1885). A French artist, he painted the famous picture of **Napoleon** leaving Elba (see p. 169). Born on 27 September 1796 at Marseille, he went to school in Gros. Initially painting biblical scenes, he gradually became more ambitious, and one of his most famous paintings was *Bénédiction et la pose de la première pierre du monument de Louis XVI*. However his *Napoléon Ier quittant l'île d'Elbe,* painted in 1836 provides a dramatic image of the proud ex-emperor about to gamble everything on returning to France. This painting was, itself, not without controversy. Initially it was planned to hang the painting in one of the historical galleries at Versailles. However this was stopped after Louis-Napoleon, a nephew of Napoleon Bonaparte (and later Napoleon III) tried to stage a rebellion against the French government, planning to march on Paris as his uncle had done in 1815. This made the painting potentially subversive and it ended up at the Musée Naval et Napoléonien du Cap d'Antibes. Joseph Beaume died on 11 September 1885 in Paris.

References: Barbara Ann Day-Hickman, *Napoleonic Art: Nationalism and the Spirit of Rebellion in France (1815–1848)*, Newark: University of Delaware Press, 1999, p. 115.

BECHI, STANISLAO ELBANO (1828–1863). An Italian soldier, he was born in **Portoferraio**, the son of Alexis Becchi who had served in the Napoleonic forces and then was a major in the Tuscan artillery. Stanislao Bechi served in the Italian forces after Unification, and then went to Poland to help the Poles fighting the Russians. He was promoted to colonel and led the Poles but were eventually overwhelmed by the Russians and in December 1863 when he was taken prisoner and then executed at Włocławek, in spite of protests from Italy and elsewhere. Funds were raised for his widow and children who later moved to England. In 1938 the Italian military reburied his remains in Italy, with a memorial erected at Włocławek.

References: Niccolò Tommaseo, *Stanislao Bechi, documenti della sua vita e della sua morte*, Firenze: Tip. Barbèra, 1864.

BEECHAM, JOHN ARTHUR (1922–1944). A petty officer in the British Royal Navy, he was the son of Albert E. and Gertrude W. Beecham, of Didcot, Berkshire. Mentioned in Despatches, he was serving on a landing craft during the attack on Elba on 17 June 1944, he the landing craft was sunk and Beecham was posted as missing, presumed killed. He is commemorated on the Plymouth Naval Memorial (panel 85, column 2).

BEECHER, KENNETH PAUL (1924–1944). An able-bodied seaman in the British Royal Navy, he was born in late 1924 in Cardiff, Wales, the son of Archie Beecher and Alice (née Tobin) of Cardiff. Joining the Royal Navy, was amongst the group that stormed ashore on the island of Elba at **Marina di Campo** on 17 June 1944. Under very heavy fire from the Germans, most of the attackers, including Kenneth Beecher, were killed. His body may be one of the six unidentified bodies initially interred in the local cemetery at Marina di Campo, and later reburied at Bolsena War Cemetery on the Italian mainland, the headstone bearing the caption 'Known Unto God'. He is commemorated on the Plymouth Memorial (panel 85, column 2).

References: *The war dead of the British Commonwealth and Empire; the register of the names of those who fell in the 1939–1945 war and have no other grave than the sea: Plymouth Naval Memorial*, Maidenhead: Imperial War Graves Commission, 1952, p. 42.

BELLECOUR, CESARE DE LAUGIER, COMTE DE (1789–1871). An Italian soldier, he was born on 5 October 1789 at Portoferraio, from a noble family originally from Nancy. During the French Revolution, the family had to flee with all their property seized by the revolutionaries. The family arrived on Elba but Cesare decided to support **Napoleon** and served in the French forces in Spain and then the 1812 invasion of Russia. Later serving Murat, the brother-in-law of Napoleon Bonaparte in Naples, he joined the army of the Grand Duchy of Tuscany and was then posted to Venice. His memoirs, *Gli italiani in Russia* ('The Italians in Russia', 1826), *Fasti e vicende militari degli italiani dal 1801 al 1815* ('A chronology of military events of the Italians from 1801 to 1815, 1829–31', 13 vols), and *Concisi ricordi di un soldato napoleonico* (Concise memories of a Napoleonic soldier, 1870) were important contributions to literature on the **Napoleonic Wars**, and he also wrote about the Italian Legion that went to Montevideo, Uruguay. He died in Fiesole.

BENTINCK, Lord WILLIAM HENRY CAVENDISH (1774–1839). Later the governor-general of India, he went to Elba to visit **Napoleon** in 1814. He had been born on 14 September 1774 at Burlington House, London, the second son of William Henry Cavendish Cavendish-Bentinck, third duke of Portland (1738–1809), and Lady Dorothy Cavendish (1750–1794), the only daughter of William Cavendish, fourth duke of Devonshire. His father was a leading Whig politician and twice prime minister, but the family estates fell into debt during this period and William Bentinck jnr, after leaving Westminster School, gained a commission as ensign in the 2nd (Coldstream) Guards in 1791. He was promoted to captain in 1793 and purchased the rank of lieutenant-colonel in the following year, going with his new regiment, the 24th Light Dragoons, to Ireland. He was a member of parliament from 1796 – initially for Cornwall and then for Nottinghamshire from 1796–1803, 1812–14 and 1816–26. He served in Italy and was present at the battle of Marengo on 14 June 1800. In the following year he went to India and from 1803 to 1807 was governor of Madras. However he was recalled after news reached London of a mutiny of Indian soldiers at Vellore. He then served in the Peninsular War, and saw action at the battle of Corunna on 16 January 1809. Then the British envoy to the court of the kingdom of the Two Sicilies, he moved to Naples and became dangerously enmeshed in Neapolitan and Sicilian politics. He landed some British soldiers in northern Italy in February 1814, capturing Genoa on 19 April. Napoleon's abdication gave him the opportunity to meet the ex-emperor in Elba. William Bentinck returned to India in 1828 as governor-general and remained there until 1835. He reformed much of the administration and worked towards the abolition of suttee. Returning to England, he and his wife retired to Paris and he died there on 17 June 1839. His body was brought back to England and was buried in the family vault at Trinity Chapel, Marylebone, Middlesex.

References: John Alger, *Napoleon's British visitors and captives, 1801–1815*, New York: J. Pott, 1904, pp. 295–96; Douglas M. Peers, 'Bentinck, Lord William Henry Cavendish- (1774–1839)', *Oxford Dictionary of National Biography*, Oxford University Press, 2004; John Rosselli, *Lord William Bentinck and the British occupation of Sicily, 1811–1814*, Cambridge: Cambridge University Press, 1956; John Rosselli, *Lord William Bentinck: the making of a liberal imperialist, 1774–1839*, Berkeley: University of California Press, 1974, pp. 177–78.

BERNOTTI, ROMEO (1877–1974). An Italian admiral, he was born on 24 February 1877 at **Marciana Marina**, and joined the navy and was gradually promoted to vice-admiral and then admiral during the Mussolini government.

Described by Enrico Cernuschi and Vincent P. O'Hara as 'a brilliant theoretician', Bernotti wrote extensively on naval tactics, including many articles in *Rivista Marittima*, and was appointed deputy chief of staff of the navy in December 1927. He retired from the navy in 1939, and was appointed a senator. He died on 18 March 1974 in Rome.

References: Romeo Bernotti, *The Fundamentals of Naval Tactics*, Annapolis, Md., United States Naval Institute, 1912; Enrico Cernuschi and Vincent P. O'Hara, 'Search for a flattop: the Italian navy and the aircraft carrier 1907–2007', *Warship* 2007, pp. 61–80 at pp. 67–68.

BERTI, LUIGI (1904–1964). A writer and poet, he was born at **Rio Marina**, his parents being shipowners. He went to study seafaring in Genoa and was expected to take over the family business which involved the running of a ferry service. However with the development of faster steamships, his family business failed and he moved to Florence where he studied literature and philosophy. In 1946 he founded a literary magazine and wrote *Boccaporto* (1940); *Foscolo traduttore di Sterne* (1942); *Boccaporto secondo* (1944); *L'immaginismo* (1944); and *Storia della letteratura americana* (1961, 4 Vols). He was also was involved in translating the works of George Elliot, Hermann Melville, and William Makepeace Thackeray. He died in February 1964 in Milan.

References: Luigi Berti, *Tramonto sull'Elba*, Milan: Editrice Ceschina, 1962.

BERTRAND, HENRI GATIEN (1773–1844). The Grand Marshal of the Palace of **Napoleon** in 1813 he went with the ex-emperor to Elba. He was born on 28 March 1773 at the Château Raoul, Châteauroux, Indre, and was from a well-to-do middle class family, his father Henry Bertrand was in charge of the waters and forests in the area. He joined the army and was at the Prytanée National Militaire during the French Revolution. He then joined the army and took part in Napoleon's expedition to Egypt where he was gazetted colonel in 1798 and promoted to brigadier-general. After the battle of Austerlitz in 1805, he was appointed the emperor's aide de camp. He then worked closely with Napoleon being involved in 1809 in directing the construction of the bridges across the Danube which allowed them to win the battle of Wagram. In 1811 he was appointed governor of the Illyrian Provinces (modern-day Slovenia and Croatia), and then served in the German campaign in 1813 as commander of the IV Corps. At the battle of Leipzig on 16–19 October 1813, Bertrand managed to extricate some of the French soldiers which prevented the French army from being totally annihilated.

Comte Bertrand travelled with the ex-emperor to Elba on the *Undaunted* and was the chief assistant to Napoleon on Elba. His wife, Fanny (née Dillon), was the daughter of an Irish general who was serving in the French army. She came to Elba on 16 July 1814 and brought with her the news of the death of Josephine. She also brought one of Josephine's dresses which is still on display at the **Villa dei Mulini**.

Returning to France with Napoleon, Bertrand was at the side of Napoleon during the battle of Waterloo campaign and then followed Napoleon to St. Helena. He was condemned to death in France in 1816 but was finally granted an amnesty by King Louis XVIII after the death of Napoleon. This allowed him to return to France and in 1830 he was elected a deputy to the French National Assembly, but was defeated in the elections in 1834. In 1840 he was one of those who accompanied the Prince de Joinville to St. Helena to bring the body of Napoleon back to France. Comte Bertrand died on 31 January 1844 at Châteauroux and was buried at Les Invalides. His name appears on the Arc de Triomphe.

References: Mark Adkin, *The Waterloo Companion*, London: Aurum Press, 2001, p. 12; Michel Berthelot, *Bertrand, grand-maréchal du Palais: dans les pas d'un fidèle*, Châteauroux, Chez l'auteur, 1996; Arthur Bertrand, *Lettres sur l'expédition de Sainte-Hélène en 1840*, Paris: Paulin Éditeur, 1841; Pierre Branda, *L'île d'Elbe et le retour de Napoléon: 1814–1815*, Saint-Cloud: Soteca, 2014; Robert Christophe, *Napoleon on Elba*, London: Macdonald, 1964, pp. 44–50, 117–23; Raymond Horricks, *Napoleon's Elite*, New Brunswick: Transaction Publishers, 1995, p. 125; Norman MacKenzie, *The Escape from Elba: The Fall & Flight of Napoleon 1814–1815*, Oxford: Oxford University Press, 1982; François Rabasse, *Les indomptables, 1815: le retour de Napoléon de l'île d'Elbe jusqu'aux Tuileries*, [Brannay]: Éd. Sénones, DL 2014; Annette Surrault, *De la Campagne d'Egypte au Berry. Le général Henri-Gatien Bertrand et le savant Hervé Faye*, Issoudun: Alice Lyner Ed., 2012; Jacques de Vasson, *Bertrand, le Grand Maréchal de Sainte-Hélène*, Issoudun: Laboureur, 1935.

BETTARINI, LUIGI (1790–1850). An Italian architect, he was born in **Portoferraio** and moved to Livorno where he established his architectural practice. He was hired by **Napoleon Bonaparte** in 1814 to work on the **Villa dei Mulini**. Eleven years later, Bettarini constructed a guard post at **Fetovaia**. In 1830 he worked with Luigi Bosi on a new city plan for Livorno and in 1844 was involved in designing the vaulted roof of the Fosso Reale (Royal Canal) which now forms the Piazza della Repubblica. Bettarini also designed the ponte di Santa Trinità and the ponte di San Benedetto. He died in Livorno.

References: Giuseppe Argentieri and Luciano Bonetti, *Pittori, scultori ed architetti del passato (e non) a Livorno*, Livorno: Tipoffset Marengo, 2002.

BEVIS, KENNETH JOHN (1922–1944). A petty officer in the British Royal Navy, he was born in Birmingham, Warwickshire, the son of Sydney Arthur Bevis (1896–1976) and Mary Lilian (née Rowe, 1896–1972) of Erdington. Joining the Royal Navy, he was Mentioned in Despatches and served in the H.M.S. *Royal Scotsman*. Killing in the Allied capture of Elba on 17 June 1944, he was buried on Elba and three years later was reburied in the Bolsena War Cemetery (IV G 10) on the Italian mainland.

References: *The war dead of the British Commonwealth and Empire: the register of the names of those who fell in the 1939–1945 War and are buried in cemeteries in Italy Cemeteries 17–18: Bolsena War Cemetery, Orvieto War Cemetery*, Maidenhead: Imperial War Graves Commission, 1954, p. 14.

BIBLIOTECA COMUNALE FORESIANA. When **Napoleon Bonaparte** left Elba on 26 June 1815, he left behind a great collection of some 2,000 books which he had brought with him from Fontainebleau, or had been given during his 296 days in Elba. Located at Via Giuseppe Garibaldi 10, **Portoferraio**, it still holds many of Napoleon's books including his copy of **Arsène Thiébaut de Berneaud**'s *Voyage à l'île d'Elbe*, although these have been moved to the **Villa dei Mulini** at Portoferraio. The collection has been augmented over the years by other donations including from Giogio Roster and Alberto Reiter, and especially from Mario Foresi who gave a large collection to the library in around 1920. One of its rarest volumes is Joseph Antoir's *Herbier* which was compiled between 1810–30.

The library is open to researchers (Monday-Friday 10 – 12 noon; and Monday, Wednesday and Friday 3–7 pm). The writer **Averil Mackenzie-Grieve** in *Aspects of Elba* (1964) cites a number of documents which were held at the library including an anonymous diary from 1650, and the guard-house order book which detailed the visitors to Napoleon's Elba. In August 2015, the United Arab Emirates agreed to pay for renovation work on the Napoleon Library in Elba. This would in-volve digitisation of the library and the agreement was signed under the directives of H.H. Sheikh Mansour bin Zayed Al Na-hyan, Deputy Prime Minister and Minister of Presidential Affairs and the National Archive (NA), which is affiliated to the Minis-try of Presidential Affairs.

References: Averil Mackenzie-Grieve, *Aspects of Elba and the other islands of the Tuscan Archipelago*, London: Jonathan Cape, 1964; 'UAE signs deal to renovate Napoleon Museum's library in Italy', ArabianBusiness.com (17 August 2015).

BLACKWELL, GEORGE WILLIAM (1909–1944). A warrant officer in 293 Squadron of the British Royal Air Force Volunteer Reserve, he was born in mid–1909 in Cricklade, Wiltshire, the third of the four sons of Frederick William Blackwell (1881–1968), a clerk with the General Post Office, and Annie Elizabeth (née Poole, 1881–1968) of Wootton Bassett, Wiltshire. Serving in the Royal Air Force Volunteer Reserve, he was on a plane piloted by **Geoffrey Cooper**, and with **Hugh Hilton Hutchinson** and **Alfred Chapman Meeson** on board, flying from Bastia, Corsica, when it crashed on 19 November 1944, and all four on board were killed. They were buried in the Allied Military Cemetery at Elba, and then reburied in 1947 at the Bolsena War Cemetery (IV H 2).

References: *The war dead of the British Commonwealth and Empire: the register of the names of those who fell in the 1939–1945 War and are buried in cemeteries in Italy Cemeteries 17–18: Bolsena War Cemetery, Orvieto War Cemetery*, Maidenhead: Imperial War Graves Commission, 1954, p. 15.

BOE, GEORGE (1923–1944). A British seaman, he was born in 1923 in London, the youngest of the four sons of John William Boe (1902–1965) and Mary (née Rodwell, 1899–1977), of Stepney, London. He joined the Royal Navy and was an able seaman when he was killed when the Allied soldiers attacked Elba on 17 June 1944. He was buried on Elba and three years later was reburied in the Bolsena War Cemetery (IV G 14) on the Italian mainland.

References: *The war dead of the British Commonwealth and Empire: the register of the names of those who fell in the 1939–1945 War and are buried in cemeteries in Italy Cemeteries 17–18: Bolsena War Cemetery, Orvieto War Cemetery*, Maidenhead: Imperial War Graves Commission, 1954, p. 15.

BONAPARTE, ELISA (1777–1820).
The oldest of the sisters of **Napoleon Bonaparte**, she was the Grand Duchess of Tuscany from 1809 to 1814, and the only one of his sisters who had political power. On 19 March 1805 she was given the Principality of **Piombino** and with her husband Felice Baciocchi, became the Prince and Princess of Piombino. They were later invested as rulers of Lucca. During the time that Napoleon Bonaparte was on Elba, Elisa Bonaparte was arrested and held at the fortress of Brünn in Austria. She was later freed and as the Countess of Compignano, lived in Trieste and was believed to have been involved in some of the political machinations of the period. She died on 7 August 1820 and was the only adult sibling of Napoleon Bonaparte to survive the ex-emperor. She was buried at Bologna.

References: Emmanuel de Beaufond, *Élisa Bonaparte, princesse de Lucques et de Piombino*, Paris: L'Univers, 1895; Jean de Beaufort, *Élisa Bonaparte, princesse de Lucques et Piombino, grande-duchesse de Toscane (1777–1820)*, Paris: Au journal L'Univers, 1895; Raymond Horricks, *Napoleon's Elite*, New Brunswick: Transaction Publishers, 1995, pp. 50–51; Norman MacKenzie, *The Escape from Elba: The Fall & Flight of Napoleon 1814–1815*, Oxford: Oxford University Press, 1982; Florence Vidal, *Élisa Bonaparte*, Paris: éd. Pygmalion, 2005.

BONAPARTE, LETIZIA (1750–1835). The widowed mother of **Napoleon Bonaparte**, and known as the Madame Mère, she accompanied him into exile on Elba, and was to outlive her famous son. Born on 24 August 1750 at Ajaccio, Corsica, she was the daughter of Giovanni Geronimo Ramolino (1723–1755), Captain of Corse Regiments of Chivalry and Infantry in the Army of the Republic of Genoa, and his wife Angela Maria Pietrasanta (c.1725–1790). She was 13 when she married Carlo Buonaparte, an Ajaccio lawyer, and they had 13 children – five of whom died in infancy. Napoleon Bonaparte's dramatic rise to Emperor of France resulted in all the surviving children gaining senior titles. Joseph Bonaparte became king of Naples and Sicily and king

28

of Spain. Lucien Bonaparte became the Prince of Canino and Musignano. Elisa Bonaparte became Grand Duchess of Tuscany; Louis Bonaparte became king of Holland, Pauline Bonaparte became the Sovereign Princess and Duchess of Guastalla; Caroline Bonparte became the Grand Duchess of Berg and Cleves, and later the Queen Consort of Naples; and Jérome Bonaparte was the King of Westphalia.

Letizia's husband died on 24 February 1785 when she was 35, and helped look after her children but never learned to speak French. In 1804 she was given the title Madame Mère de l'Empereur [Madam, the Mother of His Majesty the Emperor], being paid an allowance of 25,000 francs per month. When Napoleon Bonaparte went to Elba, she accompanied him into exile. She arrived on the island on 2 August and took up residence at Portoferraio, and also stayed with him at the house of **Cerbone Vadi** at **Marciana**. As part of the agreement with the Allied powers, the French Bourbon government was to pay her and the rest of the Napoleon Bonaparte's relatives an allowance of 2,500,000 francs. When he returned to France, she moved to Rome and lived there with her younger half-brother Joseph Fesch. She died on 2 February 1835, aged 85. She had outlived her husband by nearly 50 years, and her famous son by 14 years.

References: Pierre Branda, *L'île d'Elbe et le retour de Napoléon: 1814–1815*, Saint-Cloud: Soteca, 2014; Robert Christophe, *Napoleon on Elba*, London: Macdonald, 1964, p. 102f; Alain Decaux, *Letizia, mère de l'Empereur*, Paris: éd. Amiot Dumont, 1951; François Duhourcau, *La Mère de Napoleon: Letizia Bonaparte*, Paris: éd. Excelsior, 1933; Raymond Horricks, *Napoleon's Elite*, New Brunswick: Transaction Publishers, 1995, pp. 53–55; Félix Hippolyte Larrey (Baron Larrey de l'Institut de France), *Madame Mère*, Paris: E. Dentu Editeur, 1892, 2 Vols; Éric Le Nabour, *Letizia Bonaparte: La mère exemplaire de Napoléon Ier*, Paris: éd. Pygmalion, 2003; Norman MacKenzie, *The Escape from Elba: The Fall & Flight of Napoleon 1814–1815*, Oxford: Oxford University Press, 1982.

BONAPARTE, NAPOLEON. *See* **Napoleon I.**

BONAPARTE, PAULINE (1780–1825). The second sister of **Napoleon Bonaparte** who joined her brother in exile on Elba, she was born on 20 October 1780 at Ajaccio, Corsica, the sixth child of Carlo Buonaparte and **Letizia Bonaparte** (née Ramolino). The family had to flee Corsica to mainland France in 1793 and with the British occupying Corsica, the money from the family estates never reached them meaning the Bonapartes lived a humble existence for a period. Being refugees from Corsica, they received payments from the government and moved to Marseille where Pauline hoped to marry Louis-Marie Stanislas Fréron, the proconsul of Marseille. However her mother objected and she married General Charles Leclerc in French-occupied Milan on 14 June 1797. Leclerc was later appointed the governor general of Saint-Domingue (Haiti) which had just rebelled against French rule. His task was to lead the expeditionary force to the West Indies. This was disastrous with a large number of soldiers lost to yellow fever. Pauline herself fell ill and Leclerc died from the disease on 1 November 1802.

Returning to Europe, she made her way to the French capital and sorted out her husband's estate. She married Camillo Borghese, 6th Prince of Sulmona in 1803 and three years later became Princess and Duchess of Guastalla. When Napoleon abdicated, she was one member of the family who remained totally loyal to her brother. With Napoleon Bonaparte on his way from Fontainebleau to the south coast of France after his abdication, Pauline met with him at Bouillidou on 26 April and the pair spoke for four hours. Pauline Bonaparte's biographer Len Ortzen has suggested plausibly that much of the discussion would have been about money with Pauline holding some very valuable jewels. She certainly wanted to go to Elba with her brother but said that she was unwell and had to delay her departure for 'five or six days'. However instead of heading to Elba straight away, she left for Naples where she met with Marshal Joachim Murat, the king of Naples, and her youngest sister Caroline. Murat had not remained loyal to Napoleon Bonaparte in the final military crisis in early 1814 but even if he had done so, his small army would not have been effective against the massive forces raised by the British, Austrians, Prussians, Russians and others. Naples remained a good location for Bonapartist intrigue and undoubtedly Pauline's discussions there would have touched on this.

Then on 30 May 1814, Pauline Bonaparte left for Elba, arriving there on 2 June 1814. She came ashore while her brother was out of **Portoferraio** and some locals thought that she was the Marie-Louise and cheered 'Long live the Empress!' She then headed to the **Villa dei Mulini** with Napoleon giving up his room for her and he slept on a camp-bed in the next room. Pauline quickly recognised the change in circumstances but felt that it was important that Napoleon had a residence outside Portoferraio. She gave a jewel to her brother which helped with the payment for, and the renovation of **Villa San Martino**. After a meeting with Count **Bertrand**, she left on the following day, heading back to Murat, undoubtedly with messages from the ex-emperor, and also to give her time to sort out her own affairs. This involved selling her two residences in Paris. The Austrians had finished drinking their way through her wine cellar at the Hôtel de Charost, but she managed to negotiate its sale to the Duke of Wellington who had just been appointed the British ambassador to Paris. She also made arrangements for particular items to be sent to Portoferraio. These included West Indian rum which she loved to drink in moderation, and also a billiard table, various clocks and carpets.

When Pauline Bonaparte returned to Elba on 1 November, she took up permanent residence on the top floor of the Villa dei Mulini, taking over nine rooms – one of which had originally been planned for Marie-Louise – it was now reasonably clear that she was not going to share her husband's exile on Elba. One of these nine rooms Pauline gave to her local servant, Madame Ducluzel. Pauline started decorating the villa with some flair. There had already been improvements since her first visit, and she played her part at the small court on Elba. After one performance held at the Villa dei Mulini, Pauline encouraged her brother to build a theatre. This took shape over the winter and the **Teatro dei Vigilanti** was opened in January 1815. With Napoleon's mother and Pauline now on Elba, the three often spent their evenings playing cards. Napoleon had always harboured a desire to return to power, and although his initial work on Elba diverted his attention, he finally resolved to return.

Most historians note that Pauline decided to host a masked ball at the Teatro dei Vigilanti which she did on 25 February to help cover her brother's move which saw his secret departure from Elba on the following evening.

However Flora Fraser, in her biography of Pauline Bonaparte, came to a slightly different view. She noted that Pauline sent invitations and when **Neil Campbell** received his on 16 February, he replied that he could not come as he would be going to Livorno to consult a doctor. When Napoleon was told of this, he decided that the time had come to leave Elba, and the absence of Campbell would be the best occasion for this. Pauline gave her brother a diamond necklace worth 500,000 francs which he then took with him to help defray any costs.

After the 100 Days, and Napoleon being exiled to St. Helena, she moved to Rome along with her mother where they had the protection of Pope Pius VII. She died on 9 June 1825 in Florence.

References: W. N. C. Carlton, *Pauline: Favourite Sister of Napoleon*, London: Thornton Butterworth, 1931; Flora Fraser, *Venus of Empire: The Life of Pauline Bonaparte*, London: John Murray, 2009; Raymond Horricks, *Napoleon's Elite*, New Brunswick: Transaction Publishers, 1995, pp. 51–53; Norman MacKenzie, *The Escape from Elba: The Fall & Flight of Napoleon 1814–1815*, Oxford: Oxford University Press, 1982; Len Ortzen, *Imperial Venus: Pauline Bonaparte*, London: Constable, 1974.

BORGHESE, PAULINE. *See* **Bonaparte, Pauline**.

BORGIA, CESARE (1475/6–1507). The illegitimate son of Pope Alexander VI and his long-time mistress Vannozza dei Cattanei, his father had hoped that he would have a career in the church with his older brother Juan as the military commander. However Cesare detested his brother who proved to be an ineffectual soldier. With his father as pope, Cesare Borgia sought to carve out a power base in the Romagna and increase the power of the papacy. Financed through the sale of offices, Cesare Borgia fielded a large army and on 1 June 1501 attacked Piombino and when he finally took the city, it gave him control of Elba. However the death of Pope Alexander VI in 1503 led to the end of Cesare's plans, and Elba was back in the hands of Tuscany. Cesare Borgia then went to Spain where he died on 12 March 1507.

References: Christopher Hibbert, *The Borgias and Their Enemies*, London: Constable, 2009; Averil Mackenzie-Grieve, *Aspects of Elba and the other islands of the Tuscan*

32

Archipelago, London: Jonathan Cape, 1964, pp. 61–62; Rafael Sabatini, *The Life of Cesare Borgia*, London: Stanley Paul, 1923; William Harrison Woodward, *Cesare Borgia: a biography*, London: Chapman and Hall, 1913.

BOYD, ROBERT T. (d. 1944). A US airman killed on a reconnaissance flight to Livorno, he was from New York and served as second lieutenant with the 347th American Air Force Fighter Squadron. He was flying a Bell P–39 Airacobra 42–8971 with **Milton Harber** when their plane crashed at Elba on 4 April 1944. Awarded the Purple Heart Medal, he is buried at the Florence American Cemetery.

BRIGGS, THOMAS DEVLIN (1917–1944). A British seaman, he was born in 1917 at Castle Ward, Cumberland, the third and youngest son, and eighth and youngest child of Ralph Briggs (1879–1946) and Dorothy (née Devlin, 1880–1950) of Scotswood, Newcastle-on-Tyne. He served as a petty officer with H.M.S. *Copra* (combined operations), and was killed on the first day of the Allied attack on Elba on 17 June 1944. He was buried on Elba and three years later was reburied in the Bolsena War Cemetery (IV G 19) on the Italian mainland.

References: *The war dead of the British Commonwealth and Empire: the register of the names of those who fell in the 1939–1945 War and are buried in cemeteries in Italy Cemeteries 17–18: Bolsena War Cemetery, Orvieto War Cemetery*, Maidenhead: Imperial War Graves Commission, 1954, p. 15.

BRIGNETTI, DUILIO (1926–1993). An Italian pentathlete, he was born on 17 August 1926 in **Marciana Marina**, and competed in the 1948 London Olympics and the 1952 Helsinki Olympics. In the Berne Modern Pentathlon Competition in 1950 he won silver in the modern pentathlon, and bronze in the team event. He died on 7 February 1993 in Rome.

BRIGNETTI, RAFFAELE (1921–1978). An Italian writer, he was born on 21 September 1921 on the island of Giglio, his ancestors being from Camógli moving to Elba during the Napoleonic Wars. Raffaele Brignetti's father then took up the position of lighthouse keeper at Forte Focardo at **Capoliveri**. The young Brignetti went to the **Porto Azzurro** primary school, travelling each day by boat. He then went to high school at **Portoferraio** and later moved to Rome but his studies were interrupted by **World War II**. He served in the Italian forces in Greece, and after the deposing of Mussolini in September

1943, was captured by the Germans and spent nearly two years as a prisoner of war. Afterwards he completed his thesis on writers on maritime matters, working as a journalist in Rome for *Il Tempo*, *Il Giornale* and *Corriere della Sera*. Partially paralysed from a car accident in 1961, he continued writing with his book *Il gabbiano azzurro* (The Blue Seagull, 1967) winning the Viareggio Prize. Four years later his book *La spiaggia d'oro* (The golden beach, 1971) won the Strega Prize. He died on 7 February 1978 in Rome.

References: Renato Bertacchini, 'Voce Raffaele Brignetti', *Dizionario biografico degli italiani*, Vol. 34 (1988); Birgitte Grundtvig, Martin L. McLaughlin, and Lene Waage Petersen, *Image, Eye and Art in Calvino: writing visibility*, London: Legenda, 2007, p. 153.

BRITISH COMMUNITY. British travellers came to Elba in 1814–15 to meet Napoleon Bonaparte but few stayed for long. John **Macnamara** moved to Elba soon afterwards and gradually and there was a small British community. During the twentieth century, several more prominent Britons moved to Elba including **Margaret Lane** and **Caitlin Thomas** (widow of Dylan Thomas) who moved there in search of better weather. Since the emergence of the tourism industry in the 1960s, a number of Britons have bought or rented holiday homes on the island.

References: Vernon Bartlett, *A Book about Elba*, London: Chatto & Windus, 1965.

- C -

CAMBRONNE, PIERRE (1770–1842). A French general, he commanded the detachment of the Imperial Guard which accompanied **Napoleon Bonaparte** into exile on Elba in 1814. He was born on 26 December 1770 at Nantes, France, and volunteered to join the Grenadiers in 1792. He then served under General Charles François Dumouriez in Belgium, in Le Vendée, and then served at the battle of Quiberon before heading to Ireland in the expedition in 1796. He later served in the Army of the Alps and was gazetted Colonel at the battle of Jena in 1806. He was given command of the 3rd Regiment of the Voltigeurs of the Guard in 1810, and promoted to baron of the First Empire in the same year. He then served in Spain and Russia, taking part in fighting against the Austrians in 1813.

Appointed a major in the Imperial Guard in 1814, he accompanied the ex-emperor to Elba where he was responsible for security on the island. With British visitors coming to the island, and also spies, Bonapartist agents and possibly also Royalist assassins, his role was very important. Returning with Napoleon for the 100 Days, he was involved in capturing the castle of Sisteron on 5 March 1815. He was created a count when Napoleon arrived in Paris, and Cambronne then served at the battle of Ligny and at Waterloo where he protected the emperor at the end of the battle. In command of the Old Guard, when the British general Sir Charles Colville, asked him to surrender, he is reported to have shouted 'La garde meurt et ne se rend pas!' ('The Guard dies and does not surrender!'), although there was another account that he shouted out the expletive 'Merde!'. Cambronne was tried for treason in France but was acquitted and appointed by King Louis XVIII as commandant at Lille with the rank of Brigadier in 1820. He was later created a Viscount and returned to Nantes where he died on 29 January 1842.

References: Mark Adkin, *The Waterloo Companion*, London: Aurum Press, 2001, p. 12; Pierre Branda, *L'île d'Elbe et le retour de Napoléon: 1814–1815*, Saint-Cloud: Soteca, 2014; Robert Christophe, *Napoleon on Elba*, London: Macdonald, 1964, p. 67f;

Raymond Horricks, *Napoleon's Elite*, New Brunswick: Transaction Publishers, 1995, pp. 127; Norman MacKenzie, *The Escape from Elba: The Fall & Flight of Napoleon 1814–1815*, Oxford: Oxford University Press, 1982; 'Pierre Cambronne', in Charles Mullié, *Biographie des célébrités militaires des armées de terre et de mer de 1789 à 1850*, Paris: Poignavant et compie, 1852.

CAMPBELL, Sir NEIL (1776–1827). A British army office, he was tasked with escorting **Napoleon Bonaparte** to Elba in 1814. Born on 1 May 1776, he was the son of Captain Neil Campbell (1734–1791) of Duntroon, Scotland, and his wife Jean (née Campbell, 1751–1798) of Blandfield. When he was 21, he was commissioned ensign in the 6th West India Regiment and some 19 months later he exchanged this with a position in the 67th Regiment, and was the commanding officer in the Turks and Caicos Islands in the Caribbean. He then purchased a lieutenancy in the 57th Regiment and then saw service in the Rifle Brigade.

Posted to Guadeloupe in January 1810, he then served in the Peninsular War as colonel of the 16th Portuguese Infantry and was involved in the fighting at Ciudad Rodrigo and Salamanca. At the battle of Bautzen on 20–21 May 1813 he briefly saw Napoleon across the battlefield. He was then attached to Lord Cathcart's mission to the Russian Court, and was serving in the column commanded by the Russian Marshal Prince Peter Wittgenstein (1769–1843). Leading a Russian cavalry charge at the battle of Fère-Champenoise on 24 March 1814, he was badly wounded by a Cossack who mistook him for a French officer. His baggage which included his official and military papers were lost during the fighting. Following a slow recovery, he accompanied the Allied soldiers as they entered Paris on 31 March 1814. It was Lord Carthcart who suggested him to Lord Castlereagh as the British commissioner who should accompany Napoleon Bonaparte to the island of Elba.

Neil Campbell had the task of going to Fontainebleau and then escorting the ex-emperor to Elba. It was a difficult task because Napoleon Bonaparte was not a prisoner and was going to an island where he would become a sovereign prince. Campbell always acted with respect and had a difficult task getting Napoleon to Fréjus. He kept a detailed diary of this, and also the voyage to Elba. Neil Campbell found that he was able to talk at great length to the ex-emperor. In his diary he noted:

General Bertrand had constantly impressed upon me, that as the island of Elba does not afford the supplies necessary for Napoleon's table, and as he has only with him the baggage which accompanied him in the campaign, he was in want of many things, which would oblige him to have recourse to the Continent. Although Napoleon could himself have ordered them, yet, in order to show his confidence in the Commissioners, he had directed his intentions to be fully detailed in a note; it was to the same purport as that before given, and sent to Lord Castlereagh.

Napoleon is perfectly conversant with all the details of naval affairs, 8 such as the cost and daily expense of a ship-of-war, the number of rounds for service on board, the difference between French and British line-of-battleships, the ropes in the case of the former being worked upon the upper-deck, so that more men were exposed.

He is extremely inquisitive as to all points respecting our navy, its establishment, discipline, &c., and General Bertrand daily puts similar questions to Captain Usher and myself, which are doubtless desired by Napoleon; for on other occasions it has been evident that the General himself has no curiosity or interest in anything connected with naval affairs.

One morning Napoleon described to Captain Usher, by my interpretation, the system for his marine conscripts, which he was persuaded would succeed. It was immaterial to him whether the youth was from a seaport or from the interior. He went into the navy at fourteen. For a certain number of years he remained in harbour, in order to practise getting under weigh and anchoring, which were considered the most difficult parts of a seaman's duty, then to run out on a voyage of four or five months,

On the landing at Elba himself, Campbell wrote:

The same afternoon we were off Porto Ferrajo in Elba, it being too calm for the frigate to enter the harbour. General Drouot with Count Clam and Lieutenant Hastings were sent on shore to take possession. I accompanied them. The inhabitants appeared to view us with great curiosity. We were conducted, in the first instance, to the house of General d'Alhesme, senior officer, who informed us that, two days before, an officer had arrived from Paris with orders dated April 18, for the embarkation of all stores, and notifying the appointment of the Provisional Government; in consequence of which the General and his troops had given in their adhesion to Louis XVIII, and mounted the white flag. At the same time the General expressed his desire to do whatever should be agreeable to Napoleon.

In reading out quotations from his instructions in my presence, General Drouot stated to General d'Alhesme, on the part of Napoleon, that he should wish to receive the names of all officers, non-commissioned officers, and privates, who might be willing to enter his service. Napoleon said last night that the whole force in the island amounted to only about 250; but I am informed that there had been more than 2,000 troops in all, although by desertion, and the discharge of discontented foreigners, they are now reduced to 600 or 700. There are two small vessels of the French marine in the harbour, the crews of which have deserted, and Napoleon intends, I believe, to retain them also.

General Drouot likewise desired a deputation of the principal inhabitants to come off in the course of the evening. They arrived about 8 p.m., consisting of all the civil and military authorities, and the frigate anchored at the same time.

For several weeks the inhabitants had been in a state of revolt, in consequence of which the troops occupied only the fortifications which surround the town of Porto Ferrajo. The General had discharged all foreign soldiers and landed them, on the Continent, on account of their disaffection. The spirit of the inhabitants is very inimical to the late Government of France, and personally to Napoleon, so that he will certainly require the French troops for his protection until his Guards arrive from France. He has also so strongly urged Captain Usher and myself to land the marines, that we could not refuse; although, as I told him last night, I presume that will not be necessary, so long as the French troops remain in the island.

During the night, by Napoleon's request, the Aide-decamp of General Roller was sent off to Piombino, to notify his having taken possession of the island of Elba in virtue of a treaty concluded with the Allies, and also to invite a renewal of communications for purposes of commerce, news, &c. The Austrian officer was the bearer of a letter to this effect, addressed to the Commandant, and signed by us the Commissioners. He however politely declined the proposal, until he had received the permission of the King of the Two Sicilies, to whom he had referred.

At daylight, May 4, Napoleon was on deck with the Captain of the port, and remained there for two hours, conversing with various officers, and making inquiries as to the anchorage, fortifications, &c.

At 8 a.m. he asked for a boat, and embarked, wearing his great coat and round hat. Count Bertrand, Captain Usher, Colonel Vincent the chief engineer, and myself accompanied him. When we were half-way across the harbour, he remarked that he was himself without a sword. Soon afterwards he asked whether the peasants of Tuscany were addicted to assassination. Evidently he is greatly afraid of falling in this way.

His purpose in crossing the harbour was to look at a house of imposing appearance near the beach. We remained there for nearly two hours, walking about and waiting for the keys.

Returning on board, he fixed upon the flag of Elba, and ordered two to be made immediately, in order that one may be hoisted upon the fortifications at 1 p.m., while he himself will disembark with another at 2 p.m. The flag is white, with a red stripe diagonally, and three bees on the stripe. It is as nearly as possible one of the flags of ancient Tuscany, and the bees formed part of his own arms as Emperor of France.

At 2 p.m. he landed, Count Bertrand, General Roller, Captain Usher, and myself being in the same boat with him. There were boats with officers upon either quarter, and others filled with musicians and inhabitants of the island. The yards of the frigate and of the two French corvettes were manned, and royal salutes fired. At the beach he was received by the prefect, clergy, &c., and the keys were presented upon a plate amid acclamations of Vive l'Empereur! We next proceeded to the church in procession, and from thence to the Hôtel-de-Ville, where all the authorities and principal inhabitants were assembled, with each of whom he conversed. After this he mounted his horse, attended by about a dozen persons, and visited part of the fortified outworks. Dinner was at 7 p.m.

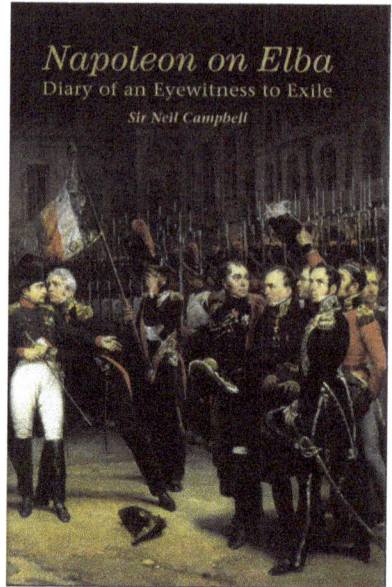

On 8 May, the *Curaçoa* arrived in Elba with **Edward Locker** on board. Locker had a copy of the preliminary peace agreement between the French provisional government and the Allied powers which had been signed on 23 April in Paris. The Austrian commissioner, **Franz Köller**, left on the *Curaçoa* on the following day. Campbell was left with the task of attending to the ex-emperor. His task was difficult as the Treaty of Fontainebleau was loosely worded and did not prevent Napoleon Bonaparte from intriguing in French politics, or even from leaving Elba. Campbell was particularly keen on keeping an eye on any Bonapartists coming to Elba, and also was worried that secret messages were being smuggled in with Napoleon's furniture which had started arriving from Italy. Campbell had agents working in Elba, and also received reports from agents on the Italian mainland. However his task was difficult and he also had to make occasional visits to the mainland.

On 16 February 1815, Campbell received his invitation to the ball being held by **Pauline Bonaparte** and replied that he could not attend as he was heading to Livorno to see his doctor as he had been suffering from deafness as a result of a head wound sustained in the Peninsula War. He was also going there to see his mistress. On the following day, Campbell left for Italy providing Napoleon Bonaparte with an opportunity to escape from Elba on 26 February. There were accusations that Campbell had been bribed but he was fully exonerated after a British enquiry. Campbell rejoined the British forces in the Southern Netherlands and was at the battle of Waterloo. He was in command of the Hanseatic Legion during the occupation of France, 1815–18, and then went to West Africa to try to locate details on the fate of Mungo Park. Promoted to major-general on 29 May 1825, he was appointed governor of Sierra Leone in West Africa after the death of the former governor, Major-

General Sir Charles Turner who had been suffering from what was believed to be malaria. Campbell did as much as he could to improve the running of the British colony based in Freetown but was regularly in conflict with the local establishment. He was soon suffering from fever, possibly malaria, and died on 14 August 1827. *See also* **Spyglass**.

References: Pierre Branda, *L'île d'Elbe et le retour de Napoléon: 1814–1815*, Saint-Cloud: Soteca, 2014; Robert Christophe, *Napoleon on Elba*, London: Macdonald, 1964; Neil Campbell, *Napoleon at Fontainebleau and Elba*, London, J. Murray, 1869; Sir Neil Campbell, *Napoleon on Elba: diary of an eyewitness to exile*, Welwyn Garden City: Ravenhall Books, 2004; Flora Fraser, *Venus of Empire: The Life of Pauline Bonaparte*, London: John Murray, 2009, p. 216; Norman MacKenzie, *The Escape from Elba: The Fall & Flight of Napoleon 1814–1815*, Oxford: Oxford University Press, 1982, pp. 39ff; H. M. Stephens, 'Campbell, Sir Neil (1776–1827)', revised by Stewart M. Fraser, *Oxford Dictionary of National Biography*, Oxford University Press, 2004.

CAPO FOCARDO. This is a cape south of **Porto Azzurro** and is the location of a seventeenth century Spanish fortress.

CAPOLIVERI. This is a commune (municipality) in the south-east of the island of Elba, and is located on top of a small hill. This places the settlement

Capoliveri.
Photograph © Antonio Scarpi / Fotolia.com

Forte Focardo at Capoliveri.
Photograph by Averil Mackenzie-Grieve.

On the road from Capoliveri.
Photograph © mor65 / Fotolia.com

in a strategic position with the gulf of **Porto Azzurro** on one side, and Golfo Stella on the other. For this reason the Italian navy built a lighthouse there in the nineteenth century.

On account of its strategic position, the Republic of Pisa built a castle there during the twelfth century. However the settlement dates back to the **Etruscans** with an Etruscan necropolis found by archaeologists. In Roman times, by tradition, the town gained its name from the fact that a debtor or other person on the run from the law was able to claim sanctuary in the town and become a free person – *caput librerum* (literally: 'free head'). This would mean that so long as they remained in the town, they would be free. This also led to some local prerogatives such as not having to pay taxes.

As well as building the castle, the **Pisans** were also responsible for the design of the church of San Michele, although only parts of the apse have survived. These present what is viewed as one of the purest Pisan architectural designs. There was also a parish church located outside the city walls. According to legend, Pope **Gregory XI**, on his return from exile in Avignon in 1376, took refuge on the island during a storm and prayed in the church.

Much of the town retains its medieval and renaissance characteristics with narrow lanes called 'chiassi', granite arches and walls around houses which have fading paintwork. There was a wall built to protect the locals from outsiders, especially from the North African Corsairs who attacked in June 1544 and again in August 1553. In the later attack, the church was destroyed, leaving only the apse.

The Forte Focardo (Focado Fortress) was built on the orders of Don Ferdinando Focardo in 1678. However the Spanish, during the War of Spanish Succession, after attacking it, pulled down the walls of the church. According to legend, it was during their attack on the town, that the verger in the parish church – outside the walls – hid himself and important church documents in a tomb in the nave of the church. However he was given away by the smell which forced him to emerge and the Spanish soldiers attending a service in the church at the time then ransacked the tomb looking for treasure. When they found none, they burned all the archival papers.

French royalist monks lived there during the French Revolution. They prayed at the Santuario della Madonna delle Grazie. Soon after the start of the French occupation of the island in 1799, a French army column ended up at Capolivieri. The locals rose up and attacked the soldiers, killing most of them. The French General Miollis arrived with reinforcements soon afterwards and took revenge on the citizens of the town. **Napoleon**, when he arrived in 1814 was greeted by the locals who reminded him of their rights including that they would not pay taxes. Napoleon then threatened to billet his soldiers in the town, and the local people paid what was owing.

The town's most famous resident was Vincenzo Silvio who was born there on 9 May 1805 and went on to play a role in the campaign for Italian Unification. The lighthouse keeper in the 1920s was the father of **Raffaele Brignetti** who was born on the island of Giglio.

In the summer months, many tourists go to Capoliveri which has a number of handicraft shops, restaurants and wine cellars. The original parish church, the Chiesa di San Mamiliano, designed by the architect Grazzini in 1752, was located in Piazza Giacomo Matteotti but was demolished in 1894 to make way for the new church.

There are some 35 kilometres of coastline around Capoliveri which also attracts many people, especially large numbers of German tourists during the summer. According to legend, in 1534 two young lovers called Lorenzo and Maria met. Their families did not like each other so the lovers chose the meet at the cove at Innammorata. However on the afternoon of 14 July 1534 pirates attacked and they killed Lorenzo. Maria then threw herself into the sea. In the eighteenth century a Spanish nobleman called Domino Cardenas was in the cove when he had a vision of a beautiful girl. This led to the annual 'Innamorata' festival in the town each year on 14 July.

The beach at Naregno, some 500 metres long, was one of the first to open in the 1960s. Lacona is one of the longest beaches on the island. Also popular are Zuccale, Lido di Capoliveri and Felciao. There are much smaller beaches of Straccoligno and Calanova, with some preferring the quiet cove at Innammorata from where tourists can swim to the Gemini Islands. Other beaches include Pareti and Morcone, with Madonna delle Grazie, Barabarca, and Norsi, having sand and gravel.

Population

1861	1,518	1911	2,773	1951	2,233	1991	2,435
1871	1,533	1921	2,635	1961	2,168	2001	3,105
1881	1,747	1931	2,424	1971	2,193	2011	3,763
1901	2,235	1941	2,431	1981	2,239		

References: Arsène Thiébaut de Berneaud, *A Voyage to the Isle of Elba*, London: Longman, Hurst, Rees, Orme and Brown, 1814, pp. 137–46; Roberto Donati, *The Island of Elba*, Terni: Fotorapidacolor, 1973, pp. 9–13; Dan Facaros and Michael Pauls, *Italy: Tuscany*, London: Cadogan Books plc, 1996, pp. 301–02; Guido Giubella, *Elba: A Garden in the Blu*, Milan: Co.Graf Editrice, 1988, pp. 64–65; Averil Mackenzie-Grieve, *Aspects of Elba*

Capraia.
Photograph by Mai-Sachme, 2005 / Wikipedia Commons.

Fort San Giorgio at Capraia.
Photograph © honzahruby / fotolia.com

44

and the other islands of the Tuscan Archipelago, London: Jonathan Cape, 1964, pp. 38f;
Miles Roddis & Alex Leviton, *Tuscany & Umbria*, Footscray: Lonely Planet, 2006, p. 191;
Christopher and Jean Serpell, *The Travellers' Guide to Elba and the Tuscan Archipelago*,
London: Jonathan Cape, 1977, pp. 194–97.

CAPRAIA. This island is the north westernmost of the seven islands in the
Tuscan Archipelago, and the third largest, after Elba and **Giglio**. Located
32 kilometres (20 miles) northwest of the island of Elba, between Elba and
Corsica, the island covers some 19 square kilometres (7 square miles) and
is of volcanic origin. It has a population of 385 (2007), and was settled by
the Greeks who called it Aegylon / Aegyllion (Αηγυλον) which means 'Goat
Place'. The Romans called it Caprara on account of the large number of wild
capers which could be found on the island. In the fourth century it was used
by Christian hermits.

It was conquered by the North African Corsairs in 1055 and these
occasionally used it as a base although the Papacy officially claimed
sovereignty over the island. Capraia was fought over in 1146–50, and then
was occupied by the Pisans. It was then owned by the Republic of Pisa, and
later the Republic of Genoa – the Genoese built the Fort San Giorgio and three
towers (Torre del Porto in 1541, the Torre del Porto in 1545; and the Torre
delle Barbici in 1699) on the island to protect it from raiders. Then in 1768

Fort San Giorgio.
Photograph by Lucarelli, 2007 / Wikipedia Commons.

Capraia.
Photograph © honzahruby / Fotolia.com

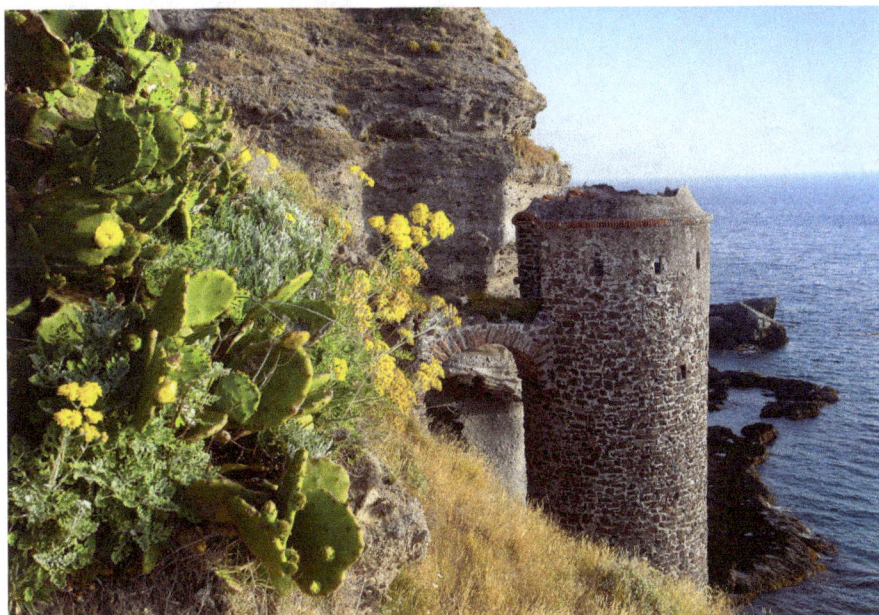

Capraia.
Photograph © honzahruby / Fotolia.com

Capraia.
Photograph © honzahruby / Fotolia.com

it was occupied by Corsican followers of **Pasquale Paoli**. The Royal Navy under **Horatio Nelson** occupied the island briefly from 1796. In 1814, it had only a small village with inhabitants surviving by fishing, and keeping goats.

On 3 May 1814 when the *Undaunted* was taking **Napoleon Bonaparte** to Elba, it passed Capraia from which a small party came on board to tell Captain **Neil Campbell** and others that the people of Elba had overthrown the French garrison and wanted to support the British in return for protection from the Royal Navy. **Thomas Ussher** sent a British officer to the island to run it for the time being. The *Undaunted* then carried on to Elba.

After the Congress of Vienna in 1815, the Republic of Genoa was annexed to the kingdom of Sardinia, and it became part of the province of Genoa in the kingdom of Sardinia, and then in the kingdom of Italy. In 1925 it was assigned to the province of Livorno, but the church recognised it as a part of the archdiocese of Genoa until 1 January 1977. From 1873 to 1986 some

48

two-thirds of the island was a penal colony, but after its closure, the whole island was opened to visitors. One of the popular sites for divers is the German Arado Ar196-A sea-plane which was dumped by the Germans in the waters some 200 metres from the village of Capraia. During its short career, it was a spotter plane and had been carried on the *Scharnhörst*, the *Gneisenau*, the *Graf Spee*, the *Lützow*, the *Scheer* and the *Prinz Eugen*, prior to being ditched at sea for reasons which have not been fully established. It seems to have been dragged to its current site by a trawler.

References: Kurt Amsler, Andrea Ghisotti, Roberto Rinaldi and Egidio Trainito, *Diving Guide to the Mediterranean Wrecks*, Shrewsbury, UK: Swan Hill Press, 1995, pp. 120–23; Norman MacKenzie, *The Escape from Elba: The Fall & Flight of Napoleon 1814–1815*, Oxford: Oxford University Press, 1982, p. 63 & 65; Miles Roddis & Alex Leviton, *Tuscany & Umbria*, Footscray: Lonely Planet, 2006, pp. 179–80; Christopher and Jean Serpell, *The Travellers' Guide to Elba and the Tuscan Archipelago*, London: Jonathan Cape, 1977, p. 41.

CAROTHERS, TERENCE BRITTAN (1907–1944). A temporary lieutenant in the British Royal Marines, he was born in 1907 in the Cape Colony, South Africa, the son of Samuel Dixon Carothers and Winifred Ellen (née Allen), and married Annabel Campbell Harper-Nelson in 1939 in Cheltenham, England. Serving on a landing craft during the attack on Elba on 17 June 1944, the landing craft was sunk with Carothers posted as missing, presumed killed. He is commemorated on the Chatham Naval Memorial (panel 79, column 1). His widow, who had been born in India, settled at Fionnhort, Isle of Mull, Scotland and died in 1982.

CAVO. This port in the north east of the island of Elba is close to **Rio Marina** and has been settled since Roman times with archaeologists unearthing remains of a Roman villa in the area. In 1849 Giuseppe Garibaldi stopped there on his way from mainland Italy to Caprera. From the late nineteenth century, it became a resort for the families of people connected with the iron industry.

References: Guido Giubella, *Elba: A Garden in the Blu*, Milan: Co.Graf Editrice, 1988, pp. 88–91.

Cavo.   Photograph © Paul Nedrack / fotolio.com.

CEMETERIES. As is the tradition in Italian towns and villages, important people were interred in churches, whilst others were buried in the grounds of churches, and this has taken place throughout Elba. The 42 British and Imperial service personnel who died in World War II on Elba and who were initially buried on the island in what was called the Allied War Cemetery in a section of the cemetery at **Marina di Campo**. These were removed in 1947 and reinterred in Plot 4 (rows G and H) at Bolsena War Cemetery, located near Lake Bolsena, 8 kilometres from the town of Montefiascone, located about halfway between Rome and Siena. The bodies of US servicemen killed in the fighting were either interred at the Florence American Cemetery or taken back to the United States, in accordance with the wishes of family members. In the cemetery at **Porto Azzurro** there is the grave of the famous World War II news correspondent **Chester Wilmot** and others who died on the **Comet Plane Crash of 1954**.

References: *The war dead of the British Commonwealth and Empire: the register of the names of those who fell in the 1939–1945 War and are buried in cemeteries in Italy Cemeteries 17–18: Bolsena War Cemetery, Orvieto War Cemetery*, Maidenhead: Imperial War Graves Commission, 1954.

Municipal cemetery near Rio nell'Elba.

Bolsena War Cemetery.   Photograph © Commonwealth War Graves Commission.

CERBOLI. This is a very small island in the Tuscan archipelago which the Romans called Cerbania. The **Pisans** built a small watch-tower on it in 1108 and this was rebuilt by the Appiani in 1567. It was also the home of many peregrine falcons and falconers were attracted to the island for this reason. In 1927 a limestone quarry was established on Cerboli by a steel company operating from Piombino. In more recent years the island was bought by the writer Carlo Cassola (1917–1987). It is now a part of the **Tuscan Archipelago** National Park.

References: Norman MacKenzie, *The Escape from Elba: The Fall & Flight of Napoleon 1814–1815*, Oxford: Oxford University Press, 1982, p. 65.

CERBONI, GIUSEPPE (1827–1917). A mathematician, he was born on 23 December 1827 at **Marciana Marina** and worked as an accountant for the government of the Grand Duchy of Tuscany. He enlisted as a volunteer in the 1848 Uprising and later served in the pay department of the Gendarmerie, and was then promoted to chief accountant at the Italian ministry of war. He devised a new system of keeping the state accounts and in 1891 resigned from the government to work as counsellor at the local auditor's office. He retired in 1895 and lived at his home at **Porto Azzurro** until his death on 14 February 1917.

References: Giuseppe Cerboni, *Genesi e sviluppo della logismografia*, Roma: Tip. elzeviriana nel Ministero delle Finanze, 1878; Giuseppe Cerboni, *Sull'ordinamento della contabilità dello Stato*, Firenze, Tip. e cart. militare di T. Giuliani, 1886; Giuseppe Cerboni, *La ragioneria scientifica e le sue relazioni con le discipline amministrative e sociali*, Roma: Ermanno Loescher, 1886–94.

CHAUTARD, J. He was the commander of the *Inconstant* on which Napoleon Bonaparte made his daring escape from Elba in 1815. He had taken control of the navy at Elba after the cowardly behaviour of **Louis Taillade**, and he took Napoleon back to France successfully evading the British ships in the Mediterranean. On 20 March 1815 Chautard was awarded the Legion of Honour.

References: Norman MacKenzie, *The Escape from Elba: The Fall & Flight of Napoleon 1814–1815*, Oxford: Oxford University Press, 1982; Philip Mansel and Torsten Riotte,

Monarchy and Exile: the politics of legitimacy from Marie de Médicis to Wilhelm II, Basingstoke, Hampshire, UK: Palgrave Macmillan, 2011.

CHESS. This game has been popular on Elba for many centuries. **Napoleon Bonaparte** certainly played chess, but many of the games attributed to him, mainly set in St. Helena, were probably later inventions. He certainly played chess on St. Helena against Marshal **Bertrand**, and it is likely that he played Bertrand in Elba as well.

There remains an active chess scene on Elba with regular tournaments which attract many Italian, and often non-Italian players. On 7 May 2007, Marco Codenotti, an Italian international master, defeated the Serbian Zivojin Ljubisavljevic. The Isolda d'Elba competition held at **Capoliveri** in May 2010 was won by Lexy Ortega from Italy, narrowly defeating Igor Naumkin from Russia, with Fabrizio Bellia from Italy coming third, and Norbert Friedrich from Germany being fourth. The Isolda d'Elba competition in May 2011 was won by Andrei Istratescu from Romania, with Gojko Laketic from Serbia being the runner-up. A 'B' competition at the same time, was won by Daniele de Nadai, with Vladyslav Pelyushenko, also from Italy as runner-up. The other players with ELO ratings of over 1700 which took part were Sergio Santinelli, Enzo Bellafiore, Alfio Pintaudi, Dari Ferro, Jorgen Kamp Nielsen (from Denmark), Luca Andreassi, and Vittorio Bolla.

References: Edward Winter, Napoleon Bonaparte and Chess, http://www.chesshistory. com/winter/extra/napoleon.html.

CHINESE COMMUNITY. Some Chinese tourists have visited Elba and there is one popular Chinese restaurant in **Portoferraio**, the Ristorante La Felicita a Portoferraio.

CHURCH OF (THE REVERENDA) MISERICORDIA. This church in **Portoferraio** was built in 1677 by the Confraternita of San Cristino was established in 1566 by Giovanni de 'Medici to hold relics connected with San Cristino, the early Christian martyr who is also the patron saint of Portoferraio. Known as the 'Chapel of the Blacks', to contrast it with the Church of the Holy Sacrament, this church has a nave and a pipe organ built by Paoli in the eighteenth century. There is a small sculpture of the Virgin and Child executed by the sculptor Tino di Camaino (c1280-c1337).

It also has a number of relics connected with **Napoleon**, in particular a bronze copy of his death mask made by Doctor Antonmarchi on St. Helena – the Church of the Holy Sacrament also in Portoferraio holds another death mask. On 5 May each year, at the suggestion of Prince **Anatole Demidoff** in 1852, a memorial mass is held for Napoleon. Demidoff left a fund which provides 500 francs for the local clergy and 400 francs for the poor of the parish, and 100 francs for the service. All these sums have long since been eroded by inflation. However the church has become a shrine for those interested in Napoleon Bonaparte.

References: Christopher and Jean Serpell, *The Travellers' Guide to Elba and the Tuscan Archipelago*, London: Jonathan Cape, 1977, p. 160.

CHURCH OF THE HOLY SACRAMENT. This church in **Portoferraio** is known locally as the 'Chapel of the Whites'. It has a bronze copy of the desk mask of **Napoleon Bonaparte** as does the Church of Misericordia (known as the Chapel of the Blacks), also in Portoferraio. On the ceiling is a painting of the Assumption of the Virgin Mary by the Florentine Baroque painter Giovanni Camillo Sagrestani (1660–1731). There is another painting by him of the Assumption of the Virgin Mary at the Musée des Beaux-Arts, Nancy, France.

References: Christopher and Jean Serpell, *The Travellers' Guide to Elba and the Tuscan Archipelago*, London: Jonathan Cape, 1977, pp. 159–60.

CIONI, RENAT (1929–2014). An Italian tenor, he was born on 15 April 1929 at **Portoferraio**, his father being a fisherman. He studied music at the Conservatorio Luigi Cherubini in Florence and started performing in Italy, and then in Switzerland, Spain, Germany, Belgium and France before making his debut in the United States in 1959. In 1970 he performed alongside Joan Sutherland. He died on 4 March 2014 at Portoferraio.

CLAM-MARTINITZ, KARL JOSEPH (1792–1840). An Austrian major, he had been born on 23 May 1792 in Prague, his father being a prominent political figure in Bohemia, and his mother Maria Anna was the daughter and heiress of Count Franz Karl von Martinitz. Initially joining the civil service, Karl then transferred to the army and served in the Legion Erzherzog Karl (Legion Archduke Charles), and was with the lancers in 1812. In the following year he fought at the battle of Kulm and was then appointed as an aide-de-camp of Field Marshal **Franz Freiherr von Köller**. In 1814 when it was decided that **Napoleon Bonaparte** should go to Elba, Köller sent Clam-Martinitz to the Allied army headquarters to urge them to make sure that the French garrison at Elba remained there until Napoleon arrived. He then travelled with Napoleon Bonaparte and Köller on the *Undaunted* which took the ex-emperor to Elba. When the *Undaunted* arrived at Elba, Major Clam-Martinitz, Baron **Jermanowski**, and **Antoine Drouot** went ashore to ensure Napoleon would be given a suitable welcome.

Clam-Martinitz left Elba with Köller soon afterwards, with the two travelling on the *Undaunted*. He then went to Vienna where he helped in the Congress of Vienna and was sent in September 1816 on a special mission by the Austrian chancellor Count Metternich. He held subsequent staff appointments in the Austrian army and died on 29 January 1840 in Vienna. He left two sons and two daughters. Both his sons were to be party leaders in the Austrian Chamber of Deputies.

References: Norman MacKenzie, *The Escape from Elba: The Fall & Flight of Napoleon 1814–1815*, Oxford: Oxford University Press, 1982, p. 46, 51, 54, 61f.

COAT OF ARMS. The coat of arms of Elba has a white background and a diagonal red stripe which is the same flag which **Cosimo de Medici** flew over Elba when he ruled the island. To these were added three bees to symbolise **Napoleon**. This design was originally from the flag designed in consultation with Napoleon on the *Undaunted* on the night of 3–4 May 1814, and has since been used as the coat of arms of Elba.

COLE, STANLEY CHRISTOPHER (1917–1944). A British naval officer, he was born in late 1917 in Wandsworth, London, the son of Christopher Albert Cole and Edith Ruth (née Sumner). He grew up in Friern Barnet. Middlesex, and joined the Royal Navy, and was commissioned lieutenant. He was killed on the first day of the Allied attack on Elba on 17 June 1944. He was buried on Elba and three years later was reburied in the Bolsena War Cemetery (IV H 20) on the Italian mainland.

References: *The war dead of the British Commonwealth and Empire: the register of the names of those who fell in the 1939–1945 War and are buried in cemeteries in Italy Cemeteries 17–18: Bolsena War Cemetery, Orvieto War Cemetery*, Maidenhead: Imperial War Graves Commission, 1954, p. 17.

COLLIER, PETER (1920–1944). A leading seaman in the British Royal Navy, he was born on 8 April 1920 in Liverpool, England, the third of the five sons of John Dearden Collier (1887–1941) and his wife Mary Elizabeth (née Crummy, 1892–1932). He joined the Royal Navy in 1938 and was amongst the group that stormed ashore at **Marina di Campo** on 17 June 1944. Under withering fire from the Germans, most of the attackers including Peter Collier were killed. His body may be one of the six unidentified bodies interred in the local cemetery, and later reburied at Bolsena War Cemetery on the Italian mainland, the headstone bearing the caption 'Known Unto God'. He is commemorated on the Plymouth Memorial (panel 85, column 2).

References: *The war dead of the British Commonwealth and Empire; the register of the names of those who fell in the 1939–1945 war and have no other grave than the sea: Plymouth Naval Memorial*, Maidenhead: Imperial War Graves Commission, 1952, p. 128.

COMET PLANE CRASH (1954). At 10.50 am, on 10 January 1954, a BOAC de Havilland Comet 1 called Yoke Peter on flight 781 crashed into the sea some 16 kilometres south of the island of Elba, between Elba and the island of **Montecristo**. The flight had originated in Singapore and was flying from Ciampino Airport in Rome to London when it broke up after an

BOAC's De Havilland Comet G-ALYP as it leaves London Airport for Johannesburg on 2 May 1952. This was the same plane that crashed on 10 January 1954 off Elba.

explosive decompression as a result of metal fatigue and all 29 passengers and six crew were killed.

The crew were named as Captain Alan Gibson DFC, aged 31, from Highcliffe, Hampshire; First Officer William John Bury, aged 33, of Gosport, Hampshire; engineer officer Francis Charles Macdonald, aged 27, of Yateley, Hampshire, steward Frank Leonard Saunders of Dover, Kent; radio officer Luke Patrick McMahon, aged 32, of Omagh, Northern Ireland; and stewardess Jean Evelyn Clarke of Huntingdon.

The famous journalist **Chester Wilmot** was on board, travelling from Rangoon to London. Travelling from Bahrain to London were Mr and Mrs J. M. Bunyan and their infant child from Stirling, Scotland; Miss Leila Yateen, of St. Mary's Hall School; Miss R. Keedoori, aged 13; Miss N. Keedoori, aged 15; Mr Bernard Butler of Bildworth, Nottinghamshire; Mr J. B. Crilly (or G. B. Grilly) of BOAC with his daughter Brenda; and a passenger surnamed Israel. Travelling from Beirut to London was Mrs R. E. Geldard, wife of a BOAC staff member, and two children Miss G. Geldard and Master M. Geldard, of Beirut; Mr S. Naamin of Damascus; Mrs E. S. Maclachlan, wife of a BOAC staff member; Mr John Yescomes Ramsden of the Shell Petroleum Company, Beirut; Mr D. Leaver; and Mr A. Crisp (Grisca). Making the journey from Singapore to London was Mr J. P. Hill of BOAC; and Mr J. P. Steel of George Wimpey and Company, and formerly a boxing champion of the British Army; and from Bangkok to London there were three passengers: Mr Francis Harold

THE SEARCH OFF ELBA FOR THE WRECK OF THE LOST COMET; AND A MEMORIAL SERVICE AT SEA.

ABOUT TO TAKE HEAVY SALVAGE GEAR ABOARD BEFORE SAILING FOR ELBA : THE BOOM DEFENCE VESSEL *BARHILL* MOVING ALONGSIDE THE SALVAGE VESSEL H.M.S. *SEA SALVOR* AT MALTA.

CONDUCTING A MEMORIAL SERVICE AT SEA FOR THE VICTIMS OF THE *COMET* CRASH : THE REV. J. FINDLOW GIVING A BLESSING, NEAR ELBA.

AT the time of writing the frigate H.M.S. *Wrangler*, commanded by Captain C. M. Parry, is carrying out an intensive search off the island of Elba for the ill-fated B.O.A.C. *Comet* which crashed into the sea on January 10 with the loss of all thirty-five people on board. So far a number of contacts with underwater objects have been registered by Asdic devices and depth-sounding equipment; and these may well prove to be important parts of the airliner. H.M.S. *Wrangler* is being joined by H.M.S. *Sea Salvor*, a salvage vessel, and the boom defence ship *Barhill* bringing underwater television equipment, an articulated diving-suit, a diving-chamber, grabs and other heavy lifting gear.

[RIGHT.] AT PORTO AZZURRO : THE BRITISH FRIGATE H.M.S. *WRANGLER*, WHICH IS CONDUCTING AN INTENSIVE AND SYSTEMATIC SEARCH OFF ELBA FOR THE WRECKAGE OF THE ILL-FATED *COMET*.

THE *COMET* SEARCH : A SCIENTIST INSPECTING AN UNDERWATER TELEVISION CAMERA WHICH CAN EXAMINE WRECKAGE AT GREAT DEPTHS.

ON BOARD H.M.S. *WRANGLER* DURING THE SEARCH OFF ELBA FOR THE WRECKAGE OF THE *COMET* : PETTY OFFICER ROSS CHECKING THE POSITIONING OF AN ADDITIONAL TELEMETER [RANGE-FINDER].

Greenhough of Horley, Surrey; Master Robert Sawyer Snelling, aged 14, from Brighton, whose father (Thomas Arthur Sawyer-Snelling, 1912–1973) worked for BOAC in Bangkok; and Captain R. V. Wolfson, general manager of BOAC's subsidiary airlines in Bangkok. From Karachi to London there were four passengers: Mrs Dorothy Beecher Baker of Wilmette, Illinois, USA, and a Hand of the Cause of God for the Baha'i Faith; Mr H. E. Schuhmann also of the United States, of the Macmillan Company, New York; Mr T. S. H. Moore; and Mrs E. Fairbrother. The last passenger was Captain Livingstone of British European Airways, who had joined the flight at Rome. The children were returning at the end of the school holidays.

A search was organised by Captain Colin McMullen. Chester Wilmot's body and those of 14 others were recovered and the local priest gave benediction as the bodies were brought ashore and taken to the cemetery chapel. They were examined by the pathologist Antonio Fornari. Local village schoolchildren brought flowers and ten of the bodies – including that of Chester Wilmot – were buried in the cemetery at **Porto Azzurro** after a service held on 18 January. A service was also held over the site where the plane crashed for those whose bodies were not recovered. Mr Lennox-Boyd, the British minister of transport, attended both services.

At a subsequent enquiry it was found that the wreckage, when recovered showed that fractures had started on the roof and then a window smashed into the back elevators, the 'back fuselage then tore away, the outer wing structure fell, then the outer wing tips and finally the cockpit broke away and fuel from the wings set the debris on fire.' There was a temporary suspension of Comet flights but they resumed soon afterwards.

The disaster was followed by another on 8 April 1954 when a Comet, als taking off from Rome, disappeared off Naples, and this led to the grounding of all Comets and a long investigation into this and other crashes at around the same time. The Comet's Certificate of Airworthiness was then revoked and line production of the Comet 1 at the Hatfield factory was suspended. Although a new Comet was designed, Britain lost its lead position in passenger plane manufacture, and never regained it. The possibility of a break-up of a plane from metal fatigue was raised six years before the Comet crash in Nevil Shute's novel, *No Highway* (London, 1948). The Comet crash was the focus of an episode of *Seconds from Disaster*, and also a British Channel 4 television programme, *A Great British Air Disaster*.

References: Accident description, http://aviation-safety.net/database/record.php?id= 19540110–1; Macarthur Job, *Air Disaster* vol. *1*, Fyshwyck, ACT, Australia: Aerospace

SALVAGING THE WRECKAGE OF THE COMET AIRLINER: WITH SEA SALVOR OFF ELBA.

PART OF THE PORT SIDE OF THE COMET'S FUSELAGE, INCLUDING THE PASSENGERS' DOOR, RECOVERED ON FEBRUARY 25: THIS PIECE WAS RAISED FIRST ON FEBRUARY 23 BUT LOST.

SWINGING INBOARD SEA SALVOR'S GRAB, HOLDING A LARGE PORTION OF FUSELAGE. THOUGH THE GRAB DAMAGES THE FRAGMENTS, THIS DAMAGE CAN BE IDENTIFIED.

A PORTION OF THE COMET'S FUSELAGE ON THE DECK OF SEA SALVOR AFTER BEING RAISED ON FEBRUARY 24, WHEN ABOUT 200 SQUARE FEET OF FUSELAGE WAS SALVED.

CLEARLY SHOWING THE LETTERS "B.O.A.C.": A FRAGMENT OF FUSELAGE SECTION BEING EXAMINED ON THE DECK OF SEA SALVOR AFTER BEING RECOVERED OFF ELBA.

THE TAIL FIN OF THE COMET AIRLINER, WHICH HAD BEEN RECOVERED BY SEA SALVOR, AFTER BEING OFF-LOADED AT THE PIER OF PORTO AZZURRO, ELBA.

On February 12 it was confirmed that the salvage fleet seeking the remains of the Comet airliner which crashed in the sea off Elba on January 10 had definitely identified a number of fragments, lying at about 400 ft., by means of an under-water television camera. On February 19 the wreckage was examined for the first time by a diver in an observation chamber. On February 21 parts of the Comet were raised by the salvage vessel, Sea Salvor; these came mainly from the baggage-hold under the passengers' cabin just astern of the main plane and included many square feet of metal skin, tarpaulins, a passenger's chair, hydraulic control gear and electric cable. On February 22 the pressure dome and part of the toilet compartments were raised and among the fragments were entangled nylon stockings, a yellow spotted necktie and a pair of child's socks. On February 23 a large fragment was being raised, but was lost in rising bad weather. This piece was successfully recovered on February 25; but on this day an under-water television camera was damaged after becoming fouled, it is thought, by one of Sea Salvor's six anchors. On February 28 Sea Salvor, after eight days at sea, was in harbour, having recovered most of the wreckage (mainly of the airliner's after-part) which lay in the area of her moorings; and on that day it was announced that Admiral Lord Mountbatten intended to pay a visit to the Comet recovery fleet on March 3. What has been done is a great achievement. How much more will be attempted was not known at the date of writing.

THE ELBA COMET DISASTER: RE-ASSEMBLING THE SALVAGED FRAGMENTS.

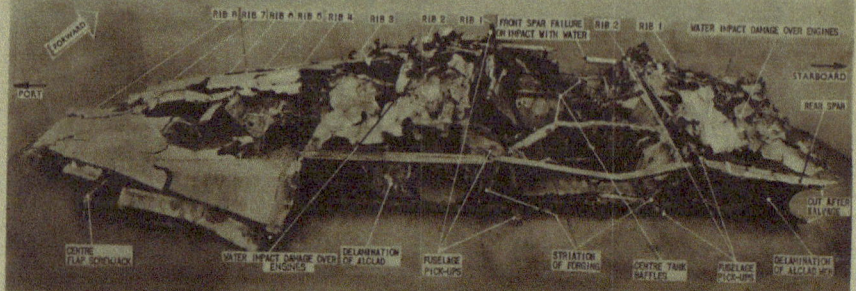

THE CENTRE SECTION OF THE PORT WING OF THE COMET "YOKE PETER."—THE FRAGMENTS WHICH WERE RECOVERED FROM THE SEA NEAR ELBA ASSEMBLED ON A FRAME TO ASSIST THOSE CONDUCTING THE INQUIRY INTO THE NAPLES AND ELBA COMET DISASTERS. IN THIS PHOTOGRAPH THE UPPER SURFACE OF THE WING IS SHOWN.

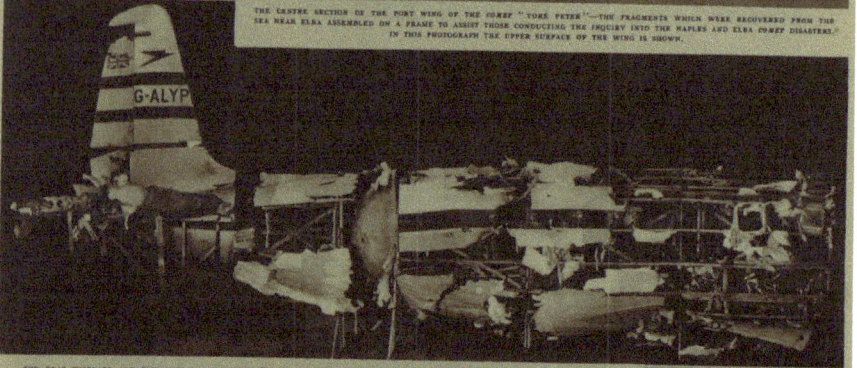

THE REAR FUSELAGE AND TAIL UNIT OF THE COMET "YOKE PETER," SEEN FROM THE STARBOARD SIDE. THIS IS A PHOTOGRAPH OF ONE OF THE WOODEN FRAMES MADE BY THE ROYAL AIRCRAFT ESTABLISHMENT TO CARRY THE SALVAGED FRAGMENTS IN THEIR APPROPRIATE POSITIONS.

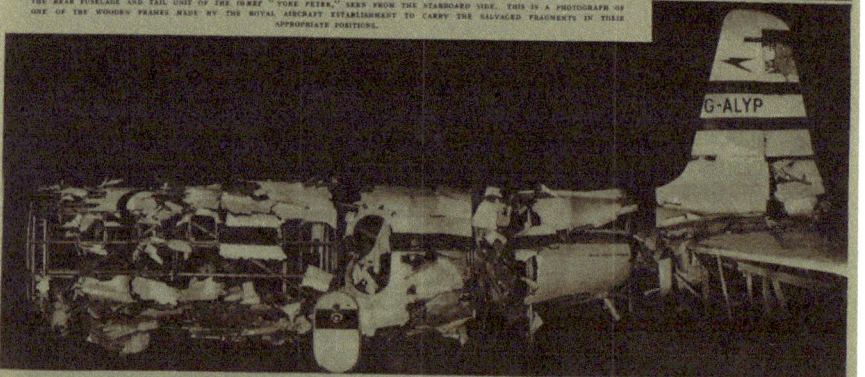

THE REAR FUSELAGE AND TAIL UNIT OF THE COMET "YOKE PETER," SEEN FROM THE PORT SIDE—IN THE CENTRE, THE DOORWAY CAN BE SEEN. THIS IS THE SAME FRAME AS THE MIDDLE PHOTOGRAPH, BUT HERE PHOTOGRAPHED FROM THE OTHER SIDE.

To assist in the investigation of the *Comet* accidents near Elba and Naples, the Royal Aircraft Establishment reconstructed the salvaged wreckage of the *Comet* "Yoke Peter" (recovered in a brilliant and prolonged salvage operation from the sea-bed near Elba) on to wooden frames so that each fragment could be seen in its proper relation. Our photographs show the tail and rear fuselage frame and the centre section of the port wing (seen from above). At the time of writing the *Comet* inquiry was still in progress. Since our last report, probably the most notable developments were as follows: Mr. Jablonsky's theory that the disasters were due to failures of the Redux adhesive was discounted, Sir Arnold Hall's statement that there was no reason why *Comet* aircraft should not go back into service after certain modifications and have "a very successful career"; and Dr. Walker's statement that although on the tests done at Farnborough the safe life of the original *Comets* should have been less than 2700 hours, nevertheless there was nothing inherent in the design which would prevent its being made a perfectly safe aircraft. As soon as possible after the inquiry the de Havilland Company hope to issue a statement on their plans for the *Comets* II. and III.

Publications Pty Ltd, 1994, pp. 11–21; Stanley Stewart, *Air Disasters: Dialogue from the Black Box*, London: Ian Allan, 1986, pp. 41–46; 'Comet airliner crashes in Mediterranean', *The Times* (11 January 1954), p. 6; 'Comet Airliner Services Suspended', *The Times* (12 January 1954), p. 6; 'Recovering the wreckage', *The Times* (13 January 1954), p. 6; Sir Miles Thomas, 'Captain V. Wolfson', *The Times* (13 January 1954), p. 8; 'Service at Sea', *The Times* (18 January 1954), p. 6; *Report of the Public Inquiry into the causes and circumstances of the accident which occurred on the 10th January, 1954, to the Comet aircraft G-ALYP*, 1955; 'Dorothy Baker – A personal reminiscence', *Bahá'í News* No 276 (December 1977), pp. 8–9; Edgar A. Haine, *Disaster in the Air*, New York: Cornwall Books, 2000, p. 211; 'Captain Colin McMullen', *The Times* (13 February 1992), p. 15; 'Captain John Morrow', *The Times* (30 September 1994), p. 19; 'Sir Arnold Hall', *The Times* (11 January 2000), p. 21; 'Anne Burns: glider pilot and air accident investigator who helped to explain the Comet disasters of 1954', *The Times* (30 January 2001), p. 23; 'Fred Jones: wreckage analyst who was involved in important investigations in the early years of jet-powered flight', *The Times* (15 September 2003), p. 26; 'The Search off Elba for the Wreck of the Lost Comet; and a Memorial Service at Sea', *Illustrated London News* (30 January 1954), p. 167; 'Salvaging the Wreckage of the Comet Airliner: With Sea Salvor off Elba', *Illustrated London News* (6 March 1954), p. 375; 'The Elba Comet Disaster: Re-Assembling the Salvaged Fragments', *Illustrated London News* (13 November 1954), p. 855.

COOPER, GEOFFREY (1923–1944). A flight sergeant in the 293 Squadron of the British Royal Air Force Volunteer Reserve, he was born in 1923 in England, the son of William and Amy Cooper of Netherfield, Nottinghamshire. He was flying an airplane with **George William Blackwell**, **Hugh Hilton Hutchinson** and **Alfred Chapman Meeson** on board, having taken off at Bastia, Corsica, and heading over Elba when it crashed on 19 November 1944 and all four were killed. They were buried in the Allied Military Cemetery at Elba, and then reinterred at the Bolsena War Cemetery (IV H 3) in 1947.

References: *The war dead of the British Commonwealth and Empire: the register of the names of those who fell in the 1939–1945 War and are buried in cemeteries in Italy Cemeteries 17–18: Bolsena War Cemetery, Orvieto War Cemetery*, Maidenhead: Imperial War Graves Commission, 1954, p. 18.

COVENEY, ERIC FRANK (1918–1944). A British sailor, he was born in 1918 in Eastry, Kent, the son of John Coveney and his wife Martha Sarah (née Nash) of Saltwood, Hythe, Kent. Joining the Royal Naval Reserve, he served with H.M.S. *Copra* (combined operations) and was killed on the first day of the Allied attack on Elba on 17 June 1944. He was buried on Elba and three years later was reburied in the Bolsena War Cemetery (Special Memorial C IV H 9) on the Italian mainland.

62

References: *The war dead of the British Commonwealth and Empire: the register of the names of those who fell in the 1939–1945 War and are buried in cemeteries in Italy Cemeteries 17–18: Bolsena War Cemetery, Orvieto War Cemetery*, Maidenhead: Imperial War Graves Commission, 1954, p. 18.

COZENS, ALEXANDER (1717–1786). A British landscape painter, he was born in 1717 in St Petersburg, the son of Richard Cozens (1674–1735), an English shipbuilder, and Mary Davenport, daughter of Robert Davenport, another shipbuilder, with some accounts fancifully claiming he was the illegitimate son of Peter the Great. Going to England, he taught at Christ's Hospital and then at Eton College, travelling in Europe. His depiction of the Isle of Elba in pencil, pen and black and grey ink, grey wash, was auctioned by Christie's King Street (London) and sold for £7,200. He died in 1786.

References: A. P. Oppe, *Alexander and John Robert Cozens*, Cambridge, Mass.: Harvard University Press, 1952; K. Sloan, *Alexander and John Robert Cozens: The Poetry of Landscape*, New Haven: Published in association with the Art Gallery of Ontario by Yale University Press, 1986; Kim Sloan, 'Cozens, Alexander (1717–1786)', *Oxford Dictionary of National Biography*, Oxford University Press, 2004.

CRACKANTHORPE, WILLIAM (1790–1888). A British visitor to Elba who met with **Napoleon Bonaparte** on the day before the former Emperor left to return to France, William Crackanthrope was born on 25 February 1790 in Cumberland, England, the son of Christopher Cookson (who assumed the surname of Crackanthorpe in 1792), and his wife Charlotte Elizabeth (née Cust). His father died when he was nine, he was educated at Sedbergh School, but his uncle Canon Cookson removed him from the school and sent him to Dr Gretton's school in Windsor. From there he proceeded to St John's College, Cambridge, matriculating in 1807 and graduating BA in 1811, and MA in 1816. He lived at Newbiggin Hall, Westmorland, and following the abdication of Napoleon on 11 April 1814, he went to the European continent, and then proceeded to Elba where he met with Napoleon on 25 February 1815 at the ball given by **Pauline Bonaparte**. On the following day, Napoleon escaped from Elba and headed to France.

In a letter William wrote from Florence to Sarah Crackanthrope, he referred to going to Elba with Mr Baillie and Mr and Mrs Orby Hunter, and they met Napoleon who chatted to them for an hour. William Crackanthorpe wrote, he showed 'a gaiety and gentlemanlike manner which quite astonished me... At intervals though he seemed to relapse into a kind of reverie, when his countenance assumed that fiendish appearance, which the light of the moon which shone upon it, perhaps rendered more horrid than it otherwise was... He still manifests the same restless disposition as ever and has already begun to make great improvements, which in the end will be extremely advantageous to the island.' He also noted that Napoleon had 'an almost fiendish expression. Crackanthorpe also write that Napoleon's house was small but he retains 'all the pomp of a court with the same ceremony as at St. Cloud of Versailles.'

Back in England, William Crackanthorpe actively supported the Liberal side of politics, and had his name put forward in the parliamentary elections in 1817 and again in 1831 but withdrew as a candidate. He was appointed the Deputy Lieutenant for Westmorland, and then High Sheriff of Cumberland in 1826. A justice of the peace and chairman of the Westmorland Poor Law Board for 40 years, Crackanthorpe rebuilt the parish church of Newbiggin and the rectory house. He was a friend of the poets Coleridge, Southey, and Wordsworth – his father's sister Ann was the mother of William Wordsworth. He was also a friend of the astronomer William Herschel. He died unmarried on 10 January, 1888 at Penrith, Cumberland; aged 97, leaving Newbiggin and other estates to his cousin Montague Hughes Cookson who took the surname of Crackanthorpe. William Crackanthorpe's papers – including his letter from Elba – were sold by Christie's, auctioneers, London, on 24 June 1992 for £3,850 and are now held at the department of manuscripts and university archives, Cambridge University Library.

References: *Alumni Cantabrigienses*; *Burke's Landed Gentry 1937*, p. 500; *Sedbergh School Register 1546 to 1895*, p. 163; David Crackanthorpe, *Hubert Crackanthorpe and English Realism in the 1890s*, Columbia: University of Missouri Press, 1977; John Worthen, *The life of William Wordsworth: a critical biography*, Chichester: Blackwell, 2014, pp. 403–04; *The Times* (11 January 1888), p. 6..

CROCCO, CARMINE (1830–1905). An Italian brigand who led a gang known as the 'Vultures', he was born on 5 June 1830 at Rionero in Vulture, then a part of the kingdom of the Two Sicilies. His father, Francesco Crocco, was the servant of a noble family, and an uncle had fought in the Napoleonic Army in the Peninsular War. Carmine Crocco came to hate the upper class which was exacerbated when his brother was beaten by a local aristocrat for

killing the lord's dog – the dog having attacked the family's chickens. Carmine's mother was beaten and lost a baby, and his father was held in jail without trial for attempted murder of the aristocrat.

Carmine Crocco worked as a shepherd and when 15, he dived into a river and saved the son of a nobleman. He was rewarded with 50 ducats, and with this money, he secured his father's release. He then joined the army of King Ferdinand II of the Two Sicilies, but deserted and was then involved in a fight to save the honour of his sister, killing the nobleman involved. He then became an outlaw. However with Giuseppe Garibaldi's Expedition of the Thousand about to collapse, the Italian patriot was eager to get any support and offered to take in deserters and brigands; Crocco joined Garibaldi but ended up in prison. Crocco was freed and came to lead a force of some 2,000 men – and in a change of sides – joined the Bourbons against the Piedmontese. He was captured by papal troops and turned over to the new Italian government who tried him and sentenced him to life in prison. At Santo Stefano, he wrote his memoirs which were published as *Gli ultimi briganti della Basilicata* (The last brigands of Basilicata, 1903). Soon afterwards he was moved to the prison at **Portoferraio** and he died there on 18 June 1905.

References: Antonio De Leo, *Carmine Cròcco Donatelli: un brigante guerrigliero*, Pellegrini, 1983; Basilide Del Zio, *Il brigante Crocco e la sua autobiografia*, Melfi: Tipografia G. Grieco, 1903; John Ellis, *A short history of guerrilla warfare*, London: Ian Allan Ltd., 1975, p. 83; Count A. Maffei and Marc Monnier, *Brigand life in Italy: a history of Bourbonist reaction*, London: Hurst and Blackett, 1865, 2 Vols; Tommaso Pedio and Mario Proto, *Come divenni brigante: autobiografia di Carmine Crocco*, Manduria: Piero Lacaita Editore, 1995.

CUISINE. Traditionally the diet of Elba includes fish or seafood, with much meat from goats. The French writer **Arsène Thiébaut de Berneaud** (1777–1850) in his *Voyage à l'île d'Elbe* (1814, English translation) noted:

The food of the inhabitants consists of dried pulse, cheese made from the milk of ewes, of which the smell and taste resemble bad grease good bacon of a light quality, salted and smoked provisions, coarse bread, fresh fish, of which the tunny is the chief, and a very few vegetables. The salted cheese of Sardinia is an article of great consumption. They also eat an immense quantity of chestnuts, the crop of which is gathered towards the end of October. After they have been dried by the fire till their double rind peels off, they are ground in the corn mill, with the upper grindstone raised to accommodate their bulk. The flour produced is not mixed with bran; it is soft, saccharine, and of a yellowish gray colour, which approaches nearer to white, in proportion as the chestnuts have been carefully picked and dried with attention. This flour combines and hardens when squeezed together. In order to preserve it, it is necessary to shut it up in a dry place, to compress it with considerable force, and to cover it over to the depth of two or three inches with ashes or sand. The Elboise make from it pollenta and pastry, far superior to any which can be manufactured from maize.

The strictest economy prevails in their use of food. It is only upon holidays, that fresh meat, and a white wine, rendered excellent by the utmost care in making, are permitted to be placed upon their tables. On ordinary days, they breakfast upon pollenta; towards noon they eat bread and beans, lentils, or some other species of pulse, boiled and with oil; and in the evening their repast is soup, and sometimes salt fish» or such as the sea yields.

Gradually more dishes were introduced and there are now a wide range of local products and dishes such as fish pasta, and sole stuffed with shrimp, as well as *risotto al nero di sepia* (cuttlefish in its own ink), and also *fagioli al fiasco* (Tuscan beans). The *ravioli all'astice* (lobster ravioli) which is served in a pepper and Parmesan sauce, and the *raviolini all'Ammoraglia* (ravioli with aubergine), often served with shrimp meat, are also popular with many gourmands. Wine in Elba is very highly regarded with Elba rosso and Elba blanco available in most restaurants and cafés around the island.

There are cafés and restaurants around Elba and many of them are highly praised in guide books. Stella Marina on Banchina Alto Fondale in **Portoferraio** is a popular restaurant for fish and seafood, being located next to the Toremar ferry jetty. The Trattoria da Zucchetta in Piazza della Repubblica, also in Portoferraio is a Neapolitan pizza restaurant dating back to 1891.

Since the arrival of tourists in the 1960s, there has been an increasing availability of foreign dishes and there is a **Chinese** restaurant and also a Japanese restaurant, the Fujion, in Marina di Campo. There is also Sir William's Irish Bar which is in Via Mangnaro in Portoferraio which serves Irish whiskey and butter.

References: Arsène Thiébaut de Berneaud, *A Voyage to the Isle of Elba*, London: Longman, Hurst, Rees, Orme and Brown, 1814, pp. 12–13; Dan Facaros and Michael Pauls, *Italy: Tuscany*, London: Cadogan Books plc, 1996, p. 304; Miles Roddis & Alex Leviton, *Tuscany & Umbria*, Footscray: Lonely Planet, 2006, p. 189; Angelo Serafin, *Il vino visto da un sommelier*, Tassotti Editore, 1973, pp. 180–82.

CULLENS, JOHN DAVID FERGUSON (1919–1944). An able seaman in the British Royal Navy, he was the son of John Dobbie Cullens and Elizabeth Dech Cullens, of Bridge of Allan, Stirlingshire. He served with H.M.S. *Copra* (combined operations) and was killed on the first day of the Allied attack on Elba on 17 June 1944. He was buried on Elba and three years later was reburied in the Bolsena War Cemetery (IV G 1) on the Italian mainland.

References: *The war dead of the British Commonwealth and Empire: the register of the names of those who fell in the 1939–1945 War and are buried in cemeteries in Italy Cemeteries 17–18: Bolsena War Cemetery, Orvieto War Cemetery*, Maidenhead: Imperial War Graves Commission, 1954, p. 18.

- D -

DA MONTEFELTRO, GUIDO (1223–1298). The lord of Urbino, and an Italian military commander, he was involved in many conflicts in central Italy during the 1270s, 1280s and 1290s. He had helped in the defence of Forlí in 1282–83 and in 1288 was hired by **Pisa** as their commander for their attack on Elba in 1293. He took the island – which had been captured by the Genoese the previous year – and in 1296 he was made lord of Montefeltro, becoming a Franciscan monk later the same year and dying in 1298 in Assisi. The Italian writer Dante Alighieri refers to Guido da Montefeltro being in hell in The Divine Comedy.

References: Dante, *The Inferno*, 27/4; Dante, *The Banquet*, 4/28/8; Richard Lansing (ed), *The Dante Encyclopedia*, New York: Garland, 2000, pp. 462–63.

DALESME, JEAN-BAPTISTE (1763–1832). He was the commander of the French garrison on Elba, he was born on 20 June 1763 at Limoges, Haute-Vienne, his father being a local printer. He was 17 when he enlisted in the infantry and served in Spain in 1782–83. Discharged from the army in 1788, after the French Revolution he rejoined the military and fought in a number of engagements and was involved in the capture of Quesnoy in 1793. However he was captured and was a prisoner in Hungary until his release in 1795. He then served as a brigadier general in Italy before being given command of the French army at Haute-Vienne. He was also elected to the French legislature in 1802, serving until 1809. After some other commands including as Major-General of the 4th Legion Reserve National Guard in Versailles, he was attached to the Rhine Army Corps and served at the battle of Essling where he was badly injured. On his recovery he was appointed a baron of the Empire and on 29 September 1810 he was appointed commander of the French troops on Elba by Prince Felix Baciocchi, the grand duke of Tuscany, and husband of **Elisa Bonaparte**.

Dalesme was still there when **Napoleon Bonaparte** arrived on the island in May 1814. Just before the arrival of the ex-emperor on the *Undaunted*, he had received news of Napoleon's abdication and was flying the white flag of the Bourbons from **Forte Falcone** and **Forte Stella**. He was worried that he was about to lose control of the island and with the arrival of Napoleon

Bonaparte, he handed over Elba and issued a proclamation on 4 May:

Inhabitants of the island of Elba: the vicissitudes natural to humanity have brought the Emperor Napoleon hither; his choice has given him to you as sovereign. Before entering these walls, your new and august monarch addressed to me the following words, which I hasten to make known to you, because they are the pledge of your future happiness: 'General, I have sacrificed my rights to the interests of mv country, reserving to myself, with the consent of all the Powers, the sovereignty and ownership of the Island of Elba. Be so good as to make the people acquainted with the new state of affairs, and the choice I have made of their island for my residence; I have selected it on account of the mildness of their manners and their climate. Tell them that they will always be the object of my most lively interest.' – Elbans I there is no need of comment on these words.

They fix your destiny. The Emperor has judged you rightly. I owe you this justice, and I render it. People of Elba, I shall soon leave you. My departure will pain me, for I love you sincerely; but the thought of your happiness will sweeten my sorrow, and in whatever place I may be I shall remain near this island in spirit, through my memory of the virtues of its inhabitants and the wishes I shall form for them.

He retired to Versailles and lived quietly. However as soon as there was news that Napoleon had landed in France, on 16 March 1815 the Royalist government of France arrested Dalesme accusing him of involvement in the escape of Napoleon from Elba.

Napoleon reappointed Dalesme as governor on Elba and was promoted to the rank of lieutenant general on 3 May. In June 1815 with the British blockading Elba, he managed to distribute grain to prevent a major riot but when he heard that Napoleon had been defeated at Waterloo, agreed to surrender Portoferraio to the Austrian government of Tuscany. He then retired to Petit Charat, near Limoges. In 1830 King Louis Philippe appointed him to run the Hotel des Invalides and he was made Grand Officer of the Legion of Honour. However he suffered from cholera and died on 13 April 1832. His name was engraved on the north side of the Arc de Triomphe.

References: Pierre Branda, *L'île d'Elbe et le retour de Napoléon: 1814–1815*, Saint-Cloud: Soteca, 2014; Robert Christophe, *Napoleon on Elba*, London: Macdonald, 1964, p. 25f; Norman MacKenzie, *The Escape from Elba: The Fall & Flight of Napoleon 1814–1815*, Oxford: Oxford University Press, 1982; Sir Henry Drummond Wolff, *The island empire, or the scenes of the first exile of the Emperor Napoleon I*, London: T. Bosworth, 1855.

DAVIS, ALAN (1923–1944). Born in 1923 in Northampton, the son of Alfred John Davis and Lily Gertrude (née Allen), of Semilong, Northampton, he served as a Sub-Lieutenant, Royal Naval Volunteer Reserve, and was posted to the H.M.S. *Armadillo* in Italy. Mentioned in Despatches, he was killed on the first day of the Allied attack on Elba on 17 June 1944. He was buried on Elba and three years later was reinterred in the Bolsena War Cemetery (IV G 2) on the Italian mainland.

References: *The war dead of the British Commonwealth and Empire: the register of the names of those who fell in the 1939–1945 War and are buried in cemeteries in Italy Cemeteries 17–18: Bolsena War Cemetery, Orvieto War Cemetery*, Maidenhead: Imperial War Graves Commission, 1954, p. 18.

DE LATTRE DE TASSIGNY, JEAN JOSEPH MARIE (1889–1952). The French commander who took Elba in June 1944, he was born on 2 February 1889 at Mouilleron-en-Pareds, in La Vendée, Brittany, coming from the same village as the politician Georges Clemenceau. He graduated 5th in his class from St Cyr, and fought with distinction in World War I, being wounded twice and being made a knight of the Legion of Honour in December 1914. He specialised in cavalry tactics and had much experience in the Rif War in Morroco where he was an officer in the French headquarters. In 1932 he was appointed to the headquarters staff of General Weygand, and three years later, was appointed the head of the French War College. With the outbreak of **World War II**, de Lattre de Tassigny was the commander of the French 14th Infantry Division until the Armistice. He was then placed in command

Jean de Lattre de Tassigny at Toulon soon after the capture of Elba.

of the Vichy French forces in Tunisia but being anti-German, was arrested and sentenced to ten years in jail. However he escaped to Algiers and was welcomed by the Free French.

With the French preparing to attack Corsica, it was decided to try out the largely inexperienced Moroccan and Senegalese troops in the attack on Elba in June 1944. This was successful in so far as the Germans on Elba were forced to withdraw and in three days Elba was in Allied hands. However the French colonial troops took part in a looting spree in which they raped many local women and only with difficulty were the French officers able to restore discipline. The attack on Corsica followed, and then there was the landing in Provence in southern France.

Jean de Lattre de Tassigny was appointed chief of staff of the NATO infantry in Europe and with the French starting to lose the war in Indochina, was sent to Vietnam and from 1950 until September 1951 he commanded the French forces. He rallied the beleaguered French forces and the Vietminh commander General Giap reported that his army now faced 'an adversary worthy of its steel'. Jean de Lattre de Tassigny gradually drove back the Vietnamese communists. In one bitter battle at Nam Dinh, he ordered that the town should be held at all costs – his only son Bernard was killed in the fighting there. However he was increasingly ill and returned to Paris where on 11 January 1952 he died from cancer. Soon after his departure from Indochina, the French started losing the war, and were forced to withdraw with the Geneva Peace Agreements in 1954 which followed their defeat at Dien Bien Phu.

References: Simonne de Lattre de Tassigny, *Jean de Lattre, mon mari*, Paris: Presses de la Cité, 1972, vol. 1: 25 September 1926 – 8 May 1945; Bernard Destremau, *Jean de Lattre de Tassigny*, Paris: Flammarion, 1999; Michel Droit, *De Lattre, maréchal de France*, Paris: Pierre Horay / Éditions de Flore, 1952; Stanley Karnow, *Vietnam: A History*, New York: Viking Press, 1983; Pierre Pellissier, *De Lattre*, Paris: Perrin, 1998.

DEL BUONO, ORESTE (1923–2003). An Italian journalist, he was born on 8 March 1923 at **Póggio** and studied in Milan. Captured by the Germans in late 1943, he spent 1½ years as a prisoner of war in Germany. A keen linguist and translator, he translated into Italian the works of many foreign authors: Raymond Chandler, Arthur Conan Doyle, Gustave Flaubert, Ian Fleming, André Gide, Gogol, Marcel Proust, Robert Louis Stevenson, Horace Walpole and

Oscar Wilde. He also wrote many books himself: *Racconto d'inverno* (The Winter's Tale, 1945), *Un intero minuto* (A full minute, 1959), *L'amore senza storie* (Love without stories, 1960), *Né vivere né morire* (Neither life nor death, 1964), *Un tocco in più*, with Gianni Rivera (A touch more, 1966), *I peggiori anni della nostra vita* (The worst years of our lives, 1971), *La parte difficile* (The hard part, 1975), *Tornerai* (I will be back, 1976), *Un'ombra dietro il cuore* (A shadow behind the heart, 1978), *Il comune spettatore* (The common spectator, 1979), *Se m'innamorassi di te* (If I fall in love with you, 1980), *La talpa di città* (The city's mole, 1984), *La nostra classe dirigente* (Our Ruling Class, 1986), *La debolezza di scrivere* (The weakness of writing, 1987), *La vita sola* (The single life, 1989), *Acqua alla gola* (Water in the throat, 1992), and *Amici, amici degli amici, maestri* (Friends, friends of friends, masters, 1994). He also wrote for the newspaper La Stampa and composed pieces about fictional interviews with historical characters. He died on 30 September 2003 in Rome.

DEMIDOFF, Prince ANATOLE NIKOLAIEVICH [Анатолий Николаевич Демидов] **(1813–1870)**. A Russian industrialist, he and his parents had been great admirers of **Napoleon Bonaparte** and married Napoleon's niece and did much to establish a museum on Elba to Napoleon. He was born on 5 April (24 March o.s.) 1813, the second son of Count Nikolai Nikitich Demidoff (1773–1828), and Baroness Elisabeta Alexandrovna Stroganova (1779–1818). His father was a diplomat in Paris and when he died, Anatole decided to remain in Western Europe, disliking the reactionary politics of Tsar Nicholas I of Russia. He did, however, run a scientific expedition to southern Russia and the Crimea which resulted in the four volume *Voyage dans la Russie méridionale et la Crimée* (1840–42). Moving to Villa San Donato at Florence, he met Jérôme Bonaparte, former king of Westphalia, in 1839 and soon afterwards preparations were made for him to marry Jérôme's daughter,

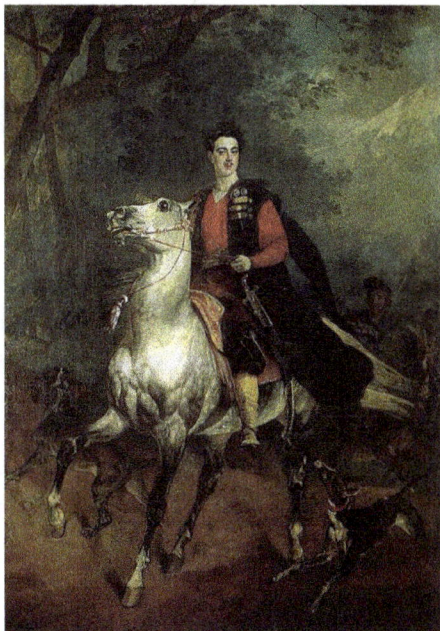

Princess Mathilde-Létizia Bonaparte. He agreed to pay a generous dowry and was created 'Prince of San Donato' which allowed Mathilde-Létizia to remain a princess although the title was never recognised in Russia.

On the island of Elba, Prince Demidoff bought Napoleon's house, **Villa San Martino**, and then helped turn it into a museum. Unfortunately many of the original items of furniture had been sold but Prince Demidoff was able to bring over some items he had found on the Italian mainland. He also established a custom by which a mass was held for Napoleon Bonaparte on 5 May each year at the **Church of (The Reverenda) Misericordia** in **Portoferraio**. Prince Demidoff's marriage was not a happy one. He had regular affairs and he and his wife separated in 1843 and she left for Paris three years later with her lover Count Émilien de Nieuwerkerke. He died on 29 April 1870.

References: Robert Christophe, *Napoleon on Elba*, London: Macdonald, 1964, pp. 194–97.

DIVING. With the increase in tourism, there has been much interest in diving around Elba and other islands in the Tuscan Archipelago. To the north of Elba, divers around **Scoglietto** often see shoals of tuna, and when diving near **Marciana Marina**, there is a state of Christ underwater, with a large anchor, about 12 feet tall, visible in the waters at Capo Vita. This anchor is said to be from a ship in the papal navy. For nudibranchs, people tend to dive off the islamd of Lammaiola, and lobsters can be seen off the island of Giuglio.

References: L. Dryjanska, 'Geotourism potential of the islands of the western Mediterranean: Case study of Elba island', European Journal of Tourism Research vol. 7 no 1 (1 January 2014), pp. 127–39; Paul Munzinger, *100 Diving Sites: Underwater Paradises Around the Globe*, New York: Paragon, 2010, pp. 18–19.

DOUGLAS, FREDERICK SYLVESTER NORTH, (1791–1819). A British politician and classical scholar, he was born on 8 February 1791 at Bedford Square, London, the son of Sylvester Douglas, Baron Glenbervie (1743–1823) from Aberdeen who moved to London where he was a member of parliament. Frederick Douglas was baptised at home and educated at Sunbury School and then Westminster School in 1801, proceeding to Christ Church, Oxford. He was admitted to Lincoln's Inn but was never called to the Bar. Instead he went to Edinburgh and in 1810 went to Greece and the Near East.

Returning to Britain from Athens in 1814 Frederick Douglas went to Elba to meet **Napoleon** telling the ex-emperor that I have come 'to see a great man'. Napoleon Bonaparte apparently 'liked him best of his English visitors on

Elba'. A member of parliament, in 1819 he spoke in support of independence for South America. He died on 21 October 1819 in Westminster. His widow married in 1825 Colonel Henry Hely Hutchinson and died on 16 July 1864.

References: John Alger, *Napoleon's British visitors and captives, 1801–1815*, New York: J. Pott, 1904, p. 295; Roland Thorne, 'Douglas, Sylvester, Baron Glenbervie (1743–1823)', *Oxford Dictionary of National Biography*, Oxford University Press, 2004; *The Record of Old Westminsters* vol. 1, p. 278; *Alumni Oxonienses* vol. 1, p. 380.

DOUGLAS, NIEL. A Scottish colonel in the British army, he accompanied **John Barber Scott**, Major **Montgomery Maxwell**, RA; Colonel **John Lemoine**, RA; and Captain Smith when they visited Napoleon Bonaparte on Elba in September 1814. John Alger wrote:

They encountered Napoleon as he was out riding, and on their saluting him he stopped for a few minutes to question them. They thought he looked more like a crafty priest than a hero... Being told by Douglas that he belonged to a Highland regiment, Napoleon asked whether they did not wear kilts (jupes). On Douglas replying in the affirmative, Napoleon asked whether he had brought his kilt with him, as he should like to see it, but Douglas was unable to gratify his curiosity.

References: John Alger, *Napoleon's British visitors and captives, 1801–1815*, New York: J. Pott, 1904, p. 296; Maxwell Montgomery, *My Adventures*, London: H. Colburn, 1845, vol. 1, pp. 189–94.

DRAGUT [Turgut Reis; درغوت] **(1485– 1565)**. A commander in the Ottoman navy, he was responsible for attacking Elba in 1553, and again two years later. Of Greek descent, he was taken prisoner by Corsairs when he was young, and soon came to embrace Islam. His skill as a sailor was quickly recognised and he was involved in fighting as a teenager, and helped with the Ottoman invasion of Egypt. In 1520 he started serving under the Ottoman naval commander Hayreddin Barbarossa, and soon started taking part in daring raids including on Capo Passero in Sicily in 1526, and then over the next seven years he attacked other ports in Sicily and in the kingdom of Naples. He commanded the rear at the battle of Preveza on

28 September 1538 which resulted in a decisive victory for the Ottoman navy. Dragut started attacking along the west coast of Italy and in 1540 sacked the island of **Capraia**.

After the death of Barbarossa in July 1546, Dragut was appointed the supreme commander of Ottoman naval forces in the Mediterranean. He attacked Malta in mid–1551, and captured Tripoli in modern-day Libya in August 1551. In the summer of 1553 Dragut led his fleet from Constantinople and having formed an alliance with the French, planned to attack Orbetello, and also Piombino and Elba. The large Ottoman fleet appeared off the coast of **Montecristo** on 7 August 1553, with the French landing on Elba and sacking Porto Longone (**Porto Azzurro**), **Rio Nell'Elba** and **Capoliveri**. Many of the Elbans took refuge in **Portoferraio** and although the Turks patrolled the seas around Elba, **Cosimo de Medici** was able to get messages to Portoferraio and from the town. Eventually the Turks withdrew but Dragut attacked again in 1555. Dragut was subsequently involved in the Great Siege of Malta and killed in the fighting there on 23 June 1565.

References: Ernle Bradford, *The Great Siege*, London: Hodder & Stoughton, 1967; Giovanni Battiste Comandé, *La Sicilia contro il corsaro Dragut (1551-'52)*, Palermo, Edizioni D.E.L.F.: 1956; Averil Mackenzie-Grieve, *Aspects of Elba and the other islands of the Tuscan Archipelago*, London: Jonathan Cape, 1964, Chapter 6; Charles Monchicourt, *Épisodes de la carrière tunisienne de Dragut (1550–1551)*, Tunis: S. A. de l'Imp. Rapide, 1918.

DROUOT, ANTOINE (1774–1847). An artillery commander, he always remained loyal to **Napoleon Bonaparte**. He was born on 11 January 1774 at Nancy, France, the son of a baker. He trained as an artilleryman and served in many battles soon after the French Revolution. He fought at the battle of Wagram, and then at Moscow and Lützen. He travelled on the *Undaunted* which took the ex-emperor to Elba, being seasick on the journey. When the *Undaunted* arrived at Elba, Drouot, Baron **Jermanowski**, and Major **Clam-Martinitz** went ashore to check that Napoleon would be given a suitable welcome. He was subsequently appointed the governor of the island.

Returning to France with Napoleon, he played an active part in the 100 Days. At the battle of Waterloo, because of rain the night before, the battlefield was muddy and Drouot felt that the French attack should be delayed because it would be easier to move the artillery on drier ground. This caused Napoleon to hold back on the attack for a few crucial hours. It was Drouot moving his artillery closer to the British lines in the afternoon that led to the British falling back and the French almost winning the battle – the tide turning suddenly with the arrival of the Prussians. With the second Bourbon Restoration, Drouot was arrested and charged but acquitted and lived quietly in in Nancy where he died on 24 March 1847.

References: Mark Adkin, *The Waterloo Companion*, London: Aurum Press, 2001, p. 12; Général Ambert, *Le général Drouot*, 9th edition, Tours: Alfred Mame et fils, 1896; Pierre Branda, *L'île d'Elbe et le retour de Napoléon: 1814–1815*, Saint-Cloud: Soteca, 2014; Robert Christophe, *Napoleon on Elba*, London: Macdonald, 1964, p. 28f; Raymond Horricks, *Napoleon's Elite*, New Brunswick: Transaction Publishers, 1995, p. 133; Norman MacKenzie, *The Escape from Elba: The Fall & Flight of Napoleon 1814–1815*, Oxford: Oxford University Press, 1982; William Serieyx, *Drouot et Napoléon, vie héroïque et sublime du Général Drouot*, Paris: Tallandier, 9th edition, 1929; Jean Tabeur, *Le général Drouot: fils de boulanger! aide de camp de l'Empereur, collection du bicentenaire de l'épopée impériale*, Paris: Teissèdre, 2004.

DUCHOQUÈ, AUGUSTO (1813–1893). An Italian politician, he was born on 5 July 1813 at **Portoferraio**. A member of the Italian senate in the 1860s, he died on 13 December 1893 in Florence.

DUDGEON, JOHN STEWART (1924–1944). A marine in the British Royal Marines, he was the son of William and Agnes Dudgeon, of Edinburgh, Scotland. John Dudgeon was killed on 17 June 1944 during the Allied attack on Elba, drowning when his landing craft sunk. His body was never identified, and he is commemorated on the Chatham Naval Memorial (panel 79, column 2).

DUMAS, ALEXANDRE (1802–1870). The famous French writer and the author of *Le Comte de Monte-Cristo* (1844; *The Count of Monte Cristo*), he visited Elba with Jérôme Bonaparte and had the idea of using the island in his story as the location of massive treasure which Edmond Dantès finds there and uses to take revenge on the people who persecuted him and caused the death of his father.

Alexandre Dumas was born on 24 July 1802 as Dumas Davy de la Pailleterie in Villers-Cotterêts in the department of Aisne, in Picardy, France,

the son of Thomas-Alexandre Dumas who had come from Saint-Domingue (now Haiti). His father, who had been promoted to general by the age of 31, had died when the young Alexandre Dumas was four leaving the family in impoverished circumstances. An avid reader, he managed to get a position in the Palais Royal working for Louis-Philippe, the duke of Orléans (later King Louis-Philippe). He took part in the July Revolution of 1830 which saw the duke of Orléans become king. Soon afterwards Dumas started writing novels.

In 1842 Alexandre Dumas went to Italy and was in Florence for a year. He met with Jérôme Bonaparte, the former king of Westphalia, and the two became friends. The two went to Elba and during the voyage Dumas heard about the island of **Montecristo** and wanted to write a story which involved the island. He may have heard the local story about Jacques Abrial who farmed on Montecristo from 1849–52. For his novel, Dumas weaved in **Napoleon**'s exile in Elba, with Edmond Dantès, an unsuspecting seafarer who had been promoted to captain of a ship, unknowlingly bringing back a letter for a Bonapartist plotter and seeing himself jailed, but managing to escape and recover a massive fortune in treasure on the island of Montecristo. The book became famous, and was translated into many languages, and has since been the subject of films, television programmes and cartoons. Dumas continued writing until his death on 5 December 1870 at Puys, near Dieppe.

References: Herbert Gorman, *The Incredible Marquis, Alexandre Dumas,* New York: Farrar & Rinehart, 1929; Frank Wild Reed, *A Bibliography of Alexandre Dumas, père,* Pinner Hill, Middlesex: J.A. Neuhuys, 1933; Miles Roddis & Alex Leviton, *Tuscany & Umbria*, Footscray: Lonely Planet, 2006, p. 192; Michael Ross, *Alexandre Dumas*, Newton Abbot: David & Charles, 1981; Harry A. Spurr, *The Life and Writings of Alexandre Dumas*, New York: Frederick A. Stokes, 1902; Marilyn S. Severson, *Masterpieces of French Literature,* Westport, Conn.: Greenwood Press, 2004, p. 59.

DUNDAS, Sir DAVID (c.1735–1820). A British military engineer, he helped take French Royalists from Toulon to Elba in 1793. Born in Edinburgh, Scotland, he was the third of the four sons of Robert Dundas, a prosperous Edinburgh merchant, and his wife, Margaret (née Melville). He attended the Royal Military Academy, Woolwich, and between 1752 and in 1756 he

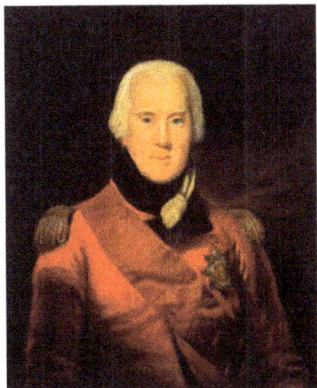

accompanied his uncle, Lieutenant-Colonel David Watson, on a survey and mapping trip of Scotland following the end of the Jacobite rebellion at Culloden in 1746. During the Seven Years' War, David Dundas was involved in British attacks on St. Malo, Cherbourg, and then served as an engineer with the British army in Germany. He then went to the Caribbean where he took part in the capture of Havana. Posted to Ireland during the American War of Independence, he remained there until the start of the French Revolutionary Wars. Sir Henry Bunbury described him as 'a tall, spare man, crabbed and austere, dry in his looks and demeanour'.

Serving in the army of the Duke of York in Flanders, he crossed France to Toulon and was appointed the second-in-command of the British and allied soldiers who, with the French royalists, were holding the city. When General Charles O'Hara was captured, Dundas took command just before the city fell. He and Admiral Samuel Hood left Toulon by sea, taking with them the British soldiers and many French royalists who were evacuated to Elba. Dundas then went to Corsica to help the insurgency led by **Pasquale Paoli**, but falling ill, he returned to Britain on sick leave. He then served in Netherlands and Germany, drawing up a new handbook for the cavalry. Taking part in the establishment of the Royal Military College at Sandhurst, he was placed in command of Kent and Sussex with Britain worried about a French invasion. He retired to live in Chelsea Hospital and died on 18 February 1820. He was buried in the grounds of the hospital.

References: R. Glover, *Peninsular preparation: the reform of the British army, 1795–1809,* Cambridge: Cambridge University Press, 1963; J. A. Houlding, *Fit for service: the training of the British army, 1715–1795*, Oxford: Clarendon Press, 1981; J. A. Houlding, 'Dundas, Sir David (1735?–1820)', *Oxford Dictionary of National Biography*, Oxford University Press, 2004.

- E -

EBRINGTON, LORD. *See* **Fortescue, Hugh**.

EDUCATION. The provision of education was largely the prerogative of the church until the arrival of **Napoleon**. When the ex-emperor started to modernise the running of Elba, he decided to establish a small school in Portoferraio modelled on the École Polytechnic in Paris. The families had to pay 300 francs a year, with the ten cadets being paid 180 francs each. They were equipped with blue trousers, riding boots, a black hat with red piping, a sword with a white sash, and sub-lieutenant's epaulettes.

The Italian ministry of education now regulates all schools on the island of Elba with school attendance compulsory for all children between the ages of six and 16, with the structure largely unchanged since 1962. There are private and public institutions and there are five stages of education: kindergarten (scuola dell'infanzia); primary school (scuola primaria); lower secondary school / middle school (scuola secondaria di primo grado or scuola media); upper secondary school (scuola secondaria di secondo grado or scuola superiore); and university (università).

ELBA, BATTLE OF. This sea battle which took place on 28 August 1652 as part of the First Anglo-Dutch War (1652–54), between the Dutch under **Johan van Galen**, and the English fleet under **Richard Badiley**. The English fleet was heading for safety in Livorno where there was a squadron under the command of Henry Appleton. The Dutch surprised the English and captured the English ship *Phoenix*, and badly damaged the English flagship, *Paragon*, which had to seek refuge in Porto Longone, Elba.

English fleet (Richard Badiley)
Paragon 52 guns (flagship)
Elizabeth 36 (Jonas Reeves)
Phoenix 36 guns (John Wadsworth). Captured by Eendracht
Constant Warwick 32 guns (Owen Cox)
Mary Rose 32 guns (hired merchantman, Jonas Poole)
William and Thomas 30 guns (hired merchantman, John Godolphin)
Thomas Bonaventure 28 guns (hired merchantman, George Hughes)
Richard and William 24 guns (hired merchantman, John Wise)

Netherlands (Johan van Galen)
Jaarsveld 44 guns (flagship)
Prinses Royaal 34 guns (Albert Cornelisz 't Hoen; killed)
Wapen van Zeeland 32 guns (Joost Willemsz Block; killed)
Eendracht 40 guns (Jacob de Boer, Vice-Admiral)
Maan 40 guns (David Janszoon Bondt; killed)
Vereenigde Provinciën/Zeven Provinciën 40 guns (Hendrick Claeszoon Swart; killed)
Haarlem 40 guns (Dirck Quirijn Verveen)
Maagd van Enkhuysen 34 guns (Cornelis Tromp)
Zeelandia 32 guns (Andries de Boer)
Jonge Prins 28 guns (Cornelis Barentszoon Slordt)

References: David C. Wallace, *Twenty-Two Turbulent Years 1639–1661*, FastPrint, 2013.

ELBA CANARY. With an increased interest in ornithology and the classification of birds during the nineteenth century, there were attempts to classify the 'Elba Canary'. According to an account written by Giovanni Pietro Olina in a book published in Rome in 1622 (and having been previously recorded by Antonio Valli da Todi in a book published in 1601), a Dutch sailor had managed to catch a few pairs of the 'Elba Canary' which were then introduced into the Low Countries where they bred freely. In the twentieth century, ornithologists came across a painting by Vincenzo Leonardi from around 1630. Held in the Royal Library at Windsor Castle, England, it shows that the Elba Canary was actually a citril finch from Corsica.

References: Tim Birkhead, *The Red Canary; The Story of the First Genetically Engineered Animal*, London: Weidenfeld & Nicolson, 2003.

ELLIS, GEORGE JAMES WELBORE AGAR, 1st Baron Dover (1797–1833). A British politician and patron of art, he was born on 14 January 1797 in London, the only son of Henry Welbore Agar-Ellis, 2nd Viscount Clifden, and his wife, Lady Caroline Spencer, eldest daughter of George Spencer, 4th duke of Marlborough. Educated at Westminster School and then Christ Church, Oxford, in 1814 he planned to visit Elba to interview **Napoleon**, intending to write a biography of the ex-emperor, but by the time he managed to get things organised, news reached him of Napoleon's escape and the 100 Days. Heading into politics, he was elected to Parliament in 1818 and urged for the British Museum to buy the Angerstein collection of paintings which then became the basis of the National Portrait Gallery.

Retaining his interest in French history, he wrote a book on the Man in the Iron Mask which was published in 1826. He died on 10 July 1833 and was buried in Twickenham, Middlesex.

References: G. F. R. Barker, 'Ellis, George James Welbore Agar-, first Baron Dover (1797–1833)', revised by H. C. G. Matthew, *Oxford Dictionary of National Biography*, Oxford University Press, 2004. *The Record of Old Westminsters* vol. 1, p. 308; *Alumni Oxonienses* vol. 2, p. 421.

ELLISTON, CECIL EDWARD (1922–1944). A marine in the British Royal Marines, he was born in late 1922 at Kendal, Cumberland, UK, the son of Cecil Edward Elliston and Elsie Kerfoot (née Waterworth), of Leigh-on-Sea, Essex. He was killed when his landing craft sank during the Allied attack on Elba on 17 June 1944, and was initially posted as missing, presumed killed. He is commemorated on the Chatham Naval Memorial (panel 79, column 2).

ENEFER, ROLAND (1924–1944). Born in 1924 at Glanford Brigg, Lincolnshire, UK, he was the son of Talbot and Ellen Enefer, of New Brumby, Scunthorpe, Lincolnshire. An able seaman in the British Royal Navy, he served with H.M.S. *Copra* (combined operations), and was killed on the first

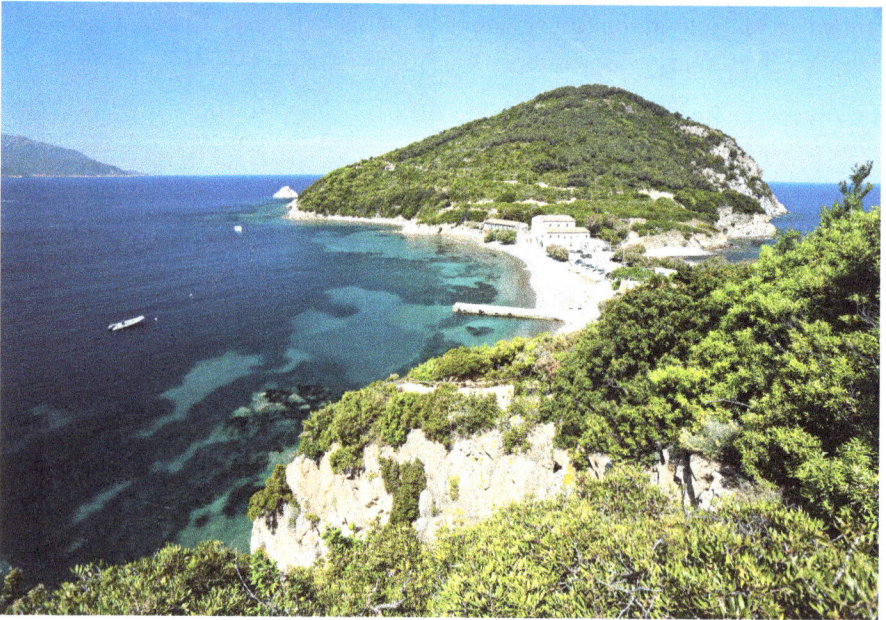

Enfola.
Photograph © Masterlu / Fotolia.com

day of the Allied attack of Elba on 17 June 1944. He was buried on Elba and three years later was reburied in the Bolsena War Cemetery (IV G 12) on the Italian mainland.

References: *The war dead of the British Commonwealth and Empire: the register of the names of those who fell in the 1939–1945 War and are buried in cemeteries in Italy Cemeteries 17–18: Bolsena War Cemetery, Orvieto War Cemetery*, Maidenhead: Imperial War Graves Commission, 1954, p. 20.

ENFOLA BEACHES. These beaches are on the strip of land which connects the Enfola peninsula and the rest of Elba. Located on the north of the island, and relatively close to **Portoferraio**, there are three beaches – one on the south side, one on the north side, and the third is off the road leading to the peninsula. It is popular on account of several hotels and also a camping ground.

ENTE VALORIZZAZIONE ELBA (EVE). This was established as the official tourist organisation on Elba and is located on the second floor of the Grattacielo, opposite the ferry pier at **Portoferraio**, at 30 Piazza della Repubblica. Over the years it has done much to help the growth of tourism on the island. In 1962 it founded the **Isola d'Elba Prize**. It has since been

Enfola.
Photograph © kletr / Fotolia.com

replaced by the **Agenzia per il Turismo dell'Archipelago Toscano**.

ERMATINGER, EDWARD (1797–1876). A well-known Canadian fur-trader and writer, he was born on 13 February 1797 on the island of Elba where his father, **Lawrence Edward Ermatinger**, was an assistant commissary general in the British army, his mother, an Italian, dying when he was an infant. He had a good education but his father had little to do with the boy's upbringing with Edward and his brother Francis going to Canada to work for an uncle, Charles Oakes Ermatinger who was in the fur trade in Canada. The two boys worked for the Hudson's Bay Company, remaining with them until 1828. After a short visit to England, Edward Ermatinger decided to change his life and moved to St Thomas where he was postmaster, and also the manager of the Bank of Upper Canada, later the Commercial Bank, and then the Bank of Montreal. A Conservative, he was elected to the Legislative Assembly in 1844 but was defeated three years later. He took up writing and was the author of *The Hudson's Bay territories; a series of letters on this important question* (Toronto, 1858), and *Life of Colonel Talbot, and the Talbot settlement, its rise and progress ...* (St. Thomas, 1859). He died on 29 October 1876 at St Thomas, Canada West (now Ontario).

References: Lois Halliday McDonald, *Fur Trade Letters of Francis Ermatinger Written to His Brother Edward During His Service with the Hudson's Bay Company, 1818–1853,* Glendale, Calif: A.H. Clark Co, 1980; L. G. Thomas, 'Ermatinger, Edward', in *Dictionary of Canadian Biography*, vol. 10, p. 273–7.

ERMATINGER, LAWRENCE EDWARD (1767–1829). He was born on 27 September 1767 in Montreal, Quebec – then recently captured by the British – the son of Lawrence Ermatinger, a Swiss merchant who had moved to Canada, and Jemima (née Oakes). Lawrence Ermatinger was assistant commissary general in the British army. Posted to Elba, he married an Italian lady and they had two children: **Edward Ermatinger**, born in February 1797; and Francis Ermatinger, born on 27 September 1798 in Portugal. Lawrence Ermatinger retired to England and died in 1829 in Oxford.

ETRUSCAN ELBA. The Etruscans were attracted to Elba on account of the iron mines on the island, and the Greek philosopher Aristotle mentions the

Etruscan control of the island in his works. This came about when a combined Etruscan and Carthaginian fleet defeated a large Greek fleet at the battle of Alalia fought on a day sometime between 540 and 535 BC. Some Etruscan sites have been found on the island with archaeologists in the nineteenth century finding some Etruscan tombs in **Portoferraio**, near the house where Grand Duke **Cosimo de 'Medici** stayed in the late 1540s. In recent years there has been research into whether heavy metal poisoning had a detrimental effect on the Etruscan settlements on Elba. Archaeologists have also found an Etruscan shipwreck off the coast of **Giglio**, one of the islands in the Tuscan Archipelago. *See also* **Ancient Elba**.

References: Alexis Catsambis, Ben Ford and Donny L. Hamilton, *The Oxford Handbook of Maritime Archaeology*, Oxford & New York: Oxford University Press, 2011, p. 371; Claudio Giardino, 'Villanovan and Etruscan Mining and Metallurgy', in Jean Macintosh Turfa (ed), *The Etruscan World*, London: Routledge, 2013, pp. 721–37; A. P. Harrison, I. Cattani and J. M. Turfa, 'Metallurgy, environmental pollution and the decline of Etruscan civilisation', *Environmental Science and Pollution Research International* vol. 17, no 1 (January 2010), pp. 165–80; John MacIntosh Turfa, *The Etruscan World*, London and New York: Routledge, 2013.

- F -

FAIRBANKS, DOUGLAS, Jr (1909–2000). The famous US actor, he was the commander of an American PT boat during the Allied landing at Elba on 17 June 1944. Born on 9 December 1909 in New York City, the son of Douglas Fairbanks and Anna Beth (née Sully), his parents divorced when he was nine. His father had been a famous actor in the early days of the US film industry. Douglas Jr was raised by his mother in New York, then lived in Paris and London. When he was only 14, he was given a role in a film, and made his name during the silent film era, and continued through to the talkies becoming a famous actor and with a host of film appearances which made him wealthy. In 1941 he was appointed by US President Franklin D. Roosevelt as a special envoy to South America and was then called up to serve in the US Navy as a reserve officer. He was attached to the Commando staff of Lord Louis Mountbatten in Britain and then after studying beach landings by commandos, he returned to the United States where the US forces were preparing for Operation Torch which would involve the landing of Allied soldiers in North Africa.

Fairbanks wrote of his experiences in World War II in the second volume of his memoirs, *A Hell of a War* (1993). After the war, Douglas Fairbanks jnr returned to Hollywood and starred in many films. He was an Anglophone and the College of Arms in London granted him a coat of arms. He died on 7 May 2000, aged 90, and was buried in the Hollywood Forever Cemetery, alongside his father.

References: Douglas Fairbanks jnr, *The Salad Days: an autobiography*, London: Collins, 1988; Douglas Fairbanks jnr, *A Hell of a War*, New York: St. Martin's, 1993.

FAIRWEATHER, GEORGE P. (d. 1944). A British able seaman in the Royal Navy, he served with H.M.S. *Copra* (combined operations) and was killed on the first day of the Allied attack on Elba on 17 June 1944. He was buried on Elba and three years later was reburied in the Bolsena War Cemetery (IV G 20) on the Italian mainland.

References: *The war dead of the British Commonwealth and Empire: the register of the names of those who fell in the 1939–1945 War and are buried in cemeteries in Italy Cemeteries 17–18: Bolsena War Cemetery, Orvieto War Cemetery*, Maidenhead: Imperial War Graves Commission, 1954, p. 20.

FALETTI, GIORGIO (1950–2014). An Italian comedian, he was born on 25 November 1950 at Asti, near Turin, and studied law. He then decided to go on the stage and became a comedian on a number of shows, as well as writing with three of his books translated into English: *I Kill* (2010); *I am God* (2011); and *The Killer in My Eyes* (2012). In ill-health in recent years, he moved to live at **Capoliveri**, Elba. He died on 4 July 2014 in Turin, from lung cancer.

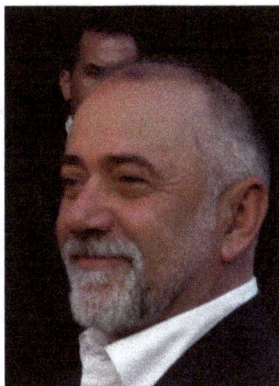

FAUNA. In prehistoric times, Elba was connected to the mainland and archaeologists have found evidence of large cave bears, rhinoceros and hippopotamus on Elba. Later there were still bears, as well as stags and roe deer, and also wild goats. Gradually, however, with Elba an island, and with a growing human population, the number and variety of animals was heavily reduced.

There are a number of species native to Elba, and also generally Sardinia and Corsica. Most are small reptiles or insects and include the the Tyrrhenian tree-frog (*Hyla sarda*), the cricket *Rhacocleis tyrrhenica*, the butterfly *Hipparchia neomiris*, the spider *Phyllodactylis europaeus*. There are also a number of local bird species such as the Corsican venturone (*Serinus citrinella corsicanus*), and the Sardinian magnanina (*Sylvia sarda*), as well as the Corsican sea-gull (*Larus audouinii*). The Greek tortoise (*Testudo lutea*) can also be seen around the island.

There are also some species which arrived on the island during the Pleistocene period. These include a flat worm, the alpine Crenobia, which lives along ditches, and the cricket *Omocestus ventralis*. There is a third group of species which arrived in more recent times. These generally come from the mainland and include some mammals such as moufflons (*Ovis musimom*) and wild boars (*Sus scrofa*) both introduced in the 1970s, both of which can easily be seen on the Monte Capanne. There are also wild cats (*Felis silvestrìs*), martens (*Martes martes*), hares (*Lepus capensis*), and dormice (*Glis glis*), with

Mouflon.
Painting by R. Lydekker F.R.S.

hedgehogs (*Erinaceus europaeus*) also being quite common. There are also the Noctule bat (*Vesperugo noctula*), and the horseshoe bat (*Rhinolophidae*). New introductions include the lizard, the *Podarcis muralis colosii*; the cricket, *Phyllodromica nagidi*; and a butterfly, the *Coenonympha elbana*.

Other reptiles found on Elba include a range of snakes such as vipers (*Vipera aspis francisciredi*); grass collared snakes (*Natrix natrix helvetica*); the non-venomous biacco (*Coluber viridiflavus*); the coluber liscio (*Coronella austriaca*); the gecko 'verrucoso' (*Hemidactylus turcicus*) brought over from Asia Minor; the green lizard (*Lacerta virìdis*); another lizard (*Podarcis sicula campestris*); the common toad (*Bufo bufo*), the tree-frog (*Hyla sarda*), the green frog (*Rana esculenta*), and the 'smeraldino' toad (*Bufo viridis*).

Ornithologists have long been fascinated by the variety of birds on Elba with many species similar to those seen in Tuscany on the Italian mainland. The birds of prey include the barn owl (*Tyto alba*); the horn owl (*Otus scops*); the little owl (*Athene noctua*); the buzzard (*Buteo buteo*); the common kestrel (*Falco tinnunculus*); and the peregrine falcon (*Falco peregrinus brookei*). Occasionally it has also been possible to see the Eurasian hobby or 'lodolaio' (*Falco subbuteo*); the European honey buzzard (*Pernis apivorus*); the red-footed falcon (*Falco vespertinus*); and the short-toed snake eagle or 'biancone' (*Circaetus gallicus*).

There is a range of birds on Elba – including many imperial sea-gulls (*Larus cachinnans michahellis*), the Alpine accentor (*Prunella collaris*) in the hilly areas; and the European reed warbler (*Acrocephalus scirpaceus*) in marshy areas. Other birds regularly seen in Elba include the imperial crow (*Corvus corax*) and the red partridge (*Alectoris rufa*). The song thrush (*Tordo*) is regarded as a game bird and has long been served in restaurants. For hunters, the roe deer has been reintroduced to the island. *See also* **Elba Canary**.

References: N. M. G. Ardenghi, G. Galasso, E. Banfi, A. Zoccola, B. Foggi and L. Lastrucci, 'A taxonomic survey of the genus Vitis L. (Vitaceae) in Italy, with special reference to Elba Island (Tuscan Archipelago)', *Phytotaxa* vol. 166, no. 3 (25 April 2014), pp. 163-98; G. Chiatante, A. Meriggi, D. Giustini, and N. E. Baldaccini, 'Density and habitat requirements of red-legged partridge on Elba Island (Tuscan Archipelago, Italy)', *Italian Journal of Zoology* vol. 80, no 3 (September 2013), pp. 402–11; Gianpasquale Chiatante, 'Habitat selection of Dartford WarblerSylvia undataon Elba Island (Tuscan Archipelago, Italy)', *Bird Study* vol. 61, no 3 (2 July 2014), pp. 438–43; Leonardo Dapporto, 'Core and satellite butterfly species on Elba island (Tuscan Archipelago, Italy): A study on persistence based on 120 years of collection data', *Journal of Insect Conservation* vol. 13, no 4 (2009), pp.421-28; Dr. Sergio Maria Frugis, 'Italy with Corsica, Sardinia, Sicily and other islands in the western Mediterranean', in James Ferguson-Lees,

Quentin Hockliffe and Ko Weeres (eds.), *A guide to bird-watching in Europe*, London: The Bodley Head, 1975, pp. 223–41 at p. 240; Duilio Lamonico, Leonardo Forbicioni and Giuliano Frangini, 'A New Hybrid in the Genus Ophrys (Orchidaceae) from the Elba Island (Central Italy)', *Annales Botanici Fennici* vol. 48, no 5 (2011), pp. 435-38; Frank Licher and Michael Kuper, 'Typosyllis tyrrhena (polychaeta, Syllidae, Syllinae), a new species from the island Elba, Tyrrhenian sea', *Italian Journal of Zoology* vol. 65, no 2 (1998), pp. 227–33; Christopher and Jean Serpell, *The Travellers' Guide to Elba and the Tuscan Archipelago*, London: Jonathan Cape, 1977, pp. 84–86; G. Szpunar, G. Aloise, M. G. Filippucci, 'Suncus etruscus (Soricomorpha, Soricidae): A new species for Elba Island (Tuscan Archipelago, Italy)', *Italian Journal of Zoology* vol. 75, no 4 (2008), pp.445-47; Jean-Claude Thibault and Gilles Bonaccorsi, *The birds of Corsica: an annotated checklist*, Tring: British Ornithologists' Union, 1999.

FEAST DAYS. In addition to public holidays, there are a large number feast days celebrated on Elba.

Easter Monday	Pilgrimage to the Shrine of the Madonna del Monte, above **Marciana**.
29 April	San Cristino, patron saint of **Portoferraio**.
1–3 May	Minor pilgrimages to the Madonna del Monte above Marciana.
5 May	Service held at the **Church of Misericordia**, Portoferraio, to commemorate the death of **Napoleon**.
May (moveable)	Feast of the Ascension, with pilgrimages to the Shrine of Santa Lucia near Portoferraio.
15 July	SS Giacomo and Quirico, the patron saints of **Rio nell'Elba**.
7 August	San Gaetano, patron saint of Campo.
12 August	Santa Chaia, patron saint of Marciana Marina.
15 August	Major pilgrimages to Madonna del Monte above Marciana.
16 August	San Rocco, patron saint of **Rio Marina**.
29 August	Traditional procession of the Misericordia Brotherhood to San Rocco Church, Portoferraio.
8 September	Nativity of the Virgin Mary, the patron of **Porto Azzurro**.
8–15 September	Pilgrimages to Madonna di Monserrato.
25 November	Santa Caterina, patron saint of Marciana Alta.
8 December	Immaculate Conception of the Virgin Mary; feast celebrated at **Capoliveri**, in honour of the Madonna della Grazie.

See also **Public holidays**.

Fetovaia Bay.
Photograph © Antonio Scarpi / Fotolia.com

FIRE BRIGADE. Napoleon is credited with establishing the first formal government fire brigade in Paris. Although this has been queried by some historians, **Napoleon Bonaparte** certainly formed the first fire brigade on the island of Elba in 1814, this being one of the ex-emperor's first major local reforms and it was made up from local engineers and others. The fire brigade (Vigili del Fuoco) has been modernised and reorganised many times since then. Its headquarters today are at Piazza Duchoque in Portoferraio.

FETOVAIA. A village on the south-west coast of Elba, there are several theories as to how it dervives its name which may be connected with the sighting of a dolphin off the coast, or coming from either the fertile land or from the occasional dead fish which used to wash up on the beach. A guard post, designed by **Luigi Bettarini**, was built there in 1825 and it is now a private residence. Because of the sandy beach, it became popular with the advent of tourism, with hotels built there.

References: Christopher and Jean Serpell, *The Travellers' Guide to Elba and the Tuscan Archipelago*, London: Jonathan Cape, 1977, pp. 210–11.

FLAG. On his way to Elba, **Napoleon** tried to design a suitable flag for his new kingdom, and which would be flown on ships from Elba. Very soon

after the *Undaunted* arrived at **Portoferraio** on 3 May 1814, he asked **André Ponds de l'Hérault** to come up with a design. **Thomas Ussher** later related that Napoleon 'had with him a book in which were represented all the flags of Tuscany, ancient and modern, and he asked me my opinion on the one he had chosen'. The historian **Norman MacKenzie** noted that **Giuseppe Balbiani** referred to the book as it had pictures of banners and coats of arms connected with Elba. Napoleon decided to adapt the flag **Cosimo de Medici** had used on Elba. This was white with a red diagonal. He added to this three bees – bees being part of his arms as emperor of France. The initial plan was for the bees to be blue, but with the planned flag being red, white and blue, Napoleon thought that this might be criticised as an imitation of the tricolour, and had the bees in gold. Ussher noted that Napoleon had explained that there were 'three bees because they represent the people of Elba that has had three rulers and now, with me, they are finally united under a single banner'.

The tailor on the *Undaunted* then stitched up two of these flags, one of which was sent ashore to fly from Fort Stella, and the other to fly from the barge of the *Undaunted* on which the new King of Elba would travel from the ship to the shore. One of these original flags is held at the **Villa dei Mulini** in Portoferraio.

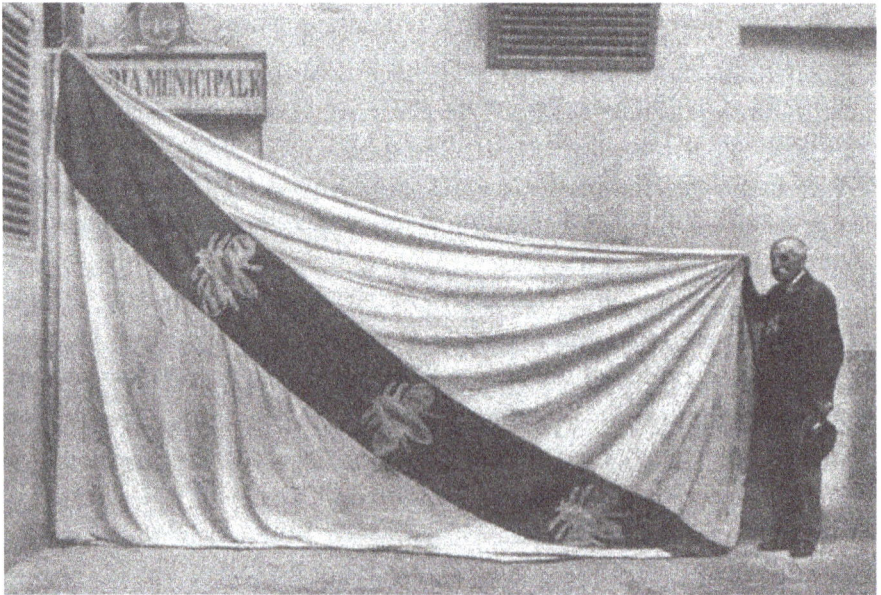

One of the original flags at Portoferraio.

References: Norman MacKenzie, *The Escape from Elba: The Fall & Flight of Napoleon 1814–1815*, Oxford: Oxford University Press, 1982, pp. 73–74.

FLEURY de CHABOULON, PIERRE ALEXANDRE ÉDOUARD (1779–1835). A young French government official, he went to Elba in 1815 and brought messages to the island from Bonapartists in France. He was 16 when he joined the National Guard and was later appointed the sub-prefect of Château-Salins (Doubs). In 1814 he was appointed the prefect of Reims and helped organise the French soldiers to resist the Allied invasion. During the Bourbon Restoration in 1814, he went to Italy and from there to Elba.

After **Napoleon**'s return to France, Fleury de Chaboulon worked for Napoleon and took messages to the Emperor of Austria and on other personal assignments. After the battle of Waterloo, he went to London, and wrote a memoir about the 100 Days called *Les Cent-Jours: Mémoires pour servir à l'histoire de la vie privée, du retour, et du règne de Napoléon en 1815*. He returned to France and became a director of the insurance company, Royale Incendie, and then Royale Vie. After the revolution of July 1830, he returned to the State Council and in 1834 he was elected for Meurthe. He died on 28 September 1835.

References: Pierre Fleury de Chaboulon, *Les Cent-Jours: Mémoires pour servir à l'histoire de la vie privée, du retour, et du règne de Napoléon en 1815*, Londres, C. Roworth, 1820; Norman MacKenzie, *The Escape from Elba: The Fall & Flight of Napoleon 1814–1815*, Oxford: Oxford University Press, 1982.

FLORA. The flora of Elba is known as 'macchia Mediterranea', and is similar to that of many other parts of the Mediterranean. This results in a variety of climbing plants, and some evergreen vegetation, with the holly tree (*ilex*) being very common. There were primitive forests of cork-oaks but these have nearly all been cut down since medieval times. There are also isolated carob, myrtle, and plane trees, as well as some Judas trees. Because sheep-farming was not introduced to Elba, it remains one of the most 'green' islands in the Mediterranean, and to improve the island, during the 1950s there was much planting of chestnuts and especially pine trees on deforested slopes.

References: Gianfranco Barsotti, *Flora, vegetazione ed ambiente delle isole dell'arcipelago toscano*, Ospedaletto, Pisa: Pacini, 2008; G. Battipaglia, D. E. Micco, W. A. Brand, M. Saurer, G. Aronne, P. Linke and P. Cherubini, 'Drought impact on water use efficiency and intra-annual density fluctuations in Erica arborea on Elba (Italy)', *Plant, Cell & Environment* vol. 37, no 2 (February 2014), pp. 382-91; Guido Giubella, *Elba: A Garden in the Blu*, Milan: Co.Graf Editrice, 1988, pp. 92–93; Teresa Fossi Innamorati, 'La flora vascolare dell'isola d'Elba (Archipelago Toscana)', *Webbia* vol. 36, no 2 (1983), pp. 273–411; vol. 43, no 2 (1989), pp. 201–67; vol. 45, no 1 (1991), pp. 137–85; vol. 49, no 1 (1994), pp. 93–123; Oleg Polunin and Anthony Julian Huxley, *Flowers of the Mediterranean*, London: Chatto and Windus, 1965; Christopher and Jean Serpell, *The Travellers' Guide to Elba and the Tuscan Archipelago*, London: Jonathan Cape, 1977, pp. 83–84.

FOOTBALL. The most popular sport for men and boys remains football/soccer and two of the major clubs are U.S.D. ELBA 2000 located in Capoliveri, and A.S.D. BONALACCIA located at Campo nell'Elba.

References: U.S.D. ELBA 2000, http://www. usdelba2000capoliveri.org/

FORESI, RAFFAELLO (1820–1876). An Italian writer and amateur geologist, he was born on 20 November 1820 at Portoferraio, the son of Iacopo Foresi and Maria (née Guarelli). He studied at the faculty of literature at the University of Pisa and moving to Florence, from 1845 he started to write on Florentine music. In 1858 he established a monthly magazine, *Il piovano Arlotto*, with the help of his brother Alessandro Forsi and a friend Pietro Fanfani. It covered aspects of philosophy and theology. He then decided to work on the geology of Elba and worked with Louis Celleri, a mineralogist, and together collected enough material to establish the Museo Foresi at Portoferraio. Many of the geological specimens are held at the **Museo Archeologico** del Distretto Minerario.

FORTE FALCONE. Built on orders of **Cosimo de Medici** in the late 1540s, it is located on the highest point of **Portoferraio** and was the location of

Fort Stella dominating Portoferraio.

Photograph © Malgorzata Paula / Fotolia.com

lookouts over many centuries. This was one of the locations of the French garrison on Elba in April 1814 just before **Napoleon Bonaparte** arrived on the island. It was from this fort that on 4 May 1814 one of the two flags of the new principality of Elba was flown as Napoleon came ashore. The area around is limestone has been quarried over many centuries. Now controlled by the Italian Navy, the fort is not open to the public.

References: Guido Giubella, *Elba: A Garden in the Blu*, Milan: Co.Graf Editrice, 1988, pp. 36–37; Norman MacKenzie, *The Escape from Elba: The Fall & Flight of Napoleon 1814–1815*, Oxford: Oxford University Press, 1982, p. 64; Christopher and Jean Serpell, *The Travellers' Guide to Elba and the Tuscan Archipelago*, London: Jonathan Cape, 1977, pp. 168–69.

FORTE STELLA. This was originally built on orders of **Cosimo de Medici** in the late 1540s and it gets its name from its shape which resembles a star. It is located at Portoferraio and was one of the locations of the French garrison on Elba in April 1814. Located on Via della Stella, it is open from 9 am to 7 pm from Easter through to September, with a small admission charge.

References: Norman MacKenzie, *The Escape from Elba: The Fall & Flight of Napoleon 1814–1815*, Oxford: Oxford University Press, 1982, p. 64; Christopher and Jean Serpell, *The Travellers' Guide to Elba and the Tuscan Archipelago*, London: Jonathan Cape, 1977, p. 161.

FORTESCUE, HUGH, 2nd Earl Fortescue (1783–1861). A British politician, he was born on 13 February 1783 at the Army Pay Office, Whitehall, London, the oldest son of Hugh Fortescue, 3rd Baron and 1st Earl Fortescue (1753–1841), and his wife, Hester (née Grenville, 1760–1847), daughter of the politician George Grenville. He was educated at Eton College, and Brasenose College, Oxford. In 1804 he took up a seat in the British Parliament supporting his uncle Lord Grenville. Re-elected, and then defeated in elections, in June 1814, during his maiden speech, he urged for the end of slavery. In December of that year he went to Elba and there met with **Napoleon** on the evening of 6 December 1814, and chatted with him on another occasion. His account which was subsequently published as *Memorandum of Two Conversations* (1823), showed an admiration for the

former emperor. Returning to Britain, he was returned to parliament but lost his seat in 1820 and again in 1826, but managed a big victory in 1830. He was lord steward of the household in the government of Lord Russell from 1846 to 1850, and died on 14 September 1861. His first wife was Lady Susan Ryder and they had three sons. After her death he married Elizabeth, widow of Sir Marcus Somerville, and daughter of Piers Geale of Clonsilla, co. Dublin. She died on 4 May 1896, aged 91.

References: John Alger, *Napoleon's British visitors and captives, 1801–1815*, New York: J. Pott, 1904, pp. 297–99; R. Brent, *Liberal Anglican politics: whiggery, religion, and reform, 1830–1841*, Oxford: Clarendon Press, 1987; Lord Ebrington, *Memorandum of two conversations between the Emperor Napoleon and Viscount Ebrington at Porto Ferrajo, on the 6th and 8th of December, 1814*, London: J. Ridgway, 1823; D. R. Fisher, 'Fortescue, Hugh, second Earl Fortescue (1783–1861)', *Oxford Dictionary of National Biography*, Oxford University Press, 2004; *The Eton School Lists from 1791 to 1850*, p. 17, 23; *Alumni Oxonienses* vol. 2, p. 480.

FREMANTLE, Sir THOMAS FRANCIS (1765–1819). A British naval officer, he was born on 20 November 1765 in Buckinghamshire, the third son of John Fremantle (1737–1784) of Aston Abbots in Buckinghamshire, and his wife, Frances Edwards (1740–1810), daughter of John Edwards of Bristol. When he was twelve, he joined the Royal Navy serving on the *Hussar* off the coast of Portugal. He later served on the *Jupiter* and was on the *Phoenix* and survived when that ship sank in October 1780 after being caught in a hurricane which pushed the vessel onto the coast of Cuba. Based at Jamaica until 1787, in May 1793 he was promoted to captain of the Tartar and served in the Mediterranean.

Fremantle sailed his ship into Toulon when the British and their allies captured the port on 27 August 1793. He served with Horatio Nelson who had a high opinion of him, and in 1796 they evacuated Britons and others from Livorno (Leghorn), then on 10 July 1796 Fremantle was involved in the capture of the island of Elba. In the following year he married Elizabeth 'Betsey' Wynne, and they had nine children.

During the rest of the **Napoleonic Wars**, Fremantle served in many engagements including the battle of Copenhagen and then at the battle of Trafalgar on the *Neptune*. In 1818 he was appointed commander-in-chief of the Royal Navy in the Mediterranean, but fell ill and died on 19 December 1819, and was buried in Naples. His oldest son, also called Thomas Francis Fremantle, inherited the title. His second son Charles Howe Fremantle became an admiral in the Royal Navy.

References: J. K. Laughton, 'Fremantle, Sir Thomas Francis (1765–1819)', revised by Roger Morriss, *Oxford Dictionary of National Biography*, Oxford University Press, 2004, revised May 2009; Piers Mackesy, *The war in the Mediterranean, 1803–1810*, Cambridge, Mass.: Harvard University Press, 1957

- G -

GELSI, MICHELE (1968–   ). An Italian **footballer**, he was born on 9 July 1968 in **Portoferraio** and made his debut at 17, playing for Florence. He played for Parma in 1988–89, and then for Pescara, 1989–92, playing 103 marches and scoring seven goals. He played for Perugia, 1992–93; and Udinese, 1993–94, then was back in Perugia in 1994, before returning to Pescara, 1994–2000, playing 202 games and scoring 42 goals. Gelsi then played for Livorno, Lucchese, Arezzo, Mantova and then for Renato Curi Angolana.

GENEALOGY. When tracing family trees, one should always start with elderly relatives. If ancestors moved from Elba to another country, it is always best to exhaust the records of that country first to ensure you have has the exact surname and first names of any migrant ancestor, and as many details about the date and place of birth, especially exactly in which part of Elba they resided.

For civil registration (stato civile), the registering of births, marriages and deaths started in Tuscany (which included Elba) from 1808 when the French occupied the area. This was influenced by the administrative reforms by **Napoleon** in France. Many people were not registered, and initially most who did so were wealthier or middle class residents in cities or towns. These records from 1808 to 1866 are held in the State Archives in Florence. Birth certificates give the name, date and place of birth, names of both parents, mother's maiden name and father's occupation. Details on marriage and death are included as a marginal entry in the register on many certificates from 1900. Marriage certificates have the date and place of the marriage, the names and ages of both parties, as well as their places of birth, names of parents including the maiden names of mothers, names of witnesses, and the occupation and addresses of the bride, groom, parents and witnesses. Death certificates have the name of the deceased, date and place of death, occupation and address, and also the date and place of birth, as well as the names of parents and addresses if they are still alive, and also the name of any spouse. The recent records are held at the Civil Registry Office (Ufficio di Stato Civile) in **Portoferraio**.

Church records include information on baptisms, marriages and burials. Traditionally parish registers were kept in the local church, with the local priest being the custodian. Older records are often held at the local state **archives**.

There are some official archival records, as well as private records, held in the Communal Archives in **Portoferraio**. There are 102 provincial archives with the records for the commune of Rio nell'Elba held in Livorno. The Archivio di Stato di Livorno (State Archive of Livorno, Via Fiume 40, Livorno) was originally created in 1941. It holds the parish records for Memoria dei Sacramenti from 1540 to 1870, and the registers of births, marriages and deaths from 1804 to 1874. For central records, the Archivio centrale dello Stato (Central Archives of the State) was formed in 1875 as the Royal Archives, and is located in Rome.

If possible, a researcher should try to visit Elba to see the location of ancestors, and also to check local records, the local library and cemeteries. However for many cemeteries in Italy, burial plots are only for a short period – 30 or 50 years – unless people are buried inside churches or in family mausoleums or vaults. The graves are then often cleared and the bones left in an ossuary.

Information on Italians who migrated overseas are held in the Registri dell' Emigrazione, in state archives and at the Ministero dell'Interno in Rome. Most of these remain closed to the public, but records for some countries to where migrants moved such as the United States, Australia, Argentina etc allow access to their records. The number of records now available online is increasing rapidly and many details could also be available on subscription sites online such as ancestry.com and geneanet.org (for French records).

For British records, many of those who went to Elba were connected with the Royal Navy. Some of are now listed online, and there are many guides to the records, the major work being written by N. A. M. Rodger.

References: Angus Baxter, *In Search of Your European Roots: a complete guide to tracing your ancestors in every country in Europe*, Baltimore: Genealogical Publishing Co., 1994, pp. 163–71; Terra Castiglia Brockman, *A student's guide to Italian American Genealogy*, Phoenix, Arizona: Oryx Press, 1996; John Philip Colletta, *Finding Italian Roots: the complete guide for Americans*, Baltimore: Genealogical Publishing Co., 1993; Bette Leone, *How to trace your Italian ancestors, for Australians and New Zealanders*, Sydney: Hale & Iremonger, 1994; E. Lucchetti, M. Tasso, P. Pizzetti, S. de Iasio and G. U. Caravello, 'Similarities in the surnames of island and continental populations of the north-western Mediterranean area', *Journal of Biosocial Science* vol. 40, no 3 (May 2008), pp. 359–77; N. A. M. Rodger, *Naval Records for Genealogists*, London: Her Majesty's Stationery Office, 1988.

GEOLOGY. The deposits of copper and iron on Elba led to the Etruscans and later the Romans occupying the island, and the iron mines employed many people until World War II. However geologists have not just been interested in the iron – the copper deposits having long since run out – but also in many other minerals, with the western part of Elba being formed with granite, tourmaline, beryl, serpentine and porphyry, with the central zone having diabase and serpentine, with the east being far more complex.

References: M. Benvenuti, A. Dini, M. D'Orazio, L. Chiarantini, A. Corretti, and P. Costagliola, 'The tungsten and tin signature of iron ores from Elba island (Italy): A tool for provenance studies of iron production in the Mediterranean region', *Archaeometry* vol. 55, no 3 (1 June 2013), pp. 479-506; Dan Bowman, Valentina Rosas and Enzo Pranzini, 'Pocket beaches of Elba Island (Italy) – Planview geometry, depth of closure and sediment dispersal', *Estuarine, Coastal and Shelf Science* vol. 138 (2014), pp. 37–46; A. Caggianelli, G. Ranalli, A. Lavecchia, D. Liotta, and A. Dini, 'Post-emplacement thermo-rheological history of a granite intrusion and surrounding rocks: the Monte Capanne pluton, Elba Island, Italy', *Geological Society, London, Special Publications* vol. 394, no. 1 (23 May 2014), pp. 129–43; Guido Giubella, Elba: *A Garden in the Blu*, Milan: Co.Graf Editrice, 1988, pp. 11–13; G. Massa, 'The tectonic evolution of eastern Elba Island: New hypothesis (Tuscany, Italy)', *Rendiconti Online Societa Geologica Italiana* vol. 29 (1 October 2013), pp. 97–100; Karl F. Nordstrom, Nancy L. Jackson and Enzo Pranzini, 'Beach Sediment Alteration by Natural Processes and Human Actions: Elba Island, Italy', *Annals of the Association of American Geographers* vol. 94, no 4 (2004), pp.794–806; S. A. F. Smith, R. E. Holdsworth, and C. Collettini, 'Interactions between low-angle normal faults and plutonism in the upper crust: insights from the Island of Elba, Italy', *The Geological Society of America Bulletin* vol. 123, nos 1–2 (Jan–Feb, 2011), pp. 329–47.

GIGLIO. One of the islands in the **Tuscan Archipelago**, this is south of Elba and administraively, is a part of the province of Grosseto. It gets is name from Aegilium (Goat Island) which comes from the Ancient Greek, Αιγύλλιον (little goat). The island has been inhabited since prehistoric times, and probably was an Etruscan military base, and then used by the Romans. In 805 Emperor Charlemagne donated it to the abbey of the Tre Fontane in Rome, and it flourished for a period but was attacked by the Corsairs from North Africa on many occasions. The writer **Raffaele Brignetti** was born on the island in 1921. On 13 January 2012 the cruise liner *Costa Concordia* ran aground close to the island, with 32 people killed. The remaining 4,200 passengers and crew were taken to Giglio where the local people helped them before they were taken to mainland Italy.

References: Alexis Catsambis, Ben Ford and Donny L. Hamilton, *The Oxford Handbook of Maritime Archaeology*, Oxford & New York: Oxford University Press, 2011, p. 371;

Giglio

Gorgona.
Photograph by Giovanni Spinozzi, 30 September 2010 / Wikipedia Commons.

Averil Mackenzie-Grieve, *Aspects of Elba and the other islands of the Tuscan Archipelago,* London: Jonathan Cape, 1964, pp. 113–25; John MacIntosh Turfa, *The Etruscan World,* London and New York: Routledge, 2013.

GIOVANELLI, Captain. He was the author of *Breve Relazione dell'Isola dell'Elba* (1771), a book which influenced **Arsène Thiébaut de Berneaud** who wrote about Elba in 1808.

GOLF. In recent decades, golf has become a popular pastime for tourists going to Elba. The Hotel Elba Palace Golf at Fuerteventura has long been popular with golfers. Mention should also be made of the Elba Golf Club at Aquabona; and the Hermitage Golf Club. For a fee, it is also possible to play on many of the golf courses even if staying at another hotel.

References: Elba Golf Club Aquabona, http://www.elbagolfacquabona.it/; Hermitage Golf Club, http://www.golfhermitage.it/; Christopher and Jean Serpell, *The Travellers' Guide to Elba and the Tuscan Archipelago*, London: Jonathan Cape, 1977, p. 71.

GORGONA. This is a small island covering 2.23 square kilometres and is the northernmost island in the **Tuscan archipelago** being known to the ancient Greeks as Gorgòn (Γοργόν). It is mentioned briefly by Pliny and by the later Roman writer Rutilius Claudius Namatianus who wrote about it in the account of his voyage in AD 416. Because of its isolation, monks started to live there and they held the relics of St. Julia of Corsica on the island for a while. However the monastery on the island was sacked by the Saracens but rebuilt after the Republic of Pisa took control of the seas preventing more attacks by the Muslims from North Africa. The monastery was rebuilt and was mentioned in a letter by Catherine of Siena (1347–1380). Following attacks on the island and nearby areas by the North African corsairs in the early fifteenth century, the monks left the island for Calci on the mainland and took their records with them. The island is mentioned briefly by Dante in *The Divine Comedy*. However the Carthusians remained owners of the island until 1771 when they sold it to Peter Leopold I, Grand Duke of Tuscany. A fishing village was established on the island and soon the place became famous for its anchovies.

When he was young, **Napoleon Bonaparte** based a novel on the rock. It told of the friendship of an exiled Corsican patriot and an Englishman who had been shipwrecked on the island and who cherished freedom. In 1869 the island was taken over by the government and is now an agricultural penal colony. There is only one landing place on the island, Cala dello Scala, and the village is occupied by workers at the prison and also, during the summer, by descendants of former residents. Visitors to the island need to obtain prior permission from the Italian Ministry of Justice and private boats are not allowed any closer than 500 metres from the shore, except for emergencies. Forest covers some 90 per cent of the island and is one of only five islands in the world where the Corsican finch is be found.

References: Riccardo Ambrosini, *Relitti romani dell'isola d'Elba*, Lucca: M.P. Fazzi, 1982; Avner Falk, *Napoleon against himself: a psychobiography*, Charlottesville, Va.: Pitchstone Pub., 2007, p. 67; Norman MacKenzie, *The Escape from Elba: The Fall & Flight of Napoleon 1814–1815*, Oxford: Oxford University Press, 1982, p. 65; Miles Roddis & Alex Leviton, *Tuscany & Umbria*, Footscray: Lonely Planet, 2006, p. 180; Christopher and Jean Serpell, *The Travellers' Guide to Elba and the Tuscan Archipelago*, London: Jonathan Cape, 1977, p. 41.

GORI, PIETRO (1865–1911). An Italian anarchist poet and and political activist, he was born on 14 August 1865 in Messina, in Sicily, his parents being from Tuscany. The family moved to Livorno when Pietro Gori was 13. Initially he was active in the Monarchist Association but left when at the University of Pisa, and started to move in Anarchist circles. He was arrested after protesting about fellow anarchists in Chicago, USA, who had been killed in a riot. Arrested again in 1890, he spent six months in jail for taking part in an illegal demonstration in Livorno. He then moved to Milan and worked as a lawyer and helped to found the Partito Socialista Anarchico Rivoluzionario (Socialist Revolutionary Anarchist Party). Translating Karl Marx's *Communist Manifesto* into Italian, he was kept under surveillance by the police and attended the Socialist Congress in Zurich in 1893 but was expelled from it. When the Italian government introduced three laws against anarchists, Gori sought refuge in Switzerland and then went to Germany, Belgium and finally to Britain. He was eventually able to return to Italy but had to remain on the island of Elba. From 1898–1902 he was again in exile – this time in Argentina. On his return he remained in Italy moving to Portoferraio where he died on 8 January 1911 from tuberculosis. He was buried at Rosignano Marittimo on the Italian mainland. Arturo Gozzi sculpted a bas-relief on the main post office in **Portoferraio** to commemorate

Gori's connection with the town.

References: Maurizio Antonioli, *Pietro Gori, il cavaliere errante dell'anarchia: studi e testi*, Pisa: BFS, 1995; Antonio Bellandi, *Carlo Della Giacoma e Pietro Gori: musica e politica nella Livorno di fine Ottocento*, Livorno: Comune di Livorno, 2005.

GOTO, CELETEUSO. A self-styled historian – possibly a pseudonym – he wrote on Elba incorporating into his account a number of fanciful 'legends'.

References: Averil Mackenzie-Grieve, *Aspects of Elba and the other islands of the Tuscan Archipelago*, London: Jonathan Cape, 1964, p. 17.

GRANVILLE, AUGUSTUS BOZZI (1783–1872). A physician and Italian patriot, he was born on 7 October 1783 in Milan, Italy, the third son of Carlo Bozzi (1742/3–1826), postmaster-general of the Lombardo-Venetian kingdom, and his wife, Maria Antonietta (née Rapazzini). He was well-connected with his father distantly related to the Bonapartes, and his maternal grandmother being the daughter of a Cornishman who fled to Italy as a political exile. He went to the University of Pavia to read medicine, but his studies were interrupted by a brief imprisonment for expressing his republican views. In 1803 he was in Corfu where he met W. R. Hamilton, the private secretary to Lord Elgin, and the two went to Greece. He served as a physician to the Turkish navy and then to the British Royal Navy, taking the surname Granville at the deathbed request of his mother – this was the name of his Cornish ancestor. In 1809 in Portsmouth, he married Mary Ann Kerr, and they had four sons and a daughter.

Posted to the Caribbean, he brought messages to London from Simon Bolívar. He then practised as a doctor in London where he developed the use of iodine. However he could not stay away from politics and went to Italy where he urged for independence. During this time he heard that **Napoleon** was planning to escape from Elba and warned the British government but they did not take heed. Focusing on obstetrics and children's diseases, he established a dispensary for children in London and was vice-president of the British Medical Association. He became a friend of Joseph Bonaparte, and was also active in promoting the increasingly popular spa resorts. His wife died in 1861, and he died on 3 March 1872 in Dover.

References: P. B. Granville (ed.), *Autobiography of A. B. Granville*, London: H. S. King & Co., 1874, 2 Vols, Ornella Moscucci, 'Granville, Augustus Bozzi (1783–1872)', *Oxford Dictionary of National Biography*, Oxford University Press, 2004.

GRATTACIELO ('Skyscraper'). This building close to the docks in Portoferraio, the Cadogan guide called this 'a 10-storey pile of peeling paint built in the 1950s that is one of the most endearingly hideous buildings in the Mediterranean.'

References: Dan Facaros and Michael Pauls, *Italy: Tuscany*, London: Cadogan Books plc, 1996, p. 299.

GRATTAN, HENRY (c1746–1820). There was a Mr Grattan who was on Elba when Napoleon Bonaparte left the island on 26 February 1815, and John Alger has suggested that this might have been Colley Grattan (1754–c1815), the father of the journalist and novelist Thomas Colley Grattan (1791–1864). However **John MacKenzie** has identified him as Henry Grattan, Colley Grattan's second cousin once removed. Henry Grattan was born in 1789 – the year of the French Revolution – and was the son of the famous Irish politician Henry Grattan (1746–1820) and his wife Henrietta (née Fitzgerald, 1761–1820). His father went to Trinity College where he became interested in literature. He then moved to London to study law at the Middle Temple, spending much of his spare time listening to debates in the British House of Commons. He entered the Irish House of Commons soon afterwards and became a prominent debater and was the leader of the Irish Patriot Party from 1775. He then opposed the Act of Union of 1800 which merged the kingdoms of Ireland and Great Britain, but then sat in the House of Commons in London.

Henry Grattan jnr decided to follow his father into the law and was called to the Irish Bar in 1810. He then travelled and this took him to Elba. As John Alger wrote:

One Englishman at least was a spectator of Napoleon's departure from Elba. A Mr. Grattan (probably the father of Thomas Colley Grattan, the traveller and novelist) had landed on the island on the 24th February. On the evening of the 26th he noticed unusual bustle, as though something was about to happen, and at 9 p.m. he saw Napoleon, escorted by General Bertrand, come out in his sister Pauline's four-horse carriage, enter a boat, and go on board the brig *Inconstant*. Thereupon the whole flotilla got under way, the soldiers shouting 'Vive l'Empereur!' Scarcely believing his eyes, Grattan hired a boat to go alongside the brig, and thence he saw Napoleon in his grey overcoat and round hat pacing the quarter-deck. One of the boatmen, however, cried out that there was an Englishman on board, upon which an officer on the poop of the *Inconstant* demanded who he was and what he wanted. Grattan had to explain that he had merely come to have a look at the Emperor, whereupon he was told to be off, and he complied with alacrity, expecting every instant to be fired at or arrested.

Henry Grattan snr spoke vociferously in parliament about Napoleon's departure from Elba and demanded that the British support the Bourbons. A letter from Henry Grattan to his son about Napoleon and Elba is held at the National Library of Ireland.

On his return to Britain, Henry Grattan jnr entered politics when his father died. He contested his father's seat of Dublin City as a Whig but was defeated. However he was elected in 1826. Later that year, on 5 October in Dublin, Henry Grattan married Mary O'Kelly Harvey, and they had four daughters: Catherine; Henrietta, born in 1828 in Dublin (died on 12 March 1898 in Yorkshire); Anne, born in 1831; and Pauline, born in 1841 (died on 17 July 1908 in Wicklow, Ireland). Henry Grattan jnr was defeated in the 1830 elections but in a by-election on 11 August 1831 was elected a member of parliament for Meath and represented that seat until 1852. He died on 16 July 1859.

References: John Alger, *Napoleon's British visitors and captives, 1801–1815*, New York: J. Pott, 1904, p. 302; Henry Grattan, *The Speeches of the Right Honourable Henry Grattan*, London, Longman, Hurst, Rees, Orme and Brown, 1822; James Kelly, *Henry Grattan*, Dublin: Published for the Historical Association of Ireland by Dundalgan Press, 1993; R. B. McDowell, *Grattan: A Life*, Dublin: Lilliput Press, 2001; Norman MacKenzie, *The Escape from Elba: The Fall & Flight of Napoleon 1814–1815*, Oxford: Oxford University Press, 1982, pp. 223–26.

GREGORY XI (c.1329–1378). The Pope from 30 December 1370 until his death on 27 March 1378, he was born as Pierre Roger de Beaufort in Maumont in the modern commune of Rosiers-d'Égletons, Limousin, France. The nephew of Pope Clement VI, he was elected by the papal conclave of 1370 and became the seventh (and last) Pope to live at Avignon. He was passionate in his campaign against the Lollards who were growing in number in parts of England and Germany, supporting the burning of people deemed to be heretics. Apparently influenced by Catherine of Siena, Gregory XI decided to return the Papacy to Rome from Avignon. He went by sea and stopped at **Portoferraio** in Elba. Although he was probably there for only a day, this was the only recorded visit to the island by a serving Pope.

References: Francis Thomas Luongo, *The Saintly Politics of Catherine of Siena*, Ithaca, NY: Cornell University Press, 2006, pp. 174–76; Richard P. McBrien, *Lives of the Popes*, London: HarperCollins, 2000, pp. 245–47; G. Mollat, *The Popes at Avignon: The Babylonian Captivity of the Medieval Church*, New York: Harper & Row, 1963.

GRIFFITHS, FREDERICK HOWARD (1919–1944). A temporary sub-lieutenant with the Royal Naval Volunteer Reserve, he served on H.M.S. *Quebec*. The son of David and Marion Griffiths, of Llandovery, Carmarthenshire, he was wounded in the landings on Elba and died from his injuries on 21 June 1944. He was buried in Biguglia War Cemetery in Corsica.

GRUYER, PAUL (1868–1930). A French writer, translator and art critic, he was also the author of several books including *Napoleon: King of Elba*. Born on 13 March 1868 in Paris, he worked on translations of books before writing his own accout of Napoleon's time in Elba. In researching his book, he took the train to Piombino, and from there caught the ferry to Elba. He noted:

When I landed at Elba, I vaguely imagined I should find some bare and arid rock; a foretaste of St. Helena – and my first surprise came in seeing a picturesque country, full of variety, well worth the trouble of the journey. Moreover, this little island, half-forgotten in the sea, has remained almost precisely what it was a century ago. The modern life that has penetrated so far has not altered either its natural aspect nor its villages or towns. The Vandalism of modern improvement has spared the strange buildings and left the old walls intact. The very same houses, roads, even stones on the paths, have seen the Emperor pass. I find all the places spoken of in the memoirs of his time; every fact, every event, falls into its place in public functions and private life; there are the same names and the same families.

The history I read lives and breathes again – instead of dried phrases set in unknown scenes, the past is there, living before me. I can see them all as if they exist to-day; the Emperor, ageing a little, but always alert; inscrutable Madame Mere, the venerable Corsican; Pauline, the sweet and beautiful 'Venus'; the fair Polish lady, Walewska; the old devoted but grumbling Bertrand, the wise Drouot, the watch-dog Cambronne, making up the little Court of a day, where, under the veil of comedy, is gathering the thunder-cloud of the Return.

References: Paul Gruyer, *Napoleon, King of Elba*, Philadelphia: J. B. Lippincott Company, 1906.

GUIBERT, HERBÉ (1955–1991). A French writer and photographer, he was born on 14 December 1955, and lived in Paris, then moved to La Rochelle from 1970 to 1973. Working as a film-maker and then actor, he started work for *Le Monde* in 1978 and became an important social commentator whose writing was influenced by Jean Genet. He became a partner of Michel Foucault, and in January 1988 was diagnosed with an AIDS-related condition. He wrote about his plight in his book *À l'ami qui ne m'a pas sauvé la vie* (To the Friend Who Did Not Save My Life, 1990), and his last books helped explain the problem of HIV-AIDS. His major works are: *Zouc par Zouc, Balland* (1978); *Suzanne et Louise: roman-photo, Hallier* (1980); *L'Image fantôme* (1981); *L'Homme blessé: scénario et notes* (1983); *Le Seul Visage, photographies* (1984); *L'Image de soi ou l'Injonction de son beau moment?* (1988); *Vice, photographies de l'auteur* (1991); *Cytomégalovirus, journal d'hospitalisation* (1992); and *Photographies* (1993). He died on 27 December 1991 at Clamart, and was buried at the Hermitage of Santa Caterina d'Alessandria, **Rio dell'Elba**.

References: Bruno Blanckeman, *les Récits indécidables: Jean Echenoz, Hervé Guibert, Pascal Quignard*, Villeneuve d'Ascq: Presses universitaires du Septentrion 2000; Antoine de Gaudemar, 'La Maladie de l'amour, entretien avec Hervé Guibert', *Libération* (1 March 1990).

- H -

HALL, FREDERICK (1780–1843). The American author of *Notes on a tour in France, Italy, and Elba, with a notice of its mines of iron* (1837), he graduated from Dartmouth College, New Hampshire, in 1803, and was then a tutor at Middlebury College from 1805–06 before being appointed Middlebury's first professor of mathematics and natural philosophy. He was paid twice the salary of the college's president, Jeremiah Atwater, and was also allowed to spend two years in Europe attending lectures and collecting books and equipment. Awarded degrees from Middlebury in 1806, and also Dartmouth and Harvard in 1810, he gained his medical degree from Castleton Medical College in 1827, completing a law degree at Dartmouth in 1841. His account of his time in Elba was published in 1837. In it he noted:

Elba is about sixty miles in circumference, of an irregular oblong figure, its longer diameter running from west to east. Its surface is exceedingly uneven, being thrown into every imaginable shape; there, rising into mountains two or three thousand feet in elevation; here, sinking into deep vallies. Some of the high lands are covered with vegetation, but most of the summits of the mountains are naked, and exhibit nothing but rocks, which a hundred centuries have rendered almost as white as Parian marble. The vallies are productive, yielding grapes in vast abundance, and grain of various kinds, the fig, the orange, the watermelon, (which is here called encumber,) pears, apples, plumbs, &c. he. The number of inhabitants in the island is about fifteen thousand. They are principally in Porto Ferrajo, and the villages of Longone, Capoleon, Marinna and Campo. There is little wood on the island, and what there is, is a small growth. Jackasses, loaded with faggots, and pieces of wood two or three inches in diameter, are constantly seen coming into Porto Ferrajo from the country. The oak grows here, and the maple, and several other trees, which are common in America: but there is one here that 1 have not met with before; it is the cork tree, whose bark is thick, and is used for stoppers of bottles, to make lines float on water, he. I have cut a stick of it, which I shall have converted into a cane when I arrive in Paris.

The geological structure of Elba is different from any other part of Italy. I saw no decidedly primitive country between Avallon in France, and Naples. There may be land of this character in Italy, and the south of France, which I did not see. I infer from what I saw, that the whole country of which I speak, was of volcanic origin: in some places the lava is old, and in others young, but always bearing evident marks of igneous fusion. I have crossed the Apennines twice; once over Mount Somma, one of the highest, where I expected to find primitive rocks, but found nothing but secondary limestone, full of pores, once, doubtless, filled with gas, and a combination of other materials, which nothing but intense heat could have generated. This island presents a curious mixture of primitive and volcanic formations. The rugged mountain which you see at the right hand as you enter the harbor of Porto Ferrajo, has all the appearance of having been ejected from the earth by an internal energy; whereas those massy piles which stand on the south and east of the island, bear no obvious marks of fire, although they, too, may have been raised, at a more remote period, by that agent. I have spent a week here, and seen many of the mineral productions. I shall enumerate some of those which I have seen, without any regard to system. There are probably others which have not come under my observation.

1. Rock crystals, of various sizes, from a line in diameter to two inches; all in the form of the hexagonal pyramid at one extremity, and some at both; some diaphanous, as the purest water, and others entirely opaque.

2. Feldspar, crystallized and massive.

3. Tourmaline. It often occurs in the feldspar. I found a vast quantity of it in rolled fragments, lying along the northern shore of the island, and it must have been brought there by the waves of the sea. Some of the balls were nothing but black tourmaline, (schorl;) others were a mixture of this substance with feldspar.

4. Rubellite, in beautiful crystals, but not enveloped, like those of Chesterfield, in green tourmaline.

5. Aqua-marine, not plentiful, but sometimes found.

6. Epidote, crystallized, and in irregular masses.

7. Jasper, red, green, and brown; very abundant.

8. Porcelain earth, or decomposed feldspar, in different parts of the island. The manufacture of this article into porcelain, or China ware, might be made a source of revenue to the government, were fuel more plentiful.

9. Limestone, primitive and secondary, red, white, and sky-colored. The white is capable of being converted into a marble, little, if at all, inferior to that of Carrara. The red, too, when polished, strongly resembles the best of the Rouge Antique of Rome.

10. Arragonite, in the shape of calcareous stalactites.

11. Mica, silver white, green and black.

12. Yenite, jet black and brown, crystallized and massive. The crystals usually occur in groups, which are, occasionally, large and splendid. Formerly, yenite was abundant here, but at present good crystals are rarely to be met with, and when bought of the inhabitants, they are purchased at a high price. I have obtained, by discovery and by purchase, a good number of specimens. A large group of crystals of yenite was offered to me by a gentleman of this city, who estimated its value at the moderate sum of three hundred piastres or dollars.

I have made several mineralogical excursions, on different parts of the island. In one of them only, I will ask you to accompany me. Having provided myself with a guide, the only practical mineralogist on the island, and being furnished with little horses, accustomed to climb mountains – by the way, I had the same pony, as the guide told me, which Napoleon had rode, with a rope bridle, over the same grounds – we first pass the bay, which is two or three miles across. We then ascended a ragged mountain, probably three thousand feet in height, composed chiefly of micaceous schist and jaspery ironstone. On the almost inaccessible summit of this mountain, stand, frowning on the world below, an old tower and fort, built at an unknown period. Descending, we found on the eastern slope the ancient village of Rio, consisting of about one hundred houses. It is placed on a succession of serpentine rocks, both precious and common. We descended into a narrow valley, where the walls, along the sides of the road, were formed principally of serpentine and common jasper. After travelling a few miles further, we came to another mean and filthy village, called also Rio, but to distinguish it from the other village of the same name, and because it is situated on the margin of the sea, it is denominated Rio Marina. There was yet another lofty elevation to climb, before I could gain a view of the famous mine of specular oxide of iron, to see which was the main object of my visit to Elba. All this part of the island seemed little else but a vast ore bed, made up of the sulphuret, the sulphate, the specular and the magnetic oxides of iron. Winding our way up the mountain by a most zigzag path, we met hundreds of donkies, almost crushed to the ground by the astonishing loads of the ore, in baskets, two tied together and slung across their backs, which they were bringing down to the vessels lying in the harbor ready to receive it. I pitied the poor animals, imo pectore, as I have often done before. Indeed, the ass is the animal the most used and the most abused in Italy, always toiling from break of day to dusky eve. willing to eat anything, and yet always starved; if among the slippery ledges he makes a misstep, he is sure to be lashed for it; and yet is patient and uncomplaining, under all his hardships and cruel treatment.

The surface of the ground, in many places, exhibits a very curious appearance. The sides of the ravines, produced by the force of the water, rushing down from the highlands, look as if they were covered with a thick green moss; but, on approaching, I discovered that the substance was copperas, or the sulphate of iron crystallized. In other places, it is carpeted by nearly pure sulphur. The summit of the mountain is taken off. The removal of an immense amount of the ore, has converted a large area of the highest land into an horizontal plain. On this plain is situated a round building, called the Coliseum, in which visitors take repose, and in which, I believe, an account is kept of the labor performed by the workmen. Near to this edifice is a grotto, in the mine, made by the ancients, in which have been found hammers, wedges, arid other instruments, used by them m digging out the ore. The ore is obtained in the same manner here, that it is in America, by blasting, wedges and pounding.

I was a little surprised, on learning that no metallic iron has been obtained in modern times, from this excellent ore, in the island of Elba. The work is done elsewhere, in Sicily, Turkey, and Spain. It is all conveyed to foreign countries in the ore. It was smelted here in old times, but has not been in modern days, nor can it be, for there is no fuel here which can be spared for this purpose, no mineral coal, and next to no wood. After procuring a large variety of specimens of the different substances found in this neighborhood, I returned to Porto Ferrajo, well satisfied with my day's work, but not a little fatigued.

References: Clark A. Elliott (ed), *Biographical Index to American Science: the seventeenth century to 1920*, New York: Greenwood Press, 1990; Frederick Hall, *Notes on a tour in France, Italy, and Elba, with a notice of its mines of iron*, New Haven: B. L. Hamlen, 1837.

HALLOS, HARRY (1893–1944). A leading seaman in the British Royal Navy, he served with H.M.S. *Copra* (combined operations), and was killed on the first day of the Allied attack on Elba on 17 June 1944. He was buried on Elba and three years later was reburied in the Bolsena War Cemetery (IV G 15) on the Italian mainland. He had married Elise Bates in 1935 in Halifax, and they had three children: Geoffrey, born in 1935 in Huddersfield, Yorkshire; Gwenda, born in 1937 in Huddersfield; and Dorothy, born in 1939 in Calder, Yorkshire.

References: *The war dead of the British Commonwealth and Empire: the register of the names of those who fell in the 1939–1945 War and are buried in cemeteries in Italy Cemeteries 17–18: Bolsena War Cemetery, Orvieto War Cemetery*, Maidenhead: Imperial War Graves Commission, 1954, p. 22.

HARBER, MILTON (1924–1944). A US pilot, he was born on 26 March 1924, the son of William Edgar Harber (1897–1972), a farmer, and Frieda (née Voight, 1894–1976). A second lieutenant in the 347th American Air Force Fighter Squadron, after flying 23 patrols and 14 combat sorties, he was killed with Robert Boyd when their Bell P–39 Airacobra 42–8971 crashed on Elba on 4 April 1944. It was on a reconnaissance flight to Livorno. His body was later brought back to the United States and interred at the Roselawn Memorial Park Cemetery, San Antonio, Texas.

HARDY, Sir THOMAS MASTERMAN, Baronet (1769–1839). A British naval officer, he was born on 5 April 1769 at Martin's Town, near Dorchester, England, the second son of Joseph Hardy (1733–1785) of Portesham, Dorset, and his wife, Nanny Masterman (1737–1799), daughter of Thomas Masterman of Kingston, Dorset. His father was in the navy and at the age of was twelve, Thomas Hardy joined the Royal Navy and served on a number of ships before being promoted to lieutenant on the *Meleager* in the Mediterranean. He

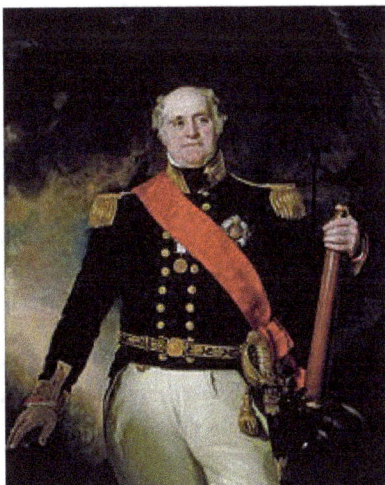

then transferred to the *Minerva* and was on the *Muntine*, a captured French brig when **Horatio Nelson** concentrated his fleet at Elba and then turned the fleet to Egypt to attack the French fleet which took place at the battle of Aboukir Bay on 1 August 1798. Hardy served with Nelson at the battle of Copenhagen, the subsequent blockade of the French port of Toulon and the pursuit of the French fleet across the Atlantic. During the battle of Trafalgar when Nelson was shot, Hardy was one of those who nursed the injured admiral and Nelson's dying words were reported to be 'Kiss me, Hardy'. Hardy was created a baronet and continued serving with distinction in the Royal Navy until he left the sea in 1827 to serve at the Admiralty. He died on 20 September 1839 at the Royal Naval Hospital, Greenwich, and was buried in its cemetery.

References: Alexander Broadley, *The Three Dorset Captains at Trafalgar*, London: J. Murray, 1906; A. M. Broadley and R. G. Bartelot, *Nelson's Hardy: his life, letters and friends*, London: John Murray, 1909; J. K. Laughton, 'Hardy, Sir Thomas Masterman, baronet (1769–1839)', revised by Andrew Lambert, *Oxford Dictionary of National Biography*, Oxford University Press, 2004.

HASTINGS, Sir THOMAS (1790–1870). A British naval officer who was on the *Undaunted* which took **Napoleon** to Elba, he was born on 3 July 1790, the oldest son of the Rev. James Hastings, rector of Martley, Worcestershire, and a distant cousin of Warren Hastings who had been governor-general of Bengal, India. He joined the Royal Navy when he was 13 and served in the English Channel and in the West Indies, serving in the Mediterranean on the *Undaunted* from 1813 to 1815. This ship conveyed Napoleon Bonaparte from Fréjus to Elba after his abdication in 1814. Hastings wrote later that Napoleon was physically 'inactive and unwieldy', and his matters were 'far from dignified or graceful' and that he 'assumed an affability which certainly did not appear natural to him.'

Thomas Hastings remained in the Mediterranean and a few other places until 1825, returning to the sea again from 1828 to 1830. Knighted in 1839, he worked on improving the design of heavy artillery and was made vice-admiral in October 1862 and admiral in April 1866. He died on 3 January 1870 at his home in London, survived by his wife Louisa Elizabeth (née Lowe).

References: A. D. Lambert, *The last sailing battlefleet: maintaining naval mastery, 1815–1850*, London: Conway Maritime Press, 1991; J. K. Laughton, 'Hastings, Sir Thomas (1790–1870)', revised by Andrew Lambert, *Oxford Dictionary of National Biography*, Oxford University Press, 2004; Norman MacKenzie, *The Escape from Elba: The Fall & Flight of Napoleon 1814–1815*, Oxford: Oxford University Press, 1982, p. 62.

HAYWARD, JACK PERCY (1920–1944). An able seaman in the British Royal Navy, he was born in 1920 in Kendal, Cumberland, the son of Percy Richard Hayward, and Maud Emily (née Barker), later of Holme Lacy, Herefordshire. Serving with H.M.S. *Copra* (combined operations), he was killed on the first day of the Allied attack on Elba on 17 June 1944. He was buried on Elba and three years later was reburied in the Bolsena War Cemetery (IV G 8) on the Italian mainland.

References: *The war dead of the British Commonwealth and Empire: the register of the names of those who fell in the 1939–1945 War and are buried in cemeteries in Italy Cemeteries 17–18: Bolsena War Cemetery, Orvieto War Cemetery*, Maidenhead: Imperial War Graves Commission, 1954, p. 22.

HEALTH CARE. Over many centuries there have been occasional epidemics in Elba, often caused by diseases in stagnant water, and also from malaria. It was struck by the plague at one stage and there is a small cemetery in the grounds of the church of San Rocco in **Portoferraio** where those who died from the disease were buried. On 1 January 1794 when the British Royal Navy brought French Royalist refugees to Portoferraio, there was an epidemic in the town at the time. Well aware of these problems, Napoleon when he took over Elba in 1814 introduced a policy of quarantine for foreign vessels arriving on Elba.

From the late eighteenth century there were two hospitals on Elba. The one in Portoferraio had 250 beds in five wards and was located west of **Forte Falcone**, and the hospital in Porto Longone (now **Porto Azzurro**) had 180 beds.

Malaria remained a problem in some parts of Elba – as it was in a few regions of Italy until **World War II**. However during the eighteenth century

Grand Duke Pietro Leopoldo II, during a land reform programme, encouraged the draining of swamps to provide more farmland and this had the effect of destroying the habitat of many mosquitoes.

The main hospital on Elba is the Ospedale Civile Elbano in Portoferraio, and has a good reputation locally. During the interwar period, its surgeon-in-chief was Guido Farina (left), one of the pioneers of cardiac surgery. With the emergence of a major tourist industry in Elba, a number of clinics have been established catering for visitors often suffering from sunburn or queasy stomach problems. There has also been a significant amount of medical research conducted in Elba, with several medical conferences held there including the European Molecular Biology Organization on 28–31 May 1981.

There have been attempts to promote the spas on Elba with the Terme San Giovanni located on the fringes of Portoferraio. However, although popular, it has never managed to develop its full potential.

References: Arsène Thiébaut de Berneaud, *A Voyage to the Isle of Elba*, London: Longman, Hurst, Rees, Orme and Brown, 1814, pp. 38–39; G. Buonomini, G. T. Sicca, and M. Manfredi, 'La malaria all'isola d'Elba' [Malaria on the Island of Elba.], *Rivista italiana d'igiene* vol. 8, nos. 1–2 (1948), pp. 1–12; M. Gabriel, C. Resch, S. Günther and J. Schmidt-Chanasit, 'Toscana virus infection imported from Elba into Switzerland', *Emerging Infectious Diseases* vol. 16, no 6 (2010), pp. 1034–36; E. Giménez-Forcada, A. Bencini, and G. Pranzini, 'Hydrogeochemical considerations about the origin of groundwater salinization in some coastal plains of Elba Island (Tuscany, Italy)', *Environmental Geochemistry and Health* vol. 32, no 3 (2010), pp. 243–57; S. Giuliani, C. Virno Lamberti, C. Sonni and D. Pellegrini, 'Mucilage impact on gorgonians in the Tyrrhenian sea', *The Science of the Total Environment* vol. 353, nos 1–3 (15 December 2005), pp. 340–49; E. Przyboś and S. Fokin, 'Habitat of Paramecium biaurelia in Italy, the Island of Elba', *Folia Biologica* (Krakow) vol. 49, nos 1–2 (2001), pp. 103–06; Christopher and Jean Serpell, *The Travellers' Guide to Elba and the Tuscan Archipelago*, London: Jonathan Cape, 1977, pp. 63–64; Harris B. Shumacker, *The evolution of cardiac surgery*, Bloomington, Ind.: Indiana University Press, 1992; Jonathan Weiland, 'Malaria in Etruria', *Etruscan Studies* vol. 14 (2010–11), pp. 97–106.

HOARE, RICHARD COLT (1758–1858). An English antiquarian and traveller, he was born on 9 December 1758 at Barnes Elms, Barnes, Surrey (now London), the son of Sir Richard Hoare, 1st Baronet (1735–1787) and his wife Frances Ann (née Acland, 1735/6–1800). Coming from a wealthy banking family, he inherited a large estate at Stourhead which allowed him to pursue his interest in archaeology and also the history of Wiltshire. He went on the Grand Tour in 1785, going to France, Italy and Switzerland, and after inheriting the baronetcy from his father two years later, he embarked on another tour in 1788 with accounts of this being published in the 1810s. On this second continental trip, he went to the island of Elba. He wrote:

Sunday, 26th April, 1789. I sailed from Piombino, at seven o'clock in the morning, in a felucca that traverses the channel from the coast of Tuscany to the Island of Elba every Sunday and Thursday; and Handed, after a passage of three hours, at the sea-port of Rio, and talked to a town of the same name about two miles up the country, placed under sortie high

Sir (Richard) Colt Hoare with his son, by Samuel Woodforde, 1795.

mountains, and in a picturesque situation. The population of this little village, amounting to two thousand souls, is considerable. I found, by recommendation, a good lodging in the house of Signor Pellegrini. In the evening, I ascended a lofty eminence, two miles distant, on which are the ruins of an old castle, called Torre del Giwe, or the Tower of Jupiter: said to have been destroyed by the celebrated Barbarossa. From this spot, to which I was led through a thick grove of ilex, or evergreen oak, there is a very extensive prospect of the adjacent coast and Mediterranean sea.

Monday, 27. I directed my steps towards Porto Ferrajo, three miles by land, and two miles by sea: though the trajet by water may be avoided by making a long detour by land. I passed under the fortress of Volterrajo, situate on a very high and rugged rock, and forming a very prominent feature in the surrounding land- scape. The mountains abound with such a variety of odoriferous plants, many of which are preserved with care in our English conservatories, that during the greater part of my ride, I almost fancied myself in a flower-garden. A brisk gale conveyed me, in less than a quarter of an hour, across the channel to Porto Ferrajo. Having delivered my name to the officer on guard (a form required from all strangers), I proceeded to view the few objects worthy of attention within the town…

On my return from Porto Ferrajo to Rio, I crossed over to a place called Le Grotte, where there are ruins of a very spacious building, situate on an eminence. Many of the subterraneous vaults exist in a perfect state, and are lined with stucco or cement both on the sides, roof, and floor: the exterior is well constructed with stones ranged in the same mariner as the opus reticulaturn, or network of the Romans. Having never heard any mention made of these ruins, and having gathered no information respecting them by the inhabitants of the island cannot hazard any conjecture; but whatever may have been their ancient destination, they certainly were constructed on a magnificent and extensive scale.

I varied my route home to Rio by following the sea-coast for some distance, and then diverged amongst the mountains opposite to the fortress of Volterrajo, which on all sides 'uprears its crested head' above the neighbouring hills, and forms, in the eyes of a landscape-painter, the principal object of attraction. In pursuing the rugged and devious path that leads through these mountainous recesses, I found many interesting subjects, and much employment for my pencil.

Tuesday, 28. The morning of this day was devoted to the iron mines at Rio, which were celebrated, in ancient as in modern times, for their extraordinary fertility in ore. Virgil, in speaking of this island, says, *Insula inexhaustis chalybum generosa metallis* and many Other classick authors have made the same allusions. During 'the progress of modern operations in these mines, the caverns opened by the ancients have been discovered, with the marks of tools on the rocks: one of these is still visible: another, which, according to my information, was a quarter of a mile in length, is now closed. The process of procuring ore is become much more easy, and all the work is carried on above ground, for the entire substance of this large mountain appears to consist of ore, and in general of the richest and most productive species. At the extremity of the above-mentioned cavern the mineral seems to decrease in good quality, and on that account was probably dis- continued by the Romans: but either new metal had been formed by nature, or the soil had fallen considerably into this cavern: for it was discovered accidentally only three years ago by the modern miners, who worked their way into it. The number of two hundred and twenty men and boys are employed in these works, and upwards of forty asses. The ore, as well as the rubbish, is driven away in carts, by two men, with great agility. Samples of this ore have been eagerly sought for by all collectors of natural history: but those beautiful specimens which were found some years ago, are no longer to be procured but with the utmost difficulty. During my visit at the mines, I witnessed two or three grand explosions. The soil is red, with a mixture of yellow ochre. The metal is not smelted in the island, but conveyed to the coast of Tuscany, where the Prince of Piombino has two foundries: the one at Fellonica, the other at Cornia, near Sughereto. This seems to have been the practice in the earliest times: for the geographer Strabo informs us that it was transported to the shores of Tuscany as soon as it was dug from the mine. 'Non enim ed in insula fornacibus liquari potest, sed statim atque effossum est, in continentem perfertur.' Strabo, lib. V.

Varro also observes that the iron could not be smelted in Elba. 'Nascii.quidem illic Jerrum, sed in stricturam non posse cogi nisi transvectum in Populoniam, Tuscicae civitatem, ipsi insulae vicinam.'

After dinner I rode to Capo Castello, on the north east side of the island, where, upon an eminence, are seen some ruins, called the Palazzo della Regina d'Elba: but I can gain no intelligence respecting the pedigree or history of this princess. The fragments still existing denote a large fabrick, though not so extensive as the one opposite to Porto Ferrajo. On examining this building, and comparing the two together, I am inclined to think that they owe their origin to the same period; for I observed three arched apartments lined with stucco, resembling exactly, both in plan and form, those alle Grotte.

With such a fascination for Elba in 1814, he was persuaded to put his account into a book which was published as *A tour through the island of Elba*. This was followed 14 years later by *Elbese scenery: a series of picturesque views in the island of Elba: formerly the residence of Napoleon Bonaparte*. Much of Hoare's energies were devoted to Wiltshire history and archaeology. He had bought Glastonbury Tor in 1786, and with Richard Cunnington took part in the first recorded excavations of Stonehenge in 1798, working on the site again in 1810, and this was detailed in his two-volume *The Ancient History of Wiltshire* (1810), with his most important work being *Ancient History of North and South Wiltshire* (1812–19). He died on 19 May 1858, and is commemorated by a monument in Salisbury Cathedral.

References: Richard Colt Hoare and John Smith, *A tour through the island of Elba,* London: John Murray, 1814; Richard Colt Hoare, *Elbese scenery: a series of picturesque views in the island of Elba: formerly the residence of Napoleon Bonaparte*, London: R. Thurston, 1828; Victoria Hutchings, 'Hoare, Sir (Richard) Colt, second baronet (1758–1838)', *Oxford Dictionary of National Biography*, Oxford University Press, 2004.

HODGSON, ALAN BURNET (d. 1944). He was appointed sub-lieutenant in the Royal Naval Volunteer Reserve on 2 October 1941, serving on H.M.S. *Salsette*. During the initial Allied attack on Elba on 17 June 1944, Hodgson led the 24 members of 'Able Commando' ashore at Marina di Campo. There had been no air bombardment of the German positions in the hope of achieving the element of surprise. However the Germans seem to have been expecting the landing and as soon as Hodgson and his men approached the shore, they came under withering fire. He was killed in the fire-fight with the initial assault driven back. He was buried on Elba and three years later was reburied in the Bolsena War Cemetery (IV H 19) on the Italian mainland.

References: Naval List, October 1942, p. 858; *The war dead of the British Commonwealth and Empire: the register of the names of those who fell in the 1939–1945 War and are buried in cemeteries in Italy Cemeteries 17–18: Bolsena War Cemetery, Orvieto War Cemetery*, Maidenhead: Imperial War Graves Commission, 1954, p. 23.

HONEYWOOD, DOUGLAS ALAN (1920–1944). An able seaman in the British Royal Navy, he was born in 1920 in Hackney, London, the son of Mrs D. Honeywood. He joined the Royal Navy, and was killed on the first day of the Allied attack on Elba on 17 June 1944. He was buried on Elba and three years later was reburied in the Bolsena War Cemetery (IV G 5) on the Italian mainland. He is also commemorated on the war memorial at Bungay, Suffolk, England.

References: *The war dead of the British Commonwealth and Empire: the register of the names of those who fell in the 1939–1945 War and are buried in cemeteries in Italy Cemeteries 17–18: Bolsena War Cemetery, Orvieto War Cemetery*, Maidenhead: Imperial War Graves Commission, 1954, p. 23.

HORNBY, Sir PHIPPS (1785–1867). A British naval officer, he was born on 27 April 1785 at Winwick, Lancashire, England, the fifth son of Geoffrey Hornby (1750–1812), rector of Winwick, and his wife, Lucy Stanley (1750–1833), daughter of James Stanley, Lord Strange, and sister of Edward, twelfth earl of Derby. Educated in Sunbury, Phipps Hornby entered the Royal Navy soon after his twelfth birthday, and served on the frigate *Latona* under Captain John Bligh, a distant relation of William Bligh of the H.M.S. *Bounty*. The young Phipps witnessed the mutiny at the Nore, and then served in North America and in the Caribbean, under **Horatio Nelson** on the *Victory* off Toulon. After taking part in a large number of other engagements, in 1799 he was commander of the *Spartan* which helped the Tuscan forces take Elba from the French. For his involvement in that campaign, he was awarded the Austrian order of St. Joseph of Würzburg. In 1814 he married a relative, Sophia Maria Burgoyne, the daughter of Lieutenant-General John Burgoyne who was famously defeated at the battle of Saratoga in 1777. Remaining in the Royal Navy for many years, he was commander-in-chief in the Pacific and was appointed vice-admiral in 1854, and full admiral four years later. He died on 19 March 1867 at his home, Little Green, near Petersfield, Hampshire.

References: Mrs F. Egerton, *Admiral of the fleet: Sir Geoffrey Phipps Hornby, a biography,* Edinburgh: W. Blackwood, 1896; J. K. Laughton, 'Hornby, Sir Phipps (1785–1867)', revised by Andrew Lambert, *Oxford Dictionary of National Biography*, Oxford University Press, 2004.

HOTELS. When **Napoleon Bonaparte** came to Elba in 1814, there was only one hotel on the island – at **Portoferraio**. Known as the Auberge Bonroux, many of the British and other tourists who came to the island

in 1814-15 stayed there. It is still in operation as the **Albergo l'Ape Elbana** (Hotel of the Bee of Elba). Gradually a few more hotels were established and with the advent of major tourism from 1950, a large numbers of hotels were built around the island. These range from luxury hotels such as the Hotel Elba Palace Golf (which has its own **golf** course, although many people uninterested in golf also stay there) and the **Hotel Hermitage**, through to bed and breakfast accommodation.

HOTEL HERMITAGE. This is located close to **Marciana Marina** in the Biodola Bay, and is the one of the most luxurious hotels on Elba. It has an infinity pool overlooking the sea, its own private sandy beach, and its own 9-hole golf course, as well as a private boat jetty, nine tennis courts, diving centre and sailing and windsurfing school.

References: Hermitage Hotel, www.hotelhermitage.it; Miles Roddis & Alex Leviton, *Tuscany & Umbria*, Footscray: Lonely Planet, 2006, p. 189.

HUGMAN, HENRY KENT (1924–1944). A British able seaman with H.M.S. *Copra* (combined operations), he was born in Southwark, London, the son of Henry A. Hugman and Jane (née Mitchell). He was badly injured during the landings on Elba on 17 June 1944 and died the same day from his wounds. He is buried in Corsica at Biguglia War Cemetery (1 A 2).

HUGO, VICTOR MARIE (1802–1885). The famous French novelist and the author of *Notre-Dame de Paris* (1831, published in English as *The Hunchback of Notre-Dame*) and *Les Misérables* (1862), he was the son of an army officer and spent part of his childhood on Elba.

Victor Hugo was born on 26 February 1802 in Besançon, in the east of France, and was the third son of Joseph Léopold Sigisbert Hugo (1774–1828) and Sophie Trébuchet (1772–1821). In June 1803 they all moved to Elba. As Paul Gruyer wrote:

In 1802, a few months after his birth, Victor Hugo was brought to the island of Elba. He was born at Besançon, where his father, Joseph Hugo, a major in the army, was quartered. At the age of six weeks he had been taken to Marseilles, a terrible journey for so young a child, and, moreover, so delicate that the doctor despaired of his life. To add to his misfortunes, his mother had been obliged to leave him, and go to Paris to present a petition for her husband's unduly retarded promotion. The father had to take charge of the baby, who cried incessantly during his mother's absence. When she returned, she brought with her an order to proceed to Elba, which had lately been incorporated with France.

The little family set off at once for Porto Ferraio and settled down there. At first, little Victor's health did not improve; for a year after his arrival at Elba he was still unable to hold up his head, 'weighted', as his admirers said, 'so heavily by his great thoughts, still in embryo.' The child was well made, however, with broad shoulders and chest, and with the help of the fine sea air and beautiful climate he had begun to develop, after three years' stay at Elba, the robust health he enjoyed all his life. His father was ordered to Italy with Joseph Bonaparte, and Victor went with his mother and brothers to Paris, rue de Clichy, at the end of 1805 or beginning of 1806.

It was at Elba that Victor lisped his first words, which a story has kept for us. Dumas père says in his Memoirs that one day in a struggle with his governess, who was threatening him for disobedience, he cried 'Cattivar' which means naughty in Italian. How had he heard the word, and why had he remembered it? There was joy all through the house when it was known the child had spoken. Thus the first word used by the poet was in a foreign language.

But Elba 'recalled no memories to the child as yet'. Nevertheless, later, a strange analogy was found between the journey to Elba made by the author of the 'Ode A la Colonne' and that by Napoleon ten years afterwards. 'The rugged and severe landscapes of this obscure place were the first scenes of nature reflected in little Victor's eyes. The young life was already in harmony with its future destiny – 'the slender thread was being silently woven into the splendid tissue of later years.'

While I read and copied the marble inscription, a black arm was suddenly thrust in front of me and a black hand brandished a black purse before my eyes. I turned hastily and drew back, startled at the sight of a man in black – 'if you can give the name of man to a mere black bag, surmounted by a peaked hood, pierced by two holes, through which looked two burning eyes. This was one of the Penitents, in quest of alms. He followed me with his black arm, hand, and bag deafening me with a little bell attached to his waist, which he rang furiously until I pacified him with two sous.

I was told that this was the usual custom when one of the confraternity died, the collection going to defray the funeral expenses.

The Hugos whilst on Elba lived in a house on Via Guerrazzi, on a longish road close to the harbour of Portoferraio, but the actual house has never been identified although some guide books claim it was the **Portoferraio Town Hall**. There was then a long voyage to Naples – which Victor Hugo did remember – and then the family headed to Paris. There Victor Hugo fell in love with Adèle Foucher, and they were secretly engaged, but only married after his mother's death because she was against the marriage. The couple had a son who died in infancy, and then four more children. Victor Hugo was travelling with his mistress when he read in the newspapers that his oldest and favourite daughter had drowned in the Seine. He was distraught by this and wrote an epic poem to demonstrate his grief.

By that time Victor Hugo was already a famous writer. He had been upset by the state of the Cathedral of Notre Dame which had been neglected in the previous decades and fascinated by the history of Paris, he wrote his book *Notre-Dame de Paris* published in 1831 and translated into English as *The Hunchback of Notre-Dame*. This immediately created a renewed appreciation of the cathedral and work started on his restoration. He then started work on *Les Misérables*. However after the coup d'état by Louis Napoleon in 1851, he left France and went to live in Brussels and then moved to the Channel Islands, staying in Jersey until 1855, and then moved to Guernsey where he lived for the next 15 years. He returned briefly to Paris in 1871 but then went back to Guernsey and in 1873 returned to France where he remained until his death on 22 May 1885.

References: Alfred Barbou, *Victor Hugo and His Times*, New York, Harper & Brothers, 1882; Pierre Branda, *L'île d'Elbe et le retour de Napoléon: 1814–1815*, Saint-Cloud: Soteca, 2014; Robert Christophe, *Napoleon on Elba*, London: Macdonald, 1964, pp. 22–23; A. F. Davidson, *Victor Hugo: His Life and Work*, London: E. Nash, 1912; John Andrew Frey, *A Victor Hugo Encyclopedia*, Westport, Conn.: Greenwood Press, 1999; Paul Gruyer, *Napoleon, King of Elba*, Philadelphia: J. B. Lippincott Company, 1906, p. 11–13; Andre Maurois, *Victor Hugo and His World*, London: Thames and Hudson, 1966; Graham Robb, *Victor Hugo: A Biography*, London: Picador, 1998, p. 14.

HUTCHINSON, HUGH HILTON (1913–1944). A British intelligence officer, he was born on 18 May 1913 at Carrara, Italy, the son of Charles Hilton Hutchinson, engineer, and his first wife Lily Muriel Raikes (née Bromage). He was educated at Eastbourne College and proceeded to his father's old college, Gonville & Caius College, Cambridge. An Italian speaker, he was appointed a captain in the intelligence corps in the British army. He was on a plane piloted by **Geoffrey Cooper**, and with **George William Blackwell** and **Alfred Chapman Meeson** on board, flying from Bastia, Corsica, when it crashed on 19 November 1944 and all four were killed. They were buried in the Allied Military Cemetery at Elba, and then reburied in 1947 at the Bolsena War Cemetery (IV H 4).

References: *The war dead of the British Commonwealth and Empire: the register of the names of those who fell in the 1939–1945 War and are buried in cemeteries in Italy Cemeteries 17–18: Bolsena War Cemetery, Orvieto War Cemetery*, Maidenhead: Imperial War Graves Commission, 1954, p. 23.

HYDE de NEUVILLE, JEAN-GUILLAUME, BARON (1776–1857).

A French Royalist agent, he was born on 24 January 1776 at La Charité-sur-Loire, Nièvre, in central France, the son of William Hyde (Guillaume Hyde), a Scottish Jacobite who had fled to France after the Rebellion of 1745. Jean-Guillaume Hyde was educated at the Collège Cardinal Lemoine and famously when he was only 17 successfully defended a man at the revolutionary tribunal at Nevers after the unfortunate Royalist had been denounced by Joseph Fouché. Hyde then worked for the exiled Prince Louis (later King Louis XVIII) and the Comte d'Artois (later King Charles X). He took part in a failed Royalist uprising in Berry in 1796 and then made an appeal to **Napoleon Bonaparte** after the 18 Brumaire Coup of 1799 to restore the Bourbons. He changed his name to Roland and ran a medical practice in Lyons. He was accused of involvement in a royalist plot in 1800–01 and five years later agreed that he should be allowed to go into exile in the Americas, settling near New Brunswick. After the Bourbon Restoration in 1814, he returned to France and worked for Louis XVIII. On his return journey, he met the British admiral Sir Sidney Smith who asked, 'Is the distance between Elba and the southern coast of France of any significance to a man who has marched from one end of Europe to the other? Wouldn't a few hours be sufficient for him to rejoin his troops?'

Hyde was also sent to Italy where he was to collect information on Bonapartists operating there. Returning to Paris with stories that Napoleon might be planning an escape, Louis XVIII sent Hyde to London ostensibly to discuss Barbary pirates in the Mediterranean, but actually to urge the British government to move Napoleon further from France. Hyde then went to Italy in October 1814. He fled during the 100 Days but became an important figure in the Second Bourbon Restoration that followed. In January 1816 King Louis XVIII appointed him the French ambassador to the United States, a post he held for five years. He declined to serve as ambassador at Constantinople and was elected to the French Chamber of Deputies for Cosne. Made a baron and then French ambassador to Portugal, he was involved in rescuing John VI there and given the title of Comte de Bemposta in Portugal. With Dom Miguel seizing the throne in 1824, Hyde suggested that Britain should intervene in the expectation that they would not and France could instead. However the government of King Charles X of France supported Miguel's opposition to the Portuguese constitution of 1822, and would not intervene. Hyde de Neuville returned to Paris and to his seat in the Chamber of Deputies. He served as minister of the navy in the moderate ministry of Baptiste Gay de Martignac and in 1830 opposed the July Revolution, resigning his seat at the exclusion of the Bourbons from the throne. He died on 28 May 1857 in Paris.

References: Jacques Faugeras, *Hide de Neuville: Irréductible adversaire de Napoléon Ier,* Paris: Édition Guénégaud, 2003; Norman MacKenzie, *The Escape from Elba: The Fall & Flight of Napoleon 1814–1815*, Oxford: Oxford University Press, 1982, pp. 167–70; Françoise Watel, *Jean-Guillaume Hyde de Neuville*, Paris: Peter Lang, 1997.

- I -

ILVATI. This is a Ligurian (Italian) tribe mentioned by the Roman writer Livy who wrote that in 197 BC, they were the only Ligurian tribe which had not yet submitted to the power of Rome. The name came from the iron found on Elba.

References: Livy, *Rome and the Mediterranean*, Harmondsworth, Middx: Penguin Books, 1976, p. 30, 97, 98.

The brig *Inconstant* (Captain Taillade) taking Napoleon to France, crossing the path of the brig *Zéphir* (Captain Andrieux). Inconstant is flying the tricolor of the French Empire, whilst the Zéphir flies the white ensign of the Kingdom of France. Soldiers of the Imperial Guard can be seen crouching on deck with Napoleon standing fore of the main mast.

L'INCONSTANT. This 337-tonne brig, built in 1811, was used by Napoleon to leave Elba and get to France in February 1815. After the defeat of France later that year it was seized by England as a war prize in 1828, renamed Swiftsure, and soon afterwards was used on the England-Australia shipping route. It was en route from Sydney to Mauritius when, on 10 July 1831, she struck a coral reef on the Great Barrier Reef and sank. The wreck was found in November 2014 off Lockhart River near Cape York Peninsula, Queensland, Australia, by Australian filmmaker and shipwreck hunter Ben Cropp.

References: 'Napoleon Bonaparte's getaway ship found in Australian waters', http://www.economylead.com/international/napoleon-bonapartes-getaway-ship-found-in-australian-waters-77390 (accessed 15 September 2015).

ISOLA D'ELBA PRIZE. This was founded in 1962 by the **Ente Valorizzazione Elba** and awards the sum of one million lire or a novel, book of poetry or an essay of outstanding cultural interest by a living European author and which is a book of poetry or an essay of outstanding cultural interest, and which had been published in Italy by 30 June of each year.

ITAVIA DE HAVILLAND CRASH (1960). The Itavia De Havilland DH114 Heron 2 crashed at Monte Capanne, near **Marciana**, on 14 October 1960 with the loss of the seven passengers and four crew. The plane was flying

Villagers from Marciana accompanying the coffins carrying the victims from the crash of the Itavia flight in 1960.

The memorial near Marciana for the victims from the crash of the Itavia flight in 1960.

from Rome to Genoa when the pilot, Ennio Scipio, aged 30, intending to divert the plane to Turin but instead headed to Elba where the plane crashed. All were killed in the crash. As well as the pilot, the other four crew were Francesco Cossu, 44, second pilot; Giovanna Pertusio, 25, hostess; and Grazia Candeloro, 20, assistant hostess. The passengers were Ernesto Cuomo Ulloa, 60, a lawyer; Silvio Schiunnack, 48, real estate agent; Giorgio Bracci, 38, a trade unionist; Elio Perugi, 32, a businessman; Naomichi Takashima, a Japanese businessman; Adelaide Rocca Dalmau, aged 40, and her daughter Maria Pia Dalmau, aged 4. The wreckage was found two days later by Antonio Amaldi Pomonte, aged 37, a local man who was searching for mushrooms. The bodies of the passengers were taken to Genoa, and those of the crew to Rome. A joint funeral was held on 20 October at the Genoa Cathedral.

References: Silvestre Ferruzzi, 'Il disastro aereo del 1960', *Lo Scoglio* no. 87 (September-December 2009); Silvestre Ferruzzi, *Il disastro aereo del 1960*, Portoferraio: rivista Lo Scoglio, 2009; Nicola Pedde, *ITAVIA: storia della più discussa compagnia aerea italiana*, sl: Eliconie Editrice, 2003; Rinaldo Taddei, *In difesa del generale Romolo Abbriata, Il disastro aereo dell'isola d'Elba*, Roma: rivista L'Eloquenza, 1965.

- J -

JERDAN, WILLIAM (1782–1869). A British journalist and antiquary, he was born on 16 April 1782 at Kelso, Roxburghshire, Scotland, the son of John Jerdan and his wife Agnes (née Stuart). His father died when William was 13, and the boy went to work for some merchants as a clerk but was regularly ill throughout his childhood. In 1806 he moved to London and was involved with a number of newspapers. In 1813 with national interest in Napoleon Bonaparte, he went to Europe to collect reports for a book and returned to London where, in 1814, he edited *A Voyage to the Isle of Elba*, translated from the French of **Arsène Thiébault de Berneaud** for the publishers Longman, Hurst, Rees, Orme, and Brown in London. The book contains a dedication to Charles Long, an important politician. Subsequently William Jerdan worked for other journals including the *Literary Gazette*, which helped to support the establishment of the Royal Geographical Society. Always interested in history, he helped to edit *The Rutland Papers* for the Camden Society and died on 11 July 1869 at Bushey Heath.

References: W. Jerdan, *The autobiography of William Jerdan: with his literary, political, and social reminiscences and correspondence during the last fifty years*, London: A. Hall, Virtue & Co., 1852–53, 4 Vols; Beverly E. Schneller, 'Jerdan, William (1782–1869)', *Oxford Dictionary of National Biography*, Oxford University Press, 2004.

JERZMANOWSKI, PAWEŁ JAN (1779–1862). He was a cavalry colonel who commanded the small detachment of Polish lancers that escorted **Napoleon Bonaparte** to Elba in April-May 1814. Paweł Jan Jerzmanowski had been born on 25 June 1779 at Mniewo, near Kielce, Poland, and was from a minor noble family. Joining the Polish light horse in 1807, he served in Napoleon's army and was awarded the Croix de l'Ordre Militaire de Virtuti Militari and created a Knight of the Empire in 1810, then raised to the rank of Baron on 30 October 1813. When the Allied armies invaded France in 1813–14, he was involved in much of the fighting against the Austrians, and when Napoleon abdicated the throne, he was in command of the 109 Polish lancers who accompanied Napoleon into exile with Jerzmanowski travelling on the *Undaunted* with the ex-emperor.

When the *Undaunted* arrived at Elba, Jermanowski, **Drouot** and Major **Clam-Martinitz** went ashore to ensure that Napoleon would be given a suitable welcome. Jerzmanowski returned with Napoleon and fought at the battle of Waterloo, being injured in the fighting at Mont-Saint-Jean. After a short time in Poland, he and his French wife returned to France and was involved in Polish émigré movements in Paris. He died on 15 April 1862, and was buried in Montmatre Cemetery.

References: Norman MacKenzie, *The Escape from Elba: The Fall & Flight of Napoleon 1814–1815*, Oxford: Oxford University Press, 1982; Jean Tranié and Juan-Carlos Carmigniani, *Les Polonais de Napoléon*, Paris: Copernic, 1982.

JORDAN, SAMSON (1831–1900). A French metallurgist and engineer, he was born on 23 June 1831 at Eaux-Vives, Switzerland, and studied engineering, and was involved in the construction of the Saint-Louis blast furnaces at Marseille in 1855, as its engineer and then director. The furnaces were built to process iron ore from Elba, and also from Spain and Algeria. He moved to Paris in 1862 and from 1865 was professor of metallurgy at the École Centrale des Arts et Manufactures, his former school, He died on 24 February 1900 in Paris.

References: Tristan Jordan, *Samson Jordan, l'histoire d'un métallurgiste*, Meudon: T. Jordan, 2009; *The Times* (2 April 1900), p. 11.

- K -

KELLY, BENEDICTUS MARWOOD (1785–1867). A British naval officer, he was born on 3 February 1785, the second son of Benedictus Marwood Kelly (1752–1836) of Holsworthy, attorney, and his wife, Mary, daughter of Arscott Coham. Joining the Royal Navy when he was 13, he served in the expedition to Ferrol, Spain, in 1800, and then in Egypt in the following year. In 1799 he was involved in the successful attack on the island of Elba. He then joined the *Temeraire* and after serving on other vessels, in 1811 he was given command of the *Dasher* which took part in the British invasion of Java. Promoted to commander, he was involved in the suppression of the Slave Trade until 1822 when he retired in ill-health. He was promoted to rear-admiral in 1852, vice-admiral five years later, and full admiral in 1863, and also actively involved in lobbying for railways. He died on 26 September 1867 leaving enough money for the establishment of Kelly College which he hoped would train boys to become naval officers in years to come.

References: A. O. V. Penny (ed), *Kelly College Register, 1877–1927*, pp. 7–24; Roger T. Stearn, 'Kelly, Benedictus Marwood (1785–1867)', *Oxford Dictionary of National Biography*, Oxford University Press, 2004.

KERSHAW, GORDON (1924–1944). An able seamen in the British Royal Navy, he was killed on the first day of the Allied attack on Elba on 17 June 1944. He was buried on Elba and three years later was reburied in the Bolsena War Cemetery (IV H 6) on the Italian mainland.

References: *The war dead of the British Commonwealth and Empire: the register of the names of those who fell in the 1939–1945 War and are buried in cemeteries in Italy Cemeteries 17–18: Bolsena War Cemetery, Orvieto War Cemetery*, Maidenhead: Imperial War Graves Commission, 1954, p. 25.

KNAPP, HENRY HARTOPP (1782–1846). A British clergyman and school master, he was born in August 1782, being baptised on 24 August at St Michael's Church, Stamford, Lincolnshire, the son of Rev. Henry Ryder, the rector of Woodford, Northamptonshire. Educated at Eton College, he proceeded to King's College, Cambridge, matriculating in 1902 and graduating BA in 1806, and MA in 1809. A Fellow of King's College, Cambridge, from 1804 to 1821, he worked as an assistant master at Eton from 1808 to 1820, and lower master from 1830–34, then ordained deacon in 1809 at Ely, and priest in 1820. His pupils included the future prime minister William Ewart Gladstone. From 1820 to 1846, he was rector of Ampthill, Bedfordshire, and spent some time living on the island of Elba. He was the author of *Helvetiorum Luctus et Querimonia; and Tempora Subseciva, Verses Serious and Comic*. He caught malaria and died from this on 18 December 1846 in Rome.

References: *Eton School Lists from 1791 to 1850*, p. 22, 29; *Alumni Cantabrigienses*.

KÖLLER, FRANZ Freiherr von (1767–1826). An Austrian general, he was the Austrian commissioner who accompanied **Napoleon Bonaparte** to Elba in May 1814. Born on 27 November 1767 at Münchengrätz, Bohemia (now in the Czech Republic), he served in the Austrian army as an officer on the general staff, 1792–94, and was gazetted colonel in 1805. Because of his extensive knowledge of languages, Franz Köller was appointed adjutant general of Prince Schwarzenberg. This saw him chosen to accompany Napoleon from Fontainebleau to the south of France and there to Elba. During the journey through France, there were demonstrations against Napoleon prompting the ex-emperor to dress in the uniform of Köller as a disguise. Köller was seasick on the *Undaunted*. During the voyage Köller noted that the ex-emperor regularly spoke about disagreements between the British, Austrians, Prussians, Russians and other allies suggesting, he (Köller) thought that there was the possibility of using this disunity to his advantage.

Köller remained on Elba until 8 May when **Edward Locker** brought over a copy of the preliminary peace agreement between the French provisional government and the Allied powers. His task over, Köller left on the following day with Locker on the *Curaçoa*. Subsequently Köller worked on other missions including to the Tsar of Russia and the King of Prussia. He was posted to Naples in 1821 and lived there until his death on 22 August 1826.

References: Egger: 'Koller Franz Frh. Von', *Österreichisches Biographisches Lexikon 1815–1950*, Vienna: Verlag der Österreichischen Akademie der Wissenschaften, 1969, vol. 4, p. 88; Norman MacKenzie, *The Escape from Elba: The Fall & Flight of Napoleon 1814–1815*, Oxford: Oxford University Press, 1982.

- L -

LANE, MARGARET WINIFRED (1907–1994). A British novelist and biographer, she was born on 23 June 1907 at Sale, Cheshire, the only child of Harry George Lane (1881–1957), newspaper editor, and Edith Webb (1884–1951), daughter of a Birmingham glass dealer. She grew up in London and was educated at St Stephen's, Folkestone, and St Hugh's College, Oxford. Entering journalism, she worked for the *Daily Express*, and was posted to the United States where she famously managed to get an exclusive interview with Al Capone. In 1934 she married Bryan Edgar Wallace, the son of the writer Edgar Wallace. She wrote a biography of her father-in-law in 1938, and soon afterwards met Francis John Clarence Westernra Plantagenet 'Jack' Hastings. Margaret obtained her divorce in 1938 but it was four years before her lover could get his divorce, having succeeded to his father's title of Earl of Huntingdon in 1939. Margaret continued writing but was restless and the couple who were devoted to each other, moved several times – Jack Huntingdon serving as parliamentary secretary to the ministry of agriculture and fisheries in the Labour government of Clement Attlee. They bought a house on the island of Elba, and wintered in Morocco. They whittled their way through the family fortune but there was enough to last their lifetime – just. Jack died on 30 January 1990, and Margaret – whose books sold well – died on 14 February 1994 in Southampton.

References: Selina Hastings, 'Lane, Margaret Winifred [married names Margaret Winifred Wallace; Margaret Winifred Hastings, countess of Huntingdon] (1907–1994)', *Oxford Dictionary of National Biography*, Oxford University Press, 2004.

LAPI, PIERRE-JOSEPH-CHRISTIAN (1766–1854). A medical doctor, Dr Christian Lapi was the commander of the National Guard on Elba in 1814. He was born on 16 March 1766 and when **Napoleon Bonaparte** arrived in May 1814 it consisted of two understrength companies. He was one of the local dignitaries who gathered when the *Undaunted* arrived at **Portoferraio** on 3 May 1814. He went to France for the 100 Days and on 3 May 1815 he was appointed general de brigade in Napoleon's new army. He died on 5 August 1854.

References: Norman MacKenzie, *The Escape from Elba: The Fall & Flight of Napoleon 1814–1815*, Oxford: Oxford University Press, 1982, p. 69; Philip Mansel and Torsten Riotte, *Monarchy and Exile: the politics of legitimacy from Marie de Médicis to Wilhelm II*, Basingstoke, Hampshire, UK: Palgrave Macmillan, 2011.

LAZENBY, GEORGE ERIC (1923–1944). A marine in the British Royal Marines, he was born in Tadcaster, Yorkshire, United Kingdom, the son of Thomas Lazenby and Nellie F. (née Potter) of Sheffield. He was serving on a landing craft during the attack on Elba on 17 June 1944, when the craft was sunk and Lazenby was posted as missing, presumed killed. He is commemorated on the Portsmouth Naval Memorial (panel 87, column 3).

LE GHIAIE. This is a pebble beach on the north side of **Portoferraio**.

LE VISTE. This is a pebble beach at **Portoferraio** under the walls at **Forte Falcone**.

LEE, JOHN (1783–1866). A British antiquary and astronomer, he was born as John Fiott on 28 April 1783 in Totteridge, Hertfordshire, England, the oldest son of John Fiott (1752–1797), merchant of London, and his wife, Harriet Lee (1763–1794), daughter of William Lee of Totteridge Park, Hertfordshire. His father's family were originally from Dijon, Burgundy. Educated at Mackworth in Derbyshire, he proceeded to St. John's College, Cambridge, and in 1807 travelled in northern Europe managing to get to Copenhagen as it was being captured by the British. He served in the Walcheren expedition and in 1811 went to Greece, also going to Syria, taking part in robbing a tomb in Samos. In 1813 he was in Spain, and in May 1814 he decided to go to Italy. He was on the island of Elba when **Napoleon** arrived there on 6 April 1814.

Returning to Britain, his uncle died in 1815 leaving him significant land and he assumed the surname Lee. He was involved in a range of community activities also being a justice of the peace and High Sheriff of Buckinghamshire.

Fascinated by astronomy, he helped to found the Astronomical Society (later the Royal Astronomical Society), and was its treasurer from 1831 to 1840, and president in 1861–62. He was also involved in the founding of the British Meteorological Society, and also was its treasurer and president. He died on 25 February 1866 in his home, Hartwell House. His wife Cecilia (née Rutter) had died in 1854.

References: *Memoir of John Lee*, London, 1870; Anita McConnell, 'Lee, John (1783–1866)', *Oxford Dictionary of National Biography*, Oxford University Press, 2004.

LEMOINE, JOHN (1762–1821). A British colonel in the Royal Artillery – later a general – he went with **John Barber Scott**, Major **Montgomery Maxwell**, RA; Captain Smith and Colonel **Niel Douglas** to visit Napoleon Bonaparte on Elba in September 1814.

John Lemoine was born on 14 November 1762 in London, the son of Philip and Mary Lemoine, and was baptised on 27 November 1762 at St James, Westminster. The boy surnamed Lemoine who won a scholarship to Eton College and studied there from 1772 was possibly an older brother. John was commissioned second lieutenant in the Royal Artillery on 30 June 1780 and was then promoted to first lieutenant on 9 September 1785 and captain-lieutenant and captain on 14 August 1794, captain on 8 January 1799 and major in the army on 1 January 1805. He was then appointed major in the Royal Artillery on 10 March 1806 and gazetted lieutenant-colonel on 1 June 1806 and colonel in the army three days later. On 4 July 1806 at the battle of Maida in Calabria, Italy, Lemoine commanded the British artillery – three six-pound guns – and Sir John Stuart mentioned him in his despatches, 'The judgement and effect with which our artillery was directed by Major Lemoine, was, in our dearth of cavalry, of most essential use; and I have great pleasure in reporting the effective services of that valuable and distinguished corps.' Lemoine then served under **William Bentinck** in the attack on Genoa in May 1814. It was not until 20 December 1814 that Lemoine was promoted to colonel in the Royal Artillery. He died in December 1821, and was buried on 8 December at St. Martin in the Fields.

References: John Alger, *Napoleon's British visitors and captives, 1801–1815*, New York: J. Pott, 1904, p. 296; Richard Hopton, *The Battle of Maida 1806: Fifteen Minutes of Glory*, London: Leo Cooper, 2002; John Philippart, *The Royal Military Calendar, or Army Service and Commission Book ...*, London: A. J. Valpy, 1820, Volume 4, p. 153.

LEWENDON, EDWARD GEORGE (1924–1944). An able seaman in the British Royal Navy, he was born in late 1924 in Reading, Berkshire, England, the son of Frederick George Lewendon (1895–1959), and his wife (née Norris), of Reading. He served in the Royal Navy and was killed on the first day of the Allied attack on Elba on 17 June 1944. He was buried on Elba and three years later was reburied in the Bolsena War Cemetery (IV G 6) on the Italian mainland.

References: *The war dead of the British Commonwealth and Empire: the register of the names of those who fell in the 1939–1945 War and are buried in cemeteries in Italy Cemeteries 17–18: Bolsena War Cemetery, Orvieto War Cemetery*, Maidenhead: Imperial War Graves Commission, 1954, p. 26.

LIBRARY. *See* **Biblioteca Comunale Foresiana**.

LOCKER, EDWARD HAWKE (1777–1849). A British hospital administrator and watercolour painter who visited Elba and met with **Napoleon**, he was born on 9 October 1777 at East Malling, Kent, the fourth of the five surviving children of Captain William Locker (1731–1800) and his wife, Lucy Parry (1746/7–1780), daughter of Admiral William Parry and granddaughter of Commodore Charles Brown. Educated at Eton College, he joined the Royal Navy at the age of 18 and became a clerk in the navy pay office. He travelled with Admiral Edward Pellew to the East Indies, and later in the North Sea and in the Mediterranean. Roger Quarm in the *Dictionary of National Biography* notes, 'During this time he was a prize agent, engaged in the distribution of prize money, from which he himself derived considerable benefit.'

An accomplished watercolour painter, he went to Elba, arriving on 8 May 1814 on the *Curaçoa* and visited Napoleon at **Portoferraio** whom he described in 'The Plain Englishman'. His official task was to present Napoleon Bonaparte with a copy of the preliminary peace agreement which was signed by the new provisional French government in Paris and the Allied powers.

Napoleon was handed the document in the presence of **Franz Köller** and **Neil Campbell**, as well as **Thomas Ussher** and Captain Towers who sailed the *Curaçoa*. Napoleon read it and made no comment, giving it back to Locker.

On his return to Britain Locker married Eleanor Mary Elizabeth Boucher, the daughter of Rev. Jonathan Boucher, and in 1819 was appointed the secretary to the Royal Naval Hospital at Greenwich, becoming the civil commissioner five years later. He did much to maintain the hospital and a Painted Hall was added to the hospital, furnished with works from naval families. He retired in 1844 and died on 16 October 1849 at Iver, Buckinghamshire. His watercolours are held by Victoria and Albert Museum and the British Museum in London, the National Maritime Museum at Greenwich, and the Victoria Art Gallery, Bath.

References: *Eton School Lists from 1791 to 1850*, p. 5, 12; Kevin Littlewood and Beverley Butler, *Of ships and stars: maritime heritage and the founding of the National Maritime Museum, Greenwich*, London: The Athlone Press, 1998; Norman MacKenzie, *The Escape from Elba: The Fall & Flight of Napoleon 1814–1815*, Oxford: Oxford University Press, 1982, p. 82; P. Newell, *Greenwich Hospital, a royal foundation, 1692–1983*, Holbrook: Trustees of Greenwich Hospital, 1984; Roger Quarm, 'Locker, Edward Hawke (1777–1849)', *Oxford Dictionary of National Biography*, Oxford University Press, 2004.

LOWE, Sir HUDSON (1769–1844). A British army officer and colonial governor, he was born on 28 July 1769 at Galway, Ireland, the son of Hudson Lowe (d. 1801) and his wife, the daughter of J. Morgan of Galway. Hudson Lowe jnr was born when his father, an army surgeon from Lincolnshire, England, was serving in Galway, and went with his father to Jamaica and then to North America. He went to England to attend school, and then joined the East Devon militia and then the 50th Foot, his father's regiment. He was appointed a lieutenant in 1791, and promoted to captain four years later. His regiment was then posted to Gibraltar and he served in the fighting in Toulon in 1793 and was with the British soldiers who captured Corsica in 1794. After two years in the British army garrison at Ajaccio, he was posted to Elba where he served as the deputy judge-advocate. He was then posted to

Lisbon and Minorca, and helped to raise the Corsican Rangers, a unit of some 200 Corsicans who opposed **Napoleon Bonaparte**. They fought in Egypt but with the Peace of Amiens, were disbanded in Malta. With the resumption of war 14 months later, Lowe was sent back to Malta to raise a new unit which was to be called the Royal Corsican Rangers. They fought in Italy, especially in Naples, but were forced to surrender to the French at Capri after enduring a 13-day siege. The unit later served in the Ionian Islands and then in 1813 was sent to help with the Russian German Legion, a military unit formed from German soldiers who deserted during the Retreat from Moscow, and he was present at the battle of Leipzig.

Attached to the forces of Marshal von Blücher, Lowe rode from Paris to Calais with a single Cossack guard and was the first officer to bring the news of Napoleon's abdication to England. After Napoleon's return to France in 1815, he fell out with the Duke of Wellington and was sent to Genoa and then served in the occupation of Toulon. His next task was to take Napoleon Bonaparte to St. Helena and was appointed 'lieutenant-general of his Majesty's army in St. Helena and governor of that island'. Lowe never got on with Napoleon and after the ex-emperor's death, Brigadier-General John Pine Coffin was appointed to succeed him as governor. Back in Britain Lowe was involved in court action against Barry O'Meara, Napoleon's doctor on St. Helena. He died on 10 January 1844 at his home, Charlotte Cottage, near Sloane Street, Chelsea, London. His papers survived and many of them were published in three volumes as *Captivity of Napoleon at St. Helena, from the Letters and Journals of Sir Hudson Lowe* (1853).

References: H. M. Chichester, 'Lowe, Sir Hudson (1769–1844)', revised by John Sweetman, *Oxford Dictionary of National Biography*, Oxford University Press, 2004; Robert Christophe, *Napoleon on Elba*, London: Macdonald, 1964, p. 70; Desmond Gregory, *Napoleon's Jailer: Lt. General Sir Hudson Lowe: A Life*, Cranbury, NJ and London: Associated University Presses, 1996; G. C. Kitching, 'Sir Hudson Lowe and the East India Company', *The English Historical Review* vol. 63, no 248 (July 1948), pp. 322–41; Earl of Roseberry, *Napoleon: the last phase*, London: Harper & Brothers, 1900.

- M -

MACDONALD, EDWARD ARMSTRONG (1921/2–1944). A sub-lieutenant from the Royal Indian Navy Volunteer Reserve, he was the son of Frank Macdonald and Elsie Macdonald, of Kingstown, Co. Dublin, Irish Republic. Mentioned in Despatches, he served on the H.M.S. *Royal Scotsman*, and was killed on the first day of the Allied attack on Elba on 17 June 1944, aged 22. He was buried on Elba and three years later was reburied in the Bolsena War Cemetery (IV H 10) on the Italian mainland.

References: *The war dead of the British Commonwealth and Empire: the register of the names of those who fell in the 1939–1945 War and are buried in cemeteries in Italy Cemeteries 17–18: Bolsena War Cemetery, Orvieto War Cemetery*, Maidenhead: Imperial War Graves Commission, 1954, p. 27.

McGRANN, GEORGE (1926–1944). A British seaman, he was born on 20 March 1926 at Birkenhead, England, the son of William McGrann and Bertha (née Hayes). In January 1943, aged only 16, and against the wishes of his mother, he joined the Royal Navy and was trained on H.M.S. *Ganges*, then served on H.M.S. *Armadillo* in Scotland. The training in Scotland involved preparing for amphibious landings. He received further training in Corsica and then, serving with H.M.S. *Copra* (combined operations), was involved in storming the beaches on 17 June 1944 at the Golfo di Campo on the south coast of Elba. Coming under heavy fire, he and some other British attackers were killed. Initially he was buried in the village cemetery at **Marina di Campo**, but in 1947 he was reburied at the Bolsensa War Cemetery (IV H 7).

References: Bill McGrann, Operation Brassard: The Invasion of Elba, http://www.bbc.co.uk/history/ww2peopleswar/stories/85/a2943885.shtml; *The war dead of the British Commonwealth and Empire: the register of the names of those who fell in the 1939–1945 War and are buried in cemeteries in Italy Cemeteries 17–18: Bolsena War Cemetery, Orvieto War Cemetery*, Maidenhead: Imperial War Graves Commission, 1954, p. 27.

MacKENZIE, NORMAN IAN (1921–2013). The author of *The Escape from Elba: The Fall & Flight of Napoleon 1814–1815* (1982), he was born on 18

August 1921 in Deptford, London, the son of Kenneth MacKenzie, a draper and door-to-door salesman, and Helen L. (née Williamson). Educated on a scholarship at Haberdashers' Aske's School, he won a scholarship to the London School of Economics, studying under, and being influenced by Harold Laski. Graduating in 1943, he joined the Independent Labour Party, and was briefly a member of the Communist Party of Great Britain. He was trained in guerrilla warfare at Osterley Park, London, and was based in Sussex for a period, to organize resistance against the Germans should they invade Britain. Invalided out of the Royal Air Force with a stomach ulcer, he joined the staff of the magazine *New Statesman* in 1943, and remained with them for 19 years. He undertook some undercover work for the British government and stood in the general elections in 1951 and 1955 as a Bevanite Labour candidate. In 1957 he helped establish the Campaign for Nuclear Disarmament. He married Jeanne Sampson in 1945 and they collaborated on *The Time Traveller: The Life of H.G. Wells* (1973). He then worked on a number of other biographies including *Dickens: A Life* (1979) and was the editor of *The Diaries of Beatrice Webb* (1982–85).

With Anthony Brown, he wrote three novels set during the Napoleonic Wars under the pseudonym Anthony Forrest: *Captain Justice: Secret Agent against Napoleon* (1981), about the British prisoners held at Verdun, set in 1804; *The Pandora Secret* (1982) about the US inventor Robert Fulton being extricated from France, also in 1804; and *A Balance of Dangers* (1984) about the siege of Copenhagen in 1807. His book on Napoleon in Elba was the first in English for a long time that focused largely on the events in Elba itself, coming 18 years after Robert Christophe's *Napoleon on Elba* was published in English. David Chandler savagely reviewed it although much of his criticism was that MacKenzie was a polymath, and not for the

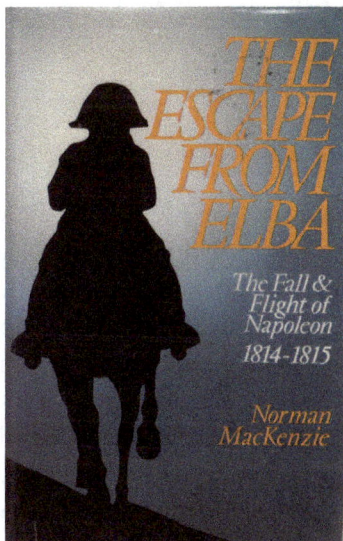

content of the book itself. Apart from that, the book was generally well-received and it brought together much detail that had not been made accessible in a single volume before. Norman MacKenzie's wife died four years later from cancer, and he married Gillian Ford, and retired from his position as professor of education at the University of Sussex, to live in Lewes where he remained active in the Open University which awarded him an honorary doctorate noting that he had 'the virtues of the 19th-century polymath and the visions fitted for the 21st century'. He died on 18 June 2013.

References: *The Writers Directory,* 13th edition, 1996–1998, p. 946; Hugh Purcell, 'Norman MacKenzie', *The Guardian* (24 June 2013); 'Norman MacKenzie', *The Daily Telegraph* (5 July 2013); Adrian Smith, 'Norman Mackenzie: editor, teacher, writer, spy?', *New Statesman* (28 June 2013); reviews of his books by Donald D. Horward, *Military Affairs*, Vol. 47, no. 3 (October 1983), pp. 156–57; and by David G. Chandler, *The International History Review* vol. 6, no 2 (May 1984), pp. 322–25.

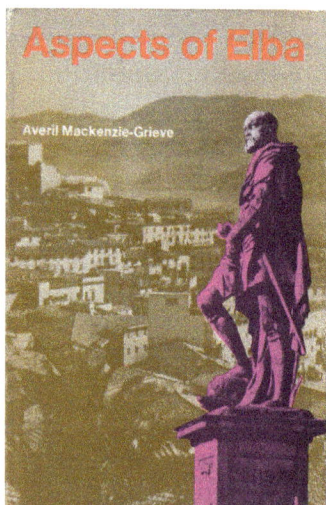

MACKENZIE-GRIEVE, AVERIL SALMOND (1903–1983). A British writer, she was born on 3 April 1903, the daughter of Robert James Mackenzie Grieve (1846–1919), a gentleman, and his wife Harriet (née Armstrong, 1863–1940). She was educated privately in England and then in Belgium and Italy, and later wrote a number of novels. In 1925 she married Cyril Drummond Le Gros Clark. Fluent in Chinese, at that time he was working on Chinese affairs in the kingdom of Sarawak, Borneo, and after some studies in China, was appointed to the Sarawak Council Negri, the body which advised the Sultan of Sarawak. On 2 May 1941 he was appointed chief secretary of Sarawak, and held that position until the Japanese invaded on 25 December of that year. He was then interned in the Batu Lintang prisoner of war camp near Kuching, and murdered by them in North Borneo (now Sarawak) on 6 July 1945.

On 6 July 1946 in Westminster, London, Averil Clark married Surgeon Commander John Joyce Keevil who was born in Argentina and then had moved to New Zealand. Averil contributed to *The Times*, *The Times Literary Supplement*, *The Sunday Times* and the British Broadcasting Corporation. She became interested in the Knights of Malta, writing about Malta and was made an officer of the Order of St. John.

When she started to research into the history of Elba, she found little serious scholarship in English about the island which prompted her to write her book *Aspects of Elba and the other islands of the Tuscan Archipelago* (1964). This involved archival research in Florence, Pisa, and, of course, Elba. Her husband died on 16 December 1957 in the Royal East Sussex Hospital, Hastings, UK, and she essentially completed the book in the following year, although she spent the next five years refining it. She retired to Sussex and died in 1983.

References: W. de B. P. Batty-Smith, *Sarawak: The Rajah's Officers 1841–1946*, Charnage, Wiltshire, UK: Nigel Batty-Smith, 1999, p. 71; Ho Ah Chon, *Kuching in Pictures 1841–1946*, Kuching: See Hua Daily News Bhd, nd, p. 113; Averil Mackenzie-Grieve, *Aspects of Elba and the other islands of the Tuscan Archipelago*, London: Jonathan Cape, 1964; Averil Mackenzie-Grieve, *Time and Chance: an autobiography*, London: Geoffrey Bles, 1970, p. 245f; 'Surgeon Commander J. J. Keevil', *The Times* (9 January 1958), p. 14; 'Napoleon's Island', *The Times* (23 January 1964), p. 15; *The International Authors and Writers Who's Who 1976*, p. 378; *The Writers Directory 1976–78*, p. 670; *The Writers Directory 1980–82*, p. 783.

MACNAMARA, JOHN (1785–1840). A visitor to Elba who met Napoleon in January 1815, John Macnamara was born on 29 June 1785, the second son of John Macnamara, of Baker Street, Portman Square, London. He was educated at Westminster School, and proceeded to Trinity College, Cambridge, matriculating in 1803, and graduating BA in 1807 and MA in 1810. Admitted to Lincoln's Inn on 17 June 1800, he was called to the Bar on 8 February 1808. Going to Elba, he interviewed **Napoleon** in January 1815. Returning to London, he died on 9 July 1840, in Half Moon Street, London.

References: *The Record of Old Westminsters* vol. 2, p. 611; *Alumni Cantabrigienses*; *Gentleman's Magazine 1840*, vol. 2, p. 217.

MADDEN, Sir GEORGE ALLAN (1771–1828). An army officer in the British and Portuguese services, he was born on 3 January 1771 in London, the eighth son and youngest child of James Madden of Cole Hill House, Fulham, Middlesex, and his wife Elizabeth. On 20 January 1771, he was baptised at St Martin-in-the-Fields, London, and after completing his schooling, worked briefly as a clerk in a merchant's office and just after his seventeenth birthday, gained a commission in the army. He then bought a commission as lieutenant in the 12th (Prince of Wales's Royal) light dragoons and served in Ireland. In

September 1793, just after being promoted to captain, the regiment was sent to Cork and there embarked for Ostend. They never got there and instead were ordered to head for Toulon which had been captured by the British and their allies. However just before they reached the port, they found that the British had left, taking with them many French royalists. The ships then made for Leghorn but were refused permission to disembark and as a result headed to Elba.

Landing at **Portoferraio**, Madden and the other cavalry officers rested their horses which had been on the ships for six months. The horses were able to be exercised but quickly the limited fodder available on Elba ran out, and the soldiers had to embark again and this time they headed for Civitavecchia in the Papal States, at the invitation of Pope Pius VI. They then embarked for Corsica and then to Spain where they were shipwrecked but the men and horses survived. They then went to Lisbon, Portugal, and from there embarked for Egypt where they fought at Alexandria. Soon afterwards, there was a regimental dispute which saw Madden court-martialled but the commander refused to confirm the proceedings and he was allowed to sell his commission and retire. He later fought a duel with one of the officers who had sided against him in the quarrel. Major Blunden fired at him and missed, whereupon Madden fired into the air and honour was maintained. Later Madden was sent to Portugal to help command a Portuguese cavalry brigade. He died on 8 December 1828 in Portsmouth, and was buried in the royal garrison church.

References: H. M. Chichester, 'Madden, Sir George Allan (1771–1828)', revised by Gordon L. Teffeteller, *Oxford Dictionary of National Biography*, Oxford University Press, 2004.

MARCIANA and **MARCIANA MARINA**. These are two settlements in the west of Elba. They were two quite distinct settlements with **Marciana** (or Marciana Alta – High Marciana') on **Monte Capanne**, and **Marciana Marina** on the coast around the old port which has beaches now very popular with tourists. The latter has grown considerably although many of the new houses have been built on the road between it and **Póggio**.

MARCIANA. This is a traditional medieval settlement close to the slopes of **Monte Capanne**, and it became a centre for the Appiani family. The town was dominated by a Pisan fortress but there is now only a shell of the fort as the whole town was sacked by the Turks in 1553. It is not open to the public but it is possible to climb up to it and look through the iron gates. The palace of the

Marciana Alta.

Appiani family (Casa degli Appiani), dates from the fifteenth century, and is located in the town but is also not open to the public. The local parish church is dedicated to St Catherine and contains the family chapel of the Appiani.

Napoleon Bonaparte visited Marciana on 21 August and stayed with **Cerbone Vadi** as he prepared for Countess Marie Walewska to visit Elba – with his (Napoleon's) mother coming to join him there four days later. When Marie Walewska arrived on 1 September, along with her brother and son, they were entertained there at the Sanctuary of the Madonna del Monte, and were initially to leave on 3 September but ended up having to go to Porto Longone (**Porto Azzurro**) from where they finally embarked.

Of most note in the town, other than the ambiance and the ability often to get away from the large tourist crowds at Marciana Marina, is the Antiquario Communale, an archaeology museum. It is open from 9 am – 1 pm, and from 4 – 7 pm, Mondays to Saturdays, from April through to September. It holds artefacts relating to prehistoric Elba, and also the Etruscan and Roman periods. **Christopher Serpell** and his wife Jean, writing in 1977 about the opening hours, complained that 'the museum custodian has in the past shown himself to be extremely casual about observing this timetable'. However that is long in the past.

Vernon Bartlett wrote of the place in 1965:

Marciana Alta, or Marciana Castello, in its proud and fantastic position over twelve hundred feet up the slope of a wooded mountain that rises steeply from the sea, claims to be the oldest community on Elba-it may have been colonized by the Greeks and it was certainly colonized by the Romans well before the birth of Christ. Its inhabitants are inclined to talk of those of Portoferraio with some disdain, and with some reason, since their town was the headquarters on Elba of the Appiani, the Princes of Piombino long before Cosimo de'Medici had begun to build the fortifications of Portoferraio. Marciana still has the old mint which produced the Appiani coinage some five centuries ago, and there is a narrow lane that leads to the Casa degli Appiani, above a charming little chapel, falling into ruins. The steps up to the house, however, were defended by so ferocious and uncomprehending a dog that I have no idea what the house looks like. I retreated, crab-wise, convinced that the animal would tear a hole in my trousers unless I managed to keep a stern eye on it.

In the middle of Marciana is a little piazza, with two or three stone benches and a stone table, sheltered by trees. It is possibly significant that the table top should consist of the fact of a disused marble sundial – time is no longer important to the old men who sit around it. But it is sad that an island with so little to remind one of its important past should treat that sundial so scurvily.

Marciana's past probably makes its present the more difficult to bear. As I have suggested elsewhere, with the disappearance of the danger of pirates, little hill towns such as. Rio and Mardana, which used to give protection to peasants and fishermen fleeing from the coastal plain, now find themselves treated at best with condescension and at worst with disdain by the descendants of those same peasants and fishermen, now living in security and relative prosperity. And this tendency is encouraged by the tourists who live in comfort in hotels by the sea, and who drive up the hill to enjoy the 'quaintness' of Marciana Alta, Póggio or Rio nell'Elba.

Marciana and Póggio are more than quaint; they are charming, and wonderfully sited in the midst of their chestnut forests. Especially in the former many of the streets are impassable for wheeled traffic, since they are wide, steep staircases; mules and donkeys replace other forms of transport. Póggio has a most attractive square with an immense view over the sea, and many of its ancient houses have been converted into flats by British and other non-Elban lovers of Elba. There is a road from Póggio to the summit of Monte Perone, from which, I had been assured I could get the best view of the central and eastern sections of the island. After hair-raising drives along some of the island's remoter roads, I arrived one afternoon with the intention of making the trip, but I took the precaution of •asking two young men at Póggio about the state of the road. It was quite possible, one told me, although I should have to drive with great care. 'Very carefully indeed', added the other. And the fact that two young Italians should advise caution so unnerved me that I abandoned the project. Luckily, on a subsequent visit, I plucked up a little more courage. Courage that was rewarded.

The road is rough, but not exceptionally narrow or alarming. Much less so, in fact, than many other roads on the island. And the view, especially in the late afternoon, is superb. Monte Perone is a preserve of the Forestry Division of the Ministry of Agriculture, and their vast plantings of pine trees layer the sides of the mountain in neat rows. From the summit, one looks down on the Gulf of Procchio on the north coast and the gulf of Campo on the south. In the distance are the honey-coloured houses of Portoferraio, and, beyond them, the hills above Porto Azzurro and the east coast. Beyond them, are the coastline of the mainland, and, very far away, the grey-blue outlines of the mountains. The island of Capraia lies on the northern horizon, and those of Pianos a, Monte Cristo and Giglio on the southern one. One looks down on an enormous relief map of central and eastern Elba and the surrounding seas.

Monte Perone is, in fact, only just over two thousand feet high. Monte Capanne exceeds this by well over a thousand feet, and near Marciana Alta there is a kind of telifirique that takes passengers to its summit. It has the dreadful name of cabinovia and its metal cages, each holding three or four standing passengers, look rather like the wire waste-paper baskets one finds in offices. The view eastwards from the summit is less spectacular than the view from Monte Perone since it is in part blocked by that mountain. But it is, after all, the highest point on Elba, and on a clear day Corsica looks magnificent (as, indeed, it should with its snow mountains and its blue sea around it).

Between Marciana and Póggio is the Fonte Napoleone, a spring of excellent mineral water which Napoleon liked to drink.

References: Vernon Bartlett, *A Book about Elba*, London: Chatto & Windus, 1965, pp. 137–38; Arsène Thiébaut de Berneaud, *A Voyage to the Isle of Elba*, London: Longman, Hurst, Rees, Orme and Brown, 1814, pp. 156–64; Roberto Donati, *The Island of Elba*, Terni: Fotorapidacolor, 1973, pp. 30–37; Guido Giubella, *Elba: A Garden in the Blu*, Milan: Co.Graf Editrice, 1988, pp. 46–47; Miles Roddis & Alex Leviton, *Tuscany & Umbria*, Footscray: Lonely Planet, 2006, p. 190; Christopher and Jean Serpell, *The Travellers' Guide to Elba and the Tuscan Archipelago*, London: Jonathan Cape, 1977, pp. 214–16.

MARCIANA MARINA. This was the port for **Marciana** and where during the fourteenth and fifteenth centuries the **Pisans** built a watch tower called the Torre Saracena which was to protect the nearby settlements from the Turks who raided the port in 1553, destroying much of it. It is now a sprawling settlement along the coast, and also straddling the road to **Póggio.**

There are three churches in Marciana Marina. San Lorenzo dates from the period of Pisan rule. The Sanctuary of San Cerbone is where **Saint Cerbone** sought refuge when on Elba. The third church was the Sanctuary of the Madonna del Monte which dates from the eleventh century. **Napoleon Bonaparte** worshipped there for two weeks, along with his Polish mistress Maria Walewska.

Vernon Bartlett wrote of this:

The road westwards from Enfola has not yet been completed-it goes as far as Viticcio, which has so magnificent a view across the Gulf of Procchio to Monte Capanne and the other western mountains that it will almost certainly become a favourite resort. One must come back again almost as far as Portoferraio to join the main road to the west. The strip of coast between La Biodola and Marciana Marina is the most sophisticated part of the island, with woods growing down to the rocks of charming little bays, each, unfortunately, already occupied by a smart hotel or an attractive private villa. It is locally known as the 'Gold Coast', since so much of it has been bought up by very rich people from Milan and other industrial cities of Northern Italy. The ordinary tourist reaches the sea only at La Biodola itself at Procchio and at Marciana Marina. The first-named has the advantage that its beach is not yet divided up into segments by rival bathing establishments, with huts, deck-chairs and coloured umbrellas (but with the handicap that nobody much seems to worry about the amount of rubbish left on the beach); Procchio has the advantage that it is also the junction for the road leading to Marina di Campo and the southwest shore of the island; Marciana Marina has the advantage that it is also a small port with a life of its own, independent of the tourist.

Perhaps that is one of the reasons for its popularity with the British, who form, I think, a larger proportion of the foreign visitors than anywhere else on the island. They are less contented than most tourists to lie and roast themselves in the sun, and at Marciana they can choose between sitting outside the cafes under the tamarisk trees, bathing in a pebbly but attractive bay with clear, deep water, and competing with the local boys fishing from the jetty. (In one form of fishing they are hopelessly out-classed. This consists of throwing in a piece of bait, which is at once surrounded by small fish. Multiple hooks attached to a very fine line are then thrown beyond the bait and, when they have sunk below it, they are manoeuvred in such a way that a fish may be harpooned when the line is sharply pulled in by the small boy at its other end.)

Emanuele Foresil remarked that Marciana Marina 'has become a favourite with the colony of bathers who arrive annually from every part, not only of Tuscany, but even from the remoter parts of Italy'. But he was writing in 1884; the last time I was there, I counted seven cars from Germany, four from Great Britain, two from Switzerland, one from France, one from Belgium and one from Austria parked along the sea-front. Nor were these cars at all out of place, for this is one of the most international places on the island; I have read somewhere that the inhabitants are mariners rather than fishermen, and one may come across them in merchant ships anywhere on the seven seas.

References: Vernon Bartlett, *A Book about Elba*, London: Chatto & Windus, 1965, pp. 137–38; Roberto Donati, *The Island of Elba*, Terni: Fotorapidacolor, 1973, pp. 22–29; Dan Facaros and Michael Pauls, *Italy: Tuscany*, London: Cadogan Books plc, 1996, p. 302; Guido Giubella, *Elba: A Garden in the Blu*, Milan: Co.Graf Editrice, 1988, pp. 45–46; Miles Roddis & Alex Leviton, *Tuscany & Umbria*, Footscray: Lonely Planet, 2006, p. 189, 190; Christopher and Jean Serpell, *The Travellers' Guide to Elba and the Tuscan Archipelago*, London: Jonathan Cape, 1977, pp. 216–17.

Marina di Campo
Photograph © Antoni Scarpi / fotolia.com.

MARINA DI CAMPO. The third port on the island of Elba (after **Portoferraio** and **Porto Azzurro**), this is on the south of the island and is a fishing town with the harbour protected by breakwaters. There is a tower dating back to Renaissance times but now nothing else older than 250 years old. **Napoleon** visited the town during his first tour of the island and stayed at a house owned by Thomas Degrosori on the night of 20 May where there is a plaque commemorating the connection.

During **World War II**, the Allies decided that this was the easiest place to land commandoes during Operation Brassard when they took the island from the Germans. There was no bombing prior to the landings as the Allies did not want to alert the enemy to the coming invasion. Commandos were landed at Marina di Campo but the Germans had anticipated the landing possibly a day or so earlier. The Germans were able to unleash withering fire as the British commandos tried to land. This caused the Allied commander to land the remainder of the commandos to the east of Marina di Campo and thus outflank the Germans. The Allied dead from the fighting were buried in a British war cemetery at Marina di Campo which was maintained by the Imperial War Graves Commission until 1947 when they were moved to

Bolsena War Cemetery on the Italian mainland.

The flat beaches which made a commando landing look so appealing to the British planners of Operation Brassard resulted in Marina di Campo in the 1950s being turned into the first tourist resort on the island. Many old houses were converted into hotels and hostels, with others built nearby to take advantage of the pleasant weather and appealing views. The **airport** was also constructed nearby.

References: Roberto Donati, *The Island of Elba*, Terni: Fotorapidacolor, 1973, pp. 39–49; Guido Giubella, *Elba: A Garden in the Blu*, Milan: Co.Graf Editrice, 1988, pp. 58–59; Christopher and Jean Serpell, *The Travellers' Guide to Elba and the Tuscan Archipelago*, London: Jonathan Cape, 1977, pp. 203–04.

MARIOTTI, CHEVALIER. A Corsican who had originally served under **Napoleon Bonaparte**, he was the French consul at Livorno during the time Napoleon was on Elba in 1814–15 and was involved in establishing – on behalf of Talleyrand and the French Royalists – a network of spies in Corsica and in southern France to get information on Bonapartists and on whether Napoleon might be planning to leave Elba. Mariotti was quickly able to report back to Talleyrand about many of the events on Elba.

References: Paul Dwyer, *Citizen Emperor: Napoleon in Power 1799–1815*, London: Bloomsbury, 2013; Norman MacKenzie, *The Escape from Elba: The Fall & Flight of Napoleon 1814–1815*, Oxford: Oxford University Press, 1982.

MAXWELL, (ARCHIBALD) MONTGOMERY (1784–1845). A colonel in the British forces, he was born on 21 June 1784 in Stoneykirk, Wigtownshire, Scotland, the son of Captain James Maxwell and his wife Elizabeth (d. 1794), and was baptised on the following day at Stoneykirk. In 1814, he travelled with some friends to Elba, describing his time there in his book, *My Adventures*:

September 21st – My gallant chief, Colonel L. [John Lemoine], with Mr. S – h [Smith] and Mr. Scott [John Barber Scott], took their departure early this morning for Leghorn, whilst Colonel D. [Douglas] and myself remained behind, intending to put ourselves on board a felucca soon, to sail for Civita Vecchia, and from thence proceed to Rome, and if possible to Naples. Colonel Campbell this morning informed us, that Marshal Bertrand would have called had he not thought we were all gone to Leghorn; and he now begged we would accept his carriage to visit St. Martin, where the emperor was preparing another chateau for himself. Colonel Campbell urged us to consent, in which case he volunteered to return and accept the offer. Neither of us seemed to like the proposition, but on talking the thing over, we expressed our thanks and assent. Colonel Campbell, before going, added, that his cousin Mr. Campbell, and Sir Gilbert Stirling, would be of the party.

Colonel D. and myself held ourselves in readiness for the excursion, at the risk of losing our passage in the felucca, which was only waiting a fair wind, and were lounging near our inn, when we espied Colonel Campbell, going to see his cousin and the baronet embark for Leghorn, having entirely forgotten his promise of seeing Count Bertrand. We could ill digest this strange forgetfulness on the part of the Scotch colonel, and returned to our hotel somewhat out of humour, which was not long indulged in; for who should almost immediately afterwards appear but Field Marshal Count Bertrand, in full fig, with all his stars and orders. After sitting a short time, and chatting most agreeably about the events of the preceding evening, &c., he asked us to take an airing with him, and politely promised to send a servant to inform us when the carriage was ready, which he did a short time afterwards, and it took us to St. Martin's, which is about three miles from Porto Ferrajo, and to which Napoleon has made a tolerable carriage road.

St. Martin's is prettily and romantically situated, in an amphitheatre of hills, itself commanding a fine view of the capital and port. It was originally a very small house, but by adding to its breadth it has been made more than double its original size, and the improvements and alterations are still going on. Napoleon's bedroom is finished, and famished in the most simple way, with a small camp-bed in one comer of it. There is an inner room that is to have a bath in it, and an outer one in which his faithful Mameluke is to sleep. One large room close to these they were painting in the Turkish style, with a jet-d'eau in its centre, to remind him of Egypt, which the count informed us his majesty constantly talked of with infinite pleasure. The grounds are also tastefully laid out, and numerous pretty alleys amidst the trees have been formed.

Count Bertrand also took us to view the sites his master has fixed on, to erect a house for his mother, and another for the Princess Pauline, as well as one for the grand marshal himself.

At a little distance there is a farm-house where Napoleon had collected a great variety of poultry, sheep, cows, and deer, as, our cicerone informed us, he intended to turn farmer. He added, that Napoleon had become quite 'knowing' as a breeder. He is expected to be here in about a week, to ruralize for a time. A very nice walk has been made by his order, to one of the hills in rear of the house, from whence (as he himself says) be can survey the whole of his dominions, and which he likes better than the immense extent of country he previously possessed.

The count brought with him his son, a fine boy, christened Napoleon. The young Napoleon made himself very agreeable, and delighted his father much by addressing us in English. The count has a fine mild expressive countenance, and a forehead bald, but full of intelligence. He pressed us to dinner, but added, that he regretted madame could not appear at table, being indisposed. We also thought it necessary to make an excuse, and his apology, on account of the countess's state of health, led to ours.

Porto Ferrajo, Sept. 22d.

The wind foul. Napoleon's capital very stupid, and Monsieur Boland's auberge very dear, by reason of the difficulty at getting over provisions from the continent; the consumption having so much increased since the arrival of Napoleon, his court, and army; and moreover, Monsieur Holand has it all his own way, being almost the only aubergiste, there having been no hotels in this retired corner of the world until lately.

To kill ennui, and make time pass – for of all annoying things, waiting for a fair wind on shore is the most disagreeable – not wishing to be on board too soon, and ever fearing to be too late, we visited the stables of Napoleon, where we whiled away an hour or two. He has about one hundred and twenty quadrupeds, and several carriages. Some of his white Arabs were very handsome, and a favourite one he had brought from Egypt with him was pointed out to us. Every horse had his name placed above the manger, and several of them were named after his great battles, such as Marengo, Austerlitz, &c. A very fine charger was pointed out to us, which carried his master during his last fatal campaign in France; he was jet black, and called Borrodino.

In the evening, as we were sitting sipping our flask of Florence wine, in rushed Peter Linnet, with flushed face, and big with importance, to in- form us, that one of Napoleon's servants wished to see us; but when the ambassador presented himself, it was with the Count and Countess Bertrand's compliments, to beg we would wave ceremony, and come and drink tea with them. We returned a polite answer, and retired to make our toilet; but before we had done so, the padrone of the felucca arrived to say, that the night was fine and the wind fair, and begged for signori to come on board immediately. We therefore called at the marshal's en passant, and left our P. P. C.'s, with our regrets at being obliged to start.

The evening was calm, the sea like a pond, without a ripple on its bosom, until its smooth surface was broken by the padrone of the Genoese felucca ordering his crew to use their sweeps; when instantly, at every stroke, all around seemed to effervesce and sparkle like liquid fire. The Mediterranean sea can be compared to no- thing but an ocean of fire-flies.

When we had pulled out to mid-channel, a breeze sprung up, but alas! it was right in our teeth, and our prudent padrone took us into Piombino for the night, where we were doomed to remain the whole of next day.

At **Piombino** he noted:

Amongst these visits, we had a long one from a knight of Malta, who thought himself vastly clever and sagacious, when he significantly whispered to us, 'that he perfectly knew the object of our journey to Elba; and that it was for the purpose of arranging plans with Napoleon, for England to place him in such situation as to menace France and Austria, and to hold him up as a rod to chastise them, should needs be.' We did not inquire of this garrulous old gentleman how this was to be accomplished.

Montgomery Maxwell returned to Britain and he married Mary Atlee on 13 October 1823 at All Saints, Wandsworth, London. He died on 21 May 1845 at Newcastle upon Tyne.

References: John Alger, *Napoleon's British visitors and captives, 1801–1815*, New York: J. Pott, 1904, p. 296; Allibone's *Critical Dictionary of English Literature: British and American authors living and deceased from the earliest accounts to the latter half of the Nineteenth Century*, Philadelphia: J.B. Lippincott, 1858–71; Maxwell Montgomery, *My Adventures*, London: H. Colburn, 1845, vol. 1, pp. 189–94.

MAYOL, JACQUES (1927–2001). A famous French diver, he was born on 1 April 1927 to a French family living in Shanghai. His father was killed in a diving accident when Jacques was young, but it did not stop him becoming keen on diving, championing free diving. Fascinated by dolphins, he made friends with one female dolphin known as 'Clown', and this led to a book on whether or not man has an aquatic origin. In around 1971 he moved to live on Elba. Mayol was the first person to get below 100 metres without a supply of oxygen or compressed air. He reached 101 metres in 1981, and 105 metres in 1983. Suffering from depression, he committed suicide by hanging himself on 23 December 2001 at his home at Calone on the island of Elba, aged 74. His body was cremated and his ashes were spread over the coast of Tuscany.

References: Jacques Mayol, *Homo Delphinus – The dolphin within man*, Reddick, Florida: Idelson-Gnocchi, 1999; Pierre Mayol and Patrick Mouton, *Jacques Mayol l'homme dauphin,* Paris: Arthaud, 2003; 'Jacques Mayol', *The Times* (26 December 2001), p. 17.

MAZZARI, RENZO (1956–   ). An Italian diver, he was born on 2 October 1956 in Portoferraio and quickly became one of the most well-known freedivers after Jacques Mayol, and known for his spearfishing. Renzo Mazzari took part in many championships around Europe wining the Euro-African championship at Marsala in 1988 for both individual and team competitions, and then the same at the 1989 World Champiuonships held at San Teodoro, Sardinia. He won the European Cup for spearfishing in 2002 at Limnos, Greece, and won the same competition at Kasos (Greece) in 2003, and then at Astypalea (Greece) in 2006. Afterwards he was forced to retire owing to ill-health.

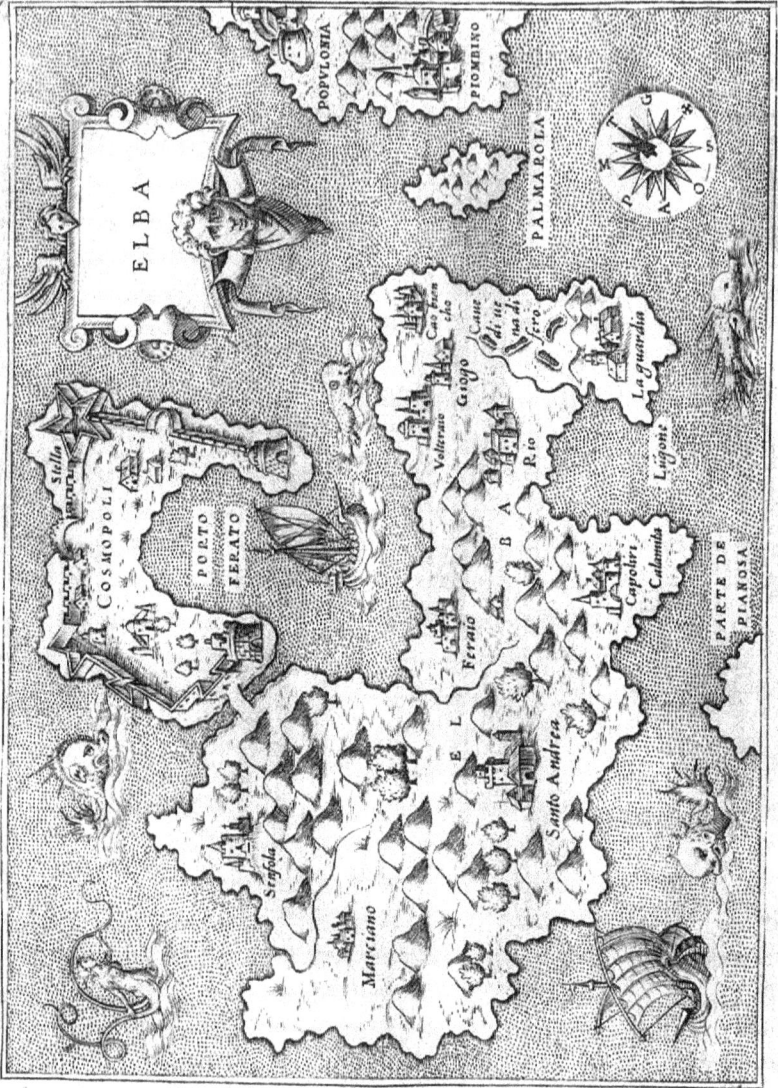

Elba in 1576.

MEDICI, COSIMO DE' (1519–1574). The second duke of Florence, and the first grand duke of Tuscany, he occupied Elba and was responsible for the construction of the town of Portoferraio. He was born on 12 June 1519 in Florence, the son of the famous soldier Giovanni dalle Bande Nere from Forlì, and Maria Salviati. He was virtually unknown in Florence when Alessandro de' Medici, the first duke of Florence, was assassinated in 1537. Alessandro's only son was illegitimate, and therefore the Medici turned to Cosimo, aged only 17, and who was from a distant branch of the family – Cosimo's maternal grandmother Lucrezia being the daughter of Lorenzo the Magnificent, himself the grandson of the original Cosimo de Medici (1389–1464). Cosimo was recognized as the head of the Florentine state by Charles V, the Holy Roman Emperor in June 1537, and then sought to expand the power of Florence.

In 1548 Cosimo de 'Medici established a major base on the island of Elba. He was eager to take advantage of a convenient source of iron, and built much of the town of **Portoferraio**, fortifying it against possible attack by the Turks. Cosimo de 'Medici had great plans for the development of Elba, taking personal charge of many of the projects. With Elba safely controlled by Florence, he launched an attack on Siena. Annexing more territory, in 1569 he was elevated to the grand duke of Tuscany by Pope Pius V. In keeping with the tradition of the Medicis, he was a patron of arts and completed the construction of the Pitti Palace. As a military leader, he enlarged the Florentine navy which took part in the battle of Lepanto in 1571 which saw the Turks defeated off the coast of Greece.

References: Eric Cochrane, *Florence in the Forgotten Centuries*, Chicago: The University of Chicago Press, 1974; Averil Mackenzie-Grieve, *Aspects of Elba and the other islands of the Tuscan Archipelago*, London: Jonathan Cape, 1964, pp. 29f, 65f; Konrad Eisenbichler (ed), *The Cultural Politics of Grand Duke Cosimo I de' Medici*, Cambridge: Cambridge University Press, 2001; Andrea M. Gáldy, *Cosimo I de'Medici as collector: antiquities and archaeology in sixteenth-century Florence*, Newcastle: Cambridge Scholars Publishing,

2009; Christopher Hibbert, *The Rise and Fall of the House of Medici*, London: Allen Lane, 1974; Paul Strathern, *The Medici: Godfathers of the Renaissance*, London: Vintage, 2007.

MEESON, ALFRED CHAPMAN (1913–1944). A British naval officer, he was born on 18 January 1913, the son of Frederick Richard Meeson and his wife Lilian (née Lang). Educated at Dulwich College, he joined the Eastern Bank and completed his BSc from the University of London. After taking a short commission in the Royal Air Force, he worked for Shell-Mex Co and then joined the Fleet Air Arm when war looked likely. He was serving in the Orkney Islands when he was recommended for a commission and served on H.M.S. *King Alfred*, being gazetted as sub-lieutenant in the Royal Naval Volunteer Reserve. Serving in the Mediterranean, he was one of the first Allied officers to land on Sicily during the Allied attack on the island. He was on a plane piloted by **Geoffrey Cooper**, and with **George William Blackwell** and **Hugh Hilton Hutchinson** on board, flying from Bastia, Corsica, when it crashed on 19 November 1944 and all four were killed. They were buried in the Allied Military Cemetery at Elba, and then reburied in 1947 at the Bolsena War Cemetery (IV H 1).

References: *Dulwich College Register 1619–1926*, p. 606; *Dulwich College Roll of Honour 1939–1945*, p. 113; *The war dead of the British Commonwealth and Empire: the register of the names of those who fell in the 1939–1945 War and are buried in cemeteries in Italy Cemeteries 17–18: Bolsena War Cemetery, Orvieto War Cemetery*, Maidenhead: Imperial War Graves Commission, 1954, p. 27.

MINERAOLOGICAL MUSEUM (Museo Archeologico del Distretto Minerario). *See* **Rio Marina**.

MISRAIR 738 CRASH (1960). An Egyptian Misrair Vickers Viscount crashed some 27½ kilometres north of Elba on 29 September 1960 with all 17 passengers and four crew killed. The flight was from Geneva to Cairo, and the plane was flying from Geneva to the first stopover at Rome. With a strong storm, after the plane crashed, the minesweepers *Pino*, *Baionetta* and *Edera* were sent to the area to search for wreckage.

Photograph © Kletr / Fotolia.com

MOBY LINES. This company, officially Moby Lines S.p.A. was established in 1959 as Navigazione Arcipelago Maddalenino (known at that time as Navarma). Its founder was Achille Onorato and it initially operated the M/S *Maria Maddalena* purchased from Denmark on the route from Sardinia to various islands off the Sardinian coast. This was successful and with the M/S *Bonaficio* from February 1966 it operated a second ferry service between Corsica and Sardinia. Gradually expanding, its ferry, the *Moby Prince*, collided with an oil tanker in the harbour at Livorno on 10 April 1991, with the loss of 140 people, with only one survivor, the ship's boy Alessio Bertrand. Run by Vincenzo Onorato, it now operates ferries between the Italian mainland, and also from the French mainland, to Elba, Corsica and Sardinia.

Ship	Built	Entered Service	Gross Tonnage	Length	Width	Pass-engers	Cars	Max. speed (knots)	Route
MS Bastia	1974	1974	1.936	75 m	13 m	400	100	18	Santa Teresa di Gallura – Bonifacio
MS Giraglia	1981	1981	2.041	75 m	13 m	400	100	18	Piombino – Cavo (Elba Island)
MS Moby Aki	2005	2005	36.284	175 m	27 m	2.200	750	29	Livorno – Olbia; Piombino – Olbia
MS Moby Ale	1969	1990	3.937	93 m	16 m	800	160	19,5	Piombino – Portoferraio
MS Moby Baby	1966	1996	4.016	101 m	18 m	1.100	100	19	Piombino – Portoferraio
MS Moby Corse	1978	2010	19.321	152 m	25 m	1.200	450	21	Genoa – Bastia
MS Moby Drea	1975	2003	22.528	185 m	27 m	1.900	500	27	Livorno – Olbia; Olbia – Genoa
MS Moby Fantasy	1976	1992	13.284	142 m	22 m	1.200	400	17	disarmed
MS Moby Lally	1974	2000	8.570	119 m	19 m	1.150	300	17.5	Piombino – Portoferraio
MS Moby Love	1975	1998	4.649	115 m	19 m	1.200	250	21	Piombino – Portoferraio
MS Moby Otta	1976	2006	22.528	185 m	27 m	1.900	500	27	Genoa – Olbia
MS Moby Tommy	2002	2007	28.915	212 m	25 m	2.200	1.000	30	Civitavecchia – Olbia
MS Moby Vincent	1974	1990	12.108	120 m	22 m	1.600	570	17.5	Livorno – Bastia
MS Moby Wonder	2001	2001	36.093	175 m	27 m	2.200	750	29	Livorno – Olbia

References: Moby, http://www.moby.it/; Miles Roddis & Alex Leviton, *Tuscany & Umbria*, Footscray: Lonely Planet, 2006, p. 186; Christopher and Jean Serpell, *The Travellers' Guide to Elba and the Tuscan Archipelago*, London: Jonathan Cape, 1977, p. 35.

MOLO MEDICEO (Medici Pier). This pier was constructed into the harbour at **Portoferraio** and was a part of the city built on the orders of Duke **Cosimo de 'Medici**. Traditionally it was the place where passengers disembarked to visit Portoferraio, although most now come through a new port to the west. From the Moleo Mediceo, there was only one entrance into the city, the **Porta a Mare**, which was heavily guarded to protect the town from attack by North African Corsairs, or indeed other attackers. On 5 May 1814 **Napoleon Bonaparte** landed on the Molo Mediceo and headed along it into Portoferraio.

MONTANARI, MARCELLO (1965–). An Italian **football**er and later football manager, he was born on 25 September 1965 in Portoferraio and played for Reggiana, 1983–84; Livorno, 1984–85; Venezia, 1985–87; Carrese, 1987–89; Lucchese, 1989–91; Inter, 1991–92; Bari, 1992–97; Lucchese, 1997–2001; and then Massese, 2001–03. He was then the manager of Reggiana, 2008–11 and from 2014.

MONTE CAPANNE. This is the highest peak in Elba, it is 3,308 feet (1,008 metres) high and from it, it is possible to see much of Elba, and to the west on a clear day one can also see Corsica. There is now a cable lift to take people close to the summit in open barred cabins.

MONTECRISTO. This island in the **Tuscan Archipelago** is located south of Elba, and is administered from **Portoferraio**. Known in ancient Greek as Oglasa (Ωγλάσσα) on account of the yellow colour of the rocks, the Etruscans used the island as a source of oak needed to stoke the fires at the iron mines on Elba. An Etruscan/early Roman altar dedicated to Jupiter was found on the island, and the Romans also operated a quarry for granite used to build some villas on Elba, and on **Giglio**.

Some Christian hermits settled on the island in the fifth century. According to local legends, the island was at this time called Montegiove ('Jove's Mountain') and inhabited by a dragon. However Mamilian (later **St. Mamilian**), the former bishop of Palermo, arrived on the island in the 450s, killed the dragon, and changed its name to Montecristo ('Christ's Mountain'). During the early seventh century Christians living on the island submitted to the monastic rule of the Benedictines and built a monastery dedicated to the memory of St. Mamilian.

Montecristo in 2008.   Wikipedia Commons.

The wealth of the abbey soon became well-known locally, and the island was part of the Republic of **Pisa**, and then administered by the Principality of **Piombino**. In 1553 the Ottoman raider **Dragut** attacked the monastery, looted it, and took the monks away as slaves. It gradually, along with some of Elba, became a part of the Stato dei Presidi ('The State of Garrisons') which was a dependency of the kingdom of Spain.

In 1802, when the Treaty of Amiens made Elba a part of France, Montecristo also became French. It was later administered by **Napoleon** from Elba, and in 1815 became part of the Grand Duchy of Tuscany. An Italian geologist Giuseppe Giuli explored the island in 1833. In October 1839 Charles Cambiagi tried to establish a colony on the island, and then Augustin Eulhardt and Joseph Keim, two German hermits, arrived there. However they all left and in 1843 an Austrian, Adolph Franz Obermüller, arrived. Some months later Charles Legrand and his girlfriend also tried to settle there, living in the old monastery. They were followed soon afterwards, in April 1844, by George Guiboud, a French agriculturalist; and some Genoese came in 1846.

The island is now famous owing to **Alexandre Dumas** and his *Le Comte de Monte-Cristo* (1844; *The Count of Monte Cristo*): 'This island was, always had been, and still is completely deserted. It is a rock of almost conical form, which looks as though it had been thrust up by volcanic force from the depth to the surface of the ocean'. Dumas visited Elba with Jérôme Bonaparte and had the idea of using the island as the location of massive treasure which the ficitional Edmond Dantès finds and uses to take revenge on the people who persecuted him and caused the death of his father. From 1849 to 1852 Jacques Abrial, a Frenchman resident in Livorno, ran a farm there.

Then, in 1852, an English adventurer, **George Watson-Taylor**, bought the island for 50,000 lire and styled himself the Count of Monte Cristo. He built the Royal Villa, planted eucalyptus trees and the Asiatic tree of heaven (*Ailanthus altissima*) which is now common all over the island. The cartographer Giovacchino Callai and the writer Vincenzo Mellini came to the island at this time. However Watson-Taylor went bankrupt and was forced to leave. In 1860 some Italian exiles were shipwrecked on the island; and on 3 June 1869 the Italian government formally purchased it from Watson-Taylor for the sum of 100,000 lire (£4,000 at the time).

In 1878, after several attempts to colonise the island, the Italian government established a penal colony there. Marquess Carlo Ginori moved there in 1889 and established his hunting ground near the villa which he restored. Then in 1896 Prince Victor Emmanuel of Savoy (later King Victor Emmanuel III) and his wife Elena of Montenegro honeymooned there and from 1899 the island was a royal hunting ground. An Italian army garrison was posted there in **World War II**, and finally in 1971 the island was turned into a nature reserve.

One of the major ecological problems with the island is the large numbers of trees of heaven which are gradually being cut down. With the penal colony closed, and the area in 1979 turned into a marine biological reserve, there have also been attempts to reduce the population of black rats. There are still many goats (*Capra hicus*), the only truly wild goats in Italy, and thousands of migratory birds still use the island. In 1988 the **Tuscan Archipelago** National Park which includes Montecristo was awarded the European Diploma of Protected Areas. Visits to Montecristo have to be part of an organised tour with the authority of the Ufficio Forestale in Follónica on the Italian mainland.

References: Vernon Bartlett, *A Book about Elba*, London: Chatto & Windus, 1965, pp. 148–49; Marco Lambertini, Arcipelago Toscano e il Parco Nazionale, Pisa: Pacini Editore, 2002; Averil Mackenzie-Grieve, *Aspects of Elba and the other islands of the Tuscan Archipelago*, London: Jonathan Cape, 1964, pp. 204–12; Richard Owen, 'Monte Cristo's treasure island unlocks the door to tourism', *The Times* (24 March 2008), p. 35; Miles Roddis & Alex Leviton, *Tuscany & Umbria*, Footscray: Lonely Planet, 2006, pp. 192–93; Peter Popham, 'Race for the riches of Montecristo', The Independent (21 August 2010); Nick Squires, 'Island of Montecristo to be bombed with poison after rat infestation', The Daily Telegraph (15 January 2012); Nick Squires, 'Plan to 'bomb' Montecristo with rat pellets may be blocked'. The Daily Telegraph (31 January 2012).

MONTE CRISTO, BATTLE OF. *See* **Elba, Battle of**.

MURRAY, WILLIAM JOHN (1922–1944). An able seaman, he was the son of William and Margaret Jane Murray. He served in the British Royal Navy and was assigned to H.M.S. *Copra* (combined operations) and was killed on the first day of the Allied attack on Elba on 17 June 1944, aged 22. He was buried on Elba and three years later was reburied in the Bolsena War Cemetery (IV G 22) on the Italian mainland.

References: *The war dead of the British Commonwealth and Empire: the register of the names of those who fell in the 1939–1945 War and are buried in cemeteries in Italy Cemeteries 17–18: Bolsena War Cemetery, Orvieto War Cemetery*, Maidenhead: Imperial War Graves Commission, 1954, p. 28.

MURZI, MANRICO (1930–   ). A journalist and poet, he was born at **Marciana Marina** and went to university in Rome to study law. He then decided to change his career path to study literature and philosophy with his thesis, *La Paura nella Letteratura Contemporanea* (Fear in Contemporary Literature). He married Ivy Pelish, a ceramics artist from New York, and they had theee daughters: Simonetta, Lauranna and Giuliana. After teaching, Muzi travelled around the Mediterranean and composed a number of highly-acclaimed poems.

MUSEO ARCHEOLOGICO DEL DISTRETTO MINERARIO. *See* **Rio Marina**.

MUSEO CIVICO ARCHEOLOGICO. Located at Via del Pretorio 66, **Marciana**, this museum was established in 1968, making it the oldest archaeological museum on the island of Elba. It is located at the foot of the medieval fortress in Marciana and has a large number of remains dating back to the Middle and Upper Paleolithic Eras, as well as from classical times. It holds many items recovered from Etruscan ships wrecked off the island, as well as later finds from Roman ships. These include amphorae from the wreck at Chiessi from the late second century AD. The museum is open from 9 am to 1 pm, and 2 pm to 7.30 pm on weekdays, and from 8 am to 1 pm on holidays. It is closed on Thursdays and also during the winter. There is a small admission fee.

MUSEO CIVICO ARCHEOLOGICO. This is in **Portoferraio** and it has an interesting collection of items relating to ancient and early medieval Elba. The museum is open from 9.30 am until 2.30 pm, and then from 6 pm until midnight from mid-June to mid-September; from 9 am to 8.30 pm from mid-September until October, and then from 10 am to 1 pm, and 3.30 to 7.30 pm from April until mid-June. There is a small admission fee.

MYNGS, Sir CHRISTOPHER (1625–1666). A British naval officer, he was baptised on 22 November 1625 at Salthouse, Norfolk, England, the son of John Myngs and Katherine Parr, daughter of Christopher Parr. Both parents of Christopher Myngs were from landowning families, although Christopher made much of the fact that his father was a shoemaker, which he was – downplaying the family connections because of his own political radicalism. He joined the British Navy and in 1651 was a supernumerary officer on the *Paragon* under **Richard Badiley**. With the outbreak of the First Anglo-Dutch War, he was second in command of the *Elizabeth* in the Battle of Elba. The *Elizabeth* was attacked by ten Dutch ships but suffered little loss, although when returning to England, the captain was killed and Myngs took over command of the ship. In 1656 he sailed for Jamaica with Oliver Cromwell keen on ensuring that the island was safe from attack. He later brought 1,400 new settlers to the island of Nevis; and in 1662 helped to capture Santiago, Cuba, and was also involved in many other actions in the West Indies. He was badly wounded fighting the Dutch on 4 June 1666, and died in London six days later. He was buried at St Mary's, Whitechapel, with his funeral being attended by Samuel Pepys and Sir William Coventry.

References: F. E. Dyer, 'Captain Christopher Myngs in the West Indies', *Mariner's Mirror* vol. 18 (1932), pp. 168–87; C. H. Firth, 'The capture of Santiago, in Cuba, by Captain Myngs, 1662', *English Historical Review* vol. 14 (1899), pp, 536–40; C. S. Knighton, 'Myngs, Sir Christopher (bap. 1625, d. 1666)', *Oxford Dictionary of National Biography*, Oxford University Press, 2004; Robert Latham (ed), *Samuel Pepys and the Second Dutch War: Pepys's navy white book and Brooke House papers*, Navy Record Society No 133 (1995).

- N -

NAPOLEON I (1769–1821). The Emperor of the French from 18 May 1804 until his abdication on 11 April 1814, and then from 20 March until 22 June 1815, he lived on the island of Elba continuously from 4 May 1814 until his departure on 26 March 1815. Born on 15 August 1789 at Ajaccio, on the island of Corsica, he was the fourth child and third son of Carlo Maria di Buonaparte, an attorney, and his wife Maria Letizia (née Ramolino).

From a moderately affluent family, Napoleon went to mainland France to study at the École Militaire and trained as an artillery officer. He was the first Corsican to graduate from the École Militaire, and in 1785 was commissioned second lieutenant in the military. He was an ardent Corsican nationalist and spent the early period of the French Revolution in Corsica where the Corsican nationalists, the revolutionaries and the Royalists were fighting each other. He came to support the Jacobins and was promoted to lieutenant colonel in the Corsican militia. His first major military engagement was at Toulon which was being held by French Royalists and the British. As an audacious artilleryman, he came up with a plan to attack the city leading to its capture as the British evacuated the French Royalists to the island of Elba.

Napoleon was then given command of the artillery of the Army of Italy, as the French forces were advancing into Italy. However with the fall of Maximilian Robespierre and the Thermidorian Reaction in July 1794, Napoleon was placed under house arrest. He was released two weeks later and was once again placed in charge of the artillery – on this occasion in Paris. In 1797, in command of the Army of Italy, he led the invasion of Lombardy and defeated the Austrians. Fighting 18 major battles, Napoleon became a hero in France. He then led a large French force to Egypt but the French navy was destroyed at the Battle of Aboukir Bay on 1–3 August 1798. Nevertheless Napoleon was able to return to France where he staged his coup d'état on 18 Brumaire (9 November 1799) making himself First Consul of France. This was followed by another major foray into Italy and the French forces attacked Elba which they had held briefly for four months in 1799. However in this assault on Elba, the French forces were involved in a protracted siege of **Portoferraio**. With the signing of the Treaty of Amiens, Napoleon established peace with Britain and as a part of the terms of the treaty, Elba was ceded to the French and became a part of France, sending a representative to the French

David's famous painting of Napoleon, a copy of which is at the Villa dei Mulini.

legislature.

The peace did not last long with Britain declaring war on France in May 1803. On 2 December 1804 Napoleon crowned himself Emperor in Notre Dame Cathedral. He was crowned King of Italy on 26 May 1805 in Milan Cathedral. War continued in Europe with Napoleon abandoning his plans for a military invasion of Britain and decided to embark on an economic war by banning British goods from being sold in Europe. This was known as the

Continental System and was forced on all European states. When Portugal refused, Napoleon sent his army through Spain to invade Portugal which led to the Peninsular War where the British, Portuguese and some Spanish Royalists waged a bitter war sapping the strength of Napoleon's forces. When Austria broke its alliance with France in 1809, Napoleon attacked them, then prepared for an attack on the Russian army.

When Napoleon invaded Russia, the Russians withdrew drawing Napoleon and his army further and further into Russia. He defeated the Russians at the battle of Borodino and captured Moscow but was forced to withdraw, losing a large number of soldiers in the retreat. In 1813 France faced attack by the Prussians, Austrians, Russians, British, Spanish, Portuguese and Swedes. In the battle of Leipzig, 16–19 October 1813, Napoleon lost more than 90,000 killed or wounded and his depleted forces retreated into France which was then invaded.

Napoleon started negotiating with his adversaries but was never seriously interested in reaching a peace agreement with them. He sought to divide them causing them to distrust each other while he manoeuvred his armies backwards and forwards launching the Six Days' Campaign, 10–14 February 1814. This blunted the attacks on France by the Coalition, and on 4 April 1814, Marshal Ney and other French marshals confronted Napoleon at Fontainebleau and demanded that Napoleon accept the inevitable and abdicate. He had prevaricated but on that day he finally abdicated in favour of his son, with Queen Marie-Louise as regent. Tsar Alexander I of Russia felt this still allowed Napoleon to return as emperor or regent in some form, and on 6 April Napoleon signed an unconditional abdication, saying farewell to his troops at Fontainebleau and headed into exile on Elba.

Napoleon had been promised that he could retain his title as emperor and was given sovereignty over Elba, but had to endure a difficult journey from Fontainebleau to the French coast coming upon unexpected groups of French Royalists on the way. Eventually he arrived at the port of Fréjus, and from there boarded the *Undaunted* for

Napoleon at Avignon.

Napoleon arriving at Portoferraio.

Elba. The island authorities had scarcely any notice of his arrival. However they rallied the local populace. Imbert de Saint-Amand in his biography of Marie Louise notes:

By noon the troops were under arms, and the authorities assembled at the wharf. The Emperor's landing at three o'clock was announced by a salute of twenty-one guns from the English frigate and as many from the guns of the fortress. Napoleon was at once harangued by the authorities of the island, and he responded very nearly in these words: – The mildness of your climate, and the romantic scenery of your island, have decided me to choose it, among all my vast domains, for the place of my abode. I hope that you will know how to appreciate this preference, and that you will love me like submissive children; you will then find me always disposed to have for you the solicitude of a father.

As soon as Napoleon had finished this little speech, three violinists and two violoncellists who accompanied the Elban officials began to play; the Emperor placed himself under a canopy, and was conducted in procession to the church, where the Te Deum was intoned. Strange irony of fate – the fallen sovereign of an immense empire causing the Te Deum to be chanted because he has lost all his dominions except the Island of Elba!

The ceremony ended, Napoleon went to the town hall, where he was to lodge. The hall which was ordinarily used for public balls had been ornamented with a few little pictures and some chandeliers. In the middle of it a throne had been hastily erected, and decorated with gilded paper and fragments of scarlet cloth. Many of the crowd that followed the sovereign were allowed to enter. He urged the mayors to maintain order in their communes, and the pastors to preach concord among their flocks. Then the new colors were hoisted, as we learn from the subjoined official report:

British cartoons showing Napoleon in Elba.

'To-day, May 4, 1814, His Majesty the Emperor Napoleon, having taken possession of the Island of Elba, General Drouot, governor of the island in the name of the Emperor, raised the new flag above the forts; a white ground crossed diagonally with a red band sown with three bees upon a ground of gold. This standard was saluted by the batteries of the coast forts, the English frigate *Undaunted* and the French men-of-war which were in the harbor. In witness whereof, we, commissioners of the Allied Powers, together with General Drouot and General Dalesme, have signed this report.'

The next morning Napoleon went out on foot at five o'clock to visit all the public institutions. He did not come in until nine o'clock, having overwhelmed with questions every one he met. He commanded various alterations. He would have liked to transform the barracks of Saint Francis at once into a palace wherein he might take up his residence. On May 6, he started very early to go and see the mines at Rio. He examined everything with scrupulous attention, and gave great praise to the director of the mines. He was occupying himself as diligently with an island twenty leagues in circumference and containing twelve thousand inhabitants, as he had done with the gigantic empire which extended from Rome to Dantzig. The same day, with a view to gaining the affections of the Elbans, he contributed sixty thousand francs toward the construction of roads long contemplated, but never begun for want of funds. He possessed this sum in uncoined gold, and he had it minted, in order that his generosity might produce a greater effect when his servants carried it in sacks across the town. Nobody talked of anything but his immense treasures and the prodigies he was going to perform. The people were enthusiastic for their new sovereign: he inflamed their southern imaginations.

On his second day on Elba, Napoleon starting looking for a more appropriate residence and decided on the **Villa dei Mulini** with conversions started on the property whilst the ex-emperor travelled around the island. It was during this time that Napoleon, on Monte Orello, said to **Neil Campbell**, 'Well, it certainly is a very small island.' After reading **Arsène Thiébaut de Berneaud**'s book, Napoleon recognised the importance of the iron mines and headed there on 6 May. Finally on 21 May the Villa dei Mulini was ready for him to move in and five days later the six hundred men from his Imperial Guard arrived on Elba and were quartered in the forts at Portoferraio and also in the monastery of San Francesco.

Napoleon had hoped that some of his close family might come to Elba and his sister **Pauline Bonaparte** arrived at Portoferraio on 2 June. She had met with Napoleon on his journey from Fontainebleau to Fréjus and had then gone to Naples to talk to her brother-in-law Joachim Murat, the king of Naples. Pauline was only on Elba for a day – leaving jewellery which allowed her brother to buy the Villa San Martino. During the rest of June Napoleon travelled around Elba and also formally 'annexed' the island of **Pianosa**.

On 16 July, Fanny Bertrand, the wife of Count **Bertrand**, arrived on Elba to join her husband. She brought with her the news of the death of Josephine and also a dress of Josephine's as a keep-sake for the ex-emperor. Two weeks

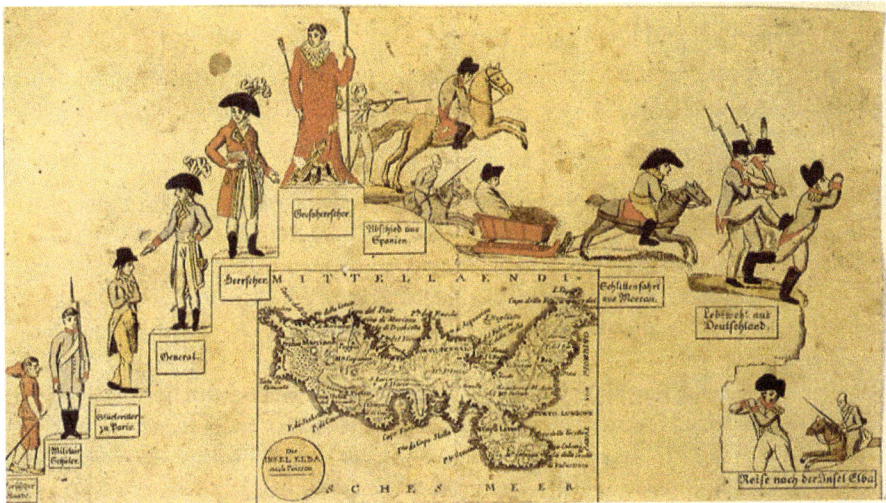

later, on 2 August, **Letizia Bonaparte**, Napoleon's mother, arrived on Elba and took up residence in Portoferraio.

There had been some expectation from the local populace that Marie-Louise of Austria, Napoleon's wife, might come to live on Elba and when Pauline arrived some had thought she was the empress. Napoleon went to **Marciana** on 21 August with the arrival of his mistress Countess Marie Walewska imminent. He hoped to keep this visit quiet as it might put off his wife from joining him in exile. Napoleon's mother joined her son at Marciana on 25 August, and on 1 September Marie Walewska along with her brother and her son arrived from Naples and went to Marciana where they were reunited with Napoleon at the Sanctuary of the Madonna del Monte. Two days later Marie Walewska and her party went to Marciana Marina to leave but there was a bad storm and in the end went to Porto Longone (**Porto Azzurro**) where on 4 September they embarked and left Elba.

Napoleon visited Pianosa from 12–17 September, and came up with plans for settling the island. With winter looming, on 1 November 1814 Pauline Bonaparte returned to Elba and was given the top floor of the Villa dei Mulini.

Since his arrival on Elba, Bonapartist agents had visited the ex-emperor and tried to persuade him to return to France. And some Italian nationalists tried to get him to go to Italy to spark an uprising there. Initially he had no plans to leave Elba as seen by the many changes he made to the island, and some of the plans he was working on through that winter of 1814–15. The Treaty of Fontainebleau was so vague that it did not prevent Napoleon from intriguing in French politics, and did not even stipulate that he could not leave Elba. Napoleon was soon bored with life on the small island and found the social scene dull, and he became restless.

Many foreigners, particularly a largely number of British tourists, came to see Napoleon. John Alger in *Napoleon's British visitors and captives, 1801–1815*, wrote:

Return however he did, and those Englishmen who had visited him at Elba cannot have been among the most startled. As early as the 29th July, less than three months after Napoleon's arrival in his little realm, General Spallannchi reported from Florence that some Englishmen had gone out of curiosity to Elba but had returned in ill-humour, the fallen monarch having barely allowed them to see him and that only in his garden. It seems from the statement of Vice-Consul Innes that the party numbered seven, including one lady, and that after being kept a long time waiting for an answer the garden interview was assigned them for the next day. A Warwickshire man who had passed through Paris and whose letter, intercepted by the Leghorn police, was signed 'Richard,' evidently his Christian name, sailed from Leghorn with his sister on the 24th November, but was told that Napoleon refused to receive curiosity-mongers. Not easily to be foiled, however, he made a second voyage and on alighting at an hotel at Porto Ferrajo on the 2nd December found covers laid for thirty Corsican functionaries in honour of the anniversary of Napoleon's coronation in 1804. Such a celebration did not argue renunciation of empire. On the following day he was allowed an audience, but nothing having been said about his sister he had to leave her outside. Napoleon, whom he found standing in a small room, advanced with an affable air and asked, 'Where do you come from?'

'Warwickshire.'

'I do not remember the name.'

'It is in the very centre of England.'

'What is your occupation?'

'General commerce, but chiefly manufactures.'

'Do you find much custom in Italy?'

'Tolerable.'

'None in France, eh?'

'None at present, for want of a commercial treaty.'

'A commercial treaty would suit you?'

'Certainly, but I do not think we shall get it.'

'I did your commerce much mischief.'

'Not so much as was supposed. Our trade found outlets out of Europe which were very profitable.'

'The troubles in Spain will open up their colonies to you?'

'Yes, but at first they will be jealously closed.'

'Your licence system was bad. It was semi-robbery.'

'This kind of conversation' (says Richard), 'lasted about an hour, and then turned on France. ... He asked me whether I was in Paris during the Peace of Amiens. 'Yes.' 'You found it now much altered'. 'Yes, much larger than in 1802.' 'It is a fine city,' he added. ... I took the opportunity of reminding him of my sister, but he took no notice. He then conversed for a few minutes, making altogether half an hour. On getting up to leave he asked me to introduce my sister, whom he received with the greatest affability, keeping up a conversation with her till a carriage was heard coming, when he bowed and we retired. ... He frequently put his fingers into a small snuff-box, but did not seem to take much notice of its contents. He asked me whether I thought the Bourbons were really popular in France. He told me he had found the heat more trying in Russia in the month of August than in any other part of Europe, and he explained the reason. I remarked evident signs of interest and inquisitiveness when speaking of the Bourbons. He twice asked me whether they were popular in France and what was said of them, and was not satisfied with a vague reply.'

Frederick Douglas, M.P., son of Lord Glenbervie, on his way home from Athens had a courteous reception, which did not however prevent him from speaking and voting in 1815 for the renewal of the war.

'Why have you come?' asked Napoleon.

'To see a great man.'

'Rather to see a wild beast,' rejoined Napoleon, who inquired whether Douglas had seen Murat or the Pope. The latter, said Napoleon, 'is an obstinately resigned old man. I

Elba from *Cassell's History of England*; 1872 edition; and 1901 edition

did not treat him properly. I did not go the right way to work with him.' As to the state of France, Douglas reported that there was much enthusiasm for the Bourbons, though there were a few malcontents. 'Yes,' remarked Napoleon, 'people who belong to whatever party pays them and make much stir in order to get money.' Napoleon went on to complain of the treachery of his officers, of the pamphleteers who styled him a usurper, of his brothers for not having seconded him, and of the sovereigns who had abandoned him. Douglas reported that he could no longer mount a horse, and that he had fallen into profound apathy. Perhaps Napoleon intentionally gave him this erroneous impression, knowing that he was on his way to Paris, which he reached in January 1815.

Lord William Bentinck, afterwards Viceroy of India, with a friend were sumptuously regaled, but we have no record of the conversation, and an English lady 'of angelical beauty/ whom Pons does not name, but who may have been Lady Jersey, for he says she showed the Emperor continued sympathy during the St. Helena captivity, was received with marked favour. When, on her return to London, she saw the Russian and Prussian sovereigns pass by, she said to the fashionable gathering round her, 'Those men cannot seem imposing to persons who like me have had a close view of the Emperor Napoleon.' Another visitor in September 1814 was John Barber Scott, of Bungay, Suffolk, ultimately a Fellow of Emmanuel College, Cambridge, but then a graduate twenty-two years of age, who was accompanied by Major (Patrick ?) [actually Montgomery] Maxwell, R.A., Colonel (afterwards General) John Lemoine, R. A., Captain Smith, and Colonel Niel Douglas.

They encountered Napoleon as he was out riding, and on their saluting him he stopped for a few minutes to question them. They thought he looked more like a crafty priest than a hero. On being told that Scott was a Cantab he said, 'What, Cambridge, Cambridge? Oh yes, you are a young man; you will be a lawyer. Eh, eh, you will be Lord Chancellor?' Being told by Douglas that he belonged to a Highland regiment, Napoleon asked whether they did not wear kilts (jupes). On Douglas replying in the affirmative, Napoleon asked whether he had brought his kilt with him, as he should like to see it, but Douglas was unable to gratify his curiosity.

Equally short, or even shorter, had been the interview of Sir Gilbert Starling [Stirling] and a Mr. Campbell.

One visitor said he was as pleased to have spent nine days at Elba as if he had won £30,000. Napoleon, however, refused audiences to Englishmen whom he suspected of simple curiosity or of exultation at his fall. When he went to Longone, the second town in the island, there were numerous English visitors, and it was remarked to him that they followed him wherever he went. He replied, 'I am an object of curiosity; let them satisfy themselves. They will go home and amuse the gentlemans (sic) by describing my acts and gestures.' He added in a sad tone, 'They have won the game; they hold the dice.'

Yet so far from showing him disrespect, Pons states that these sixty visitors of all classes vied in extolling him. Pons also acknowledges thac Colonel Campbell, though deputed by his Government to watch Napoleon, veiled his supervision so carefully that only the closest observation could detect it.

But the principal visitor, and the only one invited to dinner, was Lord Ebrington, afterwards Earl of Fortescue and in 1839–1841 Viceroy of Ireland. He first waited on the Emperor at 8 p.m. on the 6th December, and for three hours walked up and down the room with him. 'You come from France; tell me frankly,' said Napoleon, 'whether the French are satisfied.' 'Only so-so,' replied Ebrington. 'It cannot be otherwise,' rejoined Napoleon; 'they have been too much humiliated by the peace. The appointment of the Duke of Wellington as Ambassador must have seemed an insult to the army, as also the special attentions shown him by the King. If Lord Wellington had come to Paris as a visitor, I should have had pleasure in showing him the attentions due to his great ability, but I should not have liked his being sent to me as Ambassador.'

The justice of this remark is obvious. Napoleon extolled the House of Lords as the bulwark of the English constitution. He denounced the duplicity of the Emperor Alexander, expressed esteem for the Austrian Emperor, and spoke slightingly of the King of Prussia. 'How should I be treated,' he asked Ebrington, 'if I went to England? Should I be stoned?' Ebrington replied that he would run no risk, and that the irritation formerly existing against him was daily dying out. 'I think, however,' rejoined Napoleon, 'that there would be some danger from your mob' – he used the English word – 'at London.'

'The grace of his smile and the simplicity of his manner,' says Ebrington, 'had put me quite at my ease. He himself appeared to wish me to question him. He replied without the least hesitation, with a promptitude and clearness which I have never seen equalled in any other man.'

Next day, just as Ebrington was preparing to sail, came an invitation to dinner, and this second interview lasted from seven till eleven. Napoleon inquired for the Duke and Duchess of Bedford, Whitworth, Erskine, and Holland, and spoke especially of Fox. Informed that Fox felt much flattered at his reception in 1802, Napoleon said, 'He had reason to be so. He was everywhere received like a divinity because he was known to be in favour of peace.' 'Tell Lord Grenville,' added Napoleon, 'to come and see me. I wager that you in England thought me a devil, but now that you have seen me and France also you must be somewhat disabused.' He justified the detentions of 1803. Ebrington, however, maintained that the embargo on French shipping in British ports prior to the formal declaration of war was in accordance with precedent, on which Napoleon replied, 'Yes, you considered it right because it was to your advantage; other nations who lost by it thought it wrong. I am sure that at heart you in England approved me for showing force of character. Do you not see that I am a bit of a pirate like yourselves?'

Napoleon half in earnest advocated polygamy, especially in the colonies, where a planter might have a wife of each colour, so that the two families might grow up together harmoniously. He inquired for 'my good friend Ussher' – Captain, afterwards Sir Thomas Ussher – who had conveyed him to Elba.

On surprise being expressed by Ebrington at his calm endurance of adversity, Napoleon said, 'It is because everybody was more surprised at it than myself. I have not too good an opinion of mankind, and have always distrusted fortune. Moreover, I had little enjoyment. My brothers were much more kings than I was. They tasted the sweets of royalty, while I had only the worries and cares.'

Lord John Russell, the future statesman, then twenty-three years of age, being taken by his father to Florence in the autumn of 1814, embraced the opportunity of visiting Elba. 'When I saw Napoleon,' he says, 'he was in evident anxiety respecting the state of France

Napoleon leaving Elba, by Joseph Beaume.

The *Inconstant* leaving Elba on 26 February 1815.

and his chances of again seizing the crown which he had worn for ten years. I was so struck with his restless inquiry that I expressed in a letter to my brother in England my conviction that he would make some fresh attempts to disturb France and govern Europe.'

But by far the most curious incident of Napoleon's reign at Elba was his presence at an entertainment in honour of George III.'s birthday, given on the 4th June 1814 by Captain Tower on board the frigate *Undaunted*. Napoleon, on reaching Frejus after his abdication in April, had embarked in the *Undaunted* in preference to a French vessel assigned for his passage to Elba, and had taken a fancy to the captain, Ussher. The *Undaunted* went to and from Elba and Leghorn, and it might have celebrated the royal birthday at the latter port. Napoleon afterwards thought that Colonel (ultimately Sir Neil) Campbell purposely planned the celebration at Elba. When, however, Towers invited him to come on board, and sent round invitations to the principal inhabitants of Porto Ferrajo, he readily accepted the invitation, and directed his courtiers, if such a phrase can be used, to do likewise. One of these, Pons de l'Hérault, to whom we are indebted for the fullest account of the festival – not published, however, till 1897 – was inclined indeed to regard the invitation as an insult and the festival as a bravado; but his master told him that it was the duty of British sailors to observe their sovereign's birthday wherever they might happen to be. A 'throne', says Pons, had been prepared for the Emperor on the bridge; and he continues: –

The Emperor arrived, and the ship's officers received him at the top of the ladder. Guns could not be fired, as they were not mounted, but the crew, clustered on the rigging, gave him three hearty cheers, and the Emperor looking up at them raised his hat. He then passed to the quarter-deck. There all were ranged in a circle, and the Emperor, as though quite at home, his left hand as usual in his fob, put the trivial questions which he nearly always employed on such occasions, for he did not bother himself with finding remarks appropriate to each particular individual. It was not his moment for parade. When the circle had broken up the Emperor asked for an interpreter and went to talk to the sailors, especially to a mate with whom he had several times conversed during his passage from Frejus to the isle of Elba. The entire crew seemed eager to see him again. The countenances of these good fellows expressed the very contrary of the perversity of their Government. Captain Tower sincerely admired the Emperor, and watched all his movements with a gaze full of respect and interest. He had one of those open countenances which inspire confidence. The Emperor said to me ... 'The English Government will never forgive me for having been the most determined Frenchman in breaking down its supremacy. Not that hatred actuated me, it was duty, it was love of country. All well-bred Englishmen consequently honour me. If I went to England the English Government would be afraid of my popularity and would pack me off ...'. The same cheers accompanied the Emperor on his departure, and he responded with the same salute.'

Pons, with his wife and children and the other guests, remained to the dinner and ball. Unfortunately, two of the ship's officers drank a little too much, and so misbehaved themselves as to oblige several of the ladies to withdraw. It is pathetic to think that Napoleon's next and last acquaintance with British tars was when, thirteen months later, he gave himself up to the Bellerophon, and was conveyed as a captive in the Northumberland to St. Helena.

One Englishman at least was a spectator of Napoleon's departure from Elba. A Mr.

Napoleon leaving Elba on the *Inconstant*.
By Mellini and Damame.

Grattan (probably the father of Thomas Colley Grattan, the traveller and novelist) had landed on the island on the 24th February. On the evening of the 26th he noticed unusual bustle, as though something was about to happen, and at 9 p.m. he saw Napoleon, escorted by General Bertrand, come out in his sister Pauline's four-horse carriage, enter a boat, and go on board the brig *Inconstant*. Thereupon the whole flotilla got under way, the soldiers shouting 'Vive l'Empereur!' Scarcely believing his eyes, Grattan hired a boat to go alongside the brig, and thence he saw Napoleon in his grey overcoat and round hat pacing the quarter-deck. One of the boatmen, however, cried out that there was an Englishman on board, upon which an officer on the poop of the *Inconstant* demanded who he was and what he wanted. Grattan had to explain that he had merely come to have a look at the Emperor, whereupon he was told to be off, and he complied with alacrity, expecting every instant to be fired at or arrested.

The new French government of Louis XVIII had promised to pay Napoleon some two million francs per year, however with budgetary problems in France, decided not to do this, and this seems to have led to Napoleon beginning to listen to conspirators who told him of the unpopularity of the Bourbon regime in France and how many French would welcome his return.

In January 1815 the **Teatro dei Vigilanti** was completed in a deconsecrated church. A ball was held there attended by Napoleon and most of the dignitaries on the island. On 13 February 1815, Pierre Fleury de Chaboulon arrived on Elba bringing Napoleon news that the Bourbon government was becoming increasingly hated in France and on the following day Napoleon decided that he would return to France at the first opportunity that presented itself. On 16 February, Pauline Bonaparte send out her invitations to the ball and Sir Neil Campbell replied that he would be unable to attend as he ws leaving for

Napoleon greeted by soldiers after returning to France.

Livorno which he did on the following day. This provided Napoleon with the breathing space he needed, and with preparations for his departure underway, on 23 February Napoleon forbade any ship from leaving Elba.

To cover his departure preparations, Pauline Bonaparte did give the ball on 25 February at the Teatro dei Vigilanti which was attended by Napoleon. On the following day Napoleon announced that he was going to leave Elba and farewelled many local officials. He then bade goodbye to his mother and sister, went down to Portoferraio harbour and embarked on the *Inconstant* and sailed for the French coast, landing at Golfe-Juan on 1 March. The period from his return to Paris on 20 March 1815 through to the second restoration of King Louis XVIII on 8 July 1815 was 111 days, but it has become known in history as the 'Hundred Days'.

On reaching the French coast, Napoleon proceeded to Paris with French armies sent to stop him joining his forces. Napoleon quickly mobilised his forces but was nervous about reintroducing conscription. He then struck at the British and Prussian forces north of France, pushing them back at the battles of Quatre Bras and Ligny. He then attacked the British at Waterloo and was on the verge of victory when the Prussians arrived on his flank and the French army was crushed. Napoleon headed back to France but did not have

321 NAPOLÉON ET SON ÉPOQUE. — Retour de l'Île d'Elbe (Journée du 6 mars 1815). — ND.

328 FONTAINEBLEAU. — Retour de l'Île d'Elbe (17 Mars 1815). — LL.

the resources to launch another offensive. He surrendered and was sent into exile for a second time. This time the British knew that returning him to Elba would leave Europe open to the possibility of his returning again. This time he was exiled to St. Helena in the South Pacific where he died six years later, on 5 May 1821. He was initially buried on St. Helena but in 1840 King Louis Philippe I of France obtained permission from the British to return his body to France where it was reinterred at Les Invalides in Paris.

References: John Alger, *Napoleon's British visitors and captives, 1801–1815*, New York: J. Pott, 1904, pp. 292–303; Vernon Bartlett, *A Book about Elba*, London: Chatto & Windus, 1965, Chapters 6–8; Pierre Branda, *L'île d'Elbe et le retour de Napoléon: 1814–1815*, Saint-Cloud: Soteca, 2014; Neil Campbell, *Napoleon at Fontainebleau and Elba*, London, J. Murray, 1869; Robert Christophe, *Napoleon on Elba*, London: Macdonald, 1964; Peter Hicks, 'Napoleon on Elba? An Exile of Consent', *Napoleonica La Revue* vol. 19, no 1 (2014), p. 53; Volker Hunecke, *Napoleons Rückkehr Die letzten hundert Tage – Elba, Waterloo, St. Helena*, Stuttgart: Klett-Cotta 2015; Harold Kurtz, 'Napoleon in 1815: The Escape from Elba', *History Today* vol. 15, no 7 (July 1965), pp. 449–56; Jehanne Lazaj and Alba Macripò, *Il bivacco di Napoleone: lusso imperiale "en campagne"*, Museo Nazionale delle Residenze Napoleoniche dell'isola d'Elba, Villa di San Marino – Galleria Demidoff, Portoferraio, Isola d'Elba, 28 giugno – 15 ottobre 2014, Livorno: Sillabe, 2014; Katherine Macdonogh, 'A sympathetic ear: Napoleon, Elba and the British', *History Today* vol. 44, no 2 (February 1994), pp. 29-35; Norman MacKenzie, *The Escape from Elba: The Fall & Flight of Napoleon 1814–1815*, Oxford: Oxford University Press, 1982; Roberta Martinelli and Velia Gini Bartoli, *Napoleone: imperatore, imprenditore e direttore dei lavori all'isola d'Elba*, Roma: Gangemi, 2014; François Rabasse, *Les indomptables, 1815: le retour de Napoléon de l'île d'Elbe jusqu'aux Tuileries*, [Brannay]: Éd. Sénones, DL 2014; Miles Roddis & Alex Leviton, *Tuscany & Umbria*, Footscray: Lonely Planet, 2006, p. 187; Imbert de Saint-Amand, *Marie Louise, the island of Elba and the Hundred Days*, New York, C. Scribner's Sons, 1891; J. M. Thompson, 'Napoleon's Journey to Elba in 1814, Part 1: By Land', *The American Historical Review* Vol. 55, no. 1 (October 1949), pp. 1–21; 'Part 2: By Sea', *The American Historical Review* Vol. 55, no. 2 (January 1950), pp. 301–20; George Venables Vernon, *Sketch of a Conversation with Napoleon at Elba*, London: Whittigham & Wilkins, 1863–64.

NAPOLEONIC WARS. At the start of the Napoleonic Wars, Elba was a part of the Grand Duchy of Tuscany – although in 1786 the British had expressed an interest in the island. The ideas of the French Revolution were discussed in cities and towns all over Europe, and undoubtedly some of the ideas spread to **Portoferraio**. However the first major impact on Elba was on 1 January 1794 when the British arrived in Portoferraio having evacuated the French port of Toulon, and bringing with them some 3,000 French royalist refugees. The governor of Elba at that time, Baron Knesevich, did not want them to

The British taking Portoferraio in 1796.

land and pointed out that there was an epidemic in Portoferraio at that time. However Admiral Hotham of the Royal Navy insisted on landing and the French royalists came ashore. Many were not there for very long.

In 1796 when **Napoleon Bonaparte** invaded Italy and captured Livorno, the British became anxious about the future of Elba and after giving guarantees to Baron Knesevich, they landed and from July that year used soldiers from the Royal Anglo-Corsican Regiment to make up most of the British garrison on the island. Most of the British soldiers were billeted in Fort San Giovanni which then became known as the 'English Fort'. **Horatio Nelson** came to Elba around this time, and may have used the fort as his headquarters. With Italian refugees fleeing the mainland, the population of Portoferraio swelled from 3,000 to 10,000 and the British garrison was dispersed to other bases around the island. In October 1796 when the British decided to pull out their regiment, the soldiers of the Royal Anglo-Corsican Regiment refused to leave and were disbanded.

The Grand Duke of Tuscany protested against the French holding Livorno and the British Elba, and in April 1797 both sides agreed to withdraw. However two years later, the French returned and annexed the Grand Duchy of Tuscany. With a French army at Piombino, demands were sent to Elba ordering its surrender by 29 March 1799. The new governor of the island consulted with the local officials and decided that they should yield and on 4 April 1799 a French garrison under General Montserrat arrived on the island. On 5 April he marched his men to Porto Longone (**Porto Azzurro**) which he attacked. This angered many of the locals who rose up and attacked the French. One group of French soldiers was cut off at **Capoliveri** and there the locals killed them. The French in return brought in reinforcements under General Miollis and exacted retribution on the people of Capoliveri.

General Miollis then left and Montserrat continued with his siege of Porto Longone which dragged on much longer than expected with British and Neapolitan ships bringing in supplies. Colonel de Gregorio, Marquis of Squillace rallied the local soldiers and with Captain de Farra of the Tuscan army, a general uprising against the French was launched around the island. Montserrat's soldiers were on the retreat and he himself went to Livorno to gather more supplies and reinforcements. He was sacked, and the French surrendered on 17 July 1799, which was followed by a massacre of locals in Portoferraio who had supported the French on 28 July.

It was not until 1801 that the French decided to attack again. In the meantime the Grand Duke of Tuscany, himself a refugee in Vienna, sent messages to Elba for it to hold out – as it was the only part of the Grand Duchy not in French hands. General Dupont, the French commander, launched an attack in May 1801. The fortifications at Portoferraio had been heavily reinforced and with the British helping the Elbans, the French were unable to make headway. On 4 June 1802 news arrived that the Peace of Amiens had been signed and Elba was ceded to France – and in fact became a part of metropolitan France. The Tuscan commander, Lieutenant-Colonel de Fisson, and his soldiers withdrew.

French rule over Elba saw the introduction of a much more modern administration, and Elba sent one representative to the French Corps Législatif (national assembly) in Paris. The last member of the Appiani family – with the hereditary title of Prince of **Piombino** – had died in 1801, and **Elisa Bonaparte**, sister of Napoleon, was made princess of Lucca and Piombino, and her husband, Felice Pasquale Baciocchi its prince. A new garrison of locals was raised and they fought off a half-hearted British attack in 1813. Gradually the locals turned against the French and there were open demonstrations in 1814.

With the French Bonapartist administration about to be ejected by the locals, it came as a surprise to them when news arrived that Napoleon Bonaparte had been given Elba and was planning to live there. The locals, however, took this in their stride and welcomed him when he came ashore on 4 May 1814. He was to remain on the island until the night of 26 February when he left to return to France. His attempt to take the offensive saw his armies defeated at the battle of Waterloo on 18 June 1815 and his second exile, this time in St. Helena.

References: René Chartrand, *Émigré & Foreign Troops in British Service (1): 1793–1802,* Oxford: Osprey Military, 1999, p. 35; Philip J. Haythornthwaite, *The Napoleonic Wars source book*, London: Arms and Armour Press, 1990, pp. 305–08; Norman MacKenzie, *The Escape from Elba: The Fall & Flight of Napoleon 1814–1815,* Oxford: Oxford University Press, 1982, pp. 67–68; Alan Palmer, *An Encyclopedia of Napoleon's Europe,* London: Weidenfeld and Nicolson, 1984, p. 115.

NAPOLEON'S TREE. This hackberry tree is in the garden of the **Villa San Martino** and was, according to tradition, planted by **Napoleon** when staying at the villa.

Napoleon's tree in 1888.
The Illustrated London News (22 September 1888), p. 339.

NELSON, HORATIO, Viscount Nelson (1758–1805). The famous British naval officer and victor of the battle of Trafalgar in 1805, he visited Elba in 1796 and is reputed to have stayed at Fort San Giovanni in **Portoferraio**. He was born on 29 September 1758 at Burnham Thorpe, Norfolk, England, his father being Rev Edmund Nelson and his mother was Catherine, a grandniece of Robert Walpole, acknowledged as Britain's first prime minister (although the term was not used at the time). Nelson went to the local Paston Grammar School and then went to King Edward VI's Grammar School in Norwich. When he was twelve he joined the Royal Navy and was soon appointed a midshipman. He was determined on a naval career even though he soon discovered he suffered slightly from seasickness.

He sailed to India in 1773 and three years later contracted malaria. After recovering, he was based in the Caribbean. On the island of Nevis he met Frances 'Fanny' Nisbet and the two were married. With the outbreak of the Frnch Revolutionary Wars, Nelson, now one of the better-known British naval commanders was sent in 1793 to Toulon which was held by French Royalists and British soldiers, and under attack from French revolutionaries. Nelson blockaded the French in Corsica to prevent them coming to the aid of their compatriots in Toulon, but in December 1793 Toulon finally fell and without a base on the French mainland, the British decided to capture Corsica, with Nelson blockading Bastia and then taking the town, establishing a brief period of British rule on the island. However some 2½ years later the British had to leave Corsica. Nelson helped organise the evacuation of Bastia and took the men and supplies to Elba which was now the only British base in the Mediterranean. He ensured that the British forces on Elba were well-equipped before he moved most of his supplies to Gibraltar.

After defeating the Spanish fleet at the battle of Cape St. Vincent in 1797, he was involved in fighting off Cadiz and then in the Canary Islands. The French fleet managed to get to Egypt in 1798 but Nelson found and defeated them at Aboukir Bay on 1 August 1798. He spent time in Naples where he famously courted Emma Hamilton, then in 1801 he led the British to victory in the battle of Copenhagen and four years later won his great victory at the battle of Trafalgar, dying in the battle.

References: Ernle Bradford, *Nelson: The Essential Hero*, London: Macmillan, 1977; Joel S. A. Hayward, *For God and Glory: Lord Nelson and His Way of War*, Annapolis, Md.: Naval Institute Press, 2003; Christopher Hibbert, *Nelson: A Personal History*, London: Viking, 1994; Andrew Lambert, *Nelson – Britannia's God of War*, London: Faber and Faber, 2004; Carola Oman, *Nelson*, London: Hodder & Stoughton, 1946; N. A. M. Rodger, 'Nelson, Horatio, Viscount Nelson (1758–1805)', *Oxford Dictionary of National Biography*, Oxford University Press, 2004; John Sugden, *Nelson: The Sword of Albion*, New York: Henry Holt and Co, 2013.

NOVELS. There have been many novels set around Napoleon's time on Elba. The most famous is undoubtedly Alexandre Dumas's *Le Comte de Monte-Cristo* (1844; *The Count of Monte Cristo*). This starts during the period when Napoleon is still in Elba and Edmond Dantès returns to Marseille in command of the ship – the previous captain Leclère having died. Dantès has the task of delivering a letter from Elba and this quickly gets him into trouble with the authorities resulting in him being taken off to prison. Many years later after his escape, he comes by a fortune which has been hidden on the island of Monte Cristo – based on Montecristo off the coast of Elba.

David Donachie's *An Ill Wind* (London: Alison & Busby, 2009), a part of a series on the career of fictional British Royal Navy officer Lieutenant John Pearce starts with the evacuation of Toulon in 1793, but with the Royalist refugees taken to Livorno, not Elba. Dudley Pope's *Ramage* (London: Weidenfeld & Nicolson, 1965) and *The Ramage Touch* (London: Secker & Warburg, 1979) are both set near Elba, the former with the fictional Ramage sailing from the Italian mainland past **Pianosa** and to Corsica in 1796, and the latter with Ramage sailing past **Piombino** to Porto Ercole.

There were several other famous authors who wrote about Napoleon and Elba. Lord **George Gordon Byron** (1788–1824) set his story, *On Napoleon's escape from Elba* (1815) around the departure of Napoleon. Joseph Conrad (Josef Teodor Nalecz Korzeniowski; 1857–1924) set *Suspense: A Napoleonic Novel* (unfinished at death; Garden City, N.Y.: Doubleday, Page & Co., 1925) around the shifting moods of Europe after Napoleon was exiled to Elba; and Sir Arthur Thomas Quiller-Couch (1863–1944) set his novel *Poison Island* (New York: Charles Scribner's Sons, 1907) around a Treasure Island-type story which refers to Napoleon's captivity in Elba.

Of the novels specifically written about Napoleon in Elba, Pieter Jacob Andriessen (1815–1877) wrote *Elba en Sint-Helena; of, De dubbele val van het eerste keizerrijk, 1814–1821* (Leiden: A.W. Sijthoff, 1905). Julius Bacher (1810–1889), a German writer, set his long novel *Napoleons letzte Liebe* (Berlin: Otto Janke, 1868) on Napoleon's exile in Elba where he falls in love with a young girl called Julia. The Scottish writer Sir Andrew Balfour (1873–1931) set his novel *Vengeance is Mine!* (London: Methuen & Co, 1899) around an American heroine who survives a shipwreck off the west coast of Scotland, then moves to Corsica, and then to Elba before the story continues through the Hundred Days up to the battle of Waterloo. Matilda Maria Blake set *Grantley Fenton, or when the century was young: a story told in pen and pencil* (London: Jarrold & Sons, 1902) around Napoleon's time at Elba; and Sandra Paretti's The Rose and the Sword (London: Heinemann, 1968) is about Caroline, daughter of Comte de la Romme Allery heading to Elba to be with Napoleon.

The story of Napoleon's return from Elba and the Hundred Days is the basis of many novels including Arnolt Bronnen (1895–1959) *Napoleon's Fall* (Berlin: E. Rowohlt, 1924); and Albéric Cahuet (1877–1942), *Les abeilles d'or: île d'Elbe 1815; roman* (Paris: Fasquelle, 1939). Oliver Vernon Caine (1862–?), *In the Year of Waterloo* (London: James Nisbet, 1899), is a boy's adventure story and sequel to *Face to Face with Napoleon: an English boy's adventures in the great French War* (London: James Nisbet & Co Ltd, 1898; reprinted London: A. & C. Black, 1930). Bernard Cornwell's *Sharpe's Revenge* (London: Collins, 1989) in the famous Sharpe series about the British rifleman, starts just before the battle of Toulouse, and briefly involves one of the characters sending a message to Elba to provide Napoleon with information on some of his missing treasure. William Arthur Dunkerley (1852–1941) was a prolific writer and wrote some 67 novels and books of verse with *Lauristons* (London: Methuen, 1910), published under the pseudonym John Oxenham, centring on Napoleon's flight from Elba.

Ernesto Ferrero's *N.* (Turin: Einaudi, 2000) is about Napoleon's time on Elba and his relations with a local intellectual, Martino Acquabona, whom the emperor appoints as his librarian. This results in Martino getting to know Napoleon and making plans for himself, and being tempted to kill Napoleon. The novel was the winner of Italy's Strega literary prize. Sir Alan Patrick

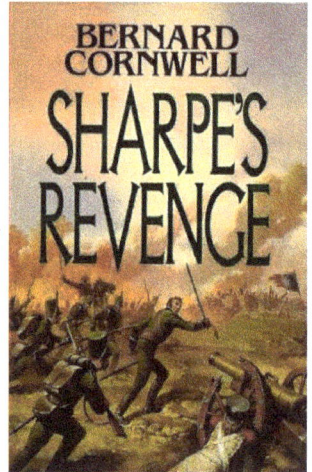

Herbert (1890–1971), *Why Waterloo?*, (London: Methuen, 1952/Garden City, New York: Doubleday, 1952) is about Napoleon's arrival at Elba.

Manuel Komroff (1890–1974) set *Waterloo: a novel* (New York: Coward-McCann, 1936) around Napoleon's escape from Elba up to his defeat at Waterloo. Eleanor Catherine Price set her children's adventure story, *Young Denys: A Story of the Days of Napoleon* (Edinburgh: W. & R. Chambers, 1896) around the life of the son of a bookseller who is a student at Winchester College and is carried off by press-gang, at sea on the *Undaunted*, managing to see Napoleon on his way to and from Elba, with Denys surviving being ship-wrecked, then is rescued by Provençals, and ends up returning to Winchester.

Joseph Roth (1894–1939) wrote *Die hundert Tage*, translated as *The Ballad of the Hundred Days* (New York, 1936) which is set around Napoleon's return from Elba told from the viewpoint of a laundress who is infatuated with him. Matthew Phipps Shiel (1865–1947), *The Man-Stealers: an Incident in the Life of the Iron Duke* (London & Philadelphia: Hutchinson, 1900) is about a French plot to kidnap Wellington in revenge for Napoleon's exile to Elba. And Ferdinand Stolle (1806–1872) wrote *Elba und Waterloo: ein historischer Roman* (Leipzig: E. Meiszner, 1838). Four other novels set on Elba are: Jan Andersen's *A Stranger Came* (London: Mills & Boon, 1964); Oriel Malet's *Horses of the Sun* (London: London Missionary Society, 1959/New York: Putnam, 1960); Denis Pitts's *The Predator* (New York: Mason Charter, 1976); and Helen Thorpe's *Bianca and Napoleon's Sergeant* (London: Robert Hale & Company, 1975). One of the more recent novels set in Elba is Jean-Philippe Toussaint's *Fuir* (2005), published in English as *Running Away* (2009). An important part of the story is set in the **Albergo l'Ape Elbana** in Portoferraio. This won the Prix Médicis in 2005.

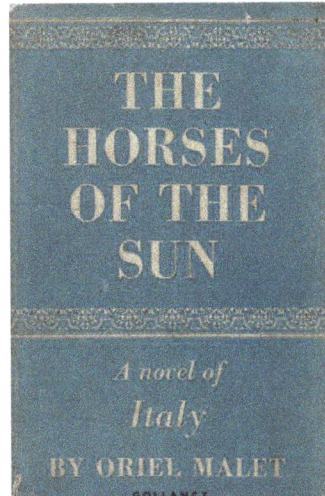

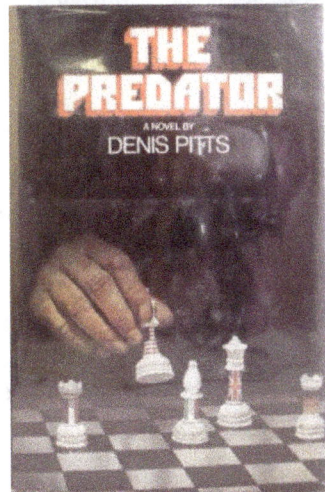

- O -

O'CONNOR, DESMOND GORDON ANTHONY (1921–1944). A sailor in the British Royal Navy, he was born on 21 February 1921 in Rangoon, Burma (now Yangon, Myanmar), the younger son of Terence Gordon O'Connor (1892–1970) and Dorothy (née Mymm, 1888–1943). Joining the Royal Navy as an able seaman, Desmond O'Connor was assigned to H.M.S. *Copra* (combined operations). He was killed on the first day of the Allied attack on Elba on 17 June 1944, and was buried on Elba and three years later was reburied in the Bolsena War Cemetery (IV G 4) on the Italian mainland.

References: *The war dead of the British Commonwealth and Empire: the register of the names of those who fell in the 1939–1945 War and are buried in cemeteries in Italy Cemeteries 17–18: Bolsena War Cemetery, Orvieto War Cemetery*, Maidenhead: Imperial War Graves Commission, 1954, p. 29.

'OIL MERCHANT'. This was the codename given to a French secret agent on Elba during the time that **Napoleon Bonaparte** was on the island. He had the task of reporting back to Chevalier Mariotti at Livorno on the movements of Napoleon. He was identified by Robert Christophe as the Italian called Alessandro Forli. He sent back details using codes, and also invisible ink, carefully evaluating information and not including gossip for the sake of it. Alessandro Forli came to **Portoferraio** on the morning of 30 November 1814, registering at the office of **Cambronne**, and seems to fit the profile of the agent. His code name may have come from the fact that he was selling olive oil to the household of **Letizia Bonaparte**, and also to the Vattani family, allowing him to collect information relatively easily. His reports were good and precise, and one dated 6 December noted that 'By and large people say that the Emperor will not show a sign of life until the Congress [of Vienna] is over.' But gradually he feared that there was the real possibility of the British working with Napoleon. When it became clear that Napoleon was preparing to leave Elba, the Oil Merchant tried to get to the Italian mainland to raise the alarm but was unable to do so because Napoleon had stopped all ships leaving Elba. He eventually managed to find somebody who would take him to **Piombino** but the boat on which he was travelling was challenged and he had to return to Portoferraio where he was watched so closely he dared not leave the island again.

References: Robert Christophe, *Napoleon on Elba*, London: Macdonald, 1964; Norman MacKenzie, *The Escape from Elba: The Fall & Flight of Napoleon 1814–1815*, Oxford: Oxford University Press, 1982.

O'NEILL, JOHN JOSEPH (d. 1944). An able seaman in the British Royal Navy, he was assigned to H.M.S. *Copra* (combined operations). He was killed on the first day of the Allied attack on Elba on 17 June 1944, and was buried on Elba and three years later was reburied in the Bolsena War Cemetery (IV G 17) on the Italian mainland.

References: *The war dead of the British Commonwealth and Empire: the register of the names of those who fell in the 1939–1945 War and are buried in cemeteries in Italy Cemeteries 17–18: Bolsena War Cemetery, Orvieto War Cemetery*, Maidenhead: Imperial War Graves Commission, 1954, p. 29.

OPERATION BRASSARD. *See* **World War II.**

ORNITHOLOGY. *See* **Fauna.**

- P -

Paduella Beach
Photograph © jarre / Fotolia.com

PADUELLA BEACH. This is a 150 metre white gravel beach near Portoferraio which has become popular with tourists.

PALMAIOLA. This is one of the islands in the **Tuscan Archipelago** and although it is only 0.08 square kilometres, it is large enough to have a watchtower which was originally built in AD 909 when the island was owned by the Republic of Pisa. The fort was restored in 1534 and a lighthouse was built on the island in 1989. It is now a part of the Tuscan Archipelago National Park.

References: Norman MacKenzie, *The Escape from Elba: The Fall & Flight of Napoleon 1814–1815*, Oxford: Oxford University Press, 1982, p. 65.

PALMER, TERENCE PATRICK (1919/20–1944). A leading seaman in the British Royal Naval Reserve, he was the son of Mary Palmer of North Shields. Mentioned in Despatches, he served on the H.M.S. *Braganza*, and was killed on the first day of the Allied attack on Elba on 17 June 1944, and was buried on Elba and three years later was reburied in the Bolsena War Cemetery (IV G 9) on the Italian mainland. His widow, Valerie Joan Palmer, lived at Kalk Bay, Cape Province, South Africa.

References: *The war dead of the British Commonwealth and Empire: the register of the names of those who fell in the 1939–1945 War and are buried in cemeteries in Italy Cemeteries 17–18: Bolsena War Cemetery, Orvieto War Cemetery*, Maidenhead: Imperial War Graves Commission, 1954, p. 29.

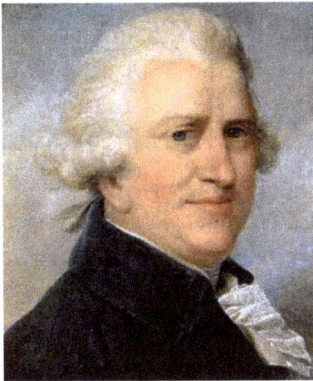

PAOLI, (FILIPPO ANTONIO) PASQUALE (1725–1807). A politician in Corsica, he was born on 6 April 1725 in the hamlet of Stretta di Morosaglia in the canton of Rostino, Corsica, the younger of the two sons of Giacinto Paoli and Dionisia Valentini. When Pasquale Paoli was 4½, a rebellion broke out in Corsica against the Genoese who were in control of the island and his father became the leader of the rebels who elected him one of their three chiefs. The island was then taken over briefly by Theodore, Baron von Neuhoff (1694–1756) who ruled as King Theodore I in 1736 before being sent into exile later that same year. With the Genoese slowly losing control of Corsica, the young Pasquale Paoli joined the Royal Regiment of Corsica then stationed in Naples, and served in the military garrison in Sicily, and then on the island of Elba.

When he returned to his native island, he became one of the leading politicians but was forced into exile to London where he met the writer James Boswell who became a close friend. Following the French Revolution, Paoli went to France where he was well-received by Maximilien Robespierre and then went back to Corsica where he hoped that there would be a constitutional monarchy in France. With the execution of King Louis XVI in Paris, there was some hope of an Anglo-Corsican kingdom but the French crushed this and Paoli again went back to Britain. He died on 5 February 1807 in his home in London. Initially he was buried at St. Pancras Church, London, and then in 1889 was reburied in Corsica.

References: M. T. Avon-Soletti, *La Corse et Pascal Paoli: essai sur la constitution de la Corse*, Ajaccio: La Marge, 1999; J. Boswell, 'An account of Corsica, the journal of a tour to that island, and memoirs of Pascal Paoli', in *Boswell on the grand tour: Italy,*

Corsica and France, 1765–1766, edited by Frank Brady and Frederick A. Pottle, New York: McGraw-Hill, 1955; Marie-Jeanne Colombani, 'Paoli, (Filippo Antonio) Pasquale (1725–1807)', *Oxford Dictionary of National Biography*, Oxford University Press, 2004; Paul-Michel Villa, *L'autre vie de Pascal Paoli*, Ajaccio: Editions A. Piazzola, 1999.

PASSANNANTE, GIOVANNI. *See* **Torre Di Passannante**.

PERTINI, SANDRO (1896–1990). The seventh president of the Italian Republic from 1978 to 1985, he was born on 25 September 1896 at Stella, in the north-west of Italy. He went to the Salesian College at Varazze and then the high school in Savona. Aged 19 when Italy entered World War I, he objected to the war but saw it as his patriotic duty to enlist and was commissioned lieutenant. After the war he joined the United Socialist Party (PSU) and lived in Florence where he completed his thesis *La Cooperazione* in 1924. He was opposed to the Fascists of Mussolini who had seized power in 1922 but he decided to leave the country and work as a mason in France. He returned to Italy and was arrested in Pisa and sent to the prison at **Pianosa** where he was held from 13 November 1931 to 9 September 1935. At his trial in 1933 at **Portoferraio**, he was jailed for ten years. He never petitioned for a pardon and was held until the deposing of Mussolini. He then served in the Italian resistance movement which fought Mussolini's new Italian Social Republic. Captured by the Germans, he was freed by partisans just ahead of his scheduled execution.

After the end of **World War II**, Pertini became a leading member of the Italian Socialist Party and always opposed the Communists who had emerged as a major force in Italian politics. He was elected to the Constituent Assembly in 1946, and in 1968 was elected president of the chamber of deputies and in 1978 was elected president of the Italian Republic holding office from 9 July 1978 to 29 June 1985. He used his position to attack organized crime, and also the Red Brigade, as well as Augusto Pinochet in Chile and the South African government. On his retirement in 1985, he was appointed senator for life. He died on 24 February 1990, aged 93.

References: Gianni Bisiach, *Pertini racconta gli anni 1915–1945*, Milan: Mondadori, 1983; Stefano Caretti and Maurizio Degl'Innocenti, *Sandro Pertini combattente per la libertà*, Manduria-Bari-Roma: Piero Lacaita Editore, 1996; Andrea Gandolfo, *Sandro Pertini: Dalla nascita alla Resistenza 1896–1945*, Rome: Aracne, 2013; Mario Guidotti, *Sandro Pertini, una vita per la libertà*, Rome: Editalia, 1987; Antonio Martino, *Pertini e altri socialisti savonesi nelle carte della R.Questura*, Rome: Gruppo editoriale L'Espresso, 2009; Raffaello Uboldi, *Il cittadino Sandro Pertini*, Milan: Rizzoli, 1982; Raffaello Uboldi, *Pertini soldato: Il dramma della prima guerra mondiale nei ricordi di un italiano*, Milan: Bompiani, 1984.

PEYRUSSE, GUILLAUME (1776–1860). He was **Napoleon Bonaparte**'s treasurer on Elba, having previously served the emperor for many years. His family came from the village of Aragon, near Carcassone in southern France. He was born on 14 June 1776, the son of Jean-Dominique Peyrusse (1734–1818), a businessman in Carcassone and the town's consul in 1769. With the French Revolution, he enlisted in the army and became the secretary to the army of the Pyrénées-Orientales, holding that position until he fell ill and was discharged on 24 July 1800. He then returned to Carcassone and worked in the family business with his father. He returned to work for the government as an employee in the treasury in October 1805 and in 1809 was trusted to be the paymaster in the embassy that went to receive Empress Marie-Louise before her marriage to Napoleon.

He travelled with the ex-emperor to the island of Elba on the *Undaunted* and during his time there he had the task of managing Napoleon's finances. This involved settling bills and paying household expenses with monies that Napoleon had brought with him. Trusted absolutely by the ex-emperor he also had the task of preparing accounts and making sure that some items were not included in general accounts, but paid from other funds, thus preventing a full scrutiny of what the ex-emperor was financing – including, obviously, the payment of agents. His task was relatively easy at the start but the failure of the government of King Louis XVIII to pay the allowance promised to Napoleon meant that his task would gradually become more difficult as Napoleon had grand ambitions for Elba. However as **Norman MacKenzie** demonstrated in his book, *The Escape from Elba* (1982), it was quite possible for Napoleon to have lasted at least four years on Elba on his own resources before there was any financial crisis.

Returning to France with Napoleon for the 100 Days, Guillaume Peyrusse was one again the state treasurer and was made an officer in the Legion of Honour on 21 June 1815 – three days after the Battle of Waterloo. With the Second Bourbon Restoration, he returned to Caracassone and worked with his father until Jean-Dominique Peyrusse died three years later. Two weeks before his father died, Guillaume Peyrusse married Marie-Antoinette Cabal Roujan, and they had a daughter. Guillaume Peyrusse was allowed to keep his title and was named a military superintendent on 21 June 1831 by the government of Louis-Philippe. He became an alderman of the city of Carcassone on 12 September that year, and was its mayor from 12 December 1832 to 5 October 1835. On 3 October 1852 during a visit to Carcassone, Prince Napoleon (later Napoleon III) met Peyrusse and on 1 July 1853 made him a Commander of the Legion of Honour. He died on 27 May 1860 and is buried in the St Vincent Cemetery in Carcassone.

References: Norman MacKenzie, *The Escape from Elba: The Fall & Flight of Napoleon 1814–1815*, Oxford: Oxford University Press, 1982; Léon Pelissier, *Lettres inédites de Guillaume Peyrusse à son frère André 1809–1814*, Paris: Plon, 1894; Roger Quentin, 'Peyrusse Guillaume Joseph (1776–1860) un trésorier de Napoléon, et sa famille', http://www.napoleon.org/fr/salle_lecture/biographies/files/472901.asp.

This photograph of Portoferraio is believed to be the first photograph taken on Elba.

PHOTOGRAPHY. John Ruskin refers to seeing daguerrotypes in Tuscany in 1846. These may have been the work of Tito Puliti (1809–1870) who worked in Florence and who probably made the first daguerrotypes in Italy which he produced on 2 September 1839. However no photographs seem to have been taken on Elba until 1855. With major interest in **Napoleon Bonaparte** and all aspects of his career, it seems likely that many photographs were taken by travellers from the 1860s. Gradually in the latter part of the nineteenth century, the production and the collecting of postcards became common, and many postcards of Elba were printed – again mainly on Napoleonic subjects. With the arrival of tourists from the 1960s, photographic development agencies became common, although with digital photography, most of these have now closed.

References: Graham Smith, 'Artists' Studies', in John Hannavy (ed), *Encyclopedia of Nineteenth-Century Photography*, New York: Routledge, 2008, vol. 1, pp. 85–86.

The west coast of the island of Pianosa.
Wikipedia Commons.

PIANOSA. This island in the **Tuscan archipelago** is flat and triangular in shape, and located 14 kilometres west of Elba. It was formally 'annexed' by

Napoleon Bonaparte in June 1814 with the ex-emperor visiting it on 12–17 September 1814. From 1858 until the mid–1990s it was a penal colony with no public access to the island. It is now possible to visit Pianosa on day trips from Elba. As part of the Archipelago Toscana National Park, it is a marine protected area and no fishing, diving or anchoring is allowed without prior permission.

References: Miles Roddis & Alex Leviton, *Tuscany & Umbria*, Footscray: Lonely Planet, 2006, p. 193.

PIAZZA CAVOUR (Portoferraio). Previously known as Piazza Granguardia, this is an open space just inside the Porta a Mare and traditionally the first place in Portoferraio any visitors. The walls have one seaward gate, the **Porta a Mare**, which was designed to protect the people of Portoferraio from an attack by the Corsairs (and also other Italians), and the Piazza Cavour, bing small and curving, would form the 'killing zone' should any attackers managed to breach the gate. On 4 May 1814 when Napoleon Bonaparte came to Elba, he entered through the Porta a Mare into the piazza heading straight on, towards the **Piazza della Repubblica**.

References: Norman MacKenzie, *The Escape from Elba: The Fall & Flight of Napoleon 1814–1815*, Oxford: Oxford University Press, 1982, p. 76.

PIAZZA DELLA REPUBBLICA. This is the central square in **Portoferraio** surrounded by cafés making it popular with tourists. On 5 May 1814 when **Napoleon** entered Portoferraio for the first time, he headed straight for the Piazza della Repubblica, through the small crowd which had gathered to attend a service in the parish church – now the Cathedral. Lined with trees it remains the commercial hub of Portoferraio.

References: Norman MacKenzie, *The Escape from Elba: The Fall & Flight of Napoleon 1814–1815*, Oxford: Oxford University Press, 1982, pp. 76–77.

PIOMBINO. This port on the Italian mainland is the location of the main ferry to Elba, and is a city on the basis of its Co-Cathedral of Sant'Animo built by the Augustinians in 1377 – and originally dedicated to St Michael. On account of its location, it has long had an influence on events on the island if Elba. The town developed during the time of the Etruscans who had a settlement at Populonia, very close to the modern-day city of Piombino.

Piombino was refounded by the Ostrogoths, and attacked by Greek pirates during the ninth century AD. From 1115 it became part of the Republic of Pisa, becoming an important port for the republic. This saw it attacked several times by the Genoese. However in 1398 Gherardo Appiani became lord of Piombino and it was briefly semi-independent of Pisa – controlling Elba, and also the islands of **Pianosa** and **Montecristo**. Although taken by **Cesare Borgia** in 1501–03, the Appianis ruled until 1634, although the Medicis from Florence did occupy it for a period. The principality of Piombino was established in 1594 and recognised by Emperor Rudolf II of Habsburg, but was annexed to the Kingdom of Etruria in 1801, and then became a part of the Grand Duchy of Tuscany in 1815.

    Maxwell Montgomery described the city in 1814:

Piombino is a small walled town belonging to Tuscany, with a citadel, and situated on a rocky promontory directly opposite to the island of Elba. It was once the capital of a principality of that name, and is now in a dilapidated condition, with a population of about three thousand. Its harbour is good, and it has considerable fisheries. The surrounding country is rich in corn, wine, and oil, but the grand allurement here, is the quantities of game of all sorts. The snipe and woodcock shooting is the best in the world, and there are wild boars in abundance. This used to be the resort of English sportsmen, and will be again.

When the French writer **Paul Gruyer** was heading to Elba to write his book on **Napoleon**, he stopped briefly at Piombino and he wrote:

Piombino is a typical old Italian town, with narrow streets, deep archways, and stone

Elba from Piombino, in the late 1930s.

towers scorched by the sun. It offers no accommodation whatever to travellers, scarcely even for one night. Facing the sea, its houses and ramparts descend abruptly into the water. Opposite is the island of Elba, outlined in violet against the sky; rocky and mountainous, its summits almost always enveloped in cloud. The distance between the mainland and the nearest point of the island is seven miles: to Portoferraio it is twelve and a half miles. A steamer conveys passengers and the mails twice a day, but these are obliged to go on board in small boats, as the shallow water does not admit of a large vessel close to shore. It frequently happens that the steamer is unable to cast anchor at all, or the small boats to put off with their load of passengers and luggage, and some little neighbouring port, or perhaps Porto Vecchio, is the starting place. Another service leaves Leghorn, and the passage, calling at Gorgona and Capraia on the way, takes eight hours.

The city's population has grown from 2,905 in 1861 to 18,649 in 1911, and 33,925 in 2001. Although there are some interesting medieval and renaissance sites in Piombino, much of the old part of the city was damaged during Allied bombing in **World War II**. Most visitors to the city head straight for the ferry terminal to go to Elba.

References: Città du Piombino, http://www.comune.piombino.li.it/; Paul Gruyer, *Napoleon, King of Elba*, Philadelphia: J. B. Lippincott Company, 1906, pp. 1–2; Maxwell Montgomery, *My Adventures*, London: H. Colburn, 1845, vol. 1, p. 194; Ettore Veruggio and Luciano Rebuffo, *Piombino*, Genova: Edoardo Garrone Raffineria petroli, 1968.

PISAN ELBA. The emerging Republic of Pisa on the Italian mainland had been keen to exploit the iron mines on Elba since at least the ninth century, in spite of them not having been active for many centuries. In 874 a fleet from Pisa defeated a Saracen fleet off the coast of Elba, and it seems likely that Pisan rule might have started soon after with the Pisans fortifying the island of Palmaiola in 909. The first documentary reference to Pisan overlordship of Elba is that their rule had been established by 1138. Certainly in 1004–05 there were Pisans fighting in Corsica and Sardinia, even sending soldiers as far as Calabria. Sending their army there led to the Moors attacking and under their leader Mujāhid al-'Āmirī (Mogehid, or Musetto). Mujāhid al-'Āmirī was able to take Sardinia and even launched an attack on the mouth of the River Arno, plundering the suburbs of Pisa. In return the Pisans launched a major attack on Mujāhid al-'Āmirī in Sardinia. They destroyed the Moorish fleet and forced him to agree to peace. However he planned to make a 'come-back'. In 1015 he launched an attack not on Sardinia as expected, but instead at Portoferraio in Elba. He left a small garrison there, then re-embarked his army and attacked near La Spezia on the mainland. This surprise assault allowed him to capture the city of Luni and his soldiers were able to forage right up to

Pisan soldiers in action.

the walls of Pisa and Genoa. This so terrified the Christian city states of Italy that they allied at the urging of Pope Benedict VII. They defeated Mujāhid al-'Āmirī at Luni and then sent their fleet to Elba. At Portoferraio, they found that the Moors, having heard of the defeat of Mujāhid al-'Āmirī, had fled. The original inhabitants then emerged from the woods and the mountains where they had taken refuge during the brief Moorish occupation.

Although Pisa would have had influence in Elba since before 1016, it might well have been in this year that Elba was formally incorporated into the Republic of Pisa. The power of Pisa grew and from 1030–35 their armed forces took parts of Sicily and also the city of Carthage in North Africa. Possibly using Elba as a base, in 1051–52, Admiral Jacopo Ciurini conquered Corsica. This then provoked the Genoese into action obliging the Pisans to form an alliance with the Normans in Italy. In 1060 the Pisan navy defeated the Genoese fleet and the Republic of Pisa grew considerably in strength, being able to launch 120 ships to help in the First Crusade (1096–99).

With Pisa expanding its power, it was also keen to protect its possessions including Elba, and built up the fortifications of the island. The Pisans were also responsible for the building of a number of churches with San Giovanni on the slopes of Mount Perone, San Lorenzo below **Marciana**, and Santo Stefano near Magazzini being examples. However the best of these is the

Church of San Michele, at **Capoliveri**, and although only parts of the apse survive, the church is believed to demonstrate the purest Pisan architectural design.

The Genoese had long wanted to challenge the power of Pisa, and take control of the iron mines of Elba, and so launched a raid on Elba in 1162. The Genoese landed near Capo San Andrea below Marciana, and on 5–6 August 1222 the Genoese fleet commanded by Alberto Doria defeated the Pisans at the battle of Meloria, signalling the start of the decline of Pisan power. In 1291 the Genoese sent Niccolò Boccanegara with 60 galleys to attack Elba. It took them four months to capture the island. The Pisans then recaptured it in 1292 but were driven out by the Genoese after only three months. Then in 1293 the Pisans retook the island under their new commander Guido da Montefeltro. To avoid further costly conflicts, the Pisans agreed to pay Genoa some 50,000 gold florins. This resulted in peace in Elba for the next hundred years but saw a gradual decline in Pisan power.

In 1376 Pope **Gregory XI** arrived on Elba, during a journey from Avignon to Rome. Eleven years later, there was a new challenge to the sea power of Pisa. This came from the Saracens or Moors from North Africa. Some ships in the normally safe Straits of **Piombino** were captured by the North Africans who were to become better known as the Corsairs. Then there were political problems in Pisa itself. The lord of Pisa, Pietro Gambacorti was assassinated in 1392 by his secretary Jacobo Appiano (I). After Jacobo Appiano died in 1398, his son Gherado sold Pisa and most of its land to Galeazzo Viscount, the duke of Milan for 200,000 florins. Gherado Appiano then moved to Piombino and established the principality of Piombino which maintained its control over Elba, Pianosa and Montecristo heralding two centuries of rule by the Appiani family.

References: Ottavio Banti, *An Illustrated History of Pisa*, Pisa: Pacini Editore, 2010; Eric Cochrane, *Florence in the Forgotten Centuries*, Chicago: The University of Chicago Press, 1974; Averil Mackenzie-Grieve, *Aspects of Elba and the other islands of the Tuscan Archipelago*, London: Jonathan Cape, 1964, Chapter 3; Christopher and Jean Serpell, *The Travellers' Guide to Elba and the Tuscan Archipelago*, London: Jonathan Cape, 1977, pp. 102–04.

POCAR, ERVINO (1892–1981). An Italian scholar of German studies and translator, he was born on 4 April 1892 at Pirano, Istria, the son of Giovanni Pocar and Giovanna Maria. He grew up speaking Slovenian as well as Italian, and then learnt German at school. He went to the University of Vienna but

Póggio.
Photograph © Masterlu / Fotolia.com

Póggio.
Photograph © bill_17 / Fotolia.com

Póggio, from an old postcard.

his studies were interrupted by **World War I**. Pocar then started working as a translator and translated the works of Lion Feuchtwanger, Franz Grillparzer, Hermann Hesse, Franz Kafka, Thomas Mann, and Erich Maria Remarque. He continued his work until his death on 17 August 1981 in Milan. Ervino Pocar loved Elba and regularly holidayed on the island with his wife Cesi de Rosa who was from **Portoferraio**.

References: Nicoletta Dacrema, *Ritratto di un germanista: Ervino Pocar*, Gorizia: Biblioteca statale isontina, 1989; Celso Macor. *Ervino Pocar*, Pordenone: Studio Tesi, 1997.

PÓGGIO ('Mountain Spur'). This is a small inland hill settlement to the west of the island and has long been a 'twin' to nearby Marciana Alta although there are key differences. At **Marciana Alta** there was a Pisan fort but at Póggio, the church dedicated to Saint Nicholas, originally built in the eight century, was a place of refuge in times of attack. Close to Póggio, on the road between Marciana Alta and Póggio, there is also a freshwater spring. **Napoleon** is said to have tasted the waters there in August 1814 when he was considering entertaining Marie Walewska at the Sanctuary of Madonna del Monte. He was suffering a chronic bladder complaint at the time and found the waters soothing. They were then bottled as Acqua di Napoleone, with the spring itself called 'Fonte di Napoleone'.

References: Roberto Donati, *The Island of Elba*, Terni: Fotorapidacolor, 1973, pp. 30–37; Guido Giubella, *Elba: A Garden in the Blu*, Milan: Co.Graf Editrice, 1988, pp. 48–50; Averil Mackenzie-Grieve, *Aspects of Elba and the other islands of the Tuscan Archipelago*, London: Jonathan Cape, 1964, pp. 97f; Miles Roddis & Alex Leviton, *Tuscany & Umbria*, Footscray: Lonely Planet, 2006, p. 189; Christopher and Jean Serpell, *The Travellers' Guide to Elba and the Tuscan Archipelago*, London: Jonathan Cape, 1977, pp. 221–24.

POLICE. Up to the **Napoleonic Wars** the policing of Elba was carried out by the army garrisons there. **Napoleon**, however, wanted a separate police force but with his departure from the island in 1815, the policing was undertaken by officers serving the magistrates appointed by the Grand Duchy of Tuscany.

There are now a number of police forces with the civil national police being the Polizia di Stato (State Police) which traces its origins back to 1852. The Guardia di Finanza (Financial Guard) work under the minister of economy and finance and focus on financial crimes such as tax evasion, smuggling, customs and illegal migration. The Arma dei Carabinieri serve as a wing of the armed forces and performs many police functions as well as being the military police for the Italian armed forces. The Polizia Penitenziaria (prison guards) operate the prison system; and the Corpo Forestale dello Stato (National Forestry Department) is responsible for law enforcement in Italian national parks and forests. The main police station on Elba is Portoferraio (tel: 112, 113). Some of the different arms of the police forces share the headquarters at Viale Alessandro Manzoni, 6, **Portoferraio**.

References: Roy D. Ingleton, *Police of the World*, London: Ian Allan Ltd, 1979, pp. 98–101.

POMFRET, FRED (1918–1944). A British able seaman with H.M.S. *Copra* (combined operations), he was born in Lancashire, the son of Fred Pomfret and Ethel (née Chadwick), of Atherton, Lancashire. He was badly injured during the landings on Elba on 17 June 1944 and died the same day from his wounds, being buried in Corsica at Biguglia War Cemetery (2 B 5).

PONCE de LEÓN y SUÁREZ de FIGUEROA, RODRIGO (c1545–1630). The third duke of Arcos, he was the Spanish governor based at Porto Longone (now **Porto Azzurro**) and in 1606 started building the Sanctuary of the Madonna di Monserrato, giving it the name Monserrat as it reminded him of Montserrat near

Barcelona. A Caballero del Toisón de Oro (knight of the Order of the Golden Fleece), he was the son of Luis Ponce de Léon, (1528–1573), the second duke, who had been a Spanish commander in Flanders. He married Teresa de Mendoza y Zúñiga Aragon, the daughter of the fifth duke of Béjar, and their son Rodrigo, born in 1602, succeeded to the title and became the fourth duke of Arcos.

PONS DE L'HÉRAULT, ANDRÉ (1772–1853). He was the administrator of the iron mines on Elba during the time of **Napoleon Bonaparte**'s residence. Born on 11 June 1772 at Sète, Hérault, France, he was the son of an innkeeper and initially he planned to become a priest. Instead he went to sea at a young age and became inspired by the French Revolution and joined the French armed forces becoming a naval officer at the age of 18. He served at the siege of Toulon – the port being in the hands of the British and French Royalists, with the revolutionaries attacking it. It was during the fighting that he met the young Napoleon Bonaparte and they became friends. However afterwards because of his support for Maximilien Robespierre, André Pons de l'Hérault was arrested and thrown into prison. He was later released but never lost any of his revolutionary zeal. He put his name to a pamphlet attacking the events of 18 Brunaire when Napoleon seized power. However because of his friendship with Bernard Germain de Lacepede, the new chancellor of the Legion of Honour, he was appointed to run the iron mines on the island of Elba which had been gifted to the Legion of Honour.

Pons de l'Hérault was one of the local dignitaries who gathered when the *Undaunted* arrived at **Portoferraio** on 3 May 1814. He then worked with Napoleon on the island with the ex-emperor remembering him from their time together at Toulon. He persuaded Pons de l'Hérault to hand over the profits from the mine to the royal household which this helped assuage **Guillaume Peyrusse**, Napoleon's treasurer, who was worried that the ex-emperor would quickly run out of money. He accompanied Napoleon Bonaparte back to France for the 100 Days and was appointed the Prefect of the Rhone with the task of defending that sector against enemy attack. When Napoleon was sent to St. Helena, he wanted to go too, but ended up wandering Europe and only returning to France in 1821. After the accession of Louis-Philippe in 1830, he obtained a political position as prefect of Jura but resigned after he clashed with Marshal Soult who was, once again, the minister of war. With the proclamation of the Second Republic in 1848, Pons de l'Hérault was exalted for his republican ideals and for his championing of universal suffrage. He was made a councillor of state, and unsurprisingly opposed the coup of Louis Napoleon in 1851. André Pons de l'Hérault died in 1853.

References: Pierre Branda, *L'île d'Elbe et le retour de Napoléon: 1814–1815*, Saint-Cloud: Soteca, 2014; Robert Christophe, *Napoleon on Elba*, London: Macdonald, 1964, pp. 44f; Raymond Horricks, *Napoleon's Elite*, New Brunswick: Transaction Publishers, 1995, pp. 206–07; Norman MacKenzie, *The Escape from Elba: The Fall & Flight of Napoleon 1814–1815*, Oxford: Oxford University Press, 1982; Pons de l'Hérault, *Souvenirs et Anecdotes de l'île d'Elbe*, Paris: Plon, 1897; *Napoléon, empereur de l'île d'Elbe, Souvenirs et anecdotes de Pons de l'Hérault*, Paris: Les éditeurs libres, 2005.

PORTA A MARE. This is a 'sea gate' into **Portoferraio** and was built by Duke **Cosimo de 'Medici**. Traditionally most people arriving in Portoferraio landed at the docks and entered the port through this gate – indeed for many years it was the only opening in the Grand Rampart which protected the town from assault by sea. It has on it an inscription from Duke Cosimo de 'Medici stating that he was the founder of the town: 'Churches, walls, houses, fortresses, and harbour, Cosimo, duke of the Florentines, erected them all from the foundations upwards, AD 1548.'. There is also another later inscription: 'Ferdinando II, grand duke of Tuscany, completed it in AD 1637, the year in which he took Victoriam Princess of Urbino, as his wife, by happy omen.'

It was still the only gate from the sea into Portoferraio on 4 May 1814 when Napoleon Bonaparte arrived, and was greeted by the local dignitaries and presented with gilded keys to symbolise the keys of the town, although these were actually from the wine cellar of **Traditi**, the mayor. He saw the inscriptions were in Latin, and were translated for him by Joseph Hutré, the deputy mayor. The ex-emperor then passed under a gilded canopy into the town. Entering through the gate, visitors then find themselves in **Piazza Cavour**. Subsequently two extra entrances were cut into the wall for cars to gain access to the old town.

References: Norman MacKenzie, *The Escape from Elba: The Fall & Flight of Napoleon 1814–1815*, Oxford: Oxford University Press, 1982, p. 75.

PORTA A TERRA (PORTOFERRAIO). The land gate into **Portoferraio**

Photograph © vinicio tullio / Fotolia.com

built by **Cosimo de 'Medici** and with the **Porta a Mare**, was one of only two original entrances into the original city.

PORTO AZZURRO. This port is located in a sheltered cove on the east of the island, and is a natural port and has been settled since medieval times. The current township owes its origins to the Spaniards who called the place Porto Longone and officially founded it on 8 May 1596, and built a fortress in 1603 to protect the settlement against attack by the Austrians and then the French. For many years the fortress was used to hold political prisoners and local criminals. The port now has a population of 3,100 residents. During the tourist season there are regular daily excursions from Port Azzurro to the island of **Montecristo**.

The old town is popular with many tourists where there are a range of hotels there and also a number in nearby resorts. The old fort, Fort San Giacomo (sometimes described as Fort Longone), was turned into a prison, but it is still possible to visit parts of it where local handicrafts are sold. The Spanish church nearby has a marble monument to General Diego d'Alarcson. The other main site in the town is The Sanctuary of the Madonna di Monserrato. It was built by the Spanish governor **José Ponce de Léon** from 1606, and the name comes from the fact that the nearby area reminded him of Montserrat near Barcelona. The most famous item in the church is a painting of the Virgin Mary which is kept inside the Sanctuary. It is considered an exact copy of the one in the Sanctuary in Spain bearing the same name. Also to those interested in twentieth century history is the Port Azzurro Cemetery which has the graves of **Chester Wilmot** and others who died in the **Comet Plane Crash** on 10 January 1954.

Many tourists to Porto Azzurro also use it as a base to visit nearby Monserrato on Lake Terranera. This settlement is north of Porto Azzurro and provides fascinating views of the area. The Reale Beach is popular with tourists and there is the nearby Rossa Beach which is much smaller and can often be found quite deserted, even in the tourist season.

References: Arsène Thiébaut de Berneaud, *A Voyage to the Isle of Elba*, London: Longman, Hurst, Rees, Orme and Brown, 1814, pp. 132–37; Roberto Donati, *The Island of Elba*, Terni: Fotorapidacolor, 1973, pp. 14–17; Dan Facaros and Michael Pauls, *Italy: Tuscany*, London: Cadogan Books plc, 1996, p. 301; Elena Giménez-Forcada, Bencini Alberto and Giovanni Pranzini, 'Hydrogeochemical considerations about the origin of groundwater salinization in some coastal plains of Elba Island (Tuscany, Italy)', *Environmental Geochemistry and Health* vol. 32, no 3 (2010), pp. 243–57; Guido Giubella, *Elba: A Garden in the Blu*, Milan: Co.Graf Editrice, 1988, pp. 68–75; Averil Mackenzie-Grieve, *Aspects of Elba and the other islands of the Tuscan Archipelago*, London: Jonathan Cape, 1964, pp. 140–54; Miles Roddis & Alex Leviton, *Tuscany & Umbria*, Footscray: Lonely Planet, 2006, pp. 191–92; Christopher and Jean Serpell, *The Travellers' Guide to Elba and the Tuscan Archipelago*, London: Jonathan Cape, 1977, pp. 184–86.

PORTO LONGONE. This was the former name of **Porto Azzurro**, the name being changed in 1947.

PORTOFERRAIO ('Iron Port'). The main port of Elba, according to tradition was where the **Argonauts** came to after they found the legendary Golden Fleece. The settlement was called Fabricia by the Romans, and later as Ferraia ('iron'), although this settlement might be in a slightly different location to where the existing town is today, and no trace has been found of the medieval town. The harbour was bought by **Cosimo de' Medici** during the sixteenth century, and the town renamed Cosmopolis, and it was during this time that the city walls were built. Over ten years from 1548, a fortress city developed with the walls designed to cope with the new developments in firearms and cannons.

In order to protect the port from attack by either the North African Corsairs or his Italian rivals, Cosimo de 'Medici allowed only two gates into the town. The main one, from the sea, was called **Porta a Mare**, and this has on it an

Portoferraio.
Photograph © Kletr / fotolia.com.

inscription by Cosimo de 'Medici stating that he built the town. The other, from the landward side, is the **Porta a Terra**. On entering through the Porta a Mare, there was only the relatively small Piazza Granguardia (now **Piazza Cavour**) which provided the 'killing zone' trapping any attackers who might have managed to break through the Porta a Mare.

The walls remained strong with Portoferraio able to withstand a siege by the French in 1801–02 only to find that the island had been ceded to France by the Treaty of Amiens. And it was to the old city that **Napoleon** arrived on 4 May 1814. Indeed when Napoleon Bonaparte arrived in Portoferraio, the Porta a Mare was still the only seaward entrance, and it was at this gate that Pietro Traditi handed him a set of gilded keys to represent the 'keys of the city' – although they were actually the keys of **Traditi**'s wine cellar.

The authorities in Portoferraio did not take much notice of the arrival of Napoleon Bonaparte, and there were not many places in the port where he could spend the night. The most obvious place was the top floor of the **Portoferraio Town Hall**. This was where, according to some traditions, the young **Victor Hugo** had lived when his father had been posted to Elba – although some biographies of the writer claim that this is not proven.

There are many other buildings in Portoferraio dating from the time of

Portoferraio in 1744.

Portoferraio in c1870.

Napoleon's arrival at Portoferraio on 4 May 1814.

Portoferraio.
Photograph © Antonio Scarpi / Fotolia.com

Napoleon Bonaparte's stay in Elba. On his arrival there was a service in the Cathedral. Two of the churches, the **Church of the Holy Sacrament** and the **Church of (The Reverenda) Misericordia** have death masks of Napoleon, and there is an annual service in the latter church to commemorate the death of Napoleon. Also of interest is the **Albergo l'Ape Elbana** (Hotel of the Bee of

Ansicht von Porto-Ferrajo auf der Insel Elba.

Elba), where many people who came to visit Napoleon in 1814–15 stayed. At that time it was called the Auberge Bonroux, and remains a relatively popular budget hotel.

Visiting the island in around 1901, **Paul Gruyer** wrote:

Porto Ferraio is an extraordinary town. Many streets are nothing but staircases, and the place is full of arches, tunnels, and ramparts covered with the sword-like aloe leaves and cactuses. Imagination takes one back to Carthage! Surely Salammbo's litter will appear on the steps, just at that corner flooded with sunlight, and up above, between those battlements outlined against the blue sky, there must be a mercenary stringing his bow and polishing his helmet…

As the evening closed in, I went down the hill to the town. Sunset is the hour when people of the South grow active after the heat of the day. The town, silent up till now, almost suddenly became active and noisy. On the public square near the harbour the townspeople walked up and down talking and exchanging greetings. Such places are the forum of Italian towns, where all affairs public and private are discussed. The shops were full of buyers. I read amongst the names: Andrea Borgia, Sweet Biscuits; Dante, Shoemaker; and farther on, Orestes and Son, Groceries and Macaroni. A decrepit old woman under an archway sold beans and baked almonds. Women drew water from the fountains in their hammered copper jugs. And as the evening wore on the noise increased. The people seemed to talk for the pleasure of talking, and children cried for the same reason. It was like Paris on some 14th July – guitars, flutes, and accordions joined in the concert. Every sound was musical. Even the street urchins shouted musically. The sounds floated to my windows, mingling in a joyous melody. In this theatrical setting they seemed like the music of an opera.

It lasted till eleven or twelve, and then, little by little, the sounds ceased. The waning moon rose, whitening the stones of the stairways and the battlemented walls, and on their terraces reappeared the shadowy form of Salammbo, mysteriously dancing and beckoning.

The next day I spent in exploring Porto Ferraio. At every turn I found the picturesque and unexpected. The Abbe Soldani, who acted as my guide, slapped me on the shoulder in a friendly way at intervals, exclaiming 'Vive la glorieuse France! Vive le glorieuse Empereur Napoleon!'

Don C. Seitz wrote in 1910:

Sunday morning is market-time at Porto Ferraio, and the town is en fête. The country people come in with their wares, and the townspeople gather in the market-place to gossip and to buy. The churches are open for those who wish to hear mass. The women ride in on large donkeys – much larger than those of Italy – sitting astride, with skirts firmly tucked in, before the panniers which balance on either side. Often a daughter or a friend rides behind. The men walk or ride in stout, two-wheeled carts, but the donkey is the rule with the ladies. They are good-looking, these people of Elba. The women are tall and straight, with fine features, aquiline noses, full lips, and noble hair. Their eyes do not flash as in Italy, but look steadily and clearly at all comers without shrinking or concern. The elder women wear gay kerchiefs for a head-dress, but the young need no adornment other than their abundant locks. The men, too, are tall, and if not as handsome in looks and bearing as

Portoferraio.
Photograph © jarre / Fotolia.com

Portoferraio.
Photograph © jarre / Fotolia.com

the splendid women, have an air of activity and independence, and somehow a suggestion of Spain about them. Here and there around the market-place stand tall fellows wrapped in bravo cloaks such as old Madrid pictures show, folded over the shoulder, with an end hiding the arm – and a knife, maybe!

There was plenty of meat in the market-place, and plenty to wear in the shops. Red overcoats of blanket stuff, and lined with heavy fur, seemed popular garments, though the December days were mild. Strangers are not plenty, but there was small staring. The innkeeper hurried to oblige with a pass to San Martino, a carriage with its single horse, and to furnish his last bottle of native wine. The other guests drank deep-red chianti from bulbous flasks. Some champagne is made on Elba, but it was not obtainable. The native wine was straw-colored, with a tang of sherry, and heady in results.

Lydia Bushnell Smith later wrote:

The city of Portoferraio rises on the slopes of a peninsula that extends from the sea to the inner bay, and is dominated by the two fortresses on their unequal heights. The higher one is toward the west, where formerly stood a Roman castle, on the ruins of which was built the larger Medicean defence, called the Falcone; the other, smaller one toward the east, is named the Stella, because of the topography of the country, which gives to it the appearance of a ray, or extension from the other. From those two heights, the wall winds down to the bay, forming, by its tongue-shaped strip of land (which has received the suggestive name of La Linguella) an almost circular basin. The bay thus protected, is the pride and joy of the Italians, who find it a magnificent playground for their squadron in time of peace, as well as a possible means of defence in time of war. It was there, and in the Gulf of Longone, that the brilliant 'maneuvers' were indulged in that called forth the admiration of the naval world. It has been admitted by the Italian Admirals, that some of the tactics used successfully in the war with Tripoli, were the result of experiments in the Elban waters. At present not a single cannon makes possible a salute to royalty. A commandant once lamenting the fact to his royal guest, said 'Sire, there are an hundred reasons why I failed to salute you; The first is that we have no cannon. I think, sir, that we can dispense with the other ninety-nine', answered His Majesty.

Gradually the town expanded but much of it was damaged during the bombing by the Germans and then by the Allies. As a result, **Christopher Serpell** and his wife Jean noted that the 'modern sector of Portoferraio is more useful than beautiful'. The town now has a population of about 11,000 and many tourists and visitors to Elba enjoy the surviving old buildings with their connections to, and associations with the Medici and with Napoleon. The main bookshop is Il Libraio, Calata Mazzini 10.

References: Vernon Bartlett, *A Book about Elba*, London: Chatto & Windus, 1965, Chapter 3; Eric Cochrane, *Florence in the Forgotten Centuries*, Chicago: The University of Chicago Press, 1974, p. 65; Arsène Thiébaut de Berneaud, *A Voyage to the Isle of Elba*, London: Longman, Hurst, Rees, Orme and Brown, 1814, pp. 105–14; Roberto Donati, *The

Portoferraio.
Photograph © jarre / Fotolia.com

Portoferraio.
Photograph © jarre / Fotolia.com

Portoferraio.
Photograph © jarre / Fotolia.com

Portoferraio.
Photograph © magati / Fotolia.com

Portoferraio.
Photograph © mor65 / Fotolia.com

Portoferraio.
Photograph © Antonio Scarpi / Fotolia.com

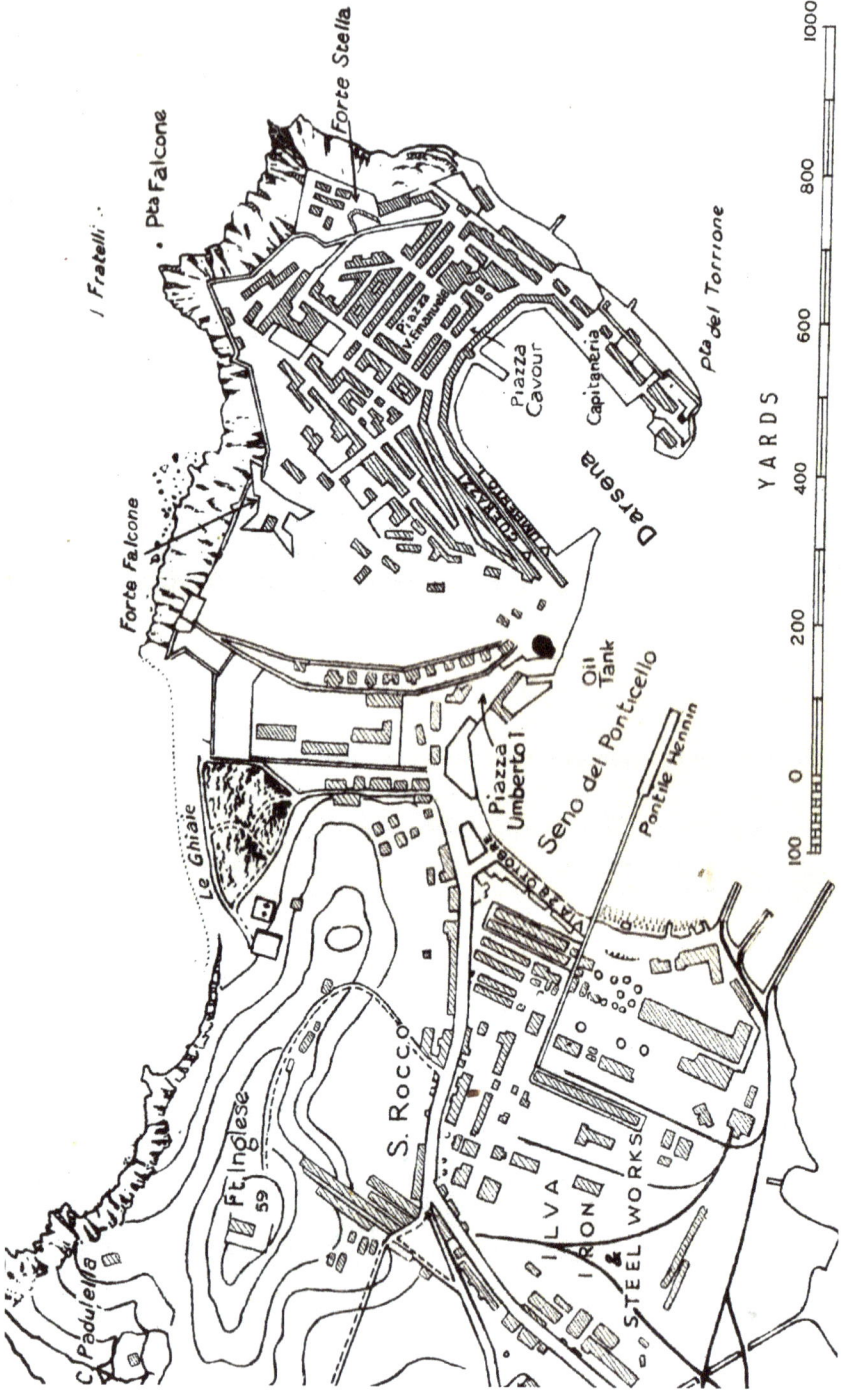

Portoferraio in the late 1930s.

The iron works in the late 1930s.

Island of Elba, Terni: Fotorapidacolor, 1973, pp. 3–7; Dan Facaros and Michael Pauls, *Italy: Tuscany*, London: Cadogan Books plc, 1996, pp. 299–301; Paul Gruyer, *Napoleon, King of Elba*, Philadelphia: J. B. Lippincott Company, 1906, p. 4f; Guido Giubella, *Elba: A Garden in the Blu*, Milan: Co.Graf Editrice, 1988, pp. 28–41; Miles Roddis & Alex Leviton, *Tuscany & Umbria*, Footscray: Lonely Planet, 2006, pp. 186–87; Don Carlos Seitz, *Elba and Elsewhere*, New York: Harper and Brothers, 1910, pp. 4–6; Christopher and Jean Serpell, *The Travellers' Guide to Elba and the Tuscan Archipelago*, London: Jonathan Cape, 1977, pp. 150–69; Lydia Bushnell Smith, *Napoleon's Elba*, Florence: Successori B. Seeber, 1914, pp. 28–30.

PORTOFERRAIO CATHEDRAL. Dedicated to the Nativity of the Blessed Virgin Mary, it was built for **Cosimo de 'Medici** from 1548 and is located in **Piazza della Repubblica**. It is not really a cathedral although it is traditionally called the Cathedral Church. Constructed in a Florentine style, it originally had only one central aisle, but in 1623 it was transformed with the addition of two side chapels, and during the eighteenth century the altar was rededicated. On 4 May 1814 when **Napoleon Bonaparte** entered Portoferraio, he passed through the crowds in the Piazza della Repubblica on his way to the cathedral where Monsignor **Arrighi**, a Corsican and distant relative of the ex-emperor, held a service of thanksgiving for him. Later when Napoleon deconsecrated the nearby and already largely disused 'Church of the Red', to turn it into the **Teatro dei Vigilanti**, the marble altar from that church was moved to the cathedral church. Open to worshippers and to the public, the church still has a wooden crucifix dating from 1549.

PORTOFERRAIO TOWN HALL. This was a bakery during the time of **Cosimo de 'Medici** and later was reported that **Victor Hugo**'s father lived there along with baby Victor Hugo in 1802, although this has not been confirmed. When **Napoleon Bonaparte** arrived on Elba on 4 May 1814, a reception was organised for him in the town hall, and the upper floor was cleared, with him living there until 21 May when he moved to the **Villa dei Mulini**.

References: Norman MacKenzie, *The Escape from Elba: The Fall & Flight of Napoleon 1814–1815*, Oxford: Oxford University Press, 1982, p. 73.

POSTAL SERVICES. Letters have been carried to and from Elba on boats since ancient times, and from the time **Napoleon** was on Elba, there are detailed records of ships coming and going, bringing and taking letters, mainly to Leghorn (Livorno). The Grand Duchy of Tuscany introduced postage stamps on 1 April 1851 and from March 1860 to 1862 it used postage stamps of the

A cover from Smryna to Elba, believed to be the only surviving registered cover from the Italian post office in Smyrna. It sold for $3,000 at Cherrystone Philatelic Auctioneers in January 2009.

kingdom of Sardinia. After then, Italian stamps were valid. For philatelists, early covers to and from Elba are scarce. There are also revenue stamps issued by Elba but these were for paying of local taxes and levies, and have no postal use – although they are often still collected by philatelists.

The main post office on Elba is located on **Piazza della Repubblica** in Portoferraio, and decorated with a bas-relief sculpted by Arturo Dazzi to commemorate the local poet **Pietro Gori**. There are smaller post offices throughout Elba. In spite of the image of Napoleon appearing on many stamps published around the world, none seem to show him at Elba. The Italian postal authorities issued a stamp with an image of **Marciana Marina** in a series celebrating tourism on 18 April 1998.

POVIA, GIUSEPPE (1972–). An Italian pop singer best-known as 'Povia', he was born on 19 November 1972 in Milan. He taught himself to play the guitar when he was 14 and started composing when he was 20. His songs became popular in 2003 with his 2005 single 'Avampost 55' about the plight of the children in Darfur, Sudan. His 2006 single, bambini fanno: Oh, sold 200,000 copies and helped to raise money to build hospitals in Darfur. Povia's family were originally from Elba, and he has performed several times at **Porto Azzurro**.

References: Giuseppe Povia, http://www.povia.net/.

PREHISTORIC ELBA. Remains have been found on Elba going back to prehistoric times and indicate a flourishing civilisation. Some chipped and flaked implements along with bones of large mammals such as the cave bear, rhinoceros and hippopotamus, have been dated as far back as 48,000 BC indicating the first wave of a Mousterian / Neanderthal culture. At that time Elba was still linked to mainland Italy. There is a change in finds from 38,000 BC indicating a second wave of the Mousterian culture, and more sophisticated weapons and implements from about 18,000 BC are linked to the arrival of Homo sapiens.

Around 10,000 BC, Elba became an island, and seafarers arrived in about 5,000–4,000 BC bringing with them much more advanced weapons and implements, or made them on the island. There is also surviving pottery from the Neolithic period. From around 3,000 BC Bronze Age cultures flourished. These are Rinaldonian and archaeologists have found arrow and spear heads, axes and also daggers fashioned from copper. From 2,000 to 700 BC, the Sub-Apennine culture in Elba flourished. They might be the tribe that the Roman historian Livy calls the **Ilvates**. From this period, pottery milk boilers, spindles, weights for looms, and razor-sharp shell scrapers have been found. It would be during this period that Elbans started travelling from the island but whether or not they fought in the Trojan Wars is clearly debateable.

References: Cyprian Brookbank, *The Making of the Middle Sea*, London: Thames & Hudson, 2013; Christopher and Jean Serpell, *The Travellers' Guide to Elba and the Tuscan Archipelago*, London: Jonathan Cape, 1977, pp. 96–97.

PUBLIC HOLIDAYS. There are 18 official public holidays on Elba.

1 January	New Year's Day.
6 January	Epiphany.
11 February	Half-holiday in honour of the Concordat (between Italy and the Vatican).
19 March	Feast Day of St Joseph.
March/April	Easter Monday.
25 April	Liberation Day (Festa della Liberazione) commemorating the end of World War II and the end of the Nazi occupation.
1 May	Labour Day.
-	Ascension Day (the sixth Thursday after Easter Sunday).
-	Corpus Domini (the ninth Thursday after Easter Sunday).
2 June	Anniversary of the Proclamation of the Republic of Italy.
29 June	Feast day of St Peter and St Paul.
15 August	Ferragosto: the Feast of the Assumption of the Virgin Mary.
4 October	The feast day of St Francis (half-holiday).
1 November	All Saints' Day.
4 November	Victory Day commemorating the victory over the Austro-Hungarian Empire in 1918.
8 December	Feast Day for the Conception of the Virgin Mary.
25 December	Christmas Day.
26 December	Boxing Day.

See also **Feast Days**.

PUBLIC TRANSPORT. Public transport on Elba is provided by buses. They generally originate from **Portoferraio** and radiate around the island, with routes designed for locals rather than tourists. Services start early in the morning and many services are cancelled during school holidays, and there is a much reduced service on Sundays and public holidays.

References: Miles Roddis & Alex Leviton, *Tuscany & Umbria*, Footscray: Lonely Planet, 2006, p. 186; Christopher and Jean Serpell, *The Travellers' Guide to Elba and the Tuscan Archipelago*, London: Jonathan Cape, 1977, p. 37–38.

- R -

RAILWAYS. There is no railway on the island of Elba, but many visitors who go to Elba travel by train to **Piombino**, and from there catch the ferry to Elba.

References: Christopher and Jean Serpell, *The Travellers' Guide to Elba and the Tuscan Archipelago*, London: Jonathan Cape, 1977, pp. 35–36.

RIO MARINA. This is the port for **Rio Nell'Elba** close to **Portoferraio** and has been in use since ancient times as a place for the loading of iron from the mines at Rio Nell'Elba. The Pisans built an octagonal watch tower there to protect both Rio Marina and Rio Nell'Elba. The **Museo Archeologico** del Distretto Minerario (Mineralogical Museum) is located at Rio Marina. It is in the Palazzo Comunale and has a wide range of rocks and mineral samples found on the island, with specimens dating back to the third millennium BC through to medieval times. The Museum is open in May and June from 11 am to 1 pm, and then from 2 pm to 7 pm. It is open by appointment at other times.

References: Roberto Donati, *The Island of Elba*, Terni: Fotorapidacolor, 1973, p. 19–21; Dan Facaros and Michael Pauls, *Italy: Tuscany*, London: Cadogan Books plc, 1996, p. 301; Guido Giubella, *Elba: A Garden in the Blu*, Milan: Co.Graf Editrice, 1988, pp. 82–87;

Photograph © tuombre / Fotolia.com

Rio Marina in the late 1930s.

Mauro Mele, Diego Servida and Domenico Lupis, 'Characterisation of sulphide-bearing waste-rock dumps using electrical resistivity imaging: the case study of the Rio Marina mining district (Elba Island, Italy)', *Environmental monitoring and assessment* vol. 185, no 7 (July 2013), pp. 5891–907; Christopher and Jean Serpell, *The Travellers' Guide to Elba and the Tuscan Archipelago*, London: Jonathan Cape, 1977, pp. 189–93.

RIO NELL'ELBA. This is an old mining centre close to **Portoferraio** and there is evidence of settlements there from Etruscan times, with some Roman sites around the mines. It derives its name from a nearby stream and there is also a spring which might have led to the original settlement there. The people in Rio are known as Riesi and are regarded as tougher and more independent than many other people on Elba.

There is an eleventh century **Pisan** castle at Rio Nell'Elba built to protect the mines and to serve as a place of refuge should the port be attacked. The town itself is regarded as rather bleak with a Spanish governor destroying many of the fortifications during the eighteenth century after the local people supported the Austrians against the Spanish. The church in the settlement dates back to medieval times.

References: Arsène Thiébaut de Berneaud, *A Voyage to the Isle of Elba*, London: Longman, Hurst, Rees, Orme and Brown, 1814, pp. 115–31; Roberto Donati, *The Island of Elba*, Terni: Fotorapidacolor, 1973, p. 18; Dan Facaros and Michael Pauls, *Italy: Tuscany*, London: Cadogan Books plc, 1996, p. 301; Guido Giubella, *Elba: A Garden in the Blu*, Milan: Co.Graf Editrice, 1988, pp. 78–81; Christopher and Jean Serpell, *The Travellers' Guide to Elba and the Tuscan Archipelago*, London: Jonathan Cape, 1977, pp. 189–93.

ROMAN ELBA. *See* **Ancient Elba**.

ROSSI, BRUNO (1915–1977). An Italian **footballer**, he was born on 7 July 1915 and played as a mid-fielder for Elbana until 1935, and then for Livorno 1936–42, and then Spezia, 1942–43, 1945–47, ending his career with Lavagnese, 1947–48. He died on 14 September 1977 at La Spezia.

ROWLEDGE, BERNARD ALBERT (1920–1944). A British seaman, he was born in mid–1920 in Solihull, Warwickshire, the son of Albert Victor Rowledge and his wife Clara Luena Rowledge (née Harvey) of Catherine de Barnes, Solihull. Working as a leading stoker in the Royal Navy, he was killed on the first day of the Allied attack on Elba on 17 June 1944, and was buried on Elba and three years later was reburied in the Bolsena War Cemetery (IV G 9) on the Italian mainland.

References: *The war dead of the British Commonwealth and Empire: the register of the names of those who fell in the 1939–1945 War and are buried in cemeteries in Italy Cemeteries 17–18: Bolsena War Cemetery, Orvieto War Cemetery*, Maidenhead: Imperial War Graves Commission, 1954, p. 31.

RUSSELL, JOHN, 1st Earl Russell (1792–1878). The British prime minister from 30 June 1846 to 23 February 1852, and again from 29 October 1865 to 28 June 1866, he was born on 18 August 1792 in Westminster, London, the third son of Lord John Russell (1766–1839) and his first wife, Georgiana Elizabeth Byng (1768–1801), the second daughter of George Byng, fourth Viscount Torrington. He was educated at Westminster School and then studied under Rev John Smith, the vicar of Woodnesborough, near Sandwich, in Kent. In 1807 his father went on a tour of Scotland taking John with him. He then went to Lisbon, and to several parts of Spain. A subsequent visit in 1812–13, allowed him to visit the battlefields of Barossa and Talavera. After this, he went to Italy and when in Florence made a detour to Elba where he hoped to meet **Napoleon Bonaparte**. He did in fact have a private audience with the former emperor on 24 December 1814. A letter from Russell to the Belgian statesman Sylvain

Van de Weyer survives:

My dear Van de Weyer,

You wish to have some account of my visit to the First Napoleon at Elba.

It is long since I paid that visit, and I can give you only glimmering recollections.

I was at Florence in December 1814, with my father and his family.

I wished very much to see Napoleon; some of my friends had been to Elba; a cousin of mine by marriage, Mr. Whitmore, was going there.

I was told that the season was bad, and that I should do well to put off my journey till the spring. But I determined to go then.

Colonel Campbell, the Commissioner of the British Government, was usually resident at Florence; he was then returning to Elba, and a brig-of-war had been placed at his disposal. I was glad to take advantage of the opportunity. He told us on the way that Napoleon had sat up late at night, revising the list of the Municipal Council of Porto Ferrajo for the ensuing year. Colonel Campbell seemed to consider this circumstance a proof that the deposed Emperor could be as busy upon a trifling affair as on the destinies of Europe. But no doubt Napoleon wished to have a municipality on whom he could rely in case of need.

The first person Whitmore and I saw at Porto Ferrajo was General Bertrand, and he introduced us to his wife, a Dillon by birth.

In conversation with General Bertrand, he asked us the meaning of a paragraph in the Courier newspaper, sent him by Colonel Campbell, to the effect that the Congress of Vienna had it in contemplation to send the Emperor to St. Helena. We had not seen the paragraph, and could not account for it. I have never referred to the Courier newspaper of that period to ascertain its wording, or guess at its origin. But it had evidently made a great impression on General Bertrand.

In the evening of that day, about eight o'clock, I went to the house at the top of the town where Napoleon resided. He received me in his drawing- room. He was dressed in uniform – a green coat, single-breasted, white breeches, and silk stockings. I was much struck with his countenance – eyes of a muddy colour and cunning expression; the fine features which we all know in his bust and on his coins; and, lastly, a most agreeable and winning smile. He was very courteous in his manner. I was with him for a long time – I think an hour and a half. He stood the whole time, only sometimes leaning on the chimney-piece.

What struck me most in his conversation was a certain uneasiness about his position – a suspicion that something serious was about to happen to him, and he seemed to have a desire to entrap me into giving him information which I was neither able nor willing to afford. With this view, as I supposed, he asked me a number of questions of little interest to him – such as, whether I was in the House of Commons or the House of Lords, whether my father had kept up much state as Lord-Lieutenant of Ireland, and whether the Lady-Lieutenant had any dame d'honneur in her suite? When I replied that she had only a young lady, who was her cousin, in the house with her, he remarked, 'C'était une dame de compagnie, pas une dame d'honneur.' These questions he would intersperse with eager enquiries respecting the state of France; and when I replied that I had not come through France, hut by sea from Portugal, he would not let me off, but asked me what Lord Holland, whom I had seen at Florence, thought of French opinion – enquiring, with much emphasis, 'L'armee est-elle contente?'

He spoke also of Italy; and when I said that Italy had no union, and therefore would probably remain quiet, he said, 'C'est vrai.' I told him that I had heard everywhere, that during his reign the robberies and pillage, which had been so common before, had almost ceased; he said quickly, 'C'était la gendarmerie.'

He seemed alarmed regarding his own safety, asking me, more than once, whether our Minister at Florence was a man to be trusted; whether fearing that he might be carried off by force, or wishing to obtain some assurance of safety and protection from Lord Burghersh, the British Minister, I cannot tell. I told him that Lord Burghersh had been attached, as a military officer, to one of the allied armies which had invaded France; but of this he seemed to know nothing.

It was evident to me that the paragraph in the Courier, which had been mentioned to me by General Bertrand, had been shown to Napoleon, and had produced a great impression upon him. He seemed to me to be meditating some enterprise, and yet very doubtful whether he should undertake it. When we heard afterwards of his expedition from Elba, the Count de Mosbourg, a minister of Murat, was asked what could have induced Napoleon to run so great a hazard; 'Un peu d'espoir et beaucoup de désespoir' was his reply. Such appeared to me to be, when I saw him, the state of his mind; and when I got to Rome, I wrote to my brother, Lord Tavistock, that I was sure Napoleon was thinking of some fresh attempt.

Napoleon seemed very curious on the subject of the Duke of Wellington. He said it was a great mistake in the English Government to send him Ambassador to Paris. 'On n'aime pas voir un homme par qui on a eti battu! He had never sent as Ambassador to Vienna a man who had entered Vienna as an officer of the French invading army. (Count Lebzeltern, the Austrian Ambassador at Rome, denied the truth of this assertion.) As I had seen a good deal of the Duke of Wellington in Spain, Napoleon asked me what were likely to be his occupations. I answered that during his campaigns the Duke had been so much absorbed by his attention to the war that I did not well understand how he could give his mind to other subjects. He remarked, rather sharply, as if he thought I was inclined to think lightly of military talents, 'Eh bien, c'est un grand jeu, belle occupation!' He spoke at some length of his plans respecting Spain. He would have divided the large landed properties in the hands of the grandees, of the monasteries, and of the clergy. He would have introduced into Spain the enlightened principles of religious toleration and facilitated commercial intercourse in the interior, etc.

I said that I thought Spain was not ready for such changes, and that the Spanish people would resist them. 'Ils succomberaient,' he said, and then the subject dropped.

He asked me whether I knew anything of what was passing at the Congress of Vienna. I said, 'Nothing.' He said he expected that each Power would have confirmed to it by treaty the territories which its forces occupied. In respect to the three great military Powers, Austria, Russia, and Prussia, this prediction was nearly verified. Mr. Pitt, however, had intended, in 1805, to give Belgium to Prussia; Lord Castlereagh gave it to the Netherlands.

Napoleon spoke of Lord Ebrington, whom he had recently seen, and said he was 'un homme fort instruit; du moins, il m'a paru un homme fort instruit' It struck me afterwards that while he had spoken to Lord Ebrington of great events of his past life – of Jaffa, of the execution of the Due d'Enghien, and other acts on which the world had passed its judgment – he spoke to me almost entirely of the existing aspect of affairs. His past history had ceased to be his main object, and his mind was busy with the present and the future. He said, 'You must be very well satisfied, you English, to have finished the war so successfully.' I answered, 'Yes, Sire, especially as at one time we thought ourselves in great danger.'

He burst out laughing, 'Ha! ha! ha! C'était le système continental, eh?'

I said, 'Yes, Sire; but as that system did not ruin us, it did us a great deal of good. For men are much governed by their physical wants.'

The interview ended soon after this. The next morning I was told that a horse from the Emperor's stable was at my disposal, and I rode to a villa which he was constructing for his summer occupation.

The day after I embarked, in the gun-brig in which I had come, for Civita Vecchia.

I remain, my dear Van de Weyer,

Yours truly,

Russell.

Lord J. Russell in his diary, wrote of Napoleon:

His manner is very good-natured, and seems studied to put one at one's ease by its familiarity; his smile and laugh are very agree- able; he asks a number of questions without object, and often repeats them, a habit which he has no doubt acquired during fifteen years of supreme command. To this I should also attribute the ignorance he seems to show at times of the most common facts. When anything that he likes is said, he puts his head forward and listens with great pleasure ... but when he does not like what he hears, he turns away as if unconcerned, and changes the subject. From this one might conclude that he was open to flattery and violent in his temper.

Sir Spencer Walpole in his Life of Lord J. Russell, adds:

Lord John was with him [Napoleon] an hour and a half, conversing on many subjects – the Russell family, Lord John's own allowance from the Duke, the state of Spain and Italy, the character of the Duke of Wellington, and the arrangements likely to be made at Vienna for the pacification of Europe. He used to say in his old age, that as the Emperor became interested in his conversation, he fell into the singular habit which he had acquired, and pulled him by the ear.

On his return to Britain he immersed himself in politics – having been elected to parliament in 1813 whilst he was overseas. In 1819 he became a strong supporter of parliamentary reform and in 1830 he was appointed paymaster of the forces and helped to lead the battle for the Reform Act of 1832. In 1845 he supported the repeal of the Corn Laws which obliged Sir Robert Peel, the Conservative Prime Minister, to follow. This split the Conservative Party and resulted in Russell becoming prime minister. His first term coincided with the Irish Famine. He was then foreign minister in the coalition government led by Lord Aberdeen. This saw him clash with Lord Palmerston but the two combined to oppose Russian expansion in the east – which led to the Crimean War. Russell then served as foreign minister under Lord Palmerston during the period of the Unification of Italy and the American Civil War. Elevated to the peerage, his second term as prime minister was brief and followed the sudden death of Lord Palmerston. He then went into retirement and died on 28 May 1878.

References: John Alger, *Napoleon's British visitors and captives, 1801–1815*, New York: J. Pott, 1904, p. 300, 319–24; *Early correspondence of Lord John Russell*, edited by R. Russell, London: T. F. Unwin, 1913, 2 Vols; John M. Prest, *Lord John Russell*, Columbia: University of South Carolina Press, 1972; John Prest, 'Russell, John [formerly Lord John Russell], first Earl Russell (1792–1878)', *Oxford Dictionary of National Biography*, Oxford University Press, 2004; J. Russell, *Recollections and suggestions, 1813–1873*, London: Longmans, Green and Co., 1875; Sir Spencer Walpole, *The life of Lord John Russell*, London: Longmans, Green & Co., 1889, 2 vols; *The Record of Old Westminsters* vol. 2, p. 808.

- S -

ST. CERBONE (d. 575). The bishop of Populonia during the Barbarian invasions of Italy, by tradition he was originally from North Africa where he was the son of Christian parents. Ordained a priest, he was persecuted by the Vandals who followed Arianism and he fled to Italy. They were caught in a storm at sea and ended up in Tuscany. He became bishop of Populonia after the death of Florentius and became unpopular for saying mass at dawn. The local people complained to Pope Vigilius and the pope sent his men to **Piombino** to bring Cerbone to Rome. When they arrived it was early in the morning and they found Cerbone eating breakfast. He was arrested on charges of heresy because he was not supposed to eat before holding mass whereas he had actually held mass already, at daybreak. On his way to Rome, his party encountered three men suffering from fever and Cerbone cured them, and also tamed some geese who following him to Rome. When the group arrived in Rome at dawn, Cerbone went to see the Pope who was still half asleep. He asked the Pope whether he heard angels singing, and Pope Vigilius agreed that he had heard something. He released Cerbonius who then returned to Piombino.

When the Ostrogoths arrived in Tuscany, Cerbonius was arrested for helping to hide some Roman soldiers. He was sentenced to death by Totila, the king of the Ostrogoths, and ordered to be fed to a wild bear. The bear, however, was terrified of Cerbonius and licked the feet of the bishop. Duly impressed, Totila exiled Cerbonius to the island of Elba. After several years on the island, Cerbonius asked to be buried in Populonia and after his death in AD 575, the ship carrying his body to the mainland ran into a heavy storm but put in at Populonia and his followers then returned to Elba just before the Lombards captured Populonia. His feast day is 10 October.

References: Sabine Baring Gould, *The Lives of the Saints*, Oxford: Oxford University, 1877, vol. 7, pp. 228–29; John Coulson, *The Saints: a concise biographical dictionary*, New York: Hawthorn Books, 1960, p. 108.

SAN GIOVANNI. This is a thermal spa near **Portoferraio**. Archaeologists found the remains of a Roman villa called Le Grotte nearby. The Lonely Planet guide was unimpressed and noted that it was 'home to a rather expensive and dull mud spa'.

References: Miles Roddis & Alex Leviton, *Tuscany & Umbria*, Footscray: Lonely Planet, 2006, p. 192.

St. Mamilian depicted on a frieze in the Cathedral at Palermo.

ST. MAMILIAN. The bishop of Palermo, he was born in that city in Sicily and was bishop until Palermo was captured by the Vandals in c450. They were followers of Arianism, a Christian sect deemed heretical by the Ecumenical First Council of Nicaea of 325. By tradition, Genseric, the king of the Vandals, exiled Mamilian to Tuscany. The bishop arrived on Elba and then went to live on the island of **Montecristo** where he is said to have defeated a dragon living there. This led to the island changing its name from Montegiove ('Jove's Mountain') to Montecristo ('Christ's Mountain'), and a community of hermits was established there. He died on 19 October 460 at Isola di Giglio.

References: Averil Mackenzie-Grieve, *Aspects of Elba and the other islands of the Tuscan Archipelago*, London: Jonathan Cape, 1964, pp. 105–06; Gloria Peria and Silvestre Ferruzzi, *L'isola d'Elba e il culto di San Mamiliano*, Portoferraio, 2010.

SANCTUARY OF MONSERRATO. This is a famous shrine north of Port Azzurro to the 'Black Madonna' and was built in 1606 by a Spanish governor who felt that the nearby mountain, Monte Castello, reminded him of the mountain of Montserrat, near Barcelona.

References: Dan Facaros and Michael Pauls, *Italy: Tuscany*, London: Cadogan Books plc, 1996, p. 301.

SANGUINETTI, ALEXANDRE (1913–1980). A prominent French politician, he was born on 27 March 1913 in Cairo, his father, a Corsican, worked in the legal department of the Egyptian foreign ministry. He studied

232

law and arts in Cairo and then in Angers and Paris, joining the Free French in **World War II**. Taking part in the landings on Elba in June 1944, he lost his left leg. Back in France he entered politics in 1946 and ten years later was appointed to the ministry of national economy. In 1959 he became the head of the private office of Roger Frey who became the minister of the interior and had the task of destroying the Secret Army Organisation (OAS). Elected to the national assembly in 1962 for Paris, he was minister of veterans and war victims under Georges Pompidou, 1966–77. He was secretary-general of the Gaullist Party, 1963–74, and then the Union des Democrates pour la République (UDR). He died on 9 October 1980.

References: Alexandre Sanguinetti, *La France et l'arme atomique,* Paris: Julliard, 1964; Alexandre Sanguinetti, *J'ai mal à ma peau de gaulliste*, Paris: Grasset, 1978; *The Times* (10 October 1980), p. 17.

SARDINIAN SEA, BATTLE OF THE. *See* **Alalia, Battle of**.

SAVI, JOHN ANGELO (1765–1831). A shipowner in India, he had been born on Elba, the son of Antonio Savi (1720–1806), an admiral of the Tuscan navy, who moved to India where he married Elizabeth, daughter of General André François de Corderan, commander of the French forces at Pondicherry and who fought Robert Clive. They had four children: Elizabeth Theresa Savi; Caroline Savi, born in 1796 (she married Charles Stuart, and died soon afterwards in 1812, aged 16); Charlotte Mary Antoinette Savi, born in 1813; and James Savi, born on 20 April 1816 (educated at Elizabeth College, Guernsey; died in 1867). Following Elizabeth's death, John Savi married Charlotte Marie Justina St Quantan who died in 1826. Dr Savi died on 29 November 1831 at Chandernagore, Bengal.

Charlotte Savi married James Hills (1801–1872) of Nishchintpur, one of the largest landowners and indigo planters in Bengal, and they had ten children with several of the sons leading distinguished military careers: Lieutenant General James Hills-Johnes (1833–1919), Major General Sir John Hills (1834–1902); and Colonel George Scott Hills (1835–1892).

References: R. H. Vetch, 'Hills, Sir John (1834–1902)', revised by Roger T. Stearn, *Oxford Dictionary of National Biography*, Oxford University Press, 2004; Elizabeth College Register 1824–1873, p. 84.

Scoglietto Island
Photograph © Kletr / fotolia.com.

SCOGLIETTO ISLAND. This rocky outcrop in the **Tuscan Archipelago**, known formally as Scoglietto di Portoferraio, was originally called Ferraiola because of its proximity to **Portoferraio**. It is the location of a lighthouse built on it in 1910, and since 1971 has been included in the Tuscan Archipelago National Park. It has become popular for scuba **diving**.

References: Paul Munzinger, *100 Diving Sites: Underwater Paradises Around the Globe,* New York: Paragon, 2010, pp. 18–19.

SCOTT, JOHN BARBER (1792–1862). The author of *An Englishman at Home and Abroad: 1792–1828*, he was the son of John Scott, a wealthy tanner of Bungay, Suffolk, England, and was educated at Emmanuel College, Cambridge, matriculating in 1810, and completing his BA in 1814. Soon afterwards, he went to Elba and visited **Napoleon Bonaparte** in September 1814. He was accompanied by Major **Montgomery Maxwell**, Colonel **John Lemoine**, Captain Smith and Colonel **Niel Douglas**.

John Scott described the meeting in his diary which as published in *Temple Bar* magazine in October 1903:

The vice consul procured us a house in the country near Longone. We were resting ourselves in it, when a beat of drums from above and a signal from Zacharia announced to us that Napoleon had gone out riding. Full of hope of meeting this extraordinary man, we walked along the road by which we understood he would probably return.

Single guards or gendarmes were posted here and there at the turning of the lanes; my companions were all in their military dress and decorations, and as we were conversing with some sentinels and viewing others in the distance they all agreed that the entire scene reminded them precisely of a patty of officers visiting the outposts on the eve of some awful engagement.

At length (in half an hour) six horse men appeared on the hill about a mile distant, and the delighted Zacharia pointing to some object, exclaimed, 'Voila Napoleon!' His cavalcade consisted of an armed avant courier followed by Napoleon, then two officers abreast, and finally the Polish lancers. We were in a lane about five yards wide; as the Emperor advanced we drew back and formed a line on his right, standing uncovered.

He stopped his horse short and touched his hat. The first impression on my mind was – Can this be the great Napoleon? Is that graceless figure, so clumsy and awkward, the figure that has awed emperors and kings, has gained victory on victory, and the sight of whom has been equivalent to one thousand men on the field of battle. Surely it is impossible? – and that countenance – it is totally devoid of expression, it appears even to indicate stupidity. Such were the thoughts that rushed through my mind, and though I soon found reason to change my opinion as far as his countenance was concerned, I still think the figure of Napoleon unmartial, clumsy, and awkward. His height appears to be about five feet seven inches, he looks about forty-five years of age, has a very large corporation, and his thighs are large – quite out of proportion. Campbell maintains that though very fat lie is a well-made man. My companions are all of my opinion.

He wore a cocked hat low over his eyes, which in some measure contributed to give him the appearance of stupidity at first sight. His hat is very high behind, low before, its brownness seems to indicate that it has seen many a campaign, it wore a cockade of white and red. His military coat was green faced with red, the skirt of it began to slope off from is high ns the waist, above that it was close buttoned, and as his neck is very short, one could hardly see his black stock. He had two shabby silver epaulettes, a shabby star on his breast as Commander of the Legion of Honour, and the three small buttons of the orders of the Legion of Honour, Reunion and Iron Cross. Under his coat appeared a red sash – the grand cordon of the Legion. His waistcoat, breeches and gloves were white His boots were old and shabby, his silver spurs were fastened with black buckles. He rode a small, brown Corsican horse, with holsters in his saddle, and a dirty bridle and bit. Although his clothes were old, his person looked clean and neat altogether. He leans very forward when riding.

While talking with us his horse suddenly lifted its hind foot. Napoleon turned quickly round as if he were nervous. He took snuff once only during the interview from a small black box on which were three cameos. His hand was particularly white, his fingers small and tapering. His hair is black and hangs down very long in candle ends (to use an expression more expressive than elegant) over his coat collar. His eyes are blue and small, eyebrows black and rather large, his nose and mouth handsome and of moderate size. His chin is not very pointed, his complexion is pale with a yellowish tinge, his forehead square and prominent. Zacharia noted the time he conversed with us. It was twenty-two minutes.

The newspaper report in *The Argus* (Melbourne, Australia) continued:

A report of the conversation is given in French by the diarist, as well as he could remember it. It consisted for the most part of questions by Napoleon about military matters, and answers by Colonel Lemoine RA, and Scott's friend Douglas. Napoleon concluded the conversation by saying with an air of great politeness, 'Continuez votre promenade, Messieurs, amusez-vous – au revoir.'

He then took off his hat, made us a low and long bow, and rode on. All the natives within sight were astonished by his taking off his hat for he has never done so to anyone since he came to the island. Our landlord told us he never bowed to man or spirit, and Colonel Campbell assured us that he has never seen him take his hat off to anyone. During the whole of our interview, there was a constant half smile on his countenance which gave one the feeling of confidence and ease. His eyes are remarkably expressive and quick, his voice is deep, his entire manner indicates great talent and he certainly inspires respect. My companions are unanimous in the opinion that he has more the appearance of a clever, craft priest than of a hero. Indeed his figure is decidedly the reverse of heroic.

John Alger summed up the incident by noting:

They encountered Napoleon as he was out riding, and on their saluting him he stopped for a few minutes to question them. They thought he looked more like a crafty priest than a hero. On being told that Scott was a Cantab he said, 'What, Cambridge, Cambridge? Oh yes, you are a young man; you will be a lawyer. Eh, eh, you will be Lord Chancellor?'

John Barber Scott returned to Bungay and was reeve in 1828–29, and on five more occasions. He died on 10 September 1862 at Bungay. His house, Scott House, was offered for sale in early 2014 for £780,000. Some coins and tokens and other memorabilia connected with him are held by the Bungay Museum.

References: John Alger, *Napoleon's British visitors and captives, 1801–1815*, New York: J. Pott, 1904, p. 296; John Barber Scott, *An Englishman at Home and Abroad: 1792–1828*, London: Heath Cranston, 1930; John Barber Scott, *An Englishman at Home and Abroad: 1792–1828, with some recollections of Napoleon*, Bungay: Morrow, 1988.

SEEWALD, RICHARD (1889–1976). A German painter and writer, he published a narrative of his visit to Elba, illustrated by some of his paintings of the island. He was born on 4 May 1889 at Arnswalde, and went to Munich to study architecture. Seewald enjoyed drawing when at high school and decided to concentrate on this and became a cartoonist. His first exhibition was held in 1919 and this allowed Seewald to travel to the Mediterranean which saw him go to Elba – his *Reise nach Elba* was published in 1921. Converting to Catholicism eight years later, he lived in Switzerland during the Nazi period in Germany and only returned to Germany in 1948. He was a professor at the Akademie der Bildenden Künste (Academy of Fine Arts) in Munich and died on 29 October 1976. He had destroyed some of his work when his wife died, and what survived was donated to the Germanischen Nationalmuseum (GNM: German National Museum), leaving the balance of his estate to the Swiss National Fund, 'Pro Helvetia'.

References: Eva Chrambach, 'Seewald, Richard Josef Michael', *Neue Deutsche Biographie*, Duncker & Humblot, Berlin 2010, vol. 24, p. 157f; Richard Seewald, *Reise nach Elba: Mit vierundzwanzig Zeichnungen*, Augsburg: Dr. Benno Filser, 1921.

SEITZ, DON CARLOS (1862–1935). An American newspaper manager, he was the author of *Elba and Elsewhere* (1910). He was born on 24 October 1862 in Portage, Ohio, the son of the Rev. J. A. S. Seitz, and graduated from the Liberal Institute in Norway, Maine, in 1880. Working as a correspondent in Albany for the *Brooklyn Eagle*, 1887–89, he was the city editor, 1889–91, and then assistant publisher of the *New York Recorder*, 1892–93, then managing editor of the *Brooklyn World*, 1893–94, becoming the advertising manager from 1895–97. He was appointed business manager from 1898 to 1923, turning to writing. He studied at St. Lawrence University, and graduated AM in 1906, then sailed for England on the *Amerika*, disembarking at Dover and it was probably on that trip that he went to Elba. He died on 4 December 1935 at Brooklyn, New York.

References: Don Carlos Seitz, *Elba and Elsewhere*, New York: Harper and Brothers, 1910; *Who Was Who in America, Vol. 1, 1897–1942*, p. 1102.

SERPELL, CHRISTOPHER HAROLD (1910–1991). The author, along with his wife Jean, of *The Travellers' Guide to Elba & the Tuscan Archipelago*, Christopher Serpell was born on 1 July 1910 in Leeds, Yorkshire, England, the oldest of the five children of Harold Wilson Serpell (1874–1948), the senior master at Leeds Grammar School, and his wife Katharine Emily (née Friend, 1887–1949). He was educated at Leeds Grammar School, and then proceeded to Merton College, Oxford, where he studied classics, graduating BA in 1934. He worked as a cub reporter with the *Yorkshire Post*, 1934–35, and then moved to London to work on *The Times*, remaining a reporter with them and on their editorial staff from 1935 to 1942. On 14 April 1939 at Crown Court Church, Covent Garden, London, he married Jean Crawford Crichton, and they had a son and three daughters: Anne V. Serpell, born on 13 July 1941 at Eynsham Hall, Oxfordshire; Camilla J. Serpell, born on 29 August 1944 in the Cotswolds, England; a third daughter, born on 2 March 1949 in Rome; and James Andrew Serpell, born on 16 February 1952 in Rome.

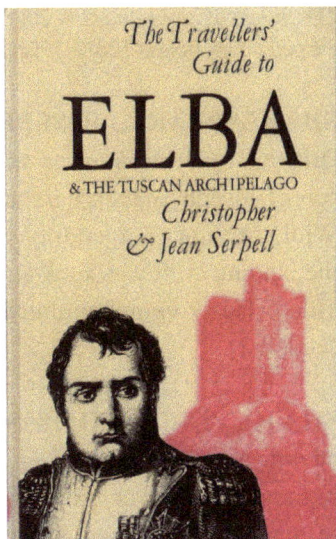

Suffering from short sightedness, he was rejected for military service and worked in the naval intelligence department of the Admiralty, serving under Ian Fleming (later the author of the James Bond books). He was a sub-lieutenant and then lieutenant with the Royal Naval Volunteer Reserve. From 1946 to 1960 he was a foreign correspondent for the British Broadcasting Corporation (BBC), and their second correspondent in Paris in July-December 1946, and then opened the office in Rome as the BBC correspondent there from December 1946 to October 1953. He and his family then moved to Washington, DC, where he was the BBC chief correspondent covering the McCarthy period, and the Cuban revolution.

In 1960 Christopher Serpell was appointed the foreign news editor of the BBC at Alexandra Palace, London. However he loved the life of a roving correspondent and became the BBC's diplomatic correspondent until 1975 when he retired. He was awarded the OBE on 1 January 1973. He had always been fascinated by Elba, and one of his first tasks in retirement was along, with his wife, to write a book on the island. This involved extensive travel around the island and even though some of the tourist information has become dated, it remains one of the best single-volume books on the island in English, and was translated into German. He died on 3 June 1991 at his home in Barnes, London. His son, educated at Westminster School, trained as a zoologist and became a journalist and broadcaster. His only brother, Michael Friend Serpell, was an assistant curator at the National Portrait Gallery.

References: Christopher and Jean Serpell, *The Travellers' Guide to Elba and the Tuscan Archipelago*, London: Jonathan Cape, 1977; *Merton College Register 1900–1964*, p.

211; *Who's Who in America 2001*, vol. 2, p. 4779 (James Andrew Serpell); 'Christopher Serpell', *The Times* (7 June 1991), p. 20.

SHAKESPEARE, JOSEPH WILLIAM (1924–1944). A marine in the British Royal Marines, he was born in Stourbridge, Worcestershire, UK, the son of Joseph Shakespeare and Alice M. (née Price), of Aston, Birmingham. While serving on a landing craft during the attack on Elba on 17 June 1944, the landing craft was sunk and Shakespeare was posted as missing, presumed killed. He is commemorated on the Chatham Naval Memorial (panel 79, section 2).

SILVIO, VINCENZO (1805–1873). Born on 9 May 1805 at **Capoliveri**, Elba, he was a medical doctor and went to Rome where he was heavily involved in the campaign for Italian Unification. He later returned to Capoliveri, and resumed his work there as a doctor, dying on Elba.

SIMS, EDWARD (1910–1944). A British lieutenant in the Royal Naval Volunteer Reserve, he was born on 18 December 1910, in Peckham, south-east London, the son of Francis William Sims, a postman, and Alice (née Avant), of 4 Milton Terrace, off Madron Street, London. With the outbreak of **World War II** in 1939, he became a part-time member of the London Fire Brigade and was reported to have been involved in fire-fighting during the first heavy German air raids on the London Docks. He then volunteered for the Royal Navy and as an ordinary seaman, he served on H.M.S. *Offa* and other vessels on convoys to Russia. Sent to the Officer Training Course at H.M.S. *King Alfred*, Brighton, he was commissioned sub-lieutenant and appointed second-in-command of Tank Landing Craft which was sent to the Mediterranean. Promoted to acting lieutenant, he was give command of H.M. Landing Craft (Flak) 15 which was involved in the landing at Elba on 17 June 1944. It picked up a cable mine in the propeller which drew the mine towards the ship and then exploded, sinking the landing craft. Edward Sims was blown over the side and not seen again. He is commemorated on the Chatham Royal Navy Memorial (79, 2). His medals are held at the Imperial War Museum, London. He left a widow, Vera May Sims, who lived in Eltham, London.

References: *The war dead of the British Commonwealth and Empire: the register of the*

names of those who fell in the 1939–1945 War and have no other grave than the sea. Memorial register 1: Chatham Memorial, Maidenhead: Imperial War Graves Commission, 1952, p. 337.

SMITH, LYDIA BUSHNELL (1862–1944). The American author of *Napoleon's Elba*, she was born on 28 December 1862 at Madison, New Haven, Connecticut, the daughter of Andrew Norman Smith and Lydia Bushnell (née Kelsey). Baptised on 3 July 1863 at Madison, she grew up in New Haven and travelled around the British Isles from June to October 1907, and then lived in Germany from October 1907 until June 1908, going to France from June 1908 to October 1911 and then settled in Italy and wrote her book on Elba which she dedicated to Rowena Ashton, 'my inspiring comrade'. She noted:

When I first desired to visit Elba, it never occurred to me that it would not be a perfectly easy matter to find the most exhaustive information concerning it. I felt especially secure, as I had an exceptionally fine library at my command (Vieusseux's, of Florence) as well as Seeber's well-stocked book-shop. Imagine then my surprise at finding the possibilities most meagre. Far from daunting me, however, it but increased my eagerness to secure my knowledge at first hand.

While making my preparations for the trip, I took delight in seeking knowledge among my friends and acquaintances. I sincerely regret that I did not tabulate all the interesting answers to my queries.

Not all would acknowledge their inability to cope with the subject. In those cases, although I could not refute their statements, I felt it the part of wisdom not to place too much credence in them.

I was told that it is a wild and uninhabited island; that it is still infested by brigands; that it is impossible to remain there more than a day or so, 'No one ever does!' The piece of information that gave me greatest joy, was that Elba is somewhere in the far, southern seas, near the lower coast of Africa, and that the voyage thither would be a long and tiresome trip. Of course that drove me to the ever-helpful Baedeker. Besides, I had a rather hazy memory as a relic of my school days, that the island is within easy distance from both the Italian and French coasts. Baedeker reassured me on this point, and added a few bits of information that stimulated my longings to see what it describes as a place which it is strongly recommended to the lover of nature.

Naturally I looked up the subject in all the 'Histories of Napoleon' available, and found various tidbits to develop a keener appetite for more. Armed with this heterogeneous collection of assumed facts, I started Elba-ward accompanied by a friend who, like myself, was equal to anything that might offer by way of experience. In fact I think we rather craved the unusual. We found it. In the first place, the approach to Elba has not been made any too easy for the tourist. If one be a good traveller by sea, the better of the two possible routes, is by steamer from Leghorn. This is a rather tiresome trip if the primary object is to reach Elba, and not to skim the Mediterranean. If one be fond of the water, however, the eight hours will be full of pleasure.

The steamer that leaves Leghorn twice weekly, makes pause at the two islands upon which Dante fiercely calls for assistance in punishing the Pisans.

Let Capraia and Gorgona move

And make a hedge across the mouth of the Arno,

So that every person in thee may drown.

It also stops before one of the most beautiful and picturesque spots on the Island, Marina di Marciana, before finally dropping anchor at Portoferraio, from which it returns on the following day by another route. This trip may be made once a week in about four hours direct from Leghorn to Portoferraio, without stopping.

The other possibility is by way of Piombino. This has the advantage of a short sea trip (lasting about one and a half hours) and one could reach the Island from Florence by mid-day. The unwary traveller might consider himself ill-used if I hesitated to elaborate the details slightly.

To begin with, we were unwise in our selection of weather. It would be much better to make special arrangements regarding that, before starting out. If this hint is made use of, there will be no further trouble. All of our discomfort, or at least the major part of it, came from the elements. Probably the average tourist is blessed with patience superior to our own, in both quality and quantity. We had made up our minds to go to Elba on a certain day, and we went. That was the beginning of our unwisdom. All the rest followed in the natural course of events. Leaving the main line (from Pisa to Rome) at Campiglia, we found ourselves hurried into a somewhat primitive train, which we were told was to start immediately. This was a bit disconcerting. We had studied our timetable most carefully, and decided that it gave us an hour and a half for luncheon. This was the more essential to our happiness, as we had made an early start in Pisa, that we might get in a little extra sight-seeing before leaving town. Thinking to fortify ourselves quite elaborately later on, we had failed to obtain the usual by-the-way treats. Being more or less philosophical, perhaps even better, being experienced travellers, accustomed to the occasional hardships encountered, we pretended that we were not ravenous. We congratulated ourselves that an earlier start from Campiglia would bring us to Piombino speedily. We would then be in sight of our destination. We assured each other that we would have all the better appetite for the delay. How fortunate that we do not always know what is in store for us!

As the train moved out of Campiglia, an occasional raindrop flecked the windowpane. As we neared the shore, it rained harder and more hard until, by the time we had reached Piombino, it came down in buckets full. There are two stations; the first, Porto Vecchio, seemed the correct one, so we gathered our belongings and prepared to alight...

No portion possesses such appealing beauty of color and contour, as is in the neighborhood of Portoferraio. The first glimpse won our hearts and made us lovers of Elba. Subsequent days and nights have developed ardent devotees.

.   In visiting the Island one can make use of the autobus that connects Portoferraio with other important localities, but, as it is run for the convenience of the post, and not for that of the occasional tourist, it may be more desirable to travel as much as possible by boat.

This is a delightful mode for the artist, the average tourist, the scientist or the historian.

Happy is the one who can travel on foot or horseback, as many otherwise inaccessible places will then be possible to him.

The greater portion of the points of interest, however, are on the coast, and are easily reached by boat. The steamers making the circuit of the Island are not luxurious, as they were intended solely for the use of the Islanders themselves, but they are reasonably clean.

As for ourselves, we have extended our stay indefinitely, in spite of the fact that our first decision was to remain but one week. The fascinations of the place have laid hold upon us and we tarry.

There are so many sketchable places for the artist, so many things of interest to the history-lover that, as yet, we do not feel we have in the least degree exhausted the resources of the island. We are conscious of the fact that we started rightly in putting ourselves in immediate touch with those persons calculated to make our stay a joy and delight. That we did so was the result of good fortune rather than good management. Those following in our footsteps may not be equally lucky, and might do worse than profit by our experience. While awaiting the boat at Piombino we entered into conversation with a pilot by the name of Frank.

Having lived in both England and the States, he had added to his native courtesy a keen desire to be of use to Anglo-Saxons. He suggested that, upon arriving at Portoferraio, we seek first the British Consul. To him he turned as the natural adviser and friend of anyone speaking the English language. We have not for a moment regretted following Frank's advice, and we pass it on for the future reference of tourists. Frank could not recall the Consul's name, but said, 'You will easily know him as the biggest, finest-looking man on the island'. The Captain of a gigantic Norwegian steamer then riding at anchor in the Ferrajo Bay, corroborated this statement, adding with open admiration, 'I heard in Norway that there was an English Consul in Elba, and no one else worth mentioning'. I would supplement this by saying that Consul Airey is ably aided and abetted in both courtesy and hospitality by his cousin, Miss Kennedy, and his daughter. One of our many causes for gratitude was an introduction to the family of Signer Del Buono. The courtesy of the Italians is too well known to need special comment. The courtesy of the Elbans, however, out-Italians even Italians, and has become almost proverbial. 'I was a stranger and you took me in', could be said by any chance guest needing entertainment for soul or body within the confines of the Island. With true Elban hospitality, the latchstring of the palatial Del Buono home in Portoferraio immediately hung outward. This was not the only courtesy extended. Plans were presently formulated that would make possible our visiting the entire Island under the pleasantest conditions. Accordingly, domestics were sent to their mountain villa, to place it in readiness for occupation; for from there we could become acquainted with other historic places. Later, when we arrived with the two charming daughters of Signor Del Buono, we found all the comforts of a modern American home. This was a surprise to us, knowing it to be in a primitive part of a primitive island, and several miles up a mountain side. The grounds were like a small park, while the panoramic expanse was even more beautiful than the Italian Lakes, and very like parts of Switzerland. The approach to Marciana Marina from Portoferraio in autobus, is a series of exquisite inland vistas, and glorious, wide-spread views of the Mediterranean. The ruggedness of the hills bordering the sea reminds one strongly of the northern coast of Wales, although the vegetation is far more luxuriant and the floral coloring more brilliant. The three-mile drive up the mountain from Marciana Marina to Póggio, lies through woods of chestnuts from which the nuts are gathered as a regular harvest, adding materially to the income of the property-owners, who are mostly prosperous peasants, cultivators of vines and fertile farms. We had found the heat of Portoferraio rather relaxing, and therefore welcomed the change to the delicious bracing air of the mountains. Dinner was served on the terrace, so our eyes feasted as well as our palates, and our ears were gladdened by the song of the nightingale. The moon was almost at its full; what more could life offer? The summons to a five-o-clock breakfast found the world still beautiful, but with the hazy softness of the early morning. The sun was not only up, but also the son of the house, a lovable boy of eleven, who was to escort the little party up the mountain to where Napoleon held court for twenty-four days on the height near the Madonna del Monte. The hot coffee proved the needed harmonizer of mood, morning and expedition, and a domestic followed our ascent with a hamper for later consideration. Our route lay first through the tiny village of Póggio, where our early advent caused quite a stir among the chickens and cats, which disputed our right of way in the narrow street. Here, as in all Elban hill towns, the majority of the streets or alleys are of steps, which bear the footprints of the donkeys and goats as well as those of their masters.

Lydia Bushnell Smith lived at Zoagli, Italy, during World War I. She died on 19 December 1944.

References: Lydia Bushnell Smith, *Napoleon's Elba*, Florence: Seeber, 1914.

SORGE, BARTOLOMEO (1929–). A Jesuit theologian, he was born on 25 October 1929 in **Rio Marina**, the son of Alfio Sorge and Anna (née Mignemi), his parents coming from Catania, Sicily. In 1938 his family moved to Castelfranco Veneto and Bartolomeo Sorge joined the Society of Jesus, and was ordained in 1958. Trained in Spain and then in Rome, he joined the editorial staff of *La Civiltà Cattolica*, the fortnightly paper of the Society of Jesus in 1966, succeeding Roberto Tucci as the director in 1973. From 1986 to 1995 he directed the Istituto di Formazione Politica Pedro Arrupe in Palermo, Sicily.

References: Bartolomeo Sorge, *Uscire dal tempio, a cura di Paolo Giuntella*, Milan: Rizzoli, 1991; *Who's Who in the World*, Third edition, 1976–1977, p. 654.

SPYGLASS. A spyglass used by Napoleon and left by him in Elba, was taken by Major **Neil Campbell** and presented in 1867 to Lord Clarence Paget, the 2nd Marquess of Anglesey. The 1st Marquess of Amglesey, Henry Paget, fought at the battle of Waterloo (when he was the 2nd Earl of Uxbridge). He famously lost his leg towards the end of the fighting. Still owned by the Marquess of Anglesey and is on display at the Waterloo Museum at Plas Newydd.

References: Edward Lowton, 'Napoleon's spyglass restored for the 200th anniversary of Waterloo', http://www.culture24.org.uk/history-and-heritage/military-history/pre-20th-century-conflict/art528716- (accessed 15 September 2015); 'Napoleon's telescope found in cellar of Welsh country house after being placed there for safekeeping 150 years ago', http://www.walesonline.co.uk/news/wales-news/napoleons-telescope-found-cellar-welsh-9424065 (accessed 15 September 2015).

STIRLING, Sir GILBERT (1779/81–1843). A Scottish baronet, he travelled to Elba with Mr Campbell and they met with **Napoleon Bonaparte**. His father was Sir James Stirling (1740–1805), 1st Baronet, of Mansfield, Ayshire, created Baronet on 19 July 1792. Gilbert succeeded to the title on his father's death on 17 February 1805. He died on 13 February 1843 and was buried at Greyfriars, Edinburgh. The baronetcy was then declared extinct.

References: John Alger, *Napoleon's British visitors and captives, 1801–1815*, New York: J. Pott, 1904, p. 296.

- T -

TAILLADE, LOUIS. A lieutenant in the French army, he had been a prisoner of war in England where he learnt to speak English. **Norman MacKenzie** wrote of him that he was 'a vain and pedantic fair-weather sailor who had left the French navy and become captain of an Elban schooner after he had married into one of the better local families.' He was given command of the small flotilla of boats under **Napoleon Bonaparte** at Elba until just before Napoleon's departure from Elba in 1815. On 10 January 1815, in spite of bad weather around the island, Taillade tried to reach the island but this resulted in the *Inconstant* being pushed ashore by the wind. There was suspicion that Taillade might have done this on purpose to prevent the vessel being used by Napoleon to leave Elba; and conversely there was also a theory that this allowed major repair work to be done on the ship which allowed Napoleon to smuggle stores on board without anybody noticing. Taillade remained in the employ of Napoleon who either did not suspect him, or was keen not to let on that he had, and the latter would have been a highly dangerous strategy as the *Inconstant* might have been lost.

Napoleon replace Taillade with **Chautard**, and Taillade seems to have travelled on the *Inconstant* when Napoleon did make his escape on 26 February 1815. He was awarded the Legion of Honour soon afterwards for his help. After the second Bourbon Restoration after the 100 Days, he moved to Washington, North Carolina. His will was on display in the local courthouse, and noted 'Testament de Louis Taillade ancien Colonel des Marvines de la Garde de l'Empreur Napolion en favereur de M. Louis LeRoy habitant en cette ville et tenant l'hotel Mansion Houye'.

References: Federal Writers' Project, *The Ocean Highway: New Brunswick, New Jersey, to Jacksonville, Florida*, New York: Modern Age Books, 1938, p. 107; Norman MacKenzie, *The Escape from Elba: The Fall & Flight of Napoleon 1814–1815*, Oxford: Oxford University Press, 1982; Philip Mansel and Torsten Riotte, *Monarchy and Exile: the politics of legitimacy from Marie de Médicis to Wilhelm II*, Basingstoke, Hampshire, UK: Palgrave Macmillan, 2011.

TATNALL, ALFRED FREDERICK (1913–1944). A leading seaman in the British Royal Navy, he was born on 13 April 1913 in London, UK, the son of Alfred Tatnall and his wife Julia (née Collins). He married Margaret Read in 1942, and they lived in Barking, Essex with their infant son. Alfred Tatnall was in a landing craft in the Allied assault on Elba on 17 June 1944 when he was killed. His body was never identified and he is commemorated on the Portsmouth Naval Memorial (panel 81, column 3). His widow died on 10 October 2008 in Strood, Kent.

TEATRO DEI VIGILANTI. This theatre was built by **Napoleon Bonaparte** in **Portoferraio** in an abandoned church known locally as the 'Church of the Red'. Napoleon oversaw the deconsecration of the church and the marble altar from there was taken to **Portoferraio Cathedral**. Much of the impetus for this was from **Pauline Bonaparte** and there was a grand opening with a gala performance attended by the ex-emperor, and also a costume ball with the sale of the boxes and the seats paying for the conversion to a theatre. It was the first time that the new anthem of Elba was played in public. The event was a great success and it was in this theatre, on 15 February 1815, that Pauline Bonaparte held a ball which helped to disguise Napoleon's preparations to leave Elba which he did on the following evening.

References: Norman MacKenzie, *The Escape from Elba: The Fall & Flight of Napoleon 1814–1815*, Oxford: Oxford University Press, 1982; Len Ortzen, *Imperial Venus: Pauline Bonaparte*, London: Constable, 1974, pp. 168–71.

TELEPHONE SERVICES. Until the 1960s there was a very limited telephone system on Elba. The Italian telephone directory for 1920–21 covered the whole country in a single volume and notes only three telephone connections in **Portoferraio**: the Banca Populare (no 1), the Società Elba (no 2) and a public telephone box with no number. In the 1936-37 directory of Tuscany, there are public telephones in all towns, 25 other numbers in Portoferraio (mostly military or business), and the only other lines in Elba were for the police in **Capoliveri**, **Marciana Marina**, Marina in Campo (now **Marina di Campo**), Portolongone (now **Porto Azzurro**) and **Rio Marina**, the prison service at Portolongone, a bank at Marciana Marina, and the Societa Ilva at Rio Marina. During **World War II**, there were two underwater cables from Piombino to the north-west of Cape Pero, and one from Marciana Marina to Point Ferraione on the island of **Capraia**, as well as one from close to Point Fetovia to Pianosa and from there to **Montecristo**.

With the influx of tourists it became necessary to upgrade the network, and there were a number of exchanges – the major ones being in Portoferraio and in Porto Azzurro. Elba was included in the telephone directory for Livorno and region. There is now an extensive service around the entire island, and also good mobile telephone connections in much of Elba.

TESEI, TESEO (1909–1941). An Italian naval officer and inventor, he was born on 3 January 1909 at **Marina di Campo** and educated at the naval academy at Livorno. He was a keen inventor and during the late 1920s and the 1930s he worked on new weapons programmes and he devised a new diving system which allowed naval divers to spend longer underwater. He took part in an abortive attack on Valletta in British-held Malta. However the explosives blew up prematurely and he was killed on 26 July 1941. He was posthumously awarded the Medaglia d'oro al valor militare (Gold Medal for military valour), and the **airport** on Elba was named after him.

THACKRAY, DENNIS CHARLES (1924–1944). An able seaman in the British Royal Navy, he was born in 1924 in Leeds, Yorkshire, the son of Harry Thackray and Maud Emily (née Greenwood) of Leeds. Serving on H.M.S. *Victory*, he was killed on the first day of the Allied attack on Elba on 17 June 1944, and was buried on Elba and three years later was reburied in the Bolsena War Cemetery (IV G 11) on the Italian mainland.

References: *The war dead of the British Commonwealth and Empire: the register of the names of those who fell in the 1939–1945 War and are buried in cemeteries in Italy Cemeteries 17–18: Bolsena War Cemetery, Orvieto War Cemetery*, Maidenhead: Imperial War Graves Commission, 1954, p. 34.

THIÉBAUT DE BERNEAUD, ARSÈNE (1777–1850). A French writer, he was the author of *Voyage à l'île d'Elbe* published in 1808. Born on 14 January 1777 at Sedan, France, he was studying at the time of the French Revolution and was 15 when he enlisted in the army and served in a hussar regiment. He fought at the battle of Kaiserslautern in December 1793 and sustained five bad injuries. He was given the rank of captain and in 1796 although only 19, was trusted with a number of special missions. Later he was involved in trips to Italy and also to the Italian islands including Elba, as well as Illyria, Greece, the Ionian Islands, and various parts of North Africa. He returned to Paris in 1808 and that was when he wrote his book on Elba. It was translated into German and published at Weimar in 1809, and translated into Dutch and published at Haarlem in 1814, as well as being translated by **William Jerdan** and published in English, and Swedish in the same year.

When Napoleon Bonaparte was to go into exile on the island of Elba he found a copy of the book in his library at Fontainebleau and it was his major source of information. It notes that 'The mountains of Elba together present only a mass of arid hills which tire the senses and impart sorrowful sensations to the soul. Rough and uneven roads, deserted cottages, ruins scattered around the countryside, wretched hamlets, two poor villages and one fortress – these, generally speaking, are all that meet the sight on the side of the island which runs along the channel of Piombino.' Much of his later work was on French agriculture. He died in January 1850 in Paris.

References: Norman MacKenzie, *The Escape from Elba: The Fall & Flight of Napoleon 1814–1815*, Oxford: Oxford University Press, 1982, p. 65; Arsène Thiébaut de Berneaud, *Voyage à l'île d'Elbe*, Paris, 1808.

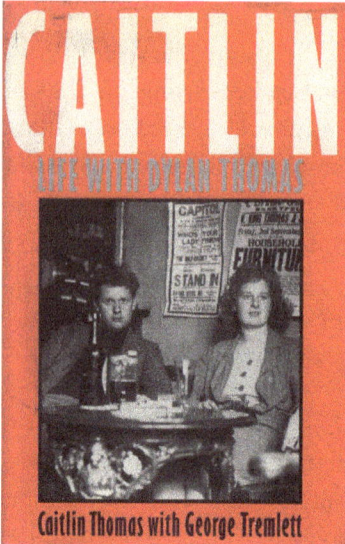

Caitlin Thomas with George Tremlett

THOMAS, CAITLIN (1913–1994). A British writer, she was born as Caitlin Macnamara on 8 December 1913 in Hammersmith, London, the youngest of the four children of Francis Macnamara (1884–1946), romantic Irishman, and his first wife, Mary (Yvonne) Majolier (1886–1973). She grew up near the New Forest but was keen on becoming a dancer and she fell in love with Casper John, the son of the painter Augustus John – she was seduced and then raped by the artist. Returning to London, she went to a dancing school and in a public house in Fitzrovia, London, met the Welsh poet Dylan Thomas whom she married in 1937. They had three children.

The couple went to Elba in 1947. Edith Sitwell was keen that Dylan Thomas not go to live in the United States so she persuaded the Society of Authors to give him a grant of £150 which this funded a trip to Italy with two children and Caitlin's sister Brigit, and Brigit's son Tobias. They went by train to Milan, then to Florence and on to Elba. Staying in **Rio Marina** for two weeks, Caitlin Thomas had an affair with the proprietor of the hotel where the group was staying. In her later writing she called him her 'beautiful Giovanni'.

With her husband drinking heavily, Caitlin also turned to alcohol, and planned to write a story of her life. When Dylan Thomas died in 1953, Caitlin was at a loose end and in August 1954, went back to Elba. With the Exchange Control Act of 1947, she was not allowed to take much money overseas for spending on pleasure, so she described the reason for her journey 'to write a book on Elba' making it a business trip. Returning to Rio Marina, she found Giovanni had a family. However they were able to resume their affair furtively although she also became involved with an eighteen-year-old who worked at the iron ore mines. Called 'Joseph' in her writings, he was keen on improving his English. She described her time in Elba in her book, *Leftover Life to Kill,* which was published in 1957. She later moved to Rome and lived with Giuseppe Fazio, a minor film actor, and finished her autobiography, *Double Drink Story,* which was published posthumously. She died on 1 August 1994 in Catania, Sicily, and was buried alongside her husband at Laugharne, Wales, following her request.

References: Paul Ferris, *Caitlin: the life of Caitlin Thomas,* London: Hutchinson, 1993, pp. 99–100, 159–68; Paul Ferris, 'Thomas, Caitlin (1913–1994)', *Oxford Dictionary of National Biography*, Oxford University Press, 2004; Caitlin Thomas, *Leftover life to kill*, Boston: Little Brown, 1957, Caitlin Thomas, with George Tremblett, *Caitlin: Life with Dylan Thomas*, London: Martin Secker and Warburg, 1986, p. 102; Caitlin Thomas, *Double drink story: a life with Dylan Thomas*, Toronto: Viking, 1997; 'Caitlin Thomas', *The Times* (2 August 1994), p. 21.

THOMAS, WILLIAM NEWELL (1924–1944). An able seaman in the Royal Navy, he was born in early 1924 at Bridgend, Monmouthshire, Wales, the son of Edward John Thomas and Rose May (née Newell) of Ogmore Vale, Glamorgan, Wales. Serving on H.M.S. *Saunders*, he was killed on the first day of the Allied attack on Elba on 17 June 1944, and was buried on Elba and three years later was reburied in the Bolsena War Cemetery (IV G 16) on the Italian mainland.

References: *The war dead of the British Commonwealth and Empire: the register of the names of those who fell in the 1939–1945 War and are buried in cemeteries in Italy Cemeteries 17–18: Bolsena War Cemetery, Orvieto War Cemetery*, Maidenhead: Imperial War Graves Commission, 1954, p. 34.

TIDDER, ALFRED (d. 1944). A leading seaman in the Royal Navy, he was attached to H.M.S. *Copra* (combined operations), and was killed on the first day of the Allied attack on Elba on 17 June 1944, and was buried on Elba and three years later was reburied in the Bolsena War Cemetery (IV G 13) on the Italian mainland.

References: *The war dead of the British Commonwealth and Empire: the register of the names of those who fell in the 1939–1945 War and are buried in cemeteries in Italy Cemeteries 17–18: Bolsena War Cemetery, Orvieto War Cemetery*, Maidenhead: Imperial War Graves Commission, 1954, p. 35.

TOREMAR. This is one of the two major ferry lines connecting Elba with other islands in the **Tuscan Archipelago** and Livorno and Piombino on mainland Italy. The name comes from the original company name Toscana Regionale Marittima S.p.A, and was founded in 1975 and has been operating on this route from 1976. In 2013 it made 8,500 crossings and transported some 1.43 million passengers. On 21 February 2014, it was appointed the official carrier of the 1814–2014 Bicentenario Napoleonico celebrations.

Name	Tonnage	Type	Passengers	Car capacity	Max. speed (kn)
Aethalia	2,780	Ferry	710	100	18
Liburna	2,677	Ferry	550 / 700	76	16.5
Rio Marina Bella	2,392	Ferry	900	120	18
Marmorica	2,386	Ferry	470	106	18
Oglasa	2,386	Ferry	470	106	18
Giovanni Bellini	1,573	Ferry	550 / 700	62	16.5
Giuseppe Rum	497	Ferry	633	40	16
Agostino Lauro Jet	415	Fast Ferry	320	-	33

References: http://www.toremar.it/en Dan Facaros and Michael Pauls, *Italy: Tuscany*, London: Cadogan Books plc, 1996, p. 298; Miles Roddis & Alex Leviton, *Tuscany & Umbria*, Footscray: Lonely Planet, 2006, p. 186; Christopher and Jean Serpell, *The Travellers' Guide to Elba and the Tuscan Archipelago*, London: Jonathan Cape, 1977, p. 15.

TORRE DEL MARTELLO (Portoferraio). This tower in Portoferraio was next to the harbour, close to the **Molo Mediceo**, and it was from there that a chain was stretched across the harbour to protect it from attack. It gained its name because of its resemblance to the shape of a hammer.

TORRE DELLA LINGUELLA (Portoferraio). This tower stands on a 'small tongue' of land – hence its name – to help protect Portoferraio from attack by sea.

TORRE DI PASSANNANTE (Portoferraio). This tower is one of those built to protect from attack by sea. It gained its name because it was used as a prison for Giovanni Passannante (1849–1910; left), an anarchist and political activist who lived in Naples. On 17 November 1878 Passannante approached a carriage taking King Umberto I on a tour of the city. Crying 'Long live Orsini! Long live the Universal Republic', he tried to stab the king with a knife which he secured shortly before the attack in exchange for his jacket. The king fought off the attacker and Passannante was arrested and charged. He cited the flour tax as leading to resentment against the government which had betrayed the ideas of the Risorgimento and left the

Two drawings of the assassination attempt on King Umberto I.

poor impoverished. He was sentenced to death on 29 March 1879 but this was commuted to life imprisonment and he was taken to **Portoferraio**.

He was locked in the tower in a small cell below sea level. There he was regularly assaulted and had to live in the cell which had no toilet facilities, and he was not allowed to talk to anybody. He soon fell ill with scurvy and could be heard screaming regularly. It was not until 1899 that there was an outcry at his treatment and he was taken from Portoferraio to an asylum in Florence where he died eleven years later. After his death his head was preserved and put on display in the Criminal Museum in Rome until 2007 when it was removed and buried secretly. The story was retold in the film *Passannante* (2011), directed by Sergio Colabona, and starred Fabio Troiano, Ulderico Pesce, Andrea Satta and Luca Lionello.

References: Giuseppe Galzerano, *Giovanni Passannante*, Casalvelino Scalo: Galzerano

The Torre di Passannante, from a contemporary postcard.

Editore, 2004; Peter Kiefer 'Anarchist's Head Is Finally Buried, but Outcry Arises Over Timing', *The New York Times* (12 May 2007), p. A5; Giuseppe Porcaro, *Processo a un anarchico a Napoli nel 1878*, Napoli: Delfino, 1975.

TRADITI, PIETRO. He was the mayor of **Portoferraio**, and one of the local dignitaries who gathered when the *Undaunted* arrived at Portoferraio on 3 May 1814. He immediately convened a meeting of the local town council and they voted that 3,000 francs be allocated to pay for illuminations to be displayd in Portoferraio, and that there be an issue of free bread for the poor. He then had a team organise the preparation of a dais made from painted plaster, covered in gold paper, with a sofa as an impromptu throne, and others to put up garlands of flowers. He also wanted to hand over ceremonial keys and because there were none for Portoferraio, he had the keys of his own cellar gilded. Whilst this was underway, Pietro Traditi had a difficult task in finding some temporary accommodation for **Napoleon Bonaparte**, and decided that the unused upper floor of the town hall could be used. He also despatched messengers to all the other worthies of Elba so they could be on hand for the disembarking of the ex-emperor on the following day.

However when Napoleon Bonaparte landed on Elba, and Traditi went to meet him, gave him the gilded keys on a silver plate and then reached for his pocket only to discover that he had forgotten to bring his speech and could not remember any of it. The ex-emperor was used to this occasionally happening and thanked the mayor for the keys and then thanked Traditi. Plaza Pietro Traditi is named after him. Another of the Traditi family, also called Pietro Traditi was the mayor of Portoferraio in 1882. The keys are at the **Villa dei Mulini**.

References: Norman MacKenzie, *The Escape from Elba: The Fall & Flight of Napoleon 1814–1815*, Oxford: Oxford University Press, 1982, p. 69, 73, 75.

TROUBRIDGE, THOMAS HOPE (1895–1949). The British Royal Navy officer who was in charge of the capturing of Elba in June 1944, he was born on 1 February 1895 at Southsea, Hampshire, the son of Admiral Sir Ernest Troubridge (1862–1926) and his wife Edith Mary (née Duffus, 1855–1900). When he was 13, Thomas Troubridge joined the Royal Navy and served in World War I. In 1936 he was appointed the British naval attaché in Berlin and in **World War II** he served as the commanding officer of the H.M.S. *Furious*, an aircraft carrier. In June 1941 he was given command of the H.M.S. *Nelson*, and in January 1942 was appointed commander of the H.M.S. *Indomitable*, another aircraft carrier. Then Rear Admiral Combined Operations and Flag Officer Commanding Overseas Assault Forces, he led the invasion of Elba in 1944. Subsequently appointed the Fifth Sea Lord, he was named the Flag Officer and Second-in-Command, Mediterranean Fleet in 1948, retiring in that year and dying on 29 September 1949 at Hawkley, Hampshire.

References: *Who was Who 1941–1950*, pp. 1165–66; *The Times* (30 September 1949), p. 4; *The Times* (1 October 1949), p. 7.

TRUSCHSESS-WALDBOURG, FRIEDRICH LUDWIG, Count (1776–1844). He was the Prussian commissioner who accompanied **Napoleon Bonaparte** to Elba in April-May 1814. He had been born on 25 October 1776 at Tangermünde, and grew up in Konigsburg (now Kaliningrad, Russia). He was the son of Major General Friedrich Ludwig, Count Truschsess-Waldbourg (1741–1807), and his first wife Albertine Wilhelmine of Ingersleben (1755–1796). He trained in Berlin with the Garde du Corps from 1793 to 1800, and then worked in Stuttgart as a chamberlain at the court of the dukes of

Württemberg. In 1806 he was the envoy of Württemberg in Vienna, and from 1806 to 1809 was the envoy in Paris. He then served King Jérôme Bonaparte who was appointed the King of Westphalia. After a stint in Italy, he went back to Prussia to work as a Prussian envoy and this saw him accompanying **Napoleon** to Elba. He then left the island. After the final defeat of Napoleon in 1815, he was the Prussian envoy to the court of the King of Sardinia in Turin; and from 1827 to 1832 he was the Prussian ambassador to The Hague. He died on 18 August 1844

References: Norman MacKenzie, *The Escape from Elba: The Fall & Flight of Napoleon 1814–1815*, Oxford: Oxford University Press, 1982; Ludwig Friedrich Truschsess-Waldbourg, *A narrative of Napoleon Buonaparte's journey from Fontainebleau to Frejus in April 1814*, London: W. Pople, 1815.

TURNBULL, WILLIAM R. (1924–1944). Born in 1924, and known as Billy, he was the son of William Turnbull and Catherine 'Kate' (née Herbertson), of Newcastle-on-Tyne. An able seaman, he served in the Royal Navy and was attached to H.M.S. *Copra* (combined operations), and was killed on the first day of the Allied attack on Elba on 17 June 1944, and was buried on Elba and three years later was reburied in the Bolsena War Cemetery (IV G 18) on the Italian mainland.

References: *The war dead of the British Commonwealth and Empire: the register of the names of those who fell in the 1939–1945 War and are buried in cemeteries in Italy Cemeteries 17–18: Bolsena War Cemetery, Orvieto War Cemetery*, Maidenhead: Imperial War Graves Commission, 1954, p. 35.

TUSCAN ARCHIPELAGO. This is the name given to the seven Italian islands located off the coast of Tuscany, together with a number of islets and shoals. The largest of these is Elba, and together with the three other northern islands: **Pianosa**, **Capraia** and **Gorgona** are in the province of Livorno. The three southern islands are **Giglio**, Giannutri and **Montecristo**, and with Giglio and Giannutri they are part of the province of Grosseto, except for Montecristo which is administered from Elba.

- U -

USSHER, Sir THOMAS (1779–1848).
A British naval officer who escorted Napoleon from France to Elba, he was born in Ireland, the son of the astronomer Dr Henry Ussher (1741–1790) and his wife, Mary (née Burne). Joining the Royal Navy, he served on a number of ships and took part in the capture of the Caribbean island of St. Lucia in May 1796. He was subsequently involved in many other actions against French and also Spanish ships in the West Indies, and was injured in fighting in Cuba. He recuperated in England in 1800–01, before returning to the sea in command of *Joseph*, and then *Colpoys* which was part of the British fleet blockading the French port of Brest. Then in the Mediterranean, he took part in the blockade of Toulon in 1813, serving on the *Undaunted*.

In April 1814, Thomas Ussher was serving on the *Undaunted* and, along with the *Euryalus* were off the coast at Marseilles when the city's mayor and some local worthies came onto his ship to inform him that **Napoleon Bonaparte** had abdicated and that a new provisional government had been formed. Soon afterwards Ussher received instructions that he was to take the ex-emperor to Elba. Ussher was asked to take the *Undaunted* to St. Tropez where he found Captain de Montcabrie and the frigate *Dryade*, the corvette *Victorieuse* and a transport ship which was to take the Imperial party to Elba. However on sailing to Fréjus it was discovered that Napoleon would rather travel on a British frigate as the French ships were flying the Bourbon flag, and on 28 April, Ussher welcomed Napoleon on board the *Undaunted*. Ussher then took the ex-emperor to Elba, weighing anchor on 30 April at **Portoferraio**, with Napoleon landing on 3 May. Gradually the ex-emperor's baggage was brought over, and Ussher then sailed for Genoa, later put in command of the *Duncan*. Ussher wrote in June 1814:

At daylight next morning Bonaparte was on deck, and remained with various officers, asking questions as to the anchorage, fortifications, etc., etc. At eight he asked me for a boat, as he intended to take a walk on the opposite side of the bay, and asked me to go with him. He wore a greatcoat and round hat. Count Bertrand, Colonel Campbell, and Colonel Vincent went with us. When about half-way he remarked that he was without a sword, and soon afterwards asked if the peasants of Tuscany were addicted to assassination.

We walked about two hours, and the peasants, considering us all as Englishmen, cried 'Vive les Anglais.' We returned on board to breakfast, and he afterwards fixed the flag of Elba, and ordered two to be made immediately, that one might be hoisted at one p.m. on the fortifications and at two p.m. he would disembark with the other. (What a childish vanity!) The flag is a white field with a red band running diagonally through it, with three bees in the band. The bees were in his arms as Emperor of France.

The boats of the island now began to assemble round the ship, crowded with people, bands of music, etc., and shouting 'Vive l'Empereur.' At two my barge was manned. He desired me to go down first; he then called Baron Koeller, Colonel Campbell, Count Kalm, and Count Bertrand. The yards were manned, and as soon as the barge shoved off a royal salute was fired, and the same by each of the French corvettes. On the beach he was received by the mayor, municipality, and the authorities, civil and military. The keys were presented on a plate, and the people seemed to receive him with great welcome, and shouts of 'Vive l'Empereur!' We proceeded to the church in procession; thence to the Hotel de Ville, where all the authorities and principal inhabitants assembled, with each of whom he conversed. After that he mounted his horse, attended by a dozen persons, and visited part of the outworks, and dined at seven o'clock.

Next morning he was up at four, and from that until ten was on foot visiting the fortifications, storehouses, magazines, etc. At two he mounted his horse, and I rode with him about two leagues into the country, over mountains and precipices, but nothing is impassable to him: He examined the country houses, and stopped at a planter's (wine merchant) and had a cold collation. He helped me to different things, which he never does to any one else. A lady came in and offered him strawberries, which he gave to me. I took an opportunity afterwards of offering him a sprig of laurel, which pleased him much. He asked me here how I liked the wine. I said it was excellent; and he immediately ordered 2000 bottles to be sent on board to the men. In short, his manner is always most agreeable and polite, and it's only when anxious to carry any point that he is passionate.

Next day we went across the island to a mountain of iron, the richest and finest mine in the world-and, what is remarkable, the revenue arising from it formerly paid his Legion of Honour. We rode through the clouds to it. I never was so fatigued in my life. The mountain is completely of iron, and is blasted with powder in the way that quarries are in England. When broken, the fragments are like pieces of diamond, of all colours. He gave me some at Elba 17 beautiful specimens of his collection. If you choose to make the college a present of one, I will send it to you.

We afterwards went through a labyrinth to a high mountain, upon the summit of which there is a temple erected by the Romans in honour of Jupiter. I suppose he consulted the oracle. At dinner we had a boar's head, and the Emperor with his usual kindness to me helped me to the eye as a great treat. I was hard set what to do. It was rudeness to refuse, but I could not stand it, and sent it away; the very idea spoiled my appetite.

Elba is a beautiful island, possessing every advantage. The bay of Porto Ferrajo is unrivalled, and the valleys are uncommonly fertile, yielding the finest vegetables of every description, and the mountains are to the summits clothed with vines. In three or four days he visited every part of the island, conceived all his plans for building palaces, stables, aqueducts, lazarettos, etc. (The latter he begged I would plan.) His constitution is of iron-always up at four, and seldom in bed before eleven. The day the transports arrived with his carriages, horses, and guards he was on his legs from four in the morning until four in the evening, under a hot sun. He then mounted his horse and rode over two or three mountains-returned at eight o'clock, and was not twenty minutes at dinner. He sent for Colonel Campbell and myself. He stopped me for a moment in the library, and hurrying over some magnificent drawings of Egypt, stopped at Cairo, and asked my opinion of it. He then said in his quick way, 'Allons!' and we walked into the garden; and there we walked for three hours, talking of Egypt. I could not help remarking to him that his constitution was of iron in being able to undergo much fatigue-'car il montait a cheval pour se defatiguer.'

The day that he was on the summit of a mountain that showed him all the island, he turned round laughing and said, 'Ah! mon ile est bien petite.' He laughed at the idea• of our being caricatured, and said 'the English had a great passion for caricaturing.' I said 'John Bull caricatured and abused people when they deserved it. I shall be caricatured nursing the King of Rome.' He often compliments the nation for generosity and liberality. In talking of Lord Wellington his admiration was unbounded. He said also that our army institutions were perfection, and that the discipline was superior to his. He also complimented my officers, and said they were the finest young men he ever saw, and that the *Undaunted* was a pattern to all other ships. He always wished to have my officers about him: a sergeant of marines, who is a great favourite, always slept in the next room to him, upon a mattress at the door.

I told him we never thought him serious in his intentions of invading England. He said that he was quite serious: his object was not to conquer England, for he knew that so high-minded a people were not to be conquered by taking their capital; but he expected to throw the country into confusion, and separate Ireland. He said his plans were on the largest scale – that in four or five years he would have had three hundred sail of the line. I asked him how he intended to man them. He said his naval conscription was fully equal to it. I told him we laughed at his naval conscripts, who were more formidable to each other than to us ...

Thomas Ussher retired in 1815 and fifteen years later, he was appointed equerry to Queen Adelaide, and then served as superintendent of the dockyards at Bermuda, and then at Halifax, Nova Scotia. He then served as commander-in-chief at Queenstown (Cork), Ireland. In 1841 he wrote *A Narrative of Events Connected with the First Abdication of Napoleon* which was reprinted in 1895 as *Napoleon's Last Voyages*. He died on 6 January 1848 at Queenstown.

References: J. K. Laughton, 'Ussher, Sir Thomas (1779–1848)', revised by Andrew Lambert, *Oxford Dictionary of National Biography*, Oxford University Press, 2004;

258

Norman MacKenzie, *The Escape from Elba: The Fall & Flight of Napoleon 1814–1815*, Oxford: Oxford University Press, 1982, p. 57f; pp. 61ff; T. Ussher, *A narrative of events connected with the first abdication of Napoleon*, Dublin: Grant and Bolton, 1841.

- V -

VADI, CERBONE. He was the mayor of **Marciana** in June 1799 leading the revolt against the French soldiers who were commanded by General Montserrat. Vadi led the Elbans to victory against the French who were forced to surrender on 17 July 1799. Although he had gained his local reputation for fighting the French, between 21 August 1814 and 5 September 1814 he hosted **Napoleon Bonaparte** and his mother **Letizia Bonaparte** when they came to Marciana.

References: Averil Mackenzie-Grieve, *Aspects of Elba and the other islands of the Tuscan Archipelago*, London: Jonathan Cape, 1964, p. 99; Christine Sutherland, *Marie Walewska: Napoleon's Great Love*, New York: Vendome Press, 1979, p. 217.

VADI, GIUSEPPE (1825–1907). An Italian patriot, he was born on 30 November 1825 at **Marciana**, the son of Giovanpaolo Vadi e Bastianina Tirati, and the grandson of **Cerbone Vadi**. Educated at the University of Pisa, Giuseppe Vadi joined the Italian patriots in May 1848 and fought the Austrians. He then returned to university and completed his law degree in 1849. From 28 January 1869 to 30 December 1878 he was mayor of Marciana, and died on 29 December 1907. On 15 July 1982, one of the main streets of Marciana was named after him.

References: Niccolò Giorgetti, *Le armi toscane e le occupazioni straniere in Toscana (1537–1860)*, Città di Castello, Tip dell' Unione arti grafiche, 1916, Volume 2, p. 184; Gherardo Nerucci, *Memorie del Battaglione universitario pisano*, Pisa: F. Mariotti 1898.

VAN GALEN, JOHAN (1604–1653). A Dutch naval commodore, and the victor of the **battle of Elba** in 1652, he was born in 1604 in Essen, and fought in the Eight Years' War against Spain, being promoted to captain in 1630 and then joined the regular army and fought around Dunkirk. In 1645 he was involved in the breaking of the Danish blockade of The Sound, fighting alongside Vice-Admiral Witte de With. After serving against the Corsair pirates of the

Barbary Coast, he retired in 1650 but was called back to service at the outbreak of the First Anglo-Dutch War. He took command of the Dutch fleet in the Mediterranean, taking over from Commander Joris van Cats. Leaving the Netherlands on 24 July 1652, he arrived at Livorno (Leghorn) on 22 August and then only six days later led his fleet against the English in the battle of Elba. He sailed on his flagship, *Jaarsveld*, and the Dutch successfully fought the English, capturing one ship and forcing many other English ships to flee to the safety of Elba. The English under **Richard Badiley**, repaired their vessels in Elba over the winter and then sought their revenge on the Dutch in the battle of Leghorn on 4 March 1653 (14 March, n.s.). The Dutch again won but during the fighting, a cannon ball smashed the right lower leg of Van Galen. His leg was amputated but he continued to direct the battle. He died on 13 March 1653 at Livorno as a result of complications from his injury.

References: David C. Wallace, *Twenty-Two Turbulent Years 1639–1661*, FastPrint, 2013.

VILLA DEI MULINI (Casa dei Mulini / Villa of the Mills). Known in Italian as the Palazzina dei Mulini, this was one of the two residences of Napoleon Bonaparte when in Elba in 1814–15 – the other was the **Villa San Martino**. Located in **Portoferraio**, the Villa dei Mulini takes its name from the two (and later four) windmills which originally stood on the promontory. In 1724 Gian Gastone de' Medici, the grand duke of Tuscany, had the site turned into a residence for the governor because of its close proximity to **Forte Stella**. There were also prisons built nearby and a home for the local magistrate. The latter had to be enlarged in 1787 but during the **Napoleonic Wars** was divided into two living quarters – one for the commander of the artillery, and the other for the commander of the engineers. The windmills were demolished in 1808.

On 5 May 1814, Napoleon's second day on Elba, he found and stayed at the Villa Dei Mulini, and it was decided that he should stay there because it was secure and also provided the ex-emperor with good views of the surrounding countryside and sea. He moved into the place on 21 May. Symbolically Napoleon joined up the two residences – at the same time as unifying Elba.

Villa dei Mulini.
Photograph © S. Engels / Fotolia.com

Paolo Bargigli worked on the site under instructions from Napoleon, and the local Elban architect **Luigi Bettarini** also worked on the site, with the painter Vincenzo A. Revelli decorating many of the walls. Pauline Bonaparte, the sister of the ex-emperor, came to stay in the villa, on the top floor, from 1 November 1814.

When Napoleon left Elba in February 1815, the house fell into disuse and was used by the military and also fanciers of racing pigeons. In 1880 the Italian state took possession of the building. In 1906, **Paul Gruyer** wrote:

At the top of the steepest street, a house with red tiles and green shutters overlooks the town: this is Napoleon's house (casa di Napoleone), the imperial palace. Outside, it is like one of the simplest Italian villas seen at Genoa or Bordighera. Part of it is now occupied by the military government. Over the door are trophies of cannon-balls, fitting emblem for a conqueror. But the spirit of the god of war is absent; a feeling of peace and happiness seems to pervade the place, as across the myrtle bushes and flowers in the garden stretches the immense horizon of the Tyrrhenian sea, blue and white like a glimpse of Paradise, the headlands outlined against gold. The prospect is brilliant, profoundly peaceful. After so many struggles, so many crushing disasters on Russian plains, after the agony of abdication, the formidable conqueror must have felt something of this ineffable peace as he gazed on the horizon. Every human being is akin, and the same feelings exist in all, in spite of surface differences, and there must have been days, hours at least, when his iron brain relaxed its tension, and a vision of a rest he had never known passed before his eyes. If it came, however, it passed rapidly out of his reach; fate impelled him on, to further battles and fresh disasters.

The exterior of the house has not changed. Inside, most of the rooms have fallen into decay, but the large salon on the first floor, with eight windows, four looking on the town and four on the sea, has remained intact. Its plaster walls are still decorated with the paintings the Emperor designed. They seem to be waiting for his return. The furniture was removed after Waterloo, and only two busts remain of the Dukes of Tuscany, Ferdinand III and Leopold II, sad and solitary on their pedestals. 1 The shutters were closed, but badly hung, and rays of light filtered through. On the dusty floor were scattered a few grains of maize; spiders had spun their webs across the corners. Did the master of the house leave it a year, or a century ago? I turned the gilded handles of one of the windows, and opening the shutters, looked out on the little garden, starred with thousands of daisies. The dazzling azure of the Tyrrhenian Sea seemed to fill the room, just as the Emperor saw it. Below the window on an asphalted path is the mark of a horse's shoe, made, they say, by the Emperor's horse while the cement was soft. This has grown already into legend, and Napoleon's horse has become as mythological as the paladin Roland's, whose hoof-marks on stones and rocks are shown all over Europe.

Don C. Seitz wrote in 1910:

Behind the castle, at the crest of the crag on the ocean side, is the Palazzo Mulini (Palace of the Mills), where the exiled Bonaparte carried on the business of his tiny kingdom, struggling to fit his vast mind to the diminutive country. It is the usual Italian building of two high stories with the sloping roof, built on a triangle around a garden where the laurel and myrtle grow, and from which still runs plainly the path down which the Emperor went from the cliff to the minute bit of beach to bathe in the gently lapping waves. Now the structure is government property, half filled with tenants of the common sort, while in a wing the tailor-made Italian officer in charge of the small garrison keeps his horse. He is a singularly 'smart' – looking officer, with mustachios that spread like eagle's wings, eye-glasses that stare piercingly, and trousers so tight as to excite two phases of wonder: one, how he gets them on, and the other how he ever gets them off again.

In 1921 on the centenary of the death of Napoleon Bonaparte, it was decided to renovate the building and in 1927 it was handed to the ministry of education and plans were drawn up but came to nothing. As a result of the bombing of Elba by the Germans and then the Allies in 1943 and 1944, the ministry of justice took over the site in March 1945 to use for prisoners sentenced to terms of hard labour. However, objections from the local authorities led to much of the site handed over to the local government in April 1948. Restoration work then took place and was finally completed in 1964 with the building becoming a Napoleonic museum open to the public at a time when the tourist industry on Elba was becoming important. It has also been furnished with many items

Villa dei Mulini.

connected with Napoleon but most of the furniture from the palace of Elisa Bonaparte from **Piombino** had been sold in the mid-nineteenth century, and some period pieces have been loaned by the Pitti Palace in Florence, and by the local government in Pisa, along with the painting of Napoleon by Jacques Louis David in the Grand Salon / Officer's Hall (Salone degli Ufficiali).

The Villa dei Mulini remains one of the major tourist attractions on Elba, and much work has gone into the care and upkeep of the building. Some items in the building have been there since the time of Napoleon, some are genuine Napoleonic items brought in from elsewhere, whilst others are reproductions to recapture the style of the small court at Elba.

Outside the villa is an inscription noting:

This august and sovereign house, where an empire collapsed and was revived, was occupied for nearly a year, during his first exile, by Napoleon the Great. The divided island of Elba having found unity through him, he solemnly pointed the way to the unity of Italy. Nostalgic for the epic of his glory, he here conceived the bold undertaking which took him away from these heights to land him on distant shores.

Entering the house, there is a small waiting room which leads into the 'grand salon' and on through to the back of the house. Decorated in pastel green with gold covings and gilt furniture, there are gold and green sofas along one wall, with a copy of David's famous painting, *Napoleon crossing the Alps* (see p. 150). There is also a small sketch by David, and the painting by Prazio Vernet, *The Death of Marshal Poniatowsky* who drowned after the battle of Leipzig. On a table in the centre of the room is an octagonal table on which there is an equestrian statue of Napoleon which dates from the Second Empire of Napoleon III. The four chests of drawers in the room date from 1840. During the time Napoleon lived in the villa, the ceiling was painted as a military marquee with coats of arms and the like. The current light green decorated design was a compromise when the house was being restored.

From the grand salon, it is possible to enter Napoleon's study which contains a writing table, armchair and cupboard. These date from the 1790s and are contemporary with Napoleon although probably not the ones he actually used. There is a framed copy of the 1814 proclamation of Napoleon, and a town plan of Portoferraio dating from the French siege (5 May 1801 – 11 June 1802) on the wall, and another by Luigi Escalapon dating from 1814; and a drawing of Portoferraio in 1759.

Beyond the study is the 'petit salon' which is Italianate and has a few armchairs, and after that is Napoleon's bedroom. This is one room in the villa which retains most of its furniture which originally came from Elisa

Bonaparte's house in Piombino. In 1814 when Napoleon arrived on Elba, and with the Austrians occupying Pimobino, Elisa Bonaparte and her husband had fled the city and so Napoleon sent over his quartermaster and others to bring some of the furniture to Elba with Napoleon quaintly remarking on the disloyalty of his sister saying, 'I have punished my sister and robbed Austria at the same time.' The ornate bed is the one in which Napoleon slept, and also on which he would lie on in the evenings while chatting to his friend, Poggi de Talavo, a Corsican and a former judge who headed Napoleon's secret police on Elba. On it is the green velvet dress owned by Josephine and brought to Elba by Marshal **Bertrand**'s wife on 16 July 1814 as a memento – Fanny Bertrand also brought the news to Napoleon of Josephine's death. There is a round marble-topped bedside table on one side of the bed, and an armchair on the other, next to a marble topped console, above which is a mirror. On the wall are paintings by Antonio Morghen's *Camp during the retreat from Russia*, and *Camp in Poland*.

In the room beyond the bedroom is the library which contained Napoleon's books brought from Fontainebleau. These include the ex-emperor's own copy of **Arsène Thiébaut de Berneaud**'s 1808 book on Elba which Napoleon read when he was going into exile. Grand Duke Leopold III of Tuscany took some of the ex-emperor's books after Waterloo, and the remainder were then taken

Napoleon's bed.

and placed in the local library, now the **Biblioteca Comunale Foresiana**. However they were subsequently restored to the villa. These include a complete set of the *Moniteur Universal* from the French Revolution through to 1813, and works by Boccaccio, Cervantes, La Fontaine, Plutarch, Rousseau and Voltaire. Some of the books are bound in red morocco bindings with 'N' stamped on them showing they were from Napoleon's own library. The wooden lectern is Italian and the mirror above the fireplace dates from the time of Napoleon but is not original to the building. The library leads back into the Grand Salon.

At the back of the building is a small passageway which takes people under the staircase through into the garden. This passes the bathroom which remained empty, and the Wardrobe Room where Napoleon's vestments were kept and looked after by Mrs Squarci, the wife of the local doctor. On one of the walls is the small flag of Elba which was hoisted over **Forte Falcone** on 4 May 1814, and the keys presented by **Pietro Traditi** are there as well as portraits of **Bertrand**, **Cambronne**, **Jermanowski**, and **Pons de l'Herault**. There is a copy of an image of Napoleon's departure from Elba on 26 February 1815, and also a photograph showing the emperor's dog – which was stuffed and is in Paris. Beyond is the guard room where some of the soldiers detailed to protect the ex-emperor would remain, and where St. Denis, his loyal bodyguard, would sleep. On the wall of this room are orders signed by **Antoine Drouot**.

Also off the grand salon is an 'Officer's Room' which has framed copies of broadsheets and other memorabilia commemorating the 100 Days including some British cartoons, and also the watercolours of the British arriving in Portoferraio on 10 July 1796, and leaving Portoferraio in 1797. Beyond that there were the kitchens but these have not survived. There is no dining room as Napoleon would eat in any room he chose, as was the custom of many rulers of his

time.

Because the building was never planned to be a palace, there are only narrow stairs to the first floor, with 20 pink marble steps leading the way to the quarters which had been prepared for Empress Marie Louise who was expected to come to Elba to live with her husband, bringing with her their son, the king of Rome. Although she never came, Pauline Bonaparte did come to the island and lived on the upper floor and served as the official hostess. The suite of four rooms has one large chandelier which dates from the time that Pauline Bonaparte lived there. The ceilings were painted in a Florentine style with spears and pikes, as well as laurel wreaths decorating the scene. However these decayed over time and in **World War II** the villa received a direct hit during an air raid with a bomb landing in the room and blowing out the original windows. The roof was subsequently repaired and has been subject to a relatively plain restoration. The bust of Napoleon is attributed to François Rude. Pauline Bonaparte's private rooms beyond are generally closed to the public, and remain unfurnished.

Outside the house is a simple garden which provides great views of Portoferraio and visitors can walk around taking in the atmosphere and views that Napoleon enjoyed during his brief stay there in 1814–15 including a good view of **Scoglietto** in the middle distance.

The Villa dei Mulini is open to the public from 9 am to 7 pm on Mondays, and from Wednesday through to Saturday, and from 9 am to 1 pm on Sundays. It remains closed on Tuesdays. It is possible to buy a joint admission ticket to both this villa and the **Villa San Martino**, some 5 kilometres away.

References: Emilia Bartolotti and Monica Guarracino, *Napoleone all'Elba: Le residenze,* Livorno: Sillabe Editore, 1998, 2009; Roberto Donati, *The Island of Elba*, Terni: Fotorapidacolor, 1973, pp. 50–57; Paul Gruyer, *Napoleon, King of Elba*, Philadelphia: J. B. Lippincott Company, 1906, pp. 6–7; *Le residenze Napoleoniche a Portoferraio*, Pisa: Settimana per i Beni Culturali e Ambientali 1986; Alessandro Pioda, *Napoleon on Elba*, Livorno, nd; Miles Roddis & Alex Leviton, *Tuscany & Umbria*, Footscray: Lonely Planet, 2006, p. 186; Don Carlos Seitz, *Elba and Elsewhere*, New York: Harper and Brothers, 1910, pp. 3–4; Christopher and Jean Serpell, *The Travellers' Guide to Elba and the Tuscan Archipelago*, London: Jonathan Cape, 1977, pp. 161–68.

VILLA SAN MARTINO. Also known by its more formal name, Villa Napoleonica di San Martino, this is one of two residences lived in by **Napoleon Bonaparte** on Elba, the other being the **Villa dei Mulini** at **Portoferraio**. Napoleon bought this property as his country residence on 2 June 1814 after the arrival on Elba of Pauline Borghese (**Pauline Bonaparte**). She gave him a

Villa San Martino.
The Illustrated London News (23 May 1868), p. 521.

jewel which he used to purchase it. **Don C. Seitz** wrote in 1910:

It is but a scant half-hour's drive from the square before the Albergo de l'Ape Elbana to the Villa Napoleon at San Martino. Visitors are rare. The single carriage at the inn is pressed into service amid proper excitement, and whirls away through the market-place, along the quay, past the ironworks, over the water-filled moat, and then into the real country, skirting the harbor for a mile or so until it makes its way up a fine valley, at the head of which stands the house, under the shadow of Monte San Martino. Little farms line the way, with here and there a pretty villa, amid its clump of trees, until the vast new country-house of Signor Del Buono bars the road. Here the innkeeper's pass is honored, and a pretty Elban woman with a bunch of keys leads through the gate and up the gravelled road to the palace.

The simple villa where the Emperor lived is unchanged in itself, but its surroundings are altered and garish. In 1851 Prince Demidoff, who married Princess Mathilde, daughter of Jerome and aunt of our Baltimore Bonapartes, bought the property and proceeded to turn it into a memorial. He built into the terrace a high, one-storied edifice, the roof of which forms an esplanade to the villa proper, of red granite, ornamented with bronze 'N's within the imperial wreath, and marked with the triple bees. Here he assembled many relics of Napoleon, which were dispersed, March 15, 1880, by his nephew and heir, Paul Demidoff. Mathilde had long before divorced Demidoff, but lived to see the new century as the last of the second Bonaparte generation.

A few sea-shells from the surrounding waters and some geological specimens remain in the great hall under the hillside, and many engravings showing events in Napoleon's day are on the walls. In the villa a few battered chairs and the bedstead used by Madame Mere remain. This bedstead is high-posted, with gilded eagles roosting on the top of each

Villa San Martino.

Villa San Martino.

post. In what was Napoleon's sleeping-room is a bedstead with broken slats, curiously curved, suggesting a square gondola, if there could be such a thing. The guide said Napoleon had slept in it. Perhaps he had.

The Emperor's bath-tub is one authentic furnishing. It is a deep, oval bowl of stone, set closely against the wall. Above it a frescoed lady reclines after her bath, clothed in the altogether, and gazing with deep satisfaction into a hand-mirror. There was no splendor at San Martino, and little comfort in the house itself beyond the bath-tub.

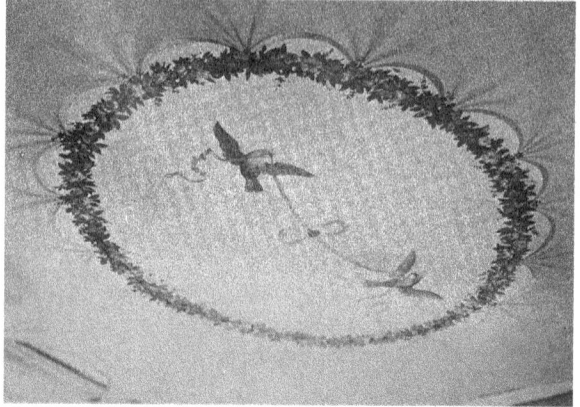

But the Salle des Pyramides, with its fountain in the floor, is still there, frescoed in drab, with such strange figures as appear on the Central Park Obelisk; and the ceiling of another room shows two doves carrying a ribbon in their bills within a circle of flowers. This is said to typify the love of Napoleon and Marie Louise, who never came to see it. Here Bonaparte met with his little court, playing cards at night with Cambronne, Bertrand, the lovely Sister Pauline, Princess Borghese, and grim old Madame Mere – cheating always when he had to in order to win, and going round the next day to pay back the money to all except his mother – who, he observed in justification, was richer than he was!

Better reminders than these scanty relics of the great are the good roads, the drained morasses, the successful mines, the improved agriculture. Elba had but ten months of its king.

The town and the harbor show in fine vistas from the villa terrace, while behind and on either side are the hills, some topped with ruins, but all in verdure clad. It is a tranquil resting-place, one that should tame the wildest mind and calm even a warrior's soul, a place to be content from struggling, away from battle, murder, and sudden death!

In the church at Porto Ferraio is an ebon coffin about which four candles are always burning. The upper part is open, and in it lies the face of Napoleon in bronze, made from Doctor Antommarchi's death-mask taken at St. Helena. On the fifth of May, the date of his death, a funeral service is said over this casket and its mask. The city hall preserves Napoleon's flag, a banner of white with a wide band of orange set at an angle across its surface from comer to comer, on which are embroidered the three golden bees, the sign manual of his kingdom! What is left of his library is also here, books left behind at the hasty flight of Sunday, February 26, 1815. The Arabian Nights and Don Quixote are conspicuous volumes. The drop-curtain of the local theatre still pictures Napoleon as Apollo watching his sheep! He saw it first raised.

The villa is open to the public from 9 am to 7 pm on Mondays, and from Wednesday through to Saturday, and from 9 am to 1 pm on Sundays. It

Villa San Martin
Photograph © padabaiashi / fotolia.com.

remains closed on Tuesdays. There is a small admission charge for adults, but it is possible to buy a joint admission ticket with the **Villa dei Mulini** in **Portoferraio**.

References: Roberto Donati, The Island of Elba, Terni: Fotorapidacolor, 1973, pp. 58–63; Don Carlos Seitz, *Elba and Elsewhere*, New York: Harper and Brothers, 1910, pp. 7–12; Christopher and Jean Serpell, *The Travellers' Guide to Elba and the Tuscan Archipelago*, London: Jonathan Cape, 1977, pp. 170–72.

VIVIAN, JOHN HENRY (1785–1855). A British industrialist and politician, he was born on 9 August 1785 in Truro, the second surviving son of John Vivian (1749/50–1826), a Cornish mining and copper-smelting entrepreneur, and his wife, Betsy (née Cranch, 1763–1816). Educated at Truro Grammar School and Lostwithiel School, he went to Germany when he was 16, and studied at the Mining Institute of the University of Freiberg. He decided to continue in the family business and was involved in improving the smelting techniques used for copper, and for establishing a secret cartel to keep the price of copper artificially high.

A keen traveller, he went to Elba in early 1815 and there met **Napoleon Bonaparte**. John Vivian wore the uniform of the Cornish militia for the audience, and subsequently published an account of their conversation. Back in Britain, he was deputy lieutenant for Glamorgan, Wales; its High Sheriff and then member of parliament for Swansea from 1832. He died on 10 February 1855. His older brother was Richard Hussey Vivian, Baron Vivian.

References: Ralph A. Griffiths, *In conversation with Napoleon Bonaparte: J. H. Vivian's visit to the island of Elba*, Newport: South Wales Record Society, 2008; reviewed by Geoffrey Ellis, *The English Historical Review* vol. 152, no. 515 (August 2010), pp. 1009–11; Edmund Newell, 'Vivian, John Henry (1785–1855)', *Oxford Dictionary of National Biography*, Oxford University Press, 2004; R. R. Toomey, *Vivian and Sons, 1809–1924: a study of the firm in the copper and related industries*, New York: Garland, 1985.

- W -

WATERTON, CHARLES (1782–1865). A British naturalist, he was born on 3 June 1782 near Wakefield, Yorkshire, the eldest son of the six children of Thomas Waterton (1738–1805), and his wife, Anne (née Bedingfeld, 1758–1819); and was a direct descendant of Sir Thomas More, the famous chancellor of King Henry VIII. A Roman Catholic, he was educated at Stonyhurst College, Lancashire, and in 1802 went to Spain to stay with two maternal uncles who had settled in Malaga. Falling ill, he moved to the family estates at Demerara, British Guiana, and managed the plantations there. His time in South America led to a fascination with the local **fauna** and on his return to Britain, travelled around Europe from 1830. On his next visit to Europe in 1840–41, he was returning home when his ship, the *Pollux*, was shipwrecked near Elba on the night of 17 June 1841. Returning to Italy, he then trekked across Germany and France, and finally arrived in Britain. He tripped over and injured himself badly on 25 May 1865, dying two days later. His first wife Anne Mary (née Edmonstone) had died in 1830; and his widow, Charlotte (née Arundel) died in 1893.

References: Julia Blackburn, *Charles Waterton*, London: Bodley Head, 1987; Brian W. Edginton, *Charles Waterton: a biography*, Cambridge: Lutterworth Press, 1996; Yolanda Foote, 'Waterton, Charles (1782–1865)', *Oxford Dictionary of National Biography*, Oxford University Press, 2004; Gilbert Phelps, *Squire Waterton*, Wakefield: EP Pub., 1976.

WATSON-TAYLOR, GEORGE GRAEME (1816–1865). An English adventurer, he bought the island of **Montecristo** in 1852 and styled himself the Count of Monte Cristo, he was the son of George Watson who had been born in Jamaica in 1770, the son of John Watson of Saul's River, Jamaica. George Watson married Anna Susannah Taylor on 6 March 1810 St James, Piccadilly, London, and they had at least three sons: Simon Watson-Taylor, born in 1811; another son; and George Watson-Taylor, born on 29 April 1816 in England.

In 1819 with the death of Joshua Smith, member of parliament for Devizes, the Watson-Taylors bought his estate at Erlestoke, Wiltshire, and George Watson-Taylor snr became member of parliament for Devizes, and used his fortune made from the sugar industry in Jamaica to wage a parliamentary campaign against the abolition of slavery. Simon Watson-Taylor married Lady Hannah Charlotte Hay (1818–1887), one of the daughters of Field Marshal George Hay, 8th Marquess of Tweeddale (1787–1876), and became a brother-in-law of the Duke of Wellington. He was a member of parliament for Devizes, Wiltshire in 1857–59.

His brother, George Watson-Taylor jnr, was baptised on 27 June 1816 at Saville Row, Westminster, London, and went to Trinity College, Cambridge, matriculating in 1839 and graduating BA in 1843 (MA 1846). A keen botanist, George was advised to find a warmer climate for his health which caused him to move to St Saviour, Jersey, in 1851 living there with his wife Victorine (née Joudioux), daughter of Jean Baptiste Joudioux. The couple then moved to the Mediterranean, and went to the island of Montecristo, south of Elba, which George Watson-Taylor bought in 1852 for 50,000 lire (then worth some £2,000). George and his wife lived on Montecristo and transformed Cala Maestra establishing a terraced garden, and introducing some foreign tree species. Their villa – later called the Villa Reale (Royal Villa) was the one used in 1896 by Prince Victor Emmanuel of Savoy (later King Victor Emmanuel III) and his wife Elena of Montenegro for their honeymoon.

Unfortunately all did not go well for George Watson-Taylor and George Cavendish-Bentinck, the conservative member of parliament for Taunton, told the British House of Commons of the problem in 1862. Bentinck noted 'When Mr Taylor purchased the island there was doing duty there a corporal ... named Durante, who was guilty of very gross misconduct towards Mr Taylor.' The exact nature of the 'misconduct' was never specified, but Taylor 'made a representation on the subject to the governor of Elba, the case was investigated, and Durante was removed.' With Italian Unification tensions arose with Italian soldiers feeling that the Watson-Taylors were too closely aligned to the former government of the Grand Duchy of Tuscany. Then on 28 April 1860 during George Watson-Taylor's birthday party, it was alleged that Mrs Taylor had told local Italian soldiers that King Victor Emmanuel was a 'bullock merchant'. They later complained that George Watson-Taylor went on to slap the corporal of the guards in the face. It appears that the Watson-Taylors left soon afterwards. Back in England, they lived at 2 Claremont Villas, Richmond, Surrey, and George died on 25 October 1865. His wife died in 1900 in Paris, France. The papers of the Taylor family in Jamaica are held by the Institute of Commonwealth Studies, University of London.

References: *Burke's Landed Gentry, 1937*, p. 2213; *Alumni Cantabrigienses*; Peter Popham, 'Race for the riches of Montecristo', *The Independent* (21 August 2010).

WEBB, JOHN RICHARD (1913–1944). A sub-lieutenant with the British Royal Navy, he was the son of Richard and Maud Webb. He served on H.M.S. *Salsette*, and was killed on the first day of the Allied attack on Elba on 17 June 1944, aged 31, and was buried on Elba and three years later was reburied in the Bolsena War Cemetery (IV G 7) on the Italian mainland. He was survived by his wife Kathleen Elizabeth Webb.

References: *The war dead of the British Commonwealth and Empire: the register of the names of those who fell in the 1939–1945 War and are buried in cemeteries in Italy Cemeteries 17–18: Bolsena War Cemetery, Orvieto War Cemetery*, Maidenhead: Imperial War Graves Commission, 1954, p. 36.

WELSH, WILLIAM McNAUGHTON (1921/2–1944). An able seaman with the British Royal Navy, he was the son of Mary Welsh of Stirling. Attached to H.M.S. *Copra* (combined operations), he was killed on the first day of the Allied attack on Elba on 17 June 1944, aged 22, and was buried on Elba and three years later was reburied in the Bolsena War Cemetery (IV G 3) on the Italian mainland.

References: *The war dead of the British Commonwealth and Empire: the register of the names of those who fell in the 1939–1945 War and are buried in cemeteries in Italy Cemeteries 17–18: Bolsena War Cemetery, Orvieto War Cemetery*, Maidenhead: Imperial War Graves Commission, 1954, p. 36.

WEMYSS, DAVID DOUGLAS (1760–1839). A British army officer, he was born in 1760 as David Douglas, taking the surname Wemyss in 1790. He served under General William Howe and then under Sir Henry Clinton during the American War of Independence; he then took part in the capture of St. Lucia in 1778, and was involved in the naval engagement off the island of Grenada, also in the West Indies, in 1779. In the French Revolutionary Wars, he served under the duke of York in Flanders, and bought his rank as lieutenant-colonel in the 18th Foot (Royal Irish). This saw him serve under Sir Charles Stuart in 1794 and was involved in the capture of Corsica. He was then appointed governor of the town of Calvi and nearby areas but the British soon had to withdraw and he left with his men for **Portoferraio**, Elba.

After a short time on Elba, he took his men to the Italian mainland, but with the French attacking, he again had to withdraw to Elba, and from there went to Gibraltar. In 1803 he was commander of the British forces in Ceylon (Sri Lanka), and back in Britain he was governor of Tynemouth Castle and Cliffe Fort. He died on 5 September 1839 at his home in Kensington, London.

References: R. Cannon (ed), *Historical record of the eighteenth, or the Royal Irish regiment of foot*, London: Parker, Furnivall & Parker, 1848; R. H. Vetch, 'Wemyss, David Douglas (1760–1839)', revised by James Lunt, *Oxford Dictionary of National Biography*, Oxford University Press, 2004.

WHITTINGTON, JOHN WILLIAM (1924–1944). An able seaman in the British Royal Navy, he was born in 1924 at St. Pancras, London, the son of Albert John Whittington and his wife Nellie (née Wilmer), of Hendon, Middlesex. Attached to H.M.S. *Copra* (combined operations), he was killed on the first day of the Allied attack on Elba on 17 June 1944, aged 19, and was buried on Elba and three years later was reburied in the Bolsena War Cemetery (IV G 21) on the Italian mainland.

References: *The war dead of the British Commonwealth and Empire: the register of the names of those who fell in the 1939–1945 War and are buried in cemeteries in Italy Cemeteries 17–18: Bolsena War Cemetery, Orvieto War Cemetery*, Maidenhead: Imperial War Graves Commission, 1954, p. 36.

WILMOT, REGINALD WILLIAM WINCHESTER 'CHESTER' (1911–1954). A war correspondent and author, he was born on 21 June 1911 in Brighton, Melbourne, Australia, the fourth and youngest child of Reginald William Ernest Wilmot, journalist, and his wife Jane Marian (née Tracy). Educated at Melbourne Grammar School, 1922–30, and then the University of Melbourne, he graduated BA and became famous for his debating skills, going on a tour to take part in debating competitions in The Philippines, Japan, the

United States, Canada and then Britain. His time in Britain allowed him to go to Germany and he was there during the Munich Crisis in September 1938. Back in Australia, he worked as an articled law clerk and with the outbreak of **World War II**, became a correspondent for the Australian Broadcasting Corporation. He was in North Africa, and also covered the Australian actions in Greece and Syria. Back in North Africa, he was in Tobruk for several months, later writing a book about the fighting there. He then went to Port Moresby to cover the Papuan campaign and then returned to Sydney where he completed his book on Tobruk. He then went to London and on D-Day, 6 June 1944, he landed in a glider in France to cover the operations there. After the war he wrote his famous book, *The Struggle for Europe* (London, 1952), which was critical of the ending of the war. As the war had been fought for Polish freedom, Wilmot felt that it was wrong to leave Poland and other states in Soviet hands. He went back to Australia in late 1953 to take part on the Christmas Day broadcast for the British Broadcasting Corporation. On his return journey to England, travelling in a BOAC Comet 1, the airliner broke up on 10 January 1954 after an explosive decompression and it crashed into the Mediterranean Sea off the coast of Elba. There were 29 on board including then children returning at the end of the school holidays. Chester Wilmot's body and those of 14 others were recovered and he was buried in the cemetery at **Porto Azzurro**. *See also* **Comet Air Crash (1954)**.

References: Neil McDonald, 'Wilmot, Reginald William Winchester (Chester) (1911–1954)', *Australian Dictionary of Biography* vol. 16, pp. 561–62; 'Possibility of Sabotage in Comet Air Disaster', *Morning Bulletin*, Rockhampton (12 January 1954), p. 1; *The Times* (13 January 1954), p. 8.

WITHNELL, WILLIAM (1908–1944). A British leading aircraftman in 983 Squadron of the Royal Air Force Volunteer Reserve, he was born in 1908 in Chorley, Lancashire, the son of Edward Withnell (1883–1934), and Mary (née Taylor, 1887–1968). In 1933, William 'Billie' Withnell married Emily Withnell, and they had one son, Keith, born on 9 January 1934 (died on 1 October 2008 in Newcastle, Australia). William Withnell was killed on the second day of the Allied attack on Elba on 18 June 1944, aged 35, and was buried on Elba and three years later was reburied in the Bolsena War Cemetery (IV H 5) on the Italian mainland.

References: *The war dead of the British Commonwealth and Empire: the register of the names of those who fell in the 1939–1945 War and are buried in cemeteries in Italy Cemeteries 17–18: Bolsena War Cemetery, Orvieto War Cemetery*, Maidenhead: Imperial War Graves Commission, 1954, p. 36.

WORLD WAR I. Although Italy had a treaty with Germany and the Austro-Hungarian Empire, it entered World War I on 23 May 1915 on the Allied side supporting Britain, France and Russia. Many young men from Elba enlisted in the Italian forces, and there is a large war memorial at **Portoferraio** commemorating those who died in the conflict. The iron industry also continued production with some 840,000 tonnes produced in 1917. Because Elba was an island, some 170 Austro-Hungarian officers were held as prisoners of war there at the **Villa dei Mulini**.

In a surprise attack on 23 May 1916, an Austrian U–27 submarine surfaced in the bay of Portoferraio and started firing at ships in the harbour and parts of the town, taking particular aim at some of the blast furnaces. The small shells did little damage to the town but the Austrians hoped that the submarine attack would cause enough consternation

British ships off the coast of Elba.

and a suitable diversion which might allow the Austrian prisoners of war to escape – which did not happen. The gunners from **Forte Falcone** opened fire on the submarine which dived and escaped, managing to sink a large Italian steamer, *Washington*, in the **Piombino** channel.

References: 'Austrian Submarine Shells Furnaces in Elba Near Villa Where Napoleon Was Confined', *The New York Times* (29 May 1916), p. 1; Philip J. Haythornthwaite, *The World War One source book*, London: Arms and Armour Press, 1992, pp. 250–59.

WORLD WAR II. Italy was neutral at the start of the war, but Benito Mussolini declared war on Britain and France on 10 June 1940. Men from Elba served in the Italian forces including in North Africa, with **Teseo Tesei** dying in an attack on the Mediterranean island of Malta. In 1943 with the Allied army landing on the Italian mainland, the Italian government sacked Mussolini and arrested him, declaring their support for the Allies. The Germans rescued Mussolini and sent many soldiers into Italy to hold back the Allied forces.

In September 1943 the German High Command decided to withdraw its forces from Corsica and wanted to use Elba as a base to support this move. The Germans demanded that Elba surrender but a citizens' committee was formed

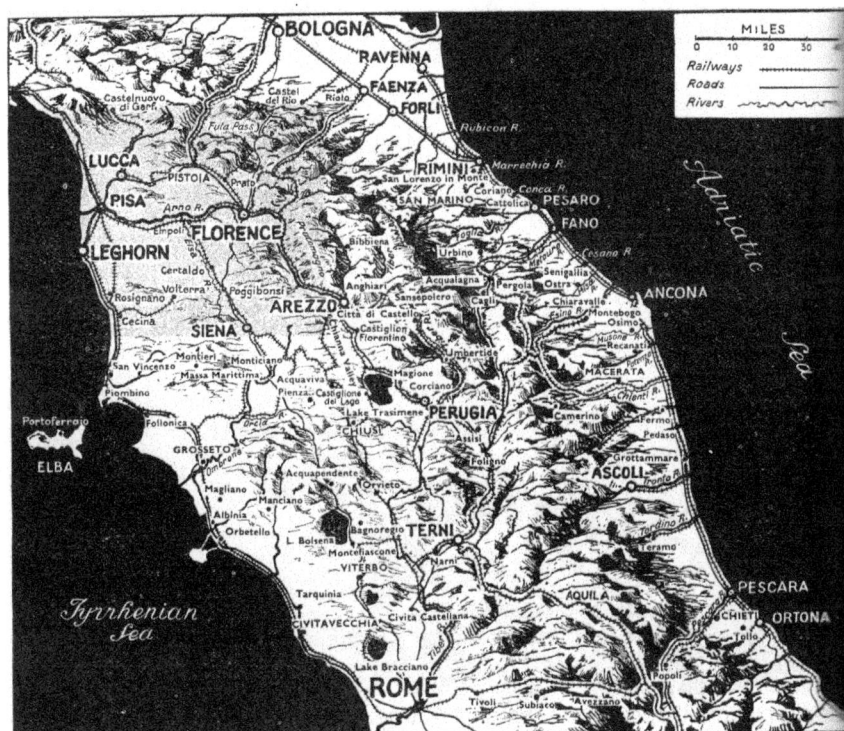

Allied assault craft landing on Elba on 17 June 1944.

and this urged the Italian military on the island to resist. With a steamer in the harbour of Portoferraio about to take supplies to Corsica, the citizens' committee stormed the ship to prevent its departure.

On 15 September 1943, German officers arrived to negotiate with the authorities on Elba. They demanded that Elba surrendered immediately or their air force would bomb the island. Most of the population knew nothing about this ultimatum and the civilians were shocked when, on the next day, 16 planes from the German air force bombed **Portoferraio** and killed 116 civilians, damaging the iron ore plant. The soldiers in the fortress hoisted a white flag and on the next day German paratroopers landed on the island. It was then the turn for the Allied forces to attack.

In a terrible incident on 22 September, *Sgarallino*, a passenger steamer, taking people from **Piombino** to Elba was torpedoed by an unidentified submarine as it approached Portoferraio harbour. Some 200 people drowned including some demobilized soldiers returning home. There were later more than 20 Allied air raids on Elba and in one of these, on 19 March 1944, more people wre killed than in the German bombing on 16 September of the previous year. Although the main targets were the port facilities and the ironworks, many bombs fell over the town. Even the local cemetery was badly damaged. Many people in Portoferraio fled the town and hid in the nearby hills.

With the Allied soldiers on the Italian peninsular briefly having to halt, it was decided it would still be possible to launch a flanking movement by attacking Elba. With many of the French troops inexperienced, it was decided that they would be sent in as not much resistance was expected. If the Allies captured Elba, it would help them control the Piombino Channel. However Adolf Hitler had decided to attach 'great importance' to holding Elba, and on 12 June Field Marshal Albert Kesselring, the German commander in Italy, had ordered that 'Elba is not to be evacuated but held', with General Alfred Jodl adding that it must be defended 'to the last man and the last cartridge', Reinforcements were sent in from 14 June. When the Allies heard of the extra shipping movements across the Piombino Channel, they thought the Germans were withdrawing.

On 4 April 1944, a US plane crashed on Elba whilst on a reconnaissance flight from Corsica to Livorno. The two officers on board, **Milton Harber** and **Robert Boyd** were killed.

Rear-Admiral **Thomas Hope Troubridge** of the Royal Navy was the naval commander for the Allied attack and Force N which would begin the attack was drawn from the French 9th Colonial Infantry Division. This

The memorial to Robert Byrd and Milton Harber.

Allied soldiers landing.

German artillery.

French soldiers landing.

Moroccan soldiers from the French colonial forces landing.

consisted of the 4th and 13th Regiments Senegalese Tirailleurs, the Bataillion de Choc Commando, a Moroccan Goumier battalion. The French were eager for more combat after liberating Corsica in September 1943.

The German reconnaissance planes spotted the invasion force heading towards Elba on 16 June 1944, but believed they were naval convoys and as a result were unprepared for the massive bombing raids which were launched with 26 Vickers Wellingtons bombing Elba on the night of 16/17 June. Their main targets were Portoferraio and Porte Longone. At midnight on 17 June the invasion fleet for Opération Brassard arrived and soldiers were landed at several different locations. The Allies had decided not to launch an air assault beforehand because this would warn the Germans of an impending assault. However the Germans were ready and waiting and presented heavy opposition to the British landing on the beaches at **Marina di Campo**. Troubridge later wrote:

The garrison of the island we had been told was under 800 Germans and reports spoke of their being preponderantly Poles and Czechs of low morale and all set for evacuation. In fact the ration strength was 2,600 Germans who fought extremely well. The defences of Campo Bay were somewhat stronger than intelligence reports had led us to believe, and were in fact, extremely formidable. They had excavated caves in the granite cliffs flanking the beaches and installed 155 mm, 88mm and machine guns in them. Behind the beaches, exactly ranged on the likely places of disembarkation were heavy mortars.

As a result, Admiral Troubridge ordered the remainder of the Allied soldiers to land on a beach to the east of Marina di Campo. The site was rocky and in normal circumstances would not be an ideal landing place. However because of this, the Germans had not protected it well, and after overcoming the natural hazards, and damaging most of the landing craft, a landing was effected and the Allied soldiers were able to come around and attack the Germans on their east flank.

The French colonial troops were commanded by General **Jean de Lattre de Tassigny** – later famous as the French commander in Indochina. The fighting was extremely vicious with Portoferraio captured on 18 June with

Jean de Lattre de Tassigny landing on Elba.

Large numbers of Allied wounded being treated before evacuation.

A wrecked German gunboat in the harbour of Marina di Campo.

More allied soldiers landing at Marina di Campo.

much of the island being in Allied hands by the following evening. However the Germans and Senegalese fought it out in the hills on the following day. On that day, 19 June, the German commander, General Franz Gall, asked permission to evacuate his forces and some 400 German troops withdrew to the mainland by the evening of 20 June.

After that, the French African soldiers were allowed to loot the place for two days, during which many women were raped, and quite a number killed. It was only with difficulty that the French officers were able to reassert their control over their troops.

Military historians have suggested that the invasion had not been necessary as it did not help the Allied soldiers on the mainland. In the fighting the Germans lost around 500 dead, with 1,995 becoming prisoners of war. The French lost 252 killed or missing, and had 635 wounded including **Alexandre Sanguinetti**, later a prominent politician, who lost a leg in the landing. The British lost 38 killed, and nine badly wounded, and a dozen landing craft. The US navy lost three sailors. The British soldiers were initially buried on Elba but in 1947 were reinterred at Bolsena War Cemetery on the Italian mainland.

German prisoners of war on Elba.

References: Jean de Lattre de Tassigny, *The History of the French First Army*, London: George Allen and Unwin Ltd., 1952; Commander Kenneth Edwards, *The Royal Navy and Allies*, London: Hutchinson, nd, pp. 128–30; vol. 3, p. David Lee, *Beachhead assault: The Story of the Royal Naval Commandos in WW2*, Mechanicsburg, Pa: Stackpole Books, 2004; Samuel Eliot Morison, 'Elba Interlude, June 1944', *Military Affairs* Vol. 21, no. 4 (Winter, 1957), pp. 182–87; Christopher and Jean Serpell, *The Travellers' Guide to Elba and the Tuscan Archipelago*, London: Jonathan Cape, 1977, pp. 129–30; Barbara Tomblin, *With Utmost Spirit: Allied Naval Operations in the Mediterranean, 1942–1945*, Lexington: University Press of Kentucky, 2004; 'Operation Brassard', http://www.combinedops.com/Elba%20-%20Op%20Brassard.htm; 'The capture of Elba', *Illustrated London News* (8 July 1944), p. 48.

WRONG, GEORGE MACKINNON (1860–1948). A Canadian clergyman and historian, he was born on 25 June 1860 at Grovesend, Canada West (now Ontario), the son of Gilbert Wrong and Christian (née Mackinnon), and was ordained an Anglican minister in 1883. From 1894 until his retirement in 1927, he was professor and head of the department of history at the University of Toronto. The author of *Elba, a hundred years after* (1915), he wrote it during

World War I noting:

There are striking parallels between Napoleon's struggle for world power a hundred years ago and that of Germany a century later. It was only in the period of the Revolution that France had begun to attain a vital national union. The older France had not been really united. Many provinces had come under the sway of the French crown, by conquest or by inheritance; but though they had one ruler they still retained in many respects their old character as separate states. There was not even free trade between these provinces. They had different modes of government, different systems of taxation and of laws. There was, it has been said, a French state but not a French nation. The ferment of the Revolution produced a France 'one and indivisible' with an intense national spirit. It was Napoleon who organized this France, who gave it unity of system, and who made its national life a homogeneous reality. Under him France had found a head who directed all the energies of the nation. He did not give France freedom. He was the Emperor of the French, their leader and war-lord. In his mind was the thought that he was the successor of Charlemagne, the great world-ruler. The realm of Charlemagne had stretched eastward far across the Rhine. Napoleon felt called upon to revive this old dominion, for the successor of Charlemagne ought to rule over the territory that Charlemagne had ruled. The Empire thus meant expansion, reunion with peoples who had been separated from it by the incidents and accidents of history.

On Napoleon, he wrote:

He was spoiled by success and came to despise all his neighbours. The English are not a military people and he regarded them as mere traders who cared only for their money bags, a nation of shop-keepers. He underestimated the power of his opponents. He took little care to treat possible enemies with diplomatic skill. To him it seemed a matter of slight moment whether one nation more or less was at war with him. In the end, as a result, he was face to face with Europe in arms. England was his arch-enemy – the tyrant of the seas as he called her. He tried to strike England by striking at Egypt. He had the fixed idea that if he could reach England, London would fall in three days and that the British Empire would then be prostrate. He believed that the Irish would help him to conquer England. He even thought that there were elements in the British Empire which would look upon him as a liberator.

In pursuing his ends Napoleon showed no patience or self-restraint. Frederick the Great, with vast ambitions, had yet moved cautiously step by step towards his goal. Napoleon would not leave anything to time. All must be done quickly by the striking of shattering blows. He could conquer people and hold them indefinitely under a military yoke. He had no belief in liberty, no insight into the fact that a strong empire can be built on only by the consent and union of those who compose it. He showed little capacity to estimate rightly political or even military forces. He fought on too extended a line, from the south of Spain to the interior of Russia. He raised up so many enemies that in the end it was certain they would overwhelm him. They knew his strength. They feared him and offered to compromise if he would abandon his dream of world-conquest. Even after the disaster in Russia it was possible for him to have retained in the north the left hank of the Rhine and in the south Nice and Savoy; but he blindly refused such terms. He would have all or nothing, and in the end his enemies saw that their only safety lay in crushing him completely.

One of his sons, Harold Verschoyle Wrong, served in the British army and was killed in action at the Battle of the Somme. Rev. George Wrong died on 29 June 1948.

References: J. B. Brebner, 'Wrong, George Mackinnon (1860–1948)', revised by Phillip Buckner, *Oxford Dictionary of National Biography*, Oxford University Press, 2004; C. Martin, 'Professor G. M. Wrong and history in Canada', in R. Flenley (ed), *Essays in Canadian history presented to George Mackinnon Wrong*, Toronto: Macmillan Co. of Canada Ltd., 1939; W. S. Wallace, 'The life and work of George M. Wrong', *Canadian Historical Review* vol. 29, no. 3 (September 1948), pp. 229–39; G. M. Wrong, *Chronicle of a family*, Toronto, 1938; *Who was Who 1941–1950*, p. 1268.

- Y -

YOUNG, Sir WILLIAM (1751–1821). A British naval officer, he was born on 16 August 1751 in England, the oldest of the five children of James Young (1717–1789), naval officer, and his first wife, Elizabeth, née Bolton (1726–1760). He joined the Royal Navy when he was ten, serving on a number of ships in home waters, and then in the Mediterranean and was the third lieutenant on the *Portland*, the flagship of Admiral James Young, in the West Indies. Promoted fast during the American War of Independence, he remained in the navy during the late 1780s. When Lord Hood attacked Toulon in 1793, Young served in operations

A FIRST RATE MAN of WAR,
taken from the DOCKYARD PLYMOUTH.

there whilst trying to establish a British base on Corsica. He was then posted to **Portoferraio**, Elba, and escorted British and allied troops under Major-General Thomas Dundas from there to Mortella Bay, Corsica, which was only effected after fighting the French. A member of the committee of conciliation during the Spithead Mutiny of April 1797, he was promoted to vice-admiral of the blue in 1799, and vice-admiral of the white two years later, finally becoming vice-admiral of the red in 1804. Elected to parliament in 1807, he was admiral of the white from 1810, and given command of the North Sea Fleet. This saw him involved in blockading the German and Dutch coasts in the last period of the **Napoleonic War**. He died on 25 October 1821 at his home in Queen Anne Street, London.

References: P. K. Crimmin, 'Young, Sir William (1751–1821)', *Oxford Dictionary of National Biography*, Oxford University Press, 2004.

APPENDIX I

Rulers of Elba

The Republic of Pisa: 850–1398

1285–1289	Ugolino della Gherardesca.
1286–1288	Nino Visconti.
1288	Ruggieri Ubaldini.
1289–1291	Guido da Montefeltro.
1202–1312	Consiglio degli Anziani.
1313–1316	Uguccione della Faggiola.
1316–1324	Gherardo della Gherardesca.
1324–1327	Rinieri della Gherardesca.
1327–1341	Fazio della Gherardesca.
1341–1347	Ranieri II della Gherardesca.
1347–1354	Andrea Gambacorta.
1354–1355	Francesco Gambacorta.
1355–1364	Marquess di Randeck e Gualtieri di Hochschiltz.
1364–1368	Giovanni dell'Agnello.
1369–1392	Pietro Gambacorta.
1392–1398	Jacopo d'Appiano.
1398	Gherardo d'Appiano.
1399–1402	Gian Galeazzo Visconti, duke of Milano.
1402–1406	Gabriele Maria Visconti.

The Lords of Appiano: 1398–1548

-	Jacobo I.
1399–1404	Gherado Appiani.

1404–1441	Jacobo II.
1441–1445	Paola.
1445–1451	Caterina.
1451–1457	Emanuele Appiani.
1457–1474	Jacobo III.
1474–1511	Jacobo IV.
1511–1545	Jacobo V.
1545–1585	Jacobo VI.
1585–1589	Alessandro.
1589–1603	Jacobo VII.

The Partition of Elba

1548	Cosimo de 'Medici

French Rule: 1646–50

Spanish Rule: 1650–1708

Grand Dukes of Tuscany

Medici dynasty

23 May 1670 – 31 Oct. 1723	Cosimo III.
31 Oct. 1723 – 9 July 1737	Giovanni Gastone.

Lorena dynasty

9 July 1737 – 18 Aug. 1765	Francesco II.

Asburgo-Lorena dynasty

18 Aug. 1765 – 22 July 1790	Pietro Leopoldo I.
22 July 1790 – 27 March 1799	Ferdinando III (1st time).

President of the Provisional Government

27 March 1799 – 5 July 1799	Rivani.
5 July 1799 – 7 July 1799	Cesare Gori (President of the Senate).

Asburgo-Lorena dynasty

7 July 1799 – 15 Oct. 1800	Ferdinando III (2nd time).

15 Oct. 1800 – 27 Nov. 1800 Grand-Ducal Commission: Giuseppe Francesco Pierallini; Antonio Cercignani; Bernardo Lessi; Giulio Piombanti.

27 Nov. 1800 – 27 March 1801 Provisional Government: Francesco Chiarenti; Enrico Pontelli; Giovanni De Ghores.

27 March 1801 – 3 Aug. 1801 Grand-Ducal Commission: Giuseppe Francesco Pierallini; Antonio Cercignani; Bernardo Lessi; Giulio Piombanti.

Kings
Borbone dynasty

3 Aug. 1801 – 27 May 1803 Ludovico I.

27 May 1803 – 10 Dec. 1807 Carlo Ludovico II.

27 May 1803 – 10 Dec. 1807 Maria Luisa (queen regent).

Governor-General

3 March 1809 – 1 Feb. 1814 Elisa Baciocchi Bonaparte (with courtesy style of Grand Duchess of Tuscany).

Grand Dukes
Asburgo-Lorena dynasty (restored)

27 April 1814 – 18 June 1824 Ferdinando III (3rd time).

18 June 1824 – 21 Feb. 1849 Leopoldo II (1st time).

21 Feb. 1849 – 27 March 1849 Giuseppe Montanelli (president of Provisional Government).

27 March 1849 – 12 April 1849 Francesco Domenico Guerrazzi (Head of the Executive Power).

12 April 1849 – 21 July 1859 Leopoldo II (2nd time).

21 July 1859 – 16 Aug. 1859 Ferdinando IV.

27 April 1859 – 10 May 1859 Ubaldino Peruzzi (president of Provisional Government).

Administrators

10 May 1859 – 16 Aug. 1859 Conte Carlo Boncompagni di Mombello (extraordinary royal commissioner).

16 Aug. 1859 – 3 Dec. 1859 Barone Bettino Ricasoli (head of government).

3 Dec. 1859 – 20 March 1860   Conte Carlo Boncompagni di Mombello (governor-general of the united provinces of central Italy).

The Kingdom of Italy / Republic of Italy

Kings of Italy

17 March 1861 – 9 January 1878 Victor Emmanuel II.

9 January 1878 – 29 July 1900   Umberto I.

29 July 1900 – 9 May 1946   Victor Emmanuel III.

9 May 1946 – 12 June 1946   Umberto II.

Provisional Heads of State

18 June 1946 – 1 July 1946   Alcide De Gasperi (acting).

1 July 1946 – 1 Jan. 1948   Enrico De Nicola.

Presidents

1 Jan. 1948 – 12 May 1948   Enrico De Nicola.

12 May 1948 – 11 May 1955   Luigi Einaudi.

11 May 1955 – 11 May 1962   Giovanni Gronchi.

11 May 1962 – 6 Dec. 1964   Antonio Segni.

6 Dec. 1964 – 29 Dec. 1964   Cesare Merzagora (acting).

29 Dec. 1964 – 29 Dec. 1971   Giuseppe Saragat.

29 Dec. 1971 – 15 June 1978   Giovanni Leone.

15 June 1978 – 9 July 1978   Amintore Fanfani (acting).

9 July 1978 – 29 June 1985   Sandro Pertini.

29 June 1985 – 28 April 1992   Francesco Cossiga.

28 April 1992 – 28 May 1992   Giovanni Spadolini (acting).

28 May 1992 – 15 May 1999   Oscar Luigi Scalfaro.

15 May 1999 – 18 May 1999   Nicola Mancino (acting).

18 May 1999 – 15 May 2006   Carlo Azeglio Ciampi.

15 May 2006 – 3 Feb. 2015   Georgio Napolitano.

3 Feb. 2015 –   Sergio Mattarella.

Prime Ministers (Presidents of the Council of Ministers)

17 March 1861 – 6 June 1861 Camillo Benso, conte di Cavour.

6 June 1861 – 4 March 1862 Bettino Ricasoli, conte di Brolio (1st time).

4 March 1862 – 9 Dec. 1862 Urbano Rattazzi (1st time).

9 Dec. 1862 – 24 March 1863 Luigi Carlo Farini.

24 March 1863 – 23 Sept. 1864 Marco Minghetti (1st time).

23 Sept. 1864 – 17 June 1866 Alfonso Ferrero, marchese di La Marmora.

17 June 1866 – 11 April 1867 Bettino Ricasoli, conte di Brolio (2nd time).

11 April 1867 – 27 Oct. 1867 Urbano Rattazzi (2nd time).

27 Oct. 1867 – 12 Dec. 1869 Conte Luigi Federico Menabrea.

12 Dec. 1869 – 10 Aug. 1873 Giovanni Lanza.

10 Aug. 1873 – 25 March 1876 Marco Minghetti (2nd time).

25 March 1876 – 23 March 1878 Agostino Depretis (1st time).

23 March 1878 – 18 Dec. 1878 Benedetto Cairoli (1st time).

18 Dec. 1878 – 12 July 1879 Agostino Depretis (2nd time).

12 July 1879 – 28 May 1881 Benedetto Cairoli (2nd time).

28 May 1881 – 29 July 1887 Agostino Depretis (3rd time).

8 Aug. 1887 – 9 Feb. 1891 Francesco Crispi (1st time).

9 Feb. 1891 – 15 May 1892 Antonio Starabba, marchese di Rudinì (1st time).

15 May 1892 – 10 Dec. 1893 Giovanni Giolitti (1st time).

10 Dec. 1893 – 10 March 1896 Francesco Crispi (2nd time).

10 March 1896 – 29 June 1898 Antonio Starabba, marchese di Rudinì (2nd time).

29 June 1898 – 24 June 1900 Luigi Pelloux.

24 June 1900 – 15 Feb. 1901 Giuseppe Saracco.

15 Feb. 1901 – 3 Nov. 1903 Giuseppe Zanardelli.

3 Nov. 1903 – 27 March 1905 Giovanni Giolitti (2nd time).

27 March 1905 – 8 Feb. 1906 Alessandro Fortis.

8 Feb. 1906 – 29 May 1906 Barone Sidney Sonnino (1st time).

29 May 1906 – 10 Dec. 1909 Giovanni Giolitti (3rd time).

10 Dec. 1909 – 30 March 1910 Barone Sidney Sonnino (2nd time).

30 March 1910 – 27 March 1911 Luigi Luzzatti.

27 March 1911 – 21 March 1914 Giovanni Giolitti (4th time).

21 March 1914 – 19 June 1916	Antonio Salandra.
19 June 1916 – 30 Oct. 1917	Paolo Boselli.
30 Oct. 1917 – 23 June 1919	Vittorio Emanuele Orlando.
23 June 1919 – 16 June 1920	Francesco Saverio Nitti.
16 June 1920 – 4 July 1921	Giovanni Giolitti (5th time).
4 July 1921 – 25 Feb. 1922	Ivanoe Bonomi (1st time).
25 Feb. 1922 – 31 Oct. 1922	Luigi Facta.
31 Oct. 1922 – 25 July 1943	Benito Mussolini.
27 July 1943 – 9 June 1944	Pietro Badoglio.
9 June 1944 – 21 June 1945	Ivanoe Bonomi (2nd time).
21 June 1945 – 10 Dec. 1945	Ferruccio Parri.
10 Dec. 1945 – 17 Aug. 1953	Alcide De Gasperi.
17 Aug. 1953 – 18 Jan. 1954	Giuseppe Pella.
18 Jan. 1954 – 9 Feb. 1954	Amintore Fanfani (1st time).
9 Feb. 1954 – 6 July 1955	Mario Scelba.
6 July 1955 – 19 May 1957	Antonio Segni (1st time).
19 May 1957 – 1 July 1958	Adone Zoli.
1 July 1958 – 15 Feb. 1959	Amintore Fanfani (2nd time).
15 Feb. 1959 – 25 March 1960	Antonio Segni (2nd time).
25 March 1960 – 26 July 1960	Fernando Tambroni.
26 July 1960 – 21 June 1963	Amintore Fanfani (3rd time).
21 June 1963 – 5 Dec. 1963	Giovanni Leone (1st time).
5 Dec. 1963 – 25 June 1968	Aldo Moro (1st time).
25 June 1968 – 13 Dec. 1968	Giovanni Leone (2nd time).
13 Dec. 1968 – 7 Aug. 1970	Mariano Rumor (1st time).
7 Aug. 1970 – 18 Feb. 1972	Emilio Colombo.
18 Feb. 1972 – 4 July 1973	Giulio Andreotti (1st time).
4 July 1973 – 2 Nov. 1974	Mariano Rumor (2nd time).
2 Nov. 1974 – 29 July 1976	Aldo Moro (2nd time).
29 July 1976 – 5 Aug. 1979	Giulio Andreotti (2nd time).
5 Aug. 1979 – 18 Oct. 1980	Francesco Cossiga.
18 Oct. 1980 – 28 June 1981	Arnaldo Forlani.

28 June 1981 – 30 Nov. 1982	Giovanni Spadolini.
30 Nov. 1982 – 4 Aug. 1983	Amintore Fanfani (4th time).
4 Aug. 1983 – 18 April 1987	Bettino Craxi.
18 April 1987 – 29 July 1987	Amintore Fanfani (5th time).
29 July 1987 – 13 April 1988	Giovanni Goria.
13 April 1988 – 23 July 1989	Ciriaco De Mita.
23 July 1989 – 28 June 1992	Giulio Andreotti (3rd time).
28 June 1992 – 29 April 1993	Giuliano Amato (1st time).
29 April 1993 – 11 May 1994	Carlo Azeglio Ciampi.
11 May 1994 – 17 Jan. 1995	Silvio Berlusconi (1st time).
17 Jan. 1995 – 18 May 1996	Lamberto Dini.
18 May 1996 – 21 Oct. 1998	Romano Prodi.
21 Oct. 1998 – 26 April 2000	Massimo D'Alema.
26 April 2000 – 11 June 2001	Giuliano Amato (2nd time).
11 June 2001 – 17 May 2006	Silvio Berlusconi (2nd time).
17 May 2006 – 8 May 2008	Romano Prodi.
8 May 2008 – 16 Nov. 2011	Silvio Berlusconi (3rd time).
16 Nov. 2011 – 28 April 2013	Mario Monti.
28 April 2013 – 22 Feb. 2014	Enrico Letta.
22 Feb. 2014 –	Matteo Renzi.